A Reader's Guide to Andrei Bely's
Petersburg

A Reader's Guide to
Andrei Bely's

Petersburg

Edited by
LEONID LIVAK

The University of Wisconsin Press

The University of Wisconsin Press
728 State Street, Suite 443
Madison, Wisconsin 53706
uwpress.wisc.edu

Gray's Inn House, 127 Clerkenwell Road
London EC1R 5DB, United Kingdom
eurospanbookstore.com

Copyright © 2019
The Board of Regents of the University of Wisconsin System
All rights reserved. Except in the case of brief quotations embedded in critical articles and reviews, no part of this publication may be reproduced, stored in a retrieval system, transmitted in any format or by any means—digital, electronic, mechanical, photocopying, recording, or otherwise—or conveyed via the Internet or a website without written permission of the University of Wisconsin Press. Rights inquiries should be directed to rights@uwpress.wisc.edu.

Printed in the United States of America

This book may be available in a digital edition.

Library of Congress Cataloging-in-Publication Data
Names: Livak, Leonid, editor.
Title: A reader's guide to Andrei Bely's *Petersburg* / edited by Leonid Livak.
Description: Madison, Wisconsin: The University of Wisconsin Press, [2018]
 | Includes bibliographical references and index.
Identifiers: LCCN 2018011399 | ISBN 9780299319304 (cloth: alk. paper)
Subjects: LCSH: Bely, Andrey, 1880–1934. Peterburg. | Bely, Andrey, 1880–1934—
Criticism and interpretation.
Classification: LCC PG3453.B84 P538 2018 | DDC 891.7/3309—dc23
LC record available at https://lccn.loc.gov/2018011399

ISBN 978-0-299-31934-2 (pbk.: alk. paper)

Contents

A Note on Translation and Transliteration	vii
Introduction LEONID LIVAK	3
On Translating *Petersburg* JOHN ELSWORTH	24

Part One. The Intellectual Context

Revolutionary Terrorism and Provocation in *Petersburg* LYNN E. PATYK	39
Petersburg and Modern Occultism MARIA CARLSON	54
Petersburg and Russian Nietzscheanism EDITH W. CLOWES	70
Neo-Kantianism in *Petersburg* TIMOTHY LANGEN	85
Petersburg and the Philosophy of Henri Bergson HILARY FINK	100
Petersburg and the New Science of Psychology JUDITH WERMUTH-ATKINSON	110
Petersburg and Contemporary Racial Thought HENRIETTA MONDRY	124

Petersburg as Apocalyptic Fiction 138
   DAVID M. BETHEA

Part Two. The Aesthetic Context

Petersburg and Music in Modernist Theory and Literature 157
   STEVEN CASSEDY

Russian Modernist Theatricality and *Life-Creation*
   in *Petersburg* 171
   COLLEEN MCQUILLEN

Petersburg and Modernist Painting with Words 186
   OLGA MATICH

Petersburg and Urbanism in the Modernist Novel 202
   TARAS KOZNARSKY

Petersburg and the Problem of Consciousness in Modernist
   Fiction 217
   VIOLETA SOTIROVA

Part Three. Aids for Reading and Studying *Petersburg*

An Annotated Synopsis of *Petersburg*'s First Edition (1913) 235
   LEONID LIVAK

Recommended Critical Literature in English 257

Contributors 259
Index 263

A Note on Translation and Transliteration

For reasons explained in the introduction, the volume's contributors have been asked to use *Petersburg*'s first, 1913 edition, as their primary text of reference. Throughout the volume, the novel's original Russian text is cited from the edition prepared and annotated by Leonid Dolgopolov: Andrei Belyi, *Peterburg* (Moscow: Nauka, 1981). Two English translations of the 1913 edition exist: one by David McDuff (London: Penguin Books, 1995) and another by John Elsworth (London: Pushkin Press, 2009). For the sake of consistency, all essays in this volume cite John Elsworth's translation, except in those cases, specified in notes, where David McDuff's translation offers linguistic nuance that is absent from its counterpart.

We use the Library of Congress system of transliteration from Cyrillic, with the exception of proper names that have a commonly accepted English spelling (e.g., Dostoevsky, Solovyov, Tolstoy, Tchaikovsky). There is no standard way of rendering the name of *Petersburg*'s author into English: we have consistently used the form "Andrei Bely," except in bibliographic references, where the writer's name is spelled according to the Library of Congress transliteration system: "Andrei Belyi."

A Reader's Guide to Andrei Bely's
Petersburg

Introduction

LEONID LIVAK

About This Book

"Something happened to art around the turn of the twentieth century," writes Gabriel Josipovici with reference to the fact that "Proust, Joyce, Picasso, Klee, Schoenberg, and Stravinsky, for all their manifest individuality, do have something in common."[1] Literary and cultural historians call that "something" *modernism*—a convenient, albeit anachronistic, shorthand for a transnational community of cultural producers and consumers who, beginning in the 1880s, grew increasingly skeptical about the philosophical pillars of the nineteenth century: the positivist cult of natural sciences as the source of ultimate truths about the universe around us; the reductively materialist understanding of human nature; and the unbridled optimism about progress that clashed with the modernists' own acute sense of spiritual and civilizational decline. Russian modernist culture matched its French-, German-, and English-speaking counterparts in the variety and intensity of artistic and philosophical production, which conveyed a new "way of experiencing the world."[2] An early recruit to modernism, the poet, critic, and novelist Andrei Bely saw it not as "an artistic school" but as a group project aimed at "reevaluating all philosophical, ethical, and religious values of European culture."[3]

Like their foreign counterparts, whose utopianism they shared and often surpassed, Russian modernists saw the ultimate purpose of creative activity in the radical transformation of human beings and life itself.[4] This programmatic desire to revolutionize the human condition, known in Russian modernist culture as the "revolution of the spirit," was driven by the sensibility of crisis—the sense of staring into a spiritual, cultural, and social chasm between past and present—and by the resultant longing for a grand new beginning that modernists consciously modeled on the Christian apocalyptic expectations of the end of the world and the ensuing establishment of Christ's millennial kingdom on earth. Few artistic works created before World War I encapsulate and articulate the sensibility, ideas, phobias, and aspirations of Russian and transnational modernism as comprehensively and extensively as Andrei Bely's magnum opus *Petersburg* (1913), whose place and importance in the literary and cultural history of twentieth-century Europe have been often compared to those of James Joyce's *Ulysses* (1922).[5]

In spite of the continuous critical rapprochement between the two modernist masterpieces—and certainly not for lack of translations, since Bely's novel exists today in four English renditions (see John Elsworth's essay in this volume)—*Petersburg* has not received its due attention from the Anglophone public and is rarely taught within the framework of literature and humanities courses at English-speaking colleges and universities. One can only conclude that, like other hermetic modernist classics, *Petersburg* presents serious challenges to nonspecialist readers as well as to instructors in Russian and comparative literature, not to mention general humanities. The essays collected in the present volume strive to make *Petersburg* more accessible: they have been written with a broad audience in mind in order to help the Anglophone reader gain a better understanding of Bely's novel and to facilitate its study in the college classroom. To this end, the volume's contributors have been asked to do what they, as academics and researchers, rarely get to do; namely, to refrain from new and original interpretations of a literary classic and to summarize instead what we already know about *Petersburg*, explicating it in the intellectual and artistic context, Russian and European, that informed the novel's creation and historical reception.

Boris Nikolaevich Bugaev (1880–1934), who used the penname Andrei Bely, was an intellectual omnivore drawn to the most diverse practices in European art and thought, which he idiosyncratically appropriated and creatively reworked. In a testimony to Bely's eclectic interests, *Petersburg* is a virtual encyclopedia of European philosophical and aesthetic currents between the turn of the century and World War I. This makes *Petersburg*—originally written for an interpretive community that shared the author's cultural knowledge and could actively explore the novel's maze of meanings—all the more difficult to understand today. Hence the structure of our book. Far from claiming to explicate *Petersburg* comprehensively, each essay explores a particular aspect of Bely's novel. If there is indeed an overarching conclusion to be drawn, it is that no single interpretation can withstand the test of *Petersburg*'s philosophical heterogeneity, aesthetic experimentalism, and—last but not least—its narrative disruptions and logical contradictions. In large part, this plurality of clashing meanings is an outcome of authorial design. But a number of problems in *Petersburg*'s intellectual economy and narrative structure arise from Bely's rapid philosophical evolution and chaotic personal circumstances at the time he was writing the novel. Another contributor to the chaos is *Petersburg*'s complex publication history. The multiplicity of analytical approaches proposed in our essay collection aims to do justice to the broad range of interpretive possibilities contained in Bely's novel, down to its seemingly trivial details.

Take, for example, Nikolai Apollonovich Ableukhov's fancy ball attire—a red domino and a black mask. This costume simultaneously anchors *Petersburg* in the social realia of contemporary Russia; mediates a mythopoetic parable of Bely's personal drama; and stakes out his novel's place in Russian modernist culture, which instrumentalized to its own ends a traditional Italian stage genre, commedia dell'arte, wherein Nikolai's costume originates. Depending on their familiarity with Russian modernism and its actors, Bely's first readers could variously interpret Nikolai's public antics as the Red Domino. For many, the costume invoked the spike in street hooliganism in 1905–6, with hoodlums in masquerade attire harassing women during the political disturbances that form *Petersburg*'s historical background.[6] The domino's red color also emblematized revolutionary violence, not least because Nikolai's role in an assassination plot recalled the use of carnival disguises by terrorists, as Lynn Patyk's essay shows. For readers privy to the theatricalization of life in modernist circles, Nikolai's commedia dell'arte disguise conveyed a special philosophy of art, discussed here by Colleen McQuillen. Finally, Bely's acquaintances saw in the masquerade dress a key to an autobiographical parable hidden in Nikolai's failed romance with Sofia Likhutina, his friend's wife. The costume linked *Petersburg*'s love triangle to Bely's tortuous affair with the wife of his friend Aleksandr Blok. Both poets lived this drama, in 1905–7, and wrote about it in terms of the commedia dell'arte plot pitting the red Harlequin (Bely) against the white Pierrot (Blok) in a contest for Columbine's heart. Replacing Harlequin's traditional, checkered and particolored suit with a patternless and monochromatic red domino, Bely wore that masquerade attire in public and subsequently bestowed it on his hero in *Petersburg*.[7]

The variety of potential meanings inherent in every aspect of Bely's novel—from prominent leitmotifs to discreet details (even colors, such as yellow, overflow with multiple connotations, as Maria Carlson, Henrietta Mondry, and Judith Wermuth-Atkinson's essays show)—calls for a broad range of interpretational approaches. Going through the essays in this volume, then, the reader will see soon enough that *Petersburg* yields a number of equally convincing, albeit often contradictory readings generated by different analytical lenses. But, as announced in its title, Bely's novel does have a stable and readily identifiable thematic core, whose meaning is unambiguous by virtue of its rootedness in the tradition of St. Petersburg's literary representation, commonly known as the "Petersburg text of Russian literature." This tradition is steeped in the mythology of the imperial capital, which the Russian cultural imagination has endowed with supernatural independent agency. In that cultural mythology, the city of Peter the Great—brought into being in 1703 as Russia's strategic "window to Europe" by the tsar's single-minded will—is forever cursed by its unnatural and cruel birth. The ostentatiously Western metropolis deliberately broke with the Russian cultural traditions embodied by Moscow when it rose up on the bones of its slave builders, who died in the thousands to erect the self-proclaimed Russian emperor's new capital in the inhospitable climate and harsh working conditions of a swampy northern wilderness.[8]

The myth codified in the "Petersburg text" was predicated on the tension between two antithetical notions of the city. On one hand, St. Petersburg was the glorious seat of imperial power where one could seek fame and fortune. An elegant "Northern Venice," it bore witness to one man's creative will, thus inspiring future creators among Peter's westernized Russian progeny. On the flip side of the city's mythology, however, St. Petersburg appeared as a haunted and morbidly unhealthy place that quashed the aspirations of ordinary folk, drove its inhabitants insane, or killed them outright by means of climate-induced, chronic physical illness and periodic natural calamities. The city was, furthermore, infused with a spiritual malaise resulting from the violent repression of traditional Russian culture during Peter's reforms. In this much darker version of St. Petersburg, the standard yellow color of governmental buildings dominating the imperial capital symbolized disease, visible in the skin tone of city residents. It also stood for madness (with state-run mental institutions popularly called "yellow houses") and prostitution, whose practitioners carried a state license informally known as the "yellow ticket." The European façade of this inhumane St. Petersburg was but a demonic illusion conjured up by Peter the Antichrist, a mirage with apocalyptic portents about the city's imminent disappearance, along with the Western civilization it embodied, into the swamps from which it had arisen.[9]

By the time Bely turned to the myth of St. Petersburg, he had many authoritative literary models at his disposal—from such foundational works of the "Petersburg text" as Aleksandr Pushkin's narrative poem *The Bronze Horseman* (1833) and story "The Queen of Spades" (1833), along with Nikolai Gogol's Petersburg tales ("Nevsky Prospect" [1835], "Nose" [1836], "Notes of a Madman" [1835], and "Overcoat" [1842]), to the subsequent elaboration of the city's myth throughout Fëdor Dostoevsky's oeuvre, most notably in *Crime and Punishment* (1866) and *The Idiot* (1868). At the turn of the twentieth century, the "Petersburg text" received a new lease on life in budding Russian modernist culture, whose apocalyptic sensibility found much fertile ground in the myth of St. Petersburg.[10] But no other Russian modernist did as much as Bely to bring the "Petersburg text" into the new century. By working St. Petersburg's mythologized history and topography into the narrative structure of his novel, Bely made the city a literary character in its own right.[11] While doing so, he systematically exploited the tradition of St. Petersburg's literary representation, positing himself as a direct continuator of Pushkin and Gogol and using the "Petersburg text" as a medium for an aesthetic and philosophical debate with Dostoevsky. This program was one he had theoretically outlined as early as 1905 but ultimately realized only in *Petersburg*.[12]

A confluence of personal and historical circumstances encouraged Bely to embrace the myth and text of St. Petersburg with a vengeance. The writer first set foot in the city on 9 January 1905, arriving there from his native Moscow on the very day the government drowned in blood a political rally in the capital's streets, unleashing the first Russian revolution. This month-long visit—during which Bely socialized with Aleksandr and Liubov' Blok, inaugurating an ill-fated romance with his friend's wife that brought Bely to the brink of suicide on another visit to the city, in September 1906—did much to amalgamate in the writer's mind the personal and social dramas forming *Petersburg*'s narrative backbone. Of course, St. Petersburg's mythology and treatment in art—recall that the heroes of Pushkin's *Bronze Horseman* and "The Queen of Spades" go mad, not least because of their living environment—fit well into Bely's association of the city with traumatic experience. The association helps explain the removal of "Saint" from the city's name in the novel's title and also the ominous patronymic "Petrovna" (the daughter of Peter) borne by Nikolai Apollonovich's love interest and Apollon Apollonovich's wife, both of whom are the sources of the male protagonists' emotional torment.

Anchoring the novel in the "Petersburg text of Russian literature," Bely turned his narrative into a panoply of citations and intertextual allusions—at times serious, at other times parodic and polemical—that gave *Petersburg*'s protagonists another, implicit dimension.[13] For Bely, intertextuality was indeed a primary tool of characterization: the reader cannot fully appreciate the story of Apollon Apollonovich Ableukhov and his estranged wife, Anna Petrovna, without tracing the couple to their Tolstoyan models—Aleksei Aleksandrovich Karenin and his wife, Anna; nor can one fully grasp the personae of Nikolai Apollonovich Ableukhov and Aleksandr Ivanovich Dudkin without recognizing their Pushkinian, Gogolian, and Dostoevskian predecessors. While our volume cannot boast an exhaustive account of *Petersburg*'s dense intertextuality, many contributors discuss, as a matter of course, various aspects of the novel's grid of literary allusions.

The book's first part explores *Petersburg*'s multifarious rapports with Russian and European intellectual life in Bely's day. This context is indispensable for a fuller appreciation of the intricate network of contemporary philosophical, theological, scientific, and political ideas that underpin the events *Petersburg* describes. This intellectual fabric informs the actions of the novel's characters and mediates the interpretation of these events and characters by Bely's narrator. Lynn Patyk explores the historical circumstances informing *Petersburg*'s terrorist intrigue, with an eye on the range of meanings—beyond politics—that intrigue had in Bely's modernist circle and in contemporary Russian society at large. Maria Carlson draws attention to Bely's fascination with Theosophy and, especially, with its offshoot—Rudolf Steiner's Anthroposophical doctrine, which freshly captivated the writer midway through his work on *Petersburg*. It has been suggested that *Petersburg* cannot be understood outside the German guru's occult science.[14] Such claims, however, should be viewed with some skepticism. Half of *Petersburg* had been written before Bely became Steiner's acolyte.[15] And even after the writer immersed himself in Anthroposophy, while finishing *Petersburg*, poor German skills slowed down his apprenticeship with Rudolf Steiner, as Bely himself admitted in letters to friends.[16] More important, as Maria Carlson and Hilary Fink show, Bely was too original, eclectic, and idiosyncratic a thinker to structure his novel in strict accordance with one specific intellectual system.

Steiner was among several German sages to leave a mark on *Petersburg*. Bely's interest in Friedrich Nietzsche's iconoclastic thought predated his work on the novel. The formative role in modernist philosophies of art and life of Nietzsche's intellectual heritage all but assured that Bely would engage with it (even parodically at times), as Edith Clowes illustrates. Nietzsche's importance in Bely's intellectual biography is echoed in *Petersburg*'s minutest details, such as the Dionysian caryatid on the façade of the institution headed by Apollon Apollonovich Ableukhov—a visual representation of the conflict between Apollinian striving for order and elemental Dionysian chaos, theorized by Nietzsche as a fundamental premise of human existence. Neo-Kantianism is yet another

German philosophical current informing the novel. As Timothy Langen explains, it shaped Bely's thought in the decade preceding his *Petersburg* project, and it is present there not only as one of the novel's competing philosophies but as the once-favorite doctrine of its young protagonist, Nikolai Ableukhov, who thus inherits more than one detail of Bely's sentimental and intellectual biography. The French thinker Henri Bergson equipped Bely with polemical tools for a critical reexamination of Nietzscheanism and Neo-Kantianism, whose philosophical virtues, Hilary Fink argues, the writer no longer took for granted during his work on *Petersburg*. Judith Wermuth-Atkinson shows that Bely's modernist search for alternatives to the materialist understanding of the world and the human being led the author of *Petersburg* to pay special attention to the new science of psychology, as elaborated by the Austrian-Jewish neurologist Sigmund Freud.

A special place in *Petersburg*'s imaginative universe is occupied by racial theories, whose narrative manifestations are explored by Henrietta Mondry. Bely, like most of his peers, was a racial thinker. He was also prone to racial conspiracy theories, which had been enthusiastically embraced in his Moscow home.[17] As a result, the writer was haunted by apprehension about the decline of the Aryan race. Aryans, understood as all Christian Europeans, were supposedly under siege by the Semites (read Jews) and the Yellow race (Asians, in the parlance of the day), with the latter unwittingly serving as a weapon of the universal Jewish plot.[18] *Petersburg*'s first readers ascribed to Bely's right-wing politics the thinly veiled anti-Semitism suffusing several characters in the novel—the double agent Lippanchenko; his informant, the sleazy journalist Neintelpfain; Lippanchenko's mistress, Zoia Fleisch; and Jewish radicals at a political rally.[19] But, as Mondry shows, Bely's racial thought went beyond politics. Fusing with modernist apocalyptic sensibility and drawing on the anti-Semitic thought of Richard Wagner, whom Bely admired as a composer and critical theorist, *Petersburg*'s racial dynamic cast Jews as agents of Russia's socio-economic disruption and as carriers of even graver existential threats—biological, spiritual, and cultural—to European civilization.

Fearing the opprobrium of political liberals, whom Bely imagined as puppets of Jewish interests, the writer expressed his racism circumspectly in *Petersburg*'s 1913 edition.[20] To be sure, the novel's anti-Semitic undercurrent was unmistakable, not least because Bely had sought inspiration in popular Jew-baiting pamphlets.[21] Symptomatically, suggesting that his friend switch prospective publishers, Blok presented a nascent modernist venture, the publishing house Sirin, which Bely ultimately chose for *Petersburg*, as a "great Aryan project" free from Jewish influence.[22] But as he prepared the novel's second, 1922 edition, Bely already had to account for Russia's changed political reality. The country's new Marxist rulers were likely to censure a novel that cast revolutionaries as proxies of a secret Jewish plot. In the novel's purged 1922 version, then, the original anti-Semitic message, while still present, became more cryptic, allowing one advocate of Bely's art to speak of the writer's intellectual evolution.[23] This was, in fact, mere adaptation to political circumstances, something Bely did continuously in Soviet Russia without relinquishing the basic tenets of his world view, including his apocalyptic racial apprehensions and conspiratorial mindset.[24]

Closing the book's first part, David Bethea demonstrates the centrality of eschatology in *Petersburg*'s narrative and stylistic economy. Eschatological thought—speculation about the end of history, framed as the demise and rebirth of the world and humankind—had special urgency in Russian modernist culture, which simultaneously anticipated, welcomed, and feared the apocalyptic scenarios it imagined. In this context, Bely's choice of St. Petersburg was anything but accidental: the thoroughly mythologized city, whose apocalyptic demise had been prophesied from its foundation, was a logical setting for the final battle of good and evil. This battle would put an end to the Antichrist's reign on earth and usher in the Second Coming of Christ, who in Bely's novel indeed roams the damned city, in the guise of a mysterious White Domino.

Our volume's second part examines *Petersburg* in the aesthetic context of Bely's day. Keenly following the latest developments in Russian and Western artistic theory and practice, equally well-versed in literature, painting, and music, Bely poured his erudition into *Petersburg* as a medium for reflecting on and realizing modernist artistic philosophy; above all, he focused on the ideal synthesis of art forms in a single oeuvre, as theorized by Richard Wagner, whose own *Gesammtkunstwerk*, or total work of art, took the form of his four-opera cycle *The Ring of the Nibelung*.[25] It is highly significant that, while writing *Petersburg* in Brussels, in the spring of 1912, Bely indulged his passion for music, attending three Wagnerian operas (*Lohengrin*, *Tristan and Isolde*, and *The Valkyrie*) to "[give his] days the coloring of the *Ring*," as he told Aleksandr Blok. There would be many other such interruptions in his work on the novel for the sake of music, without which he "simply could not live."[26] Steven Cassedy explores the role of music in Bely's novel against the backdrop of modernist musical theories and their implementation in literature. European modernists treated music as the supreme art form, wishing to integrate it, along with painting, into literary fiction. Inspired by this intellectual ferment, Bely not only devised his own theory of music in relation to other art forms but, as Cassedy shows, strove to realize his theory in *Petersburg*, whose intricate phonetic and rhythmic experiments with language explore the possibility of merging literature and music.

In contrast to their Western peers, Russian modernists took Wagner's idea of the total work of art to its logical extreme by turning their very lives, through aesthetically meaningful everyday behavior, into artistic texts that were lived before they could be written down. This practice, known in Russian modernist culture as "life-creation" (*zhiznetvorchestvo*), is exemplified in Bely's tortuous liaison with Liubov´ Blok, which the writer mythopoetically transposes in *Petersburg*, as Colleen McQuillen shows. Her essay considers Bely's novel as an exemplar of modernism's embrace of performance practices and metaphors. Explicating the role of the imagery and the vocabulary of theater and masquerade in Bely's novelistic articulation of his world view and sensibility, McQuillen illumines the complex interaction of art and life in Russian modernist experience, as encoded in *Petersburg*'s theatricalized romantic relationship between Nikolai Apollonovich Ableukhov and Sofia Petrovna Likhutina.

Heeding the programmatic modernist fusion of art forms, Olga Matich treats *Petersburg* as an expression of Bely's passion for painting. She explores the ways Bely uses verbal signs to create visual images, underlining the affinities of his style to painterly practices. Bely's choice of St. Petersburg as the novel's scene highlights such affinities, because the city was a popular subject among the modernist painters of the World of Art group, in whose eponymous journal, *Mir iskusstva*, Bely debuted as a critic.[27] A series of meaningful coincidences links *Petersburg*'s creative history to Aleksandr Benois's illustrations for Pushkin's *Bronze Horseman* and "The Queen of Spades," two cornerstones of the "Petersburg text." After its 1904 publication in *Mir iskusstva*, Benois's *Bronze Horseman* cycle was exhibited in St. Petersburg when Bely arrived there, in January 1905, for the aforementioned month-long stay, which resulted in impressions that would later inform *Petersburg*'s historical and love intrigues. Then, in late 1911, just as Bely sat down to write the opening chapters of *Petersburg*, the first edition of Pushkin's "Queen of Spades" with Benois's illustrations appeared and was soon followed by the similarly illustrated *Bronze Horseman*—events Bely was not likely to miss.[28]

In the fall of 1911, Bely also discussed painting with Henri Matisse, hosted by the Moscow art patron Sergei Shchukin, whose large collection of European modernist art was open to the public. Exchanges of this kind gave Bely a chance to stay informed even before his 1912 departure for Western Europe.[29] Abroad, his work on *Petersburg* was punctuated by visits to art galleries, where the writer saw the latest in modernist painting and regaled himself with Old Masters, from Matthias Grünewald and Jan van Eyck to Lucas Cranach and Hieronymus Bosch, whose traces Olga Matich finds in *Petersburg*'s visual texture and whom Bely particularly appreciated as precursors to "chimerical" modernist painters.[30]

Bely's artistic ecumenism and erudition make a fuller appreciation of *Petersburg* contingent on our ability to read this novel outside Russian cultural history proper, especially since it both echoed concurrent developments in transnational modernist culture and foreshadowed many of its literary practices. Thus, on one hand, *Petersburg* exemplifies transnational modernism's "metropolitan perception," its intense and continuous preoccupation with urbanism.[31] Bely's novel augured a series of modernist narratives, written in different languages but united, as Taras Koznarsky shows, by shared attention to the urban metropolis as both an active protagonist and a highly significant and indeed preferred setting in literary fiction and visual arts. On the other hand, Bely's novel marks the moment of transition between early and high modernism, in Russia and the West. The quarrel about the nature of reality was at the core of the conflict pitting Russia's positivist intelligentsia against modernists who located reality beyond rational cognition. Treating art as a privileged medium for transcendental intuition, modernists saw themselves as better realists than their materialist opponents. But, by the early 1910s, modernists increasingly looked for reality in human consciousness, coming to view the world as a construct of the psyche. This idea replaced the metaphysical bent of early Russian modernism, coinciding with the rise of the "realism of consciousness" in the West, where similar notions were being explored in the writings of Marcel Proust and Virginia Woolf, among others. In the final essay of Part Two, Violeta Sotirova looks at *Petersburg* as a case study in the larger modernist turn to consciousness as the source of reality, placing Bely's novel alongside contemporary literary experiments by his Western European peers.

With Russian modernists turning to the psyche as the source of true reality, experiments with language and narrative became means of conveying the unique relation of individual consciousness to the world.[32] *Petersburg* spearheaded this trend. Its blueprint, in fact, appeared in Bely's 1908 review of Stanisław Przybyszewski's *Homo Sapiens* (1901).[33] All that he had found admirable in the novel of the Polish modernist—its fragmented depiction of space, time, heroes, and events; its reliance on active readers to make sense of the narrative; its lack of psychological speculation as a motivating link between the inner life and actions of characters—Bely appropriated and developed in *Petersburg*, thus earning the title of "a cubist in literature."[34] *Petersburg*'s style matched its unconventional narrative. Written by a poet, this novel explored and manipulated every level of spoken and written language—from phonetics to morphology to syntax to page graphics—in order to speculate about language as a source of what people perceive as reality but what might as well be an illusion originating in the psyche. With *Petersburg*, Bely became "a writer for writers," charting the course of Russian modernist prose, whose practitioners rated his achievement as rivaling that of James Joyce.[35] That is why we open this volume with an essay by John Elsworth, the author of the most recent English translation of *Petersburg*— a task one eminent Russian-American Slavist has described as "almost insuperably hard."[36] Elsworth's essay endeavors to impart to Bely's Anglophone reader a sense of the challenges inherent in translating a text that has continuously baffled even educated native speakers of Russian. His other aim is to give the reader an idea of the inevitable losses and distortions accompanying any such translation project.

Andrei Bely's *Petersburg*: A History

Unlike the difficulties arising from *Petersburg*'s experimental style, esoteric philosophical references, dense intertextuality, and hermetic subtexts, the novel's equally challenging narrative structure is something one would be hard pressed to ascribe to authorial design alone. Bely's novel was in many ways shaped by the writer's personal circumstances and by the complex story of the book's multiple editions. Familiarity with *Petersburg*'s creative history helps us understand, if not solve, some of its narrative puzzles.

Bely initially conceived *Petersburg* as the second part in a trilogy. The poet's first foray into the novelistic genre, *The Silver Dove*, was serialized in the course of 1909. When *The Silver Dove* came out in book form, in May 1910, the author's preface described it as the first part in a trilogy, *East or West*. The trilogy's second installment—unrelated to *The Silver Dove* in plot and dramatis personae, with the exception of an episodic character (Styopka)—changed its title several times. At an early stage, in October 1911, Bely called it *A Lacquered Carriage*, referring to Senator Ableukhov's mode of transportation.[37] Two months later, submitting the novel's first three chapters to the Moscow journal *Russkaia mysl'*, Bely called his work *Evil Shadows*, alluding to the phantasmagoric nature of the city where the novel's scene was laid.[38] After the journal deemed those chapters unacceptable, Bely persevered in the project, renaming it *Petersburg* by mid-1912.[39]

Modernists flaunted their independence from the free cultural market, whose commercialism they castigated as a source of Europe's spiritual decline. But they also partook in that market. For all its elitist hermeticism and experimentalism, *Petersburg* owed its start to pragmatic monetary concerns: Bely began writing the novel in order to improve his dire financial situation. The author's economic predicament also dictated the initial breakneck pace of his work, explaining the high concentration of logical gaps in *Petersburg*'s opening chapters.

Bely had few independent sources of income and drew much of his sustenance from critical, journalistic, and literary activity. In November 1910, the writer went abroad in the company of his new romantic interest, Asya (Anna) Turgeneva. He intended to travel "for at least a year," in order to "finish the trilogy *East or West*" far from the bustle of Moscow.[40] But the travelers quickly ran out of money and cut the trip short, in May 1911, after visiting Italy, North Africa, and Palestine. Although the journey broke Bely's piggy bank, yielding not a page of the promised sequel to *The Silver Dove*, it did reenergize his anti-Western animus, which he soon poured into *Petersburg*.[41]

Bely spent the summer of 1911 frantically looking for a source of literary income. Finally, in late September, he secured a commission from *Russkaia mysl'*, brokered by fellow modernists who prevailed upon the journal's aesthetically conservative editor-in-chief, Pëtr Struve, Bely's intellectual antipode. Doubting the writer's reliability, Struve put forth stringent conditions. He refused Bely's request for an advance and gave the writer a three-month deadline to submit the novel's first half, or fifteen printer's sheets (about three hundred standard print pages) in exchange for a payout.[42] Bely had no choice but to accept: he was penniless, indebted, and homeless—cohabitation with Asya Turgeneva, whom Bely would marry only in 1914, barred the writer from his mother's place in Moscow, where he had hitherto resided. Above all, he agonized over his inability to provide for his beloved.[43] Looking back at the feverish pace of his work on *Petersburg*'s opening chapters, with no plot or character outline, Bely confessed that his stressful personal situation had "disfigured" the novel, forcing him, a year later, to try and rework those first three chapters in a rather unsuccessful attempt at remedying their "architectonic chaos."[44] That chaos gave Pëtr Struve a convenient pretext to reject the chapters Bely submitted in January 1912 and to cancel the contract for a novel that grated on the editor's aesthetic and political sensibilities.[45]

The publishing fiasco exacerbated Bely's personal circumstances, all the more so because Asya Turgeneva was eager to go to Brussels, where she wanted to continue her education as a graphic artist.[46] Borrowing money from his friend and fellow modernist poet, Aleksandr Blok, and securing an advance from the publisher K. Nekrasov, who acquired the rights to the unwritten novel in March 1912, Bely and his consort left for what was supposed to be a short trip but became a four-year expatriation, in line with the Russian tradition of producing literary masterpieces abroad. If Gogol wrote *Dead Souls* (1842) in Italy, and Dostoevsky began *The Idiot* (1868) in Geneva and finished it in Florence, *Petersburg* was mostly written in Belgium and Germany, with parts also penned in France, Switzerland, and Russia. In the two months (April–May 1912) he spent in Brussels, Bely wrote the fourth chapter and began reworking the preceding ones.[47] He was contractually obligated to finish and submit the novel by July, but his ambitious work schedule soon went off the rails.

Bely's time in Brussels was not colored solely by Wagnerian operas. The city's streets, where medieval and Renaissance architecture coexisted with modernist statements in the Art Nouveau style—echoing the writer's appreciation of the Old Masters, whom he revisited in German and Belgian museums, as prefigurations of "chimerical" modernist painters—unexpectedly became a setting for new mystical experiences. Bely and Turgeneva felt the sheer intensity of these experiences (some might call them paranoid delusions) on a daily basis and sought answers from Rudolf Steiner, whose name had been on everyone's lips in Moscow the previous autumn. In early May, they made a three-day trip to Cologne, where "the Doctor" held court.[48] Rather unsurprisingly, the impressionable and mystically inclined visitors fell under the spell of Steiner's charisma (Bely called it his "aura"), resolving to become apprentices in his occult science. This entailed not only a crash course in Anthroposophy (accompanied by German instruction since Bely's and Turgeneva's knowledge of the language was poor), but also constant travel as they followed Steiner, like groupies, on his lecture circuit—from Munich to Basel to Vitznau to Stuttgart to Berlin. Naturally, *Petersburg*'s proposed work schedule "went to hell," as Bely told Blok in December 1912, taking stock of his sporadic work on chapters 1 through 6, and asking his friend for another loan, since he was already in breach of contract with the publisher.[49] Thus, revising the novel's "chaotic" opening chapters in the fall of 1912, the writer was no less plagued by haste, thanks to pressing new commitments arising from his Anthroposophical apprenticeship, than a year earlier.[50]

In the spring of 1913, Bely's publisher, Nekrasov, set into galleys the novel's reworked first two chapters, which the writer had sent him sometime in 1912. But at that time Bely decided to switch publishers, going with the nascent modernist house Sirin, which bought from Nekrasov the rights to *Petersburg*, giving its author a more advantageous contract.[51] Nekrasov's galleys occupy an intermediate position between the original "architectonic chaos" of *Petersburg*'s opening, written in the fall of 1911, and the definitive version of the first three chapters, on which Bely worked in late 1912. The "Nekrasov redaction" has been a valuable source for literary scholars who can compare three versions of the novel's beginning, tracing the evolution of Bely's project and parsing its ultimately unresolvable contradictions.

After sending to Sirin the final version of the novel's first three chapters, in February 1913, Bely and Turgeneva left Germany for Russia, where he worked on chapters 6 and 7. In July, they left for Munich to resume their Anthroposophical studies and itinerant life among Steiner's retinue. Between August and December 1913, struggling to finish *Petersburg*, Bely traveled from Germany to Norway, then to Denmark, and back to Germany, where he shuttled between Berlin, Stuttgart, Nuremberg, Munich, and Leipzig (here, in January 1914, he made an emotionally charged pilgrimage to Nietzsche's grave). Throughout 1913, Bely increasingly viewed the *Petersburg* project as irritatingly burdensome because it was unrelated to his new life as an Anthroposophist.[52] He completed and submitted to Sirin the novel's eighth chapter and epilogue in November 1913.[53]

As its author crisscrossed Europe, *Petersburg*'s serialization began in Russia. The novel's first installment came out in the literary almanac *Sirin* in October 1913, followed by another installment in December. The final installment appeared in March 1914.[54] The completion of the novel's publication coincided with Bely and Turgeneva's move from Germany to the town of Dornach, near Basel, where they would participate in the construction of the Goetheanum— the main temple and headquarters of the Anthroposophical movement. Unexpectedly cut off from the rest of Europe by the outbreak of World War I, Bely stayed in neutral Switzerland for two years, listening to the cannonade from the French side of the border, until the Russian authorities called him up for reserve duty. In August 1916, leaving Turgeneva in Dornach, he took a circuitous route back to Russia, where he would manage to get an exemption from active military service.

Three months earlier, in April 1916, *Petersburg* had come out in book form. This was not a new edition. Eager to help Bely, whose precarious finances approached a breaking point because of the wartime slump in the literary market, Aleksandr Blok and Sirin's editor-in-chief, R. V. Ivanov-Razumnik, obtained the publisher's permission to physically remove *Petersburg*'s installments from the unsold stock of the almanac *Sirin*, bind them together, and reissue them as a separate book. The only innovation was the cover, jointly designed by Bely's colleagues, who prepared the book without the author's input.[55]

The last point is noteworthy given the reigning confusion about the dating of *Petersburg*'s first edition. The 1916 book was a straightforward reissue, without textual changes, of the novel Bely had finished in November 1913 and serialized between October 1913 and March 1914. Among the three possible chronological markers for *Petersburg*'s original edition—1913, 1914, or 1916—the year 1913 appears the most historically and textologically pertinent, particularly considering that contemporaries saw *Petersburg* as a significant literary event of 1913.[56] Part of the reason for the strong association of the novel with 1913 was the striking aesthetic novelty of the installments published in October and December of that year. Another factor was that *Petersburg* came to symbolize pre-1914 sensibility once the year 1914 became associated with the start of a war that changed the course of Russian history.[57] Pegging *Petersburg*'s first edition to 1914, let alone 1916, opens the novel to anachronistic readings, as if its conception and composition had been informed by the war. Nothing could be farther from the truth. Bely's correspondence shows that the war caught him completely by surprise, no matter how much the author and his readers have been tempted later to interpret the war and the concomitant demise of the Russian empire as prophesied by *Petersburg*'s modernist apocalypticism. Characteristically, in 1916, preparing to reissue *Petersburg* in book form, Ivanov-Razumnik cited its completion in 1913, and its resultant rootedness in antebellum realia, to dissuade a tsarist censor from retitling the novel *Petrograd*—after the wartime capital as it had been patriotically renamed in August 1914.[58]

As mentioned above, the haste, psychological stress, and constant distractions plaguing Bely's work on *Petersburg* generated a number of problems in the novel's narrative structure. Some of these problems Bely put to good aesthetic and philosophical use, for they helped convey the subjectivity of the human perception of time and reality. For example, at a 1912 public reading of the novel's early draft, Bely's attention was drawn to a factual error—there had been no trams in St. Petersburg in 1905 (the service had been launched only in 1907). The writer decided to keep the tram, thus challenging the positivist idea of time.[59] But he also self-consciously emphasized the anachronism, lest it be construed as a loss of authorial control over artistic material rather than part of a modernist philosophical statement: "In advance I must correct an inaccuracy that has crept in," says *Petersburg*'s narrator, "it is not the fault of the author, but of the author's pen: at this time trams were not yet running through the city" (24).[60] In other instances, however, problems with narrative time—detailed in the synopsis of *Petersburg*'s plot at the end of this volume—are clearly unintentional, despite Bely's efforts, in 1912, to remedy the compositional lapses of the opening chapters. These chapters, in fact, have confused even the most experienced of Bely's readers: wrestling with the problem of narrative time in *Petersburg*, the editor of its authoritative academic redaction states that the novel's action takes place "between September 31 [*sic*] and October 9, 1905," unwittingly adding one more day to the month of September in order to reconcile the novel's chronological contradictions.[61] But however hard one might try, *Petersburg*'s logical gaps cannot be entirely explained away as the author's attempt to convey the relativity of time through narrative manipulation.[62]

The subsequent rewriting to which Bely subjected *Petersburg* not only failed to address the novel's logical gaps but actually made them worse. In 1914–15, Bely still toyed with the idea of writing the third part of his proposed trilogy,

East or West, but new literary projects took precedence until, in early 1916, he gave up on the incomplete trilogy altogether.[63] In the summer of 1914, however, looking for sources of income, the writer undertook to shorten the recently published *Petersburg* "by about a hundred pages," in order to meet Georg Müller's conditions for its German translation and publication in Munich (the war delayed this publication until 1919). Bely found it "so engrossing" to reduce the length of his novel—which, in his opinion, "only benefited from abbreviation"— that he resolved "to abridge its future Russian edition as well, by about one hundred and fifty pages."[64] This new edition would have to wait a while. Desperately fighting for physical survival in the face of famine and cold during the civil war years, Bely prepared a shorter version of *Petersburg* for publication, sometime in 1919, but it never saw the light of day for economic reasons.[65] Then, in October 1921, he followed the example of many Russian artists and intellectuals, leaving for the relative material comfort of postwar Germany. The writer's expatriation was additionally motivated by his desire to reunite with Asya Turgeneva and reconnect with the Anthroposophical movement. Once in Berlin, Bely revived his plans for *Petersburg*'s second, abridged Russian edition.

This gave the author another chance to address the logical gaps in *Petersburg*'s first edition, but the final product, published in 1922, turned out to be even more confusing than the original. Personal circumstances once more conspired against Bely's artistic plans. Once again he was forced to work under time pressure, this time to earn the much-needed honorarium promised by an émigré publisher intent on selling the book in Soviet Russia (a practice that was common in the early 1920s). Even more confounding was Bely's concurrent descent into emotional torment, for which he found an outlet in binge drinking. This was the writer's way of dealing with his most serious nervous breakdown since the 1906–7 personal drama informing *Petersburg*'s romantic intrigue. The latest breakdown was tied to all that Bely found abroad: after five years of separation, Asya Turgeneva no longer wanted to be his wife; he was disappointed by the artistic and intellectual life of postwar Germany and Berlin's Russian expatriate circles; and finally, Anthroposophy proved insufficient for Bely's spiritual needs (and his Soviet passport barred him from Dornach).[66]

In this disordered state of mind, Bely undertook not only to produce *Petersburg*'s second edition but also to revise his entire literary oeuvre, making it more consonant with his current interests and concerns and more attuned to the ideological expectations of Marxist censors in Soviet Russia (which remained his target literary market). During his two years in Berlin, Bely published sixteen books of poetry and prose, half of which were reworked versions of his older writings, and the other half of which consisted of new work. It would be an understatement to say that Bely's reduction of the novel by one third at this time of duress and emotional strain was executed less thoughtfully and carefully than such a complex literary work warranted. The synopsis at the end of our volume indicates the excisions, but it does not convey the full effects of Bely's editorial ax. Summarizing the differences between *Petersburg*'s two redactions, Vladimir Alexandrov argues that the Berlin edition enhances "the narrator's highly elliptical form of communication. This is perhaps the single most important effect Bely achieved, or better to say, augmented, when he abridged the novel in 1922. He cut more or less full exchanges between characters and descriptions of events to a minimum, with the result that the new text contains numerous passages teetering on the edge of unintelligibility."[67] Without addressing the compositional imperfections of the 1913 edition, then, the Berlin redaction added a new host of problems that Leonid Dolgopolov traces to "the evident haste with which the novel was abridged, producing numerous stylistic gaffes, [narrative] inconsistencies, and lapses in logic."[68] Given all this, it is difficult to agree with the translators of *Petersburg*'s abridged edition that it constitutes the novel's "definitive text," even if its reduced size makes it more welcome in a college classroom than the original, 1913 edition, which conveys much more fully and faithfully the sensibility and world view of prewar Russian modernist culture.[69]

Upon his return to Russia in October 1923, Bely was asked by the Moscow Art Theater (MKhAT 2) to turn *Petersburg* into a play. The project soon became a delicate balancing act in view of increasingly intransigent Soviet censorship. In the play, revolutionary terrorists lost the ambiguity that had been their basic characteristic in the novel. Bely cast them as "honest and spiritually strong" fighters for a noble cause while Apollon Apollonovich's storyline lost its tragic side and became, in Bely's estimate, a Gogolian farce culminating in the senator's assassination—another politically correct departure from the novel.[70] The play's premiere, in November 1925, horrified the author as a "monstrous" and "ugly" perversion of "his" *Petersburg*.[71] But Bely's troubles with Marxist censors were only just beginning. When, in 1928, he prepared *Petersburg*'s Berlin edition for publication with further, relatively small cuts, even this politically sanitized version of the novel was banned by the gatekeepers of nascent Stalinist culture. Only the personal intervention of the head of Glavlit, the governmental body responsible for literary censorship, made the publication possible.[72] In the USSR, the Berlin edition was reissued once more, in 1935, a year after Bely's death. The intensifying Stalinist crackdown on modernism's artistic and intellectual heritage placed Bely outside the Soviet literary canon, preventing *Petersburg*'s further reprints in the USSR. The novel would not be reissued there until 1978, when it appeared in the twice-expurgated 1928 edition. In 1981, *Petersburg*'s original version—prepared by Leonid Dolgopolov to the highest standards of literary scholarship—came out for the first time since 1916.[73]

Despite Soviet proscription, *Petersburg* played an epochal role in modern Russian literature. Its importance for the evolution of Russian prose writing in the twentieth century had no equals. The novel marked a watershed in literary expression: one simply could not write Russian prose "after *Petersburg*" the way it had been written before. Even rejecting Bely's stylistic and narrative experiments, one could never lose sight of *Petersburg*'s towering example, which remained a major, if often unspoken, reference point for Russian writers in the USSR and in exile. Characteristically, fifty years after the novel's original publication, Vladimir Nabokov ranked *Petersburg* alongside James Joyce's *Ulysses*, Franz Kafka's *Metamorphosis*, and Marcel Proust's *In Search of Lost Time* in his list of "my greatest masterpieces of twentieth century prose."[74] Like the other modernist masterpieces on Nabokov's list, *Petersburg* makes for an intensely enjoyable but challenging read, for Bely expected his audience to actively participate in unraveling the work's many meanings, narrative strains, and patterns of details. The present volume aims to facilitate that task by recreating for the general Anglophone public the sociopolitical, intellectual, and artistic context informing Bely's novel.

Notes

1. Gabriel Josipovici, *The World and the Book: A Study of Modern Fiction* (London: Macmillan, 1994), 179.

2. R. V. Ivanov-Razumnik, *Russkaia literatura XX veka* (Petrograd: Kolos, 1920), 27.

3. Andrei Belyi, "Problema kul'tury" (1909), *Simvolizm* (Moscow: Musaget, 1910), 8–9.

4. Andrei Belyi, "Detskaia svistul'ka," *Vesy* 8 (1907), 58.

5. Neil Cornwell, "The Russian Joyce," *James Joyce Broadsheet* 13 (1984), 2.

6. Joan Neuberger, *Hooliganism: Crime, Culture, and Power in St. Petersburg, 1900–1914* (Berkeley: University of California Press, 1993), 30, 74–78, 155–57.

7. Vladislav Khodasevich, "Andrei Belyi," *Nekropol'. Literatura i vlast'. Pis'ma B. A. Sadovskomu* (Moscow: SS, 1996), 58–59. The publishers of John Malmstad and Robert Maguire's translation of *Petersburg* (Indiana University Press, 1978) have done a disservice to the reader by reproducing on the cover Harlequin's traditional suit instead of the domino described in the novel. See Bely's drawing of Nikolai as the Red Domino at http://stpetersburg.berkeley.edu/bely/characters.html.

8. Georgii Fedotov, "Tri stolitsy" (1926), *Litso Rossii* (Paris: YMCA-Press, 1967), 49–56.

9. Vladimir Toporov, "Peterburg i 'peterburgskii tekst russkoi literatury,'" *Peterburgskii tekst russkoi literatury* (Saint-Petersburg: Iskusstvo-SPb, 2003), 22–31, 47, 59.

10. Zara Mints, "Peterburgskii tekst i russkii simvolizm," *Poetika russkogo simvolizma* (Saint-Petersburg: Iskusstvo-SPb, 2004), 114.

11. For a map of St. Petersburg, complete with the street trajectories of the novel's protagonists, see: http://stpetersburg.berkeley.edu/bely/city.html.

12. Andrei Belyi, "Ibsen i Dostoevskii," *Vesy* 12 (1905), 49, 54; *Masterstvo Gogolia* (Moscow-Leningrad: OGIZ, 1934), 302.

13. Lidiia Ginzburg, *O literaturnom geroe* (Leningrad: Sovetskii pisatel´, 1979), 129. N. Pustygina, "Tsitatnost´ v romane Andreia Belogo 'Peterburg,'" *Trudy po russkoi i slavianskoi filologii* XXVIII.414 (1977), 80–97.

14. R. V. Ivanov-Razumnik, "Andrei Belyi," in *Russkaia literatura XX veka*, ed. S. A. Vengerov (Moscow: Mir, 1916), 3:53.

15. Monika Spivak, *Andrei Belyi—mistik i sovetskii pisatel´* (Moscow: RGGU, 2006), 70–71.

16. Andrei Bely to Aleksandr Blok (14.V.1912; 10.XI.1912), in their *Perepiska 1903–1919*, ed. A. Lavrov (Moscow: Progress-Pleiada, 2001), 457, 460, 471–72. On Bely's inadequate German, see Nikolai Berdiaev, *Samopoznanie* (Moscow: DEM, 1990), 179, 182. Aaron Shteinberg, *Druz´ia moikh rannikh let (1911–1928)*, ed. G. Nivat (Paris: Sintaksis, 1991), 122.

17. Ilona Svetlikova, *The Moscow Pythagoreans: Mathematics, Mysticism, and Anti-Semitism in Russian Symbolism* (New York: Palgrave Macmillan, 2013), 23–27.

18. Bely to Blok (June 1911), in their *Perepiska*, 408–9.

19. Marietta Shaginian, "'Peterburg' Andreia Belogo" (1914); Aleksandr Gidoni, "Omrachennyi Petrograd" (1916), in *Andrei Belyi: Pro et Contra*, ed. A. Lavrov (Saint-Petersburg: RKhGI, 2004), 395, 439–40.

20. Mikhail Bezrodnyi, "O 'iudoboiazni' Andreia Belogo," *Novoe literaturnoe obozrenie* 28 (1997), 109–12. K. Postoutenko, "N. K. i E. K. Metnery: paradoks natsional´noi samoidentifikatsii. K istorii odnogo pis´ma A. Belogo," *De Visu* 1–2 (1994), 44–48.

21. Bely to Blok (18–19.X.1911), in their *Perepiska*, 416.

22. Blok to Bely (15.XI.1912; 7.XII.1912), in their *Perepiska*, 474, 478.

23. R. V. Ivanov-Razumnik, "Peterburg," in Lavrov, *Andrei Belyi: Pro et Contra*, 635, 645.

24. Spivak, *Andrei Belyi*, 324–33.

25. Throughout this volume, the term *Gesammtkunstwerk* is cited in Wagner's original spelling (see Steven Cassedy's essay), in contrast to its current spelling with one *m*.

26. Bely to Blok (1–10.XI.1911; 14.V.1912), in their *Perepiska*, 424, 455.

27. S. S. Hoisington, "*Mednyi vsadnik* through the Eyes of Alexander Benois," *Russian Literature* 28.4 (1990), 479–506.

28. Aleksandr Ospovat, Roman Timenchik, *"Pechal´ nu povest´ sokhranit´ . . ." Ob avtore i izdateliakh "Mednogo vsadnika"* (Moscow: Kniga, 1985), 202–17.

29. Bely to Blok (4.XI.1911), in their *Perepiska*, 422–23. Iu. Rusakov, "Matiss v Rossii osen´iu 1911 goda," *Trudy Gosudarstvennogo Ermitazha* 14 (1973), 178.

30. Bely to Blok (4.IV.1912), in their *Perepiska*, 448.
31. Raymond Williams, *The Politics of Modernism: Against the New Conformists* (London: Verso, 1989), 44.
32. Leonid Livak, "Russian Modernism and the Novel," in *A History of the Modernist Novel*, ed. G. Castle (Cambridge: Cambridge University Press, 2015), 110–34.
33. Andrei Belyi, "Prorok bezlichiia," *Arabeski* (Munich: Wilhelm Fink, 1969), 3–6.
34. Nikolai Berdiaev, "Picasso" (1914); "Astral′nyi roman" (1916), *Krizis iskusstva* (Moscow: G. A. Leman, 1918), 32, 41.
35. Boris Pasternak, Boris Pil′niak, Grigorii Sannikov, "Andrei Belyi," *Izvestiia* 8 (9 January 1934), 4. Evgenii Zamiatin, "Andrei Belyi" (1934), *My* (Kishinev: Literatura artistike, 1989), 609–10.
36. Gleb Struve, "Andrey Bely Redivivus," in *Andrey Bely: A Critical Review*, ed. G. Janecek (Lexington: University Press of Kentucky, 1978), 30.
37. Bely to Blok (18–19.X.1911), in their *Perepiska*, 416.
38. Bely to Valerii Briusov (10.I.1912), "Perepiska s Andreem Belym," in *Valerii Briusov. Literaturnoe nasledstvo* 85, ed. S. Grechishkin and A. Lavrov (Moscow: Nauka, 1976), 425.
39. Bely to Blok (10.VI.1912), in their *Perepiska*, 470.
40. Bely to Blok (October 1910), in their *Perepiska*, 376.
41. Bely to Blok and M. K. Morozova (April 1911), in Belyi and Blok, *Perepiska*, 396–97.
42. Bely to Emilii Metner (29.IX.1911) and Briusov (10.I.1912), cited in Leonid Dolgopolov, "Tvorcheskaia istoriia i istoriko-literaturnoe znachenie romana A. Belogo 'Peterburg,'" in Andrei Belyi, *Peterburg*, ed. L. Dolgopolov (Moscow: Nauka, 1981), 547, 554.
43. Bely to Blok (30.X.1911; 15–16.XI.1911; 19.XI.1911), in their *Perepiska*, 419, 426–27, 429.
44. Bely to Metner (26.XII.1912), "Dopolneniia," in Belyi, *Peterburg*, 513.
45. Struve to Briusov (2.II.1912); S. Sokolov to K. Nekrasov (4.III.1912), in Dolgopolov, "Tvorcheskaia istoriia," 555–58. M. Kolerov, "Pochemu P. B. Struve otkazalsia pechatat′ 'Peterburg' A. Belogo," *De Visu* 5–6 (1994), 86–88.
46. Bely to Blok (8–9.III.1921), in their *Perepiska*, 445.
47. Andrei Belyi, "Material k biografii," in "Pis′ma Andreia Belogo k Fedoru Sologubu," *Simvolisty vblizi: Stat′i i publikatsii*, ed. A. Lavrov and S. Grechishkin (Saint-Petersburg: Skifiia, 2004), 372n5.
48. Bely to Blok (14.V.1912) and A. S. Petrovskii (10.VII.1912), in Belyi and Blok, *Perepiska*, 454, 457, 463n24.
49. Bely to Blok (10.XI.1912; December 1912), in their *Perepiska*, 471–72, 476; and to his mother, A. D. Bugaeva (18.V.1912; 11.VI.1912), *"Liubliu tebia nezhno . . ." Pis′ma Andreia Belogo k materi, 1899–1922*, ed. S. Voronin (Moscow: Reka vremen, 2013), 153–54, 156.
50. Bely to Bugaeva (24.XI.1912), in *"Liubliu tebia nezhno . . ."* 167.
51. Bely to Bugaeva (III.1913), in *"Liubliu tebia nezhno . . ."* 176.

52. Bely to R. V. Ivanov-Razumnik (1–3.III.1927), in their *Perepiska*, ed. A. Lavrov and J. Malmstad (Saint-Petersburg: Atheneum-Feniks, 1998), 495.

53. Ivanov-Razumnik to Bely (25.XI.1913), in their *Perepiska*, 34.

54. *Sirin* 1 (Saint-Petersburg, 1913), 1–148; *Sirin* 2 (1913), 1–209; *Sirin* 3 (1914), 1–276.

55. Ivanov-Razumnik to Bely (26.III.1916), in their *Perepiska*, 65.

56. R. V. Ivanov-Razumnik, "Literatura i obshchestvennost'. Russkaia literatura v 1913 godu," *Zavety* 1 (1914), 93.

57. Bely to Ivanov-Razumnik (1–3.III.1927), in their *Perepiska*, 495–96.

58. Ivanov-Razumnik's recollections, in Belyi and Ivanov-Razumnik, *Perepiska*, 66n2.

59. Vladimir Piast, "Roman filosofa" (1916), in Lavrov, *Andrei Belyi: Pro et Contra*, 399, 948n3.

60. Andrei Bely, *Petersburg*, tr. John Elsworth (London: Pushkin Press, 2009).

61. Leonid Dolgopolov, *Andrei Belyi i ego roman "Peterburg"* (Leningrad: Sovetskii pisatel', 1988), 233.

62. As does, for example, John Elsworth in his "Reprezentatsiia empiricheskogo vremeni v 'Peterburge' Andreia Belogo," in *Na rubezhe dvukh stoletii*, ed. V. Bagno et al. (Moscow: NLO, 2009), 795–805.

63. Bely to Ivanov-Razumnik (19.IV.1914; 7.XI.1915; 11.VII.1916), in their *Perepiska*, 43, 57, 70. Spivak, *Andrei Belyi—mistik i sovetskii pisatel'*, 182.

64. Bely to Ivanov-Razumnik (19.VI.1914), in their *Perepiska*, 46.

65. Bely to Ivanov-Razumnik (July 1920), in their *Perepiska*, 204, 206n5.

66. Bely to Ivanov-Razumnik (15.I.1922), in their *Perepiska*, 234–35, 254.

67. Vladimir Alexandrov, *Andrei Bely: The Major Symbolist Fiction* (Cambridge, MA: Harvard University Press, 1985), 101.

68. Dolgopolov, "Tvorcheskaia istoriia," 580–83.

69. "Translators' Introduction," in Andrei Bely, *Petersburg*, tr. Robert Maguire and John Malmstad (Bloomington: Indiana University Press, 1978), xxv.

70. Bely to Ivanov-Razumnik (17.VII.1924; 20.IX.1925; 27.IX.1925), in their *Perepiska*, 295, 328, 332.

71. Bely to Ivanov-Razumnik (6.III.1926), in their *Perepiska*, 341.

72. Bely to Ivanov-Razumnik (8.II.1928), in their *Perepiska*, 570.

73. This edition has been reissued with corrections and additional annotations: Andrei Belyi, *Peterburg*, ed. L. Dolgopolov, A. Lavrov, and S. Grechishkin (Saint-Petersburg: Nauka, 2004).

74. Vladimir Nabokov, *Strong Opinions* (New York: Vintage, 1990), 57.

On Translating *Petersburg*

JOHN ELSWORTH

I first made the acquaintance of Bely's *Petersburg* in the autumn of 1961, during my first term of postgraduate study. At that point I had read only the 1922 Berlin edition, but also had to hand the still recent first translation of the novel into English, John Cournos's version, published in 1959 and based on the same edition. In places the translation reads well, even elegantly, but it was not long before I began to notice some of its inadequacies. It was immediately clear that the translator had adopted an extremely free approach, expunging the self-conscious narrator entirely and adapting or omitting many passages for reasons that are not always easy to ascertain. He even changed the title from *Petersburg* to *St. Petersburg*, restoring the city's official title where Bely had used its popular name. However, beyond these presumably intentional alterations, it struck me then, as it has struck many another reader, that this translation abounds in quite unintentional distortions of meaning. The Russian text is frequently misread, individual Russian words are frequently misunderstood, and as a result the English text sometimes fails to make sense. One glaring example which caught my eye was the rendering of *babochkino krylo* as "a female wing," rather than "a butterfly wing."[1] It would be pointless to multiply the examples, which can be found on practically every page.

In this light, it has been extremely instructive to see the archival material recently published by Roger Keys concerning the correspondence between members of the editorial staff at Grove Press and Weidenfeld and Nicolson, prior to the publication of the translation. In a letter dated 24 April 1959, Barley Alison of Weidenfeld's wrote to Judith Schmidt at Grove: "Both Professor Bowra and Professor Berlin at Oxford have congratulated us on acquiring the English rights of this [*Petersburg*], and Berlin says he has seen your translation and shares our view that it is excellent."[2] One has to suppose that making a judgment on Cournos's translation was not high on Isaiah Berlin's agenda, and that he had not in fact found much time for it. The correspondence, relating principally to the possibility of laudatory introductions by Berlin himself and the Russian émigré poet and critic Georgii Adamovich (neither of which appeared in the published version), contains frequent mentions of Bely's stylistic innovations, of which the publishers can clearly have had only hearsay knowledge, since they are not reflected in any way in the translation.

John Cournos had been translating Russian texts since before World War I, and had first translated *Petersburg* in 1929, but had never previously succeeded in publishing it.[3] The context in which it now appeared was the aftermath of the Pasternak affair, including Boris Pasternak's forced refusal of the Nobel Prize and the worldwide fame of his novel *Doctor Zhivago* (1958). Naturally enough, publishers were seeking to keep the Russian interest alive and to find, if they could, another Russian novel which might have a similar effect. *Petersburg* cannot be said to have met that need. In the event, they had to wait a few more years until first Aleksandr Solzhenitsyn and then Mikhail Bulgakov provided what they were looking for.

A number of further years elapsed before a second attempt was made to render Bely's novel into English. This time it was the work of two distinguished professors of Russian studies, John Malmstad and Robert Maguire, who were well aware of the first translation's failings and set out to produce a version which would not be subject to any similar criticism. During those years the field of Russian-English translation had been profoundly affected by the 1964 appearance of Vladimir Nabokov's annotated translation of Aleksandr Pushkin's narrative poem *Eugene Onegin* (1825–32), and by the polemics that ensued between Nabokov and Edmund Wilson. Nabokov insisted on what he called "literal" translation, defined as "rendering, as closely as the associative and syntactical capacities of another language allow, the exact contextual meaning of the original."[4] In fact Nabokov had already put down a marker for his understanding of proper translation in the foreword to his 1958 translation of Mikhail Lermontov's

A Hero of Our Time (1840): "This is the first translation of Lermontov's novel. The book has been paraphrased into English several times, but never translated before. The experienced hack may find it quite easy to turn Lermontov's Russian into slick English clichés by means of judicious omission, amplification, and levigation; and he will tone down everything that might seem unfamiliar to the meek and imbecile reader visualised by his publisher. But the honest translator is faced with a different task."[5]

The distinction Nabokov makes here between "translation" and "paraphrase" lies at the heart of debates over the nature of literary translation that have rumbled on for years. In his recent book *Is That a Fish in Your Ear?*, David Bellos notes that traditionally, English translations of Latin and Greek texts were designed to facilitate the learning of the ancient languages rather than to be read as English texts. This situation was transformed shortly after World War II by the inauguration of the Penguin Classics series, which was intended specifically to make works of ancient literature accessible to readers with no classical training. These translations therefore needed to be couched in a readily accessible English style. Bellos calls this an "adaptive" style (305). Nabokov, it seems, would have called it paraphrase. Cournos's version of *Petersburg* might at best be called "adaptive"; it is clear that Malmstad and Maguire proposed to produce a "literal" version.

Unlike Cournos, however, they are fully aware of the novel's complexity. In their "Translators' Introduction," they give an extensive description of the novel's phonetic qualities and the way in which Bely set out to create "a world of sound."[6] They cite Bely's own statements about the dominant sound patterns which he claimed lay at the basis of the novel and gave rise to its "content." They concede that no literal translation of such features is achievable but explain that they have sought to create similar effects in English where possible. They make it clear that in their attempts to convey "some sense of this texture" in their translation, they have "eschewed 'smooth' English as consciously and deliberately as Bely did 'smooth' Russian" (xxv). Clearly, their priority has come close to the principles of translation enunciated by Nabokov: semantic accuracy takes precedence, followed by the attempt to give an impression of the text's phonetic quality, and the creation of an easily readable English text is low on the scale of desiderata. It is telling that while in their introductory material they show a flawless awareness of the importance of rhythm in Bely's novel, they make no mention of any attempt to reproduce or imitate it in translation. Nabokov, writing about the translation of *Onegin*, had insisted that seeking to reproduce the verse form, in addition to the demands he was making on the semantic level of the text, was "mathematically impossible." Given the impossibility of reproducing exactly the rhythmic character of Bely's prose, Malmstad and Maguire did not include rhythm among their aims.

As in effect the first serious attempt to render *Petersburg* into English, Malmstad and Maguire's translation attracted considerable critical attention. Clarence Brown wrote, "The work of Robert Maguire and John Malmstad is a fresh, intelligent, scrupulous and, as far as may be, faithful translation of the novel. It is, in everything but literal fact, its first appearance in the English language."[7] Alex de Jong made the point that the novel is "monstrously hard to translate," and conceded that "these two professors [. . .] have, on the face of it, done a fine job." Nevertheless, he concluded with the withering comment that they "can't really write English."[8] Critics who came to the novel without an academic basis in Russian studies tended to be less than enthusiastic. Reviewers asked whether *Petersburg* had "survived" the translation. Blake Morrison asserted, despite reservations, that it had, "not the least because (and this isn't sufficiently emphasized in the introduction) it is tense and exciting in the best narrative tradition." Robin Lane Fox, however, came to the conclusion that "this admired prose-poem has not survived its jump into English terms."[9] This same line of response is well summarized by Anthony Burgess: "If, having read this decent English rendering, we frown in perplexity at Nabokov's judgement, we shall have to conclude that the greatness is wholly resident in the language."[10] In other words, *Petersburg* is untranslatable.

Not until 1995 did any English translation of the longer, 1913 edition of *Petersburg* appear. The translator, David McDuff, offers little by way of motivation for the choice beyond the suggestion that the first edition "represents a truer fulfilment of Bely's original aim in writing the book."[11] One might respond, as Maguire and Malmstad have done in their "Translators' Introduction" (xxiv), that Bely revised the novel in 1922 precisely because at that point he believed he had not fulfilled his original aim in the first edition. The 1913 edition presents the translator with a somewhat different set of challenges from the later one, with its more convoluted syntax and its wealth of atmospheric descriptive passages that often evoke the history of the city. The translation seems to bear marks of haste. While largely accurate in its rendering of the text's meaning, it still contains numerous errors of understanding, especially in the often laconic or truncated passages of dialogue. On two occasions the word *dymiashchiisia* is translated as "smoking," once in relation to a soup tureen, and again in relation to blood, where the context clearly requires "steaming." McDuff does not identify any specific approach to the task, as Malmstad and Maguire had done, and has not succeeded in producing an English text that reads either smoothly or intentionally otherwise.

When I was approached to produce a new translation of the novel, I had to think very hard whether there was any good reason to accept. Was *Petersburg* indeed untranslatable? If I were to undertake the task, what were the criteria I would need to meet?

The first issue was the choice of edition. I was only interested in attempting a version of the original 1913 text. Not that I was concerned with interpreting Bely's intentions at either stage of composition: whatever he may himself assert afterward, an author's intentions can only be his intentions at the time of writing. Nor do I consider that the standard textological maxim to the effect that the definitive text is the last lifetime edition over which the author had full control is binding in Bely's case. He was much given to reinterpreting his own past. During his sojourn in Berlin, in 1921–23, he revised not only *Petersburg* but also his collected poetry, on which he attempted to confer a teleology not at all evident in the earlier publications.[12] Critics have not been willing to regard the 1923 edition of his poetry as definitive. My decision was based on my personal judgement that the 1913 edition was the more successful text.[13]

Given the history of previous attempts at translating *Petersburg*, none of which had fully succeeded in establishing the novel in the canon of Russian novels in English, it seemed to me that the only worthwhile undertaking was to aim for an English version that could be read pleasurably (not necessarily "easily") by a reader who was not a student of Russian and might not be well versed in Russian culture. My English text would have to be able to stand on its own without relying on explanatory material or notes. It seemed to me that the use of notes had on occasion led earlier translators to sidestep some of the greatest difficulties in translation and resort to explanation. Nothing deters the reader of a translation more than a note explaining that such-and-such a passage or expression cannot really be translated, and at the same time, of course, nothing emphasizes more clearly that the text is a translation.

If a translated text is to find a home in the culture of the target language, it must read as though, in some sense, it belongs there. I take the view that a translation must be free to exploit the full possibilities of the target language. Nothing should be a priori out of bounds. I would not try to identify in advance any specific English style to emulate. Having seen the effect of the self-denying ordinances that some translators (specifically of Bely) imposed upon themselves, I decided not to be bound by any such constraints. I would be free to introduce anachronisms, or English idioms that were not a direct translation of the Russian text, or even on occasion to use quotations from English verse, if they adequately expressed the sense of the Russian.[14] I would not seek to reproduce Russian syntactic features, even if they possessed semantic qualities, such as the tense of participles or gerunds, if the result sounded strained in English. I would also try to avoid unnatural Latinate grammar, where "Eto—ia!" is translated as "It is I!," whereas no native speaker of English would say anything other than "It's me!"

At the level of vocabulary, I would think very hard before taking the most obvious word, bearing in mind that English, with its etymological variety, has a remarkably diverse and extensive vocabulary. A case in point is the Russian word *tuman*, denoting that ubiquitous feature of the Petersburg climate: is it best rendered as "fog," or "mist," or indeed on occasion "haze"? There is, of course, no absolutely correct answer in such cases, and different translators can quite legitimately disagree. I have largely preferred the word "mist," which, as it seems to me, does the best job of expressing that vagueness and uncertainty that is such an important part of the city's literary image. In this respect, "mist" surpasses the more meteorological "fog." Other similar cases are such words as *veter*, which might be not only "wind," but also "gale" or "gust," or *mokryi*, which can be rendered not only by "wet," but also by "damp" or "sodden." A particular instance is the word *sliakot′*, used to evoke the imagined aftermath of the assassination. All other translators have used the English word "slush," which generally denotes melting snow; I have chosen "slurry," a word with much more gruesome implications.

In a small, but significant number of instances, Bely uses a substantival adjective instead of a noun to designate otherwise unidentified characters. The difficulty of turning these into English lies in the fact that adjectives in English do not work this way, and if one uses a simple adjective with an article, it comes to have a plural meaning (e.g., "the poor"). If it is to retain a singular meaning one has to add the pronoun "one." All the earlier translators have tended to go for one or the other of these essentially unsatisfactory solutions. *Neulovimyi* becomes either "the Elusive" or "the Elusive One," while *Neizvestnyi* turns into "the Unknown" or "the Unknown One." I have taken the view that these words must be translated by English nouns, and have thus arrived at "the Fugitive" and "the Incognito."

Petersburg abounds in repeated words and expressions that acquire the function of leitmotifs. All its translators have been aware of this and have endeavored to find English equivalents that can be used in all the various contexts in which they appear. Over the years since the early 1960s, as the novel has been criticized, discussed, and translated, a number of standard versions of these words have come into use in English. I became determined very early in my work on the translation to look afresh at all these words in the Russian text without considering (as far as that is possible) the English versions that had already been used. Some of them are seriously problematical since they do not merely embody recurrent images in the novel, but also invoke notions with a cultural or historical resonance. Take, for instance, the word *raznochinets*. Every student of Russian cultural history knows how this word arose in the mid-nineteenth century to denote persons "of varied rank" who did not fit into the traditional structure of Russian society. Since they came to society's attention by dint of their participation in cultural life, the word acquired connotations that are excellently expressed in Malmstad and Maguire's translation choice: an "upstart intellectual." There is, of course, no way to render this meaning with a single English word. It first occurs in the text in a situation where the only impression received of the character is a visual one. I preferred to use an expression which gave only the basic meaning of the Russian, without delving into the cultural connotations that it had acquired: "a man of uncertain status." A bit wordy, yes; but it does convey what might be observed at first sight. And as a leitmotif it retains an element of uncertainty and threat that, I think, Malmstad and Maguire's more culturally explicit translation loses.

Similar examples are the use of *osoba* to denote Lippanchenko, *neznakomets* (besides *raznochinets*) as an alternative designation of Dudkin, or *obyvatel'* in a variety of contexts, but particularly with reference to Apollon Apollonovich in the novel's later stages. *Neznakomets* is unproblematically rendered as "stranger," but the others do present some problems. *Osoba* first appears as a section title. Cournos leaves all such subtitles untranslated, but when the word recurs in the body of the text, he renders it as "personality." All the others use the surely more correct word "person," but its appearance as a subtitle complicates the issue in context. McDuff has simply "The Person," which as any kind of title seems extremely weak; Malmstad and Maguire acknowledge the contextual problem by choosing "That Person," while I decided to render what appears to me the full weight of the word in this position: "A Certain Person." The word *obyvatel'* is used to denote an ordinary person, as distinct from a person occupying a lofty status in life. Cournos's "inhabitant" fails to convey this meaning, and even Malmstad and Maguire's "solid citizen" seems slightly out of focus in the context. The sense of ordinariness is, I believe, better conveyed by the expression "the man-in-the-street" (also used by McDuff).

A general problem arising in translation from Russian to English is created by the difference between the Russian and English verb systems. Aspect apart, Russian has only one past tense, while English has at least six. The appropriate use of continuous tenses or of the pluperfect is essential for rendering precisely the meaning of a Russian sentence. It also frequently happens that English rules about the sequence of tenses are overlooked in the rendering of reported speech or the future in the past. Aspect can also be an issue, as for instance in *Petersburg*, when Dudkin and Nikolai Apollonovich are discussing the latter's encounter with Morkovin. Dudkin asks — "I nazvalsia?" — which has been understood and translated as a simple query about his name, whereas the perfective aspect was correctly rendered by John Cournos as "What did he say his name was?" (I have used, "What did he call himself?")

All translators of the novel are faced with the problem of the balance between semantics and acoustics. There is indeed no possibility of reproducing the phonetic patterns out of which Bely claimed the novel had arisen, and the policy adopted by Malmstad and Maguire of introducing alliterative passages where possible and appropriate is the only practical approach to this problem. I have followed the same principle, coming up with different results. But this is not solely a question of Bely's sound play; more crucially it is a question of the rhythmic character of the entire text. Critics have disagreed on how this rhythm is to be defined, and for the translator that question is in any case idle, since it cannot be directly imitated in English, with its different natural cadences. But this is not the same question Nabokov posed when disputing the possibility of reproducing the poetic form of *Eugene Onegin*. Malmstad and Maguire made a good case, in their approach to the task, for eschewing "smooth" English. However, that is only a negative principle that offers no indication of what should hold the text together.

There is plenty of evidence to confirm that what drew the first Russian readers of *Petersburg* to the novel, what kept them reading from page to page, despite the semantic difficulties, was the rhythm of the text.[15] This is an issue that has preoccupied Russian critics of the novel extensively, including most famously R. V. Ivanov-Razumnik, who attempted to show that there is a fundamental difference between the rhythmic character of the two main redactions and that this difference corresponds to a similar philosophical difference.[16] Modern critics have not been inclined to follow Ivanov-Razumnik's arguments in this respect, but it is beyond question that the rhythm of the prose is a dominant feature of Bely's novel. Bely repeatedly insisted that his prose was envisaged as being spoken aloud.[17] It seems strange, therefore, that none of the English translators have made any attempt to find an equivalent for this feature in English. Any literary text is in some sense an organism, where semantic and acoustic properties combine to create its meaning. It has always seemed to me that insistence on precise semantic accuracy to the detriment of all else is not a productive approach. In my translation I have not sought to create metrical form such as informs Bely's text, but I have regarded the sentence rhythm of the English as a major and essential aspect of the text.

One such example occurs in the first double-indented passage (identical in both editions), which speaks of the arrival of the Flying Dutchman, "chtoby zdes´ vozdvignut´ obmanom svoi tumannye zemli i nazvat´ ostrovami volnu nabegaiushchikh oblakov . . ."[18] Malmstad and Maguire have: "in order here to erect, by delusion, his misty lands and to give the name of islands to the wave of onrushing clouds. . . ."[19] My version reads: "to raise here as an illusion his misty lands and give the name of islands to a wave of scudding clouds. . . ."[20] It is clear that these versions are closely similar, but there are two differences. In the first place, I have disagreed with all the other translators in taking *obmanom* to be a complement rather than an agent.[21] In the second place, I have preferred "scudding" to "onrushing." Here I have to acknowledge that the choice of "onrushing" is entirely semantically correct, with its proper rendering of the meaning of the prefix. My "scudding" loses the directional force of the Russian, but I have preferred it because it retains the rhythmic pattern of the sentence, while "onrushing" adds an unwanted extra syllable. This is especially important here, since *Petersburg*'s double-indented passages always mark points of heightened lyrical tension.

A similar example where I have given sound priority over precise semantic identity is in rendering the expression, "bred, bezdna, bomba." Cournos has "delirium, an abyss, a bomb"; Malmstad and Maguire have "delirium, abyss, bomb"; McDuff has "blind delirium, bottomlessness, bomb"; while my version has "bedlam, abyss, bomb." I share entirely Malmstad and Maguire's view that the articles are unnecessary, even counterproductive, and agree that, once again, their version cannot be disputed semantically; but I take the view that the alliteration here is absolutely essential. The same consideration, I suppose, underlay McDuff's rendering, but the alliteration is not effective when the rhythm is lost.

Another fundamental feature of *Petersburg* is the introduction into the prose text of passages of verse. Not only is every chapter preceded by an epigraph from Pushkin, but verse quotations frequently occur in the body of the text. They are by no means all from classical verse, but also include popular spiritual songs and simple ditties. Malmstad and Maguire insisted quite rightly that they were too important an element of the text to be rendered simply by prose paraphrases. Cournos and McDuff have also attempted verse renderings of such passages, though they are for the most part very lame. I would go further and insist that, essential as their semantic value is, their nature as verse creates a fundamental contrast of perception with the surrounding prose. I produced new, original translations of all such passages, with the one exception of *Erlkönig* (from German), where I found I could not improve on Walter Scott's version.

Simply to print the words in a verse format, with halting rhythm and the occasional rhyme, is not satisfactory. On occasion, I have been willing to offend against semantic precision in order to preserve the verse form. After all, in such cases one is not directly translating Pushkin; one is translating Bely's quotation of Pushkin (not always accurate), used in a particular context for a particular purpose.

    The use of Russian diminutive forms is a problem that comes to the fore in *Petersburg*. It is a fallacy to imagine that a diminutive form must always denote that the thing in question is a smaller variant of something that is often bigger. Both chapter 6 and chapter 7 contain in their titles the words: *proisshestviia seren'kogo den'ka*. Cournos, as noted, omits all such titles. Malmstad and Maguire translate this as "The Events of a Gray Little Day," while McDuff seeks to do justice to the diminutive adjective as well as the noun, and comes up with "The Events of a Rather Grey Little Day." How does a day come to be little? Clearly the diminutive form here is not expressing anything to do with size, but rather, as is often the case, with the attitude of the speaker. There is absolutely no point in introducing the English word "little" to describe something of invariable duration. It seems to me that the Russian diminutive form *denëk* carries (in this context) a burden of disdain or displeasure, while the diminutive form of the adjective merely follows from that of the noun, without adding much in the way of meaning. There is no obvious or necessary way of conveying this nuance in English. My solution, which may well be subject to improvement, was to add another adjective, but avoid all definitions of size: "The Events of a Drab Grey Day."

    Another instance of misreading the burden of a diminutive form is the rendering of the word *gospodinchik*, used to refer to the secret police agent Morkovin, alias Voronkov. When first introduced, this character is described as *suetliven'kii, molchaliven'kii gospodinchik* (the second adjective is omitted in the Berlin edition). Cournos has him as simply a "fussy little man"; Malmstad and Maguire call him a "fussy little fellow"; McDuff presents him as a "bustling taciturn-like gentleman." None have fully caught the nuance of meaning in the diminutive form *gospodinchik*. It clearly contains a note of disparagement, and is not (or not principally) an indication of the man's stature. "Fellow" contains something of the dismissive attitude, but not much is gained by calling him "little." The adjectives deserve some attention, but McDuff's introduction of a nonexistent adjectival form "taciturn-like" has nothing to recommend it. I decided to leave aside all mentions of size or stature, but to try to express the note of disparagement by translating the noun as "gent." I really have no idea whether this form has any currency in American English, but I am certain that in British English it has something of the required tone, a note of false gentility or perhaps straightforward vulgarity. So Mr. Morkovin in my version is described as "a rather fidgety, rather taciturn gent." A similar issue arises in the description of Sofia Petrovna as *pustaia babënka*. "Empty-headed" is unproblematical as a rendering of the adjective, but translating the noun as "little woman" (Cournos) or simply "female" (Malmstad and Maguire, and McDuff) seems weak. Again, there is a note of disparagement which needs to come across, and I have tried to solve this by using "flibbertigibbet."

Perhaps the most intractable and challenging problem in translating *Petersburg* is how to deal with the puns that occur in the speech of Apollon Apollonovich. They tend to be embarrassingly bad and the reader is not expected to find them funny. They are mainly based upon misconstrued masculine and feminine pairs, a feature which further complicates the intrinsic untranslatability of puns in general, and which none of the novel's translators, myself included, has found it possible always to reproduce. In the fourth section of chapter 1, entitled— *Baron, borona*—Apollon Apollonovich jokes with his valet, pretending that the second of these words is a feminine equivalent of the first, and that the valet, having been brought up in the country, must be a baron (барон) because his parents owned a harrow (борона). Translators have used one or other aspect of this exchange in attempting to find an equivalent. Cournos took the rustic background of the valet to develop a pun on "sty"; Malmstad and Maguire concentrated on the "harrow" to make a pun on "a harrowing experience"; McDuff left the Russian words and offered an explanation in his notes. I resorted to the stratagem of disregarding the actual nature of the original pun and replacing it with a different pun in English, which is tenuously linked to the dialogue through reference to the valet's background—"grocer, grow, sir?" Another example occurs in the eighth section of the same chapter, when Apollon Apollonovich arrives at his office and regales his staff with an entirely unmotivated pun in which the husband of a countess (*grafinia*) becomes a decanter (*grafin*). Cournos simply translates the words as they are, making no attempt to render the pun; Malmstad and Maguire turn the husband into a "counter"; McDuff uses the Russian words with a translation, so that the pun continues to exist in Russian, but is not itself translated. I decided to turn the countess into a duchess, so that her husband could become a Dutchman.

Some problems remain unresolved. Translators are in no disagreement over the meaning of the word *sardinnitsa*. It obviously denotes a "sardine-tin" (or "sardine-can"), but does not in fact appear in any of the many Russian dictionaries I have consulted. Not only is it a sardine-tin, but a sardine-tin of "terrible import" (or "terrible contents" as other versions have it). The package containing it is evidently heavy, even a little unwieldy, as we see when it is first introduced, being carried down the stairs from Dudkin's apartment. But to an English ear, a sardine-tin is quite small, of a very specific shape, and not at all heavy. How could such a small object contain both a clockwork mechanism and enough material to cause a substantial explosion? I thought that Anglophone readers would be puzzled by this apparent inconsistency. Were Russian sardine-tins in the early twentieth century of a different shape from the standard British sardine-tin? The sardine-tin that Dudkin brings to the Ableukhov house surely has to be bigger. Was there, then, some alternative word that might be used? I considered varieties of larger fish that might appear in a larger tin. I confess that for a moment my sardines nearly turned into mackerel. But it was always clear that the sardine image could not be dropped or changed, because of its important links to the imagery of grease and slime that is a constant accompaniment to Lippanchenko and the bomb itself. The connotations of confined space that inhere in the English sardine-tin ("packed like sardines") are relevant as anticipation of the explosion, but this does not affect its size and appearance.[22] I looked for any unfamiliar connotations of the Russian word, but found no solution there. So sardine-tin it remains, but I still don't like it.

No modern translation can ever claim to be definitive. Since its publication I have certainly become aware of deficiencies in mine, and have found passages where I now consider that previous versions are more successful. No doubt *Petersburg* will be translated into English again, and future translators will find other, better solutions to its difficulties. I have become increasingly aware that my hope of producing an English text that can stand on its own is frustrated by the fact that many highly literate readers of English are so unfamiliar with Russian culture and history that the novel's many cultural, historical, and intertextual references become a real obstacle to appreciation. Perhaps it is essential to accompany an English version of such a complex novel with explanatory notes of at least the most important references. Or will potential readers be deterred by the fact that the novel was thought to need such assistance?

Notes

1. Andrey Biely, *St. Petersburg*, tr. John Cournos (New York: Grove Press, 1959), 117.
2. Roger Keys, "'An Extremist in All Things'—Georgii Adamovich on Andrei Biely: A Late Unpublished Article," in *Paraboly: Studies in Russian Modernist Literature and Culture. In Honor of John E. Malmstad*, ed. Nikolai Bogomolov et al. (Frankfurt: Peter Lang, 2011), 270.

3. Keys, "'An Extremist in All Things,'" 269. The earliest translation by John Cournos appears to be *Silence, by Leonidas Andreiyeff* (Philadelphia: Brown Brothers, 1908).

4. Vladimir Nabokov, "Introduction," in *Eugene Onegin: A Novel in Verse by Aleksandr Pushkin* (London: Routledge, 1964), 1:vii–ix; cited in David Bellos, *Is That a Fish in Your Ear?* (London: Penguin, 2012), 143.

5. Vladimir Nabokov, "Translator's Foreword," in Mikhail Lermontov, *A Hero of Our Time: A Novel* (Garden City, NY: Doubleday, 1958), xii.

6. Andrei Bely, *Petersburg*, tr. Robert Maguire and John Malmstad (Bloomington: Indiana University Press, 1978), xvii.

7. Clarence Brown, "A Bloom on the Neva," *The Guardian/Arts Guardian* (23 February 1979), 12.

8. Alex de Jong, "The Most Abstract City," *The Spectator* (24 February 1979), 18.

9. Blake Morrison, "Quis? Ego!," *The New Statesman* (2 March 1979), 296–97. Robin Lane Fox, "Small World," *The Financial Times* (24 March 1979), 15.

10. Anthony Burgess, "Time on Nevsky Prospekt," *The Observer* (25 February 1979), 37.

11. Andrei Bely, *Petersburg*, tr. David McDuff (Harmondsworth: Penguin, 1995), xxi.

12. Andrei Belyi, *Stikhotvoreniia* (Berlin: Izdatel'stvo Grzhebina, 1923).

13. I have argued this in more detail in John Elsworth, *Andrey Bely: A Critical Study of the Novels* (Cambridge: Cambridge University Press, 1983), 113–16. But see also Malmstad and Maguire's reasons for reaching the opposite conclusion in their "Translators' Introduction," xxiv–xxv.

14. I have not used this device in *Petersburg* but did employ it in my earlier translation of Andrei Bely's first novel, *The Silver Dove* (Evanston: Northwestern University Press, 2000).

15. See, for instance, P. Antokol'skii, "Posleslovie," in Andrei Belyi, *Peterburg* (Moscow: Khudozhestvennaia literatura, 1978), 340.

16. R. V. Ivanov-Razumnik, "Peterburg," *Vershiny: Aleksandr Blok, Andrei Belyi* (Petrograd: Kolos, 1923), 105–71.

17. See, for instance, Andrei Belyi, *Maski* (Moscow: GIKhL, 1932), 9–10.

18. Andrei Belyi, *Peterburg*, ed. L. Dolgopolov (Moscow: Nauka, 1981), 20.

19. Andrei Bely, *Petersburg* (Bloomington: Indiana University Press, 1978), 10.

20. Andrei Bely, *Petersburg* (London: Pushkin Press, 2009), 25.

21. I readily admit that the syntax here is ambiguous, perhaps intentionally so, but my version acknowledges a parallelism in the Russian. I would also point out in support of this reading that in a later section, referring back to this discussion of the city's founding and evoking the Bronze Horseman, we find the expression "iz obmanchivykh stran," clearly implying that "obman" denotes a quality of the place, rather than of the founding person.

22. Helene Hartmann-Flyer offers an interesting account of the way the image arises from the novel's phonetics but does not touch upon its visual qualities. See "The Time-Bomb," in *Andrey Bely: A Critical Review*, ed. G. Janecek (Lexington: University Press of Kentucky, 1978), 121–26.

Part One

The Intellectual Context

Revolutionary Terrorism and Provocation in *Petersburg*

LYNN E. PATYK

Revolutionary terrorism in Andrei Bely's *Petersburg*, and the terrorist plot at the novel's heart, has attracted surprisingly little scholarly attention. Most literary scholars have dispatched the plot in a few concise sentences as the rather incidental scaffolding supporting Bely's poetically stunning and thematically sophisticated modernist novel. Consider the following summary of the novel's political intrigue: "The basic plotline of *Petersburg* is simple. The time is the 1905 Revolution, and the place is the Imperial Russian capital, St. Petersburg. Nikolai Apollonovich Ableukhov, a student of Kantian philosophy, makes a rash promise to a revolutionary group to assassinate his father, Apollon Apollonovich, a senator and a high-ranking bureaucrat in one of the ministries. The famous revolutionary Dudkin, living clandestinely in the city, gives Nikolai a bomb to use against his father. This bomb goes off [. . .] without harming anyone."[1]

At first glance, the story line of *Petersburg* is a terrorist plot, but scholars who have sought to analyze terrorism in *Petersburg* have been stymied by the fact that terrorism in the novel is actually orchestrated by the police and is part of a provocation plot. Symptomatically, the above summary oversimplifies the novel's political intrigue: Bely's narrator is vague about the nature of Nikolai Apollonovich's promise to the revolutionary group, whereas Dudkin does not know that the bomb he delivers to Nikolai Apollonovich for safe keeping will be used in an attempt to kill his father the senator. For Bely's contemporaries, the experience of revolutionary terrorism, revolution, and provocation belonged to the very recent past and required no explanation—it was something like an inside joke, albeit a very dark one. For subsequent generations of readers, with their own experience of political violence, the novel's terrorism plot has been striking and unmistakable, but the provocation plot has grown intricate and obscure.

This chapter will help today's readers of *Petersburg* to appreciate what is behind Bely's double exposure of revolutionary terrorism as provocation—and vice versa. A short course in the symbiotic history of Russian terrorism and counterterrorism, their representation in the Russian and Western literature of Bely's day, and their particular place in Bely's modernist world view will help to shed light on the novel's fascination with political intrigue and violence.

"The Russian Method" of Terrorism and Counterterrorism

While there is no unanimity regarding the definition of terrorism, historians have reached a degree of consensus regarding its origins: Russian revolutionaries "invented" modern terrorism in the middle of the nineteenth century.[2] Recently, scholars have realized that this formulation is somewhat one-sided: Russian radicals *and* the autocratic government, as if locked in a diabolical pantomime of equal and opposite actions, "invented" terrorism *together*.[3] In the eighteenth century, the modernizing tsars Peter I and Catherine II fostered a class of westernized intellectuals who eventually came to challenge the status quo and the tsar's absolute authority. Even when this challenge took the form of mere words, the autocrat viewed it as a mortal threat and quashed the presumptuous upstart with disproportionate force. Aleksandr Pushkin's 1833 narrative poem *The Bronze Horseman* brilliantly captures this dynamic when his deranged protagonist Evgenii utters a cryptic threat and finds himself relentlessly pursued by the statue of Peter the Great, who has come terrifyingly to life. It is precisely under the sign of *The Bronze Horseman* that Bely's *Petersburg* dramatizes this dynamic, and the first several chapters of the novel alternate between the opposing perspectives of the reactionary government official, Senator Ableukhov, and the revolutionary terrorist Dudkin, each of whom perceives the other as an enemy to be obliterated. Although governmental forces enjoy an overwhelming preponderance and priority—we are told that Dudkin issues from the senator's head, as the inadvertent product of his cerebral play—the two are in fact mutually constitutive.[4]

As a modernist *historical* novel, *Petersburg* is something of an oxymoron. Its action is concentrated within a very short span of time—a few critical and tumultuous days in late September and early October 1905—which for Bely represented the symbolic culmination of a protracted, destiny-shaping struggle between the antinomies of revolution and reaction, East and West. The struggle began in earnest when Alexander II's modernizing Great Reforms (1861–1864) failed to satisfy an increasingly restive intelligentsia whose most impatient members began to advocate political violence as the only means to effect social change. On 4 April 1866, Dmitrii Karakozov's attempt to assassinate Tsar Alexander II was the precursor of increasingly bold and relentless attempts on high government officials and on the tsar himself.[5] The government overreacted to Karakozov's unprecedented act by crushing all independent political opinion with a sweeping and draconian "White Terror," essentially driving any type of political dissent deep underground. A mere three years later, the devious and charismatic agitator Sergei Nechaev produced his *Catechism of a Revolutionary*, which elaborated an all-embracing program for conspiratorial action and political terrorism, with tactics ranging from psychological manipulation to mass execution. Nechaev's own secret organization, The People's Vengeance, succeeded only in murdering a dissenting member of its own motley group, but the sweeping arrests and severe treatment of Nechaev's followers further alienated Russian society from the government.[6]

While Nechaev's methods repelled most radicals, after a cohort of young Populists (*narodniki*) were persecuted in the 1870s for their efforts to propagandize among the peasant masses, antiregime violence seemed like the only remaining option. On 31 March 1878, Vera Zasulich's unanimous acquittal by a jury for her attempted assassination of the hated Governor of St. Petersburg seemed to sanction—or at least morally condone—violent struggle against the government. And, barely a year later, the centralized and highly disciplined People's Will organization, founded in June 1879, embraced a method of terrorism based on the model of ancient tyrannicide. Early apologists for tyrannicide, including Aristotle, Cicero, and John of Salisbury, among others, condoned the murder of particular pernicious rulers and valorized the tyrant-slayer.[7] The People's Will devoted their modest resources to a systematic "emperor hunt" in the imperial capital, and, after six attempts, succeeded in assassinating Tsar Alexander II on 1 March 1881. The modus operandi employed by the People's Will became known the world over as "the Russian Method," heralding the birth of modern terrorism; but its practice of targeting particularly odious representatives of the regime does not remotely resemble the indiscriminate mass violence practiced in our own day by al-Qaeda and ISIS.

After the People's Will embraced dynamite as their preferred weapon, however, revolutionary violence became of necessity less discriminate, and ordinary

Russians feared becoming collateral damage in a dynamite attack. Terrorism therefore became genuinely terrifying at the same time that members of the People's Will adopted the word "terrorist"—which had originally referred to the radical Jacobins presiding over the Great Terror of 1793–94 in France—to refer to themselves, as well as to their strategy of political violence. Ironically, the success of the assassination led to the demise of the Executive Committee of the People's Will, whose members were expeditiously arrested and executed in the spring of 1881. In response to the terrorist juggernaut, the branch of the police charged with preventing political crimes was completely overhauled and rebranded the Sections for the Protection of Public Security and Order—referred to as the Okhrana. The Okhrana worked both cooperatively and competitively with the political arm of the police force, the Corps of Gendarmes. The Ministry of the Interior housed both the Police Department and the Okhrana, although this by no means guaranteed the efficiency or effectiveness of the empire's security apparatus.[8]

After the regicide, the newly appointed St. Petersburg Okhrana chief, Georgii Sudeikin, was determined to destroy the revolutionary movement from the inside. He pioneered the strategy of using two types of police agents: plainclothes surveillants, or "external agents," and secret, or "internal" agents within the revolutionary parties.[9] While spies and agent provocateurs had been long used in France and to a more limited degree in Russia, Sudeikin's innovation consisted in using these agents not only to obtain information, but also to wage psychological warfare, whereby the agents sought to sow discord and distrust among comrades.[10] Without question, the internal agent's position was both morally dubious and dangerous, for (s)he was required to participate fully in the revolutionaries' activities, even to the point of instigating acts of revolutionary violence, while providing the police with timely information to thwart the self-same attack. Internal agents often strategically withheld information, in order to avoid exposure, thereby becoming implicated in anti-state activities. This led, inevitably, to the question of the agent's true allegiance, but also, more importantly, to the question of the legitimacy of a government whose agents participated in terrorist attacks against it.

The radicals were not scrupulous in distinguishing between ordinary police detectives and internal agents and referred to both as provocateurs, decrying their tactics as *provokatsiia*—a word with connotations of duplicity and betrayal. Sudeikin's strategy, in fact, produced stunning results when, by feigning solidarity with the revolutionaries, he was able to convince a member of the People's Will, Sergei Degaev, to betray his terrorist comrades. When the revolutionaries learned of Degaev's betrayal, they demanded that he redeem himself by murdering Sudeikin. After fulfilling his macabre commission, Degaev escaped from

Russia to the United States, where he embarked on a new life under the assumed name of Alexander Pell and enjoyed a distinguished career as Professor of Mathematics at the University of South Dakota.[11] Degaev, however, lent his discarded name to the first notorious episode of provocation and betrayal in revolutionary history, which became known as "Degaevshchina." Police informers were thereafter terrified of meeting the same fate as their chief, Sudeikin, or for that matter Lippanchenko in Bely's *Petersburg*.

Transnational Terrorist Plots

Throughout the 1880s and 1890s, the tsarist government and secret police remained transfixed by the terrorist threat and directed their repressive forces against it, while underestimating the danger presented by the Marxist Social Democrats, who nominally rejected terrorism.[12] Meanwhile, both terrorism and counterterrorism became a transnational phenomenon as Irish nationalist Fenians waged terrorist campaigns on the British Isles, while continental anarchists of all nationalities tossed bombs into popular cafés or into public parades and gatherings. As terrorists crossed borders in flight from the authorities, so did funding and all means of material and spiritual support from sympathizers with their causes. In response, alarmed national governments (Russian, Prussian, Austro-Hungarian, and French) and their police forces made common cause. In July 1883, the director of the Russian police, Viacheslav von Plehve, established the Foreign Agency of the Russian secret police in the basement of the Russian embassy in Paris, securing the cooperation of the city's Police Prefecture. By the early 1890s, Scotland Yard lent a hand in the surveillance and investigation of Russian émigrés in London.[13] Terrorist plots had indeed become transnational ones.

The sensational violence of terrorism, with the fear and agitated excitement that it produced, was a tremendous boon for the burgeoning mass media. Inevitably, terrorism and the terrorist captured the public imagination. Littérateurs of all stripes, high- and lowbrow, capitalized on the suspense of terrorists' ticking bombs, insinuating these bombs into their preferred artistic modes: the drama (Oscar Wilde's *Vera, or the Nihilists*, 1879); the naturalist novel (Émile Zola's *Germinal*, 1884); the story of fantasy and adventure (Robert Louis Stevenson's *More New Arabian Nights: The Dynamiter*, 1885); the society novel (Henry James's *The Princess Casamassima*, 1885); and the Victorian potboiler (Joseph Hatton's *By Order of the Tsar: Anna Queen of the Ghetto*, 1890), to name just a few.[14]

Due to imperial censorship, there was no question of literary works "capitalizing" on revolutionary terrorism in Russia, although, beginning in the 1860s, a steady stream of anti-nihilist novels demonized the radicals by portraying them as morally debased morons or unscrupulous manipulators. A notable example is Fëdor Dostoevsky's brilliantly satirical and tragic *Demons* (1872), based on the Nechaev affair. Both before and after the assassination of Alexander II, Russian writers and visual artists raised the issue of revolutionary violence circumspectly. Dostoevsky's *The Brothers Karamazov* was even more topical than *Demons*, since the novel was serialized, in 1879–80, concurrently with the ongoing efforts by the People's Will to assassinate the tsar, and used the murder of the Karamazovs' despicable paterfamilias by his son(s) as an allegory for regicide. Bely's *Petersburg* is a happy hunting ground for countless references to the works that comprise Dostoevsky's "terrorism trilogy": *Crime and Punishment* (1866), *Demons*, and *The Brothers Karamazov*.[15] For example, in *Petersburg*, Dudkin's pointed question to Nikolai Apollonovich, "And so in thought you have nothing to do with any such murder?" (336), clearly echoes the Karamazov brothers' (and especially Ivan's) desire for their father's death.[16] Four years later, during the reactionary reign of Alexander III, the painter Ilya Repin turned the tables on the national fascination with patricide by depicting Ivan the Terrible's murder of his own son. Capitalizing on this tragic moment in history, Repin visually represented the father's violence as the origin story behind the lethal generational and political conflict between Russian fathers and sons in Repin's own day.

Revolutionary Terrorism and Russian Modernism

Alexander III's repressive police apparatus had effectively stifled the intelligentsia-based revolutionary movement, but by the late 1890s, drought, famine, government incompetence, and worker and peasant unrest created momentum and a genuine constituency for new oppositional movements within Russia. In 1902, disparate groupings with various populist agendas united to form the Party of Socialist Revolutionaries (PSR), which boasted many veterans of the People's Will among its members and laid claim to the predecessor's strategy of political violence. Calls for resuming the terrorist struggle preceded the party's founding, and sporadic attacks activated the heroic image and mythology of the revolutionary terrorist, as promulgated by Russian émigré writers such as Sergei Stepniak-Kravchinskii and Vladimir Burtsev.

The SRs created a specialized elite unit devoted to terrorism, called the Combat Organization (*Boevaia organizatsiia*), which was headed initially by the charismatic Grigorii Gershuni, and after Gershuni's arrest, by the terrorist-littérateur Boris Savinkov. While the SR Central Committee authorized the

Combat Organization's activities, the terrorist unit was a tightly knit conspiratorial group, characterized by its strict honor code. It enjoyed independence from the party and resented the party's interference in militant affairs. Ultimate decisions regarding the Combat Organization's terrorist operations lay with Evno Azef, a member of the SR Central Committee who served as the sole liaison between it and the terrorists. Beginning with the assassination of Minister of the Interior von Plehve in 1904, the Combat Organization staged a series of spectacular high-level political assassinations that contributed to the atmosphere of mounting revolutionary unrest. But the shock of these attacks was incomparably smaller than the shock and subsequent scandal surrounding the unmasking of Azef, a venerated SR leader, as an agent provocateur.

In his memoirs, Bely characterized von Plehve's assassination as "the great break," a break that the writer had eagerly anticipated since the turn of the century.[17] There was something of a "terrorist chic" among Russia's cultural avant-garde. Older and younger writers alike—Aleksei Remizov, Zinaida Gippius, Dmitrii Merezhkovskii, Leonid Andreev, Maksimilian Voloshin, Lev Kobylinskii, Valentin Sventitskii, Marina Tsvetaeva, and Osip Mandel'shtam, to name only some—aspired to join the elite terrorist organization, or at least to rub elbows with its members.[18] Bely subscribed to that heroic and apocalyptic strain in Russian modernism—sometimes tinged with self-parody—that sought to transform the world; but this transformation required the destruction of what had become old, outworn, and decayed. As was so often the case, Bely took this aspiration to another level: he felt himself to embody the destructive-creative force of the terrorist bomb. As John Elsworth notes: "The image of explosion was always one of Bely's favorite ways of expressing the idea of an apocalyptic transformation, and the identification of the self that undergoes spiritual transformation with a bomb recurs later in Bely's writings."[19]

Abstractly conceived, the Apocalypse held a certain sublime allure in Russian modernist culture (see David Bethea's essay in this volume); but the reality of violence was more grotesque than sublime, a fact that was not lost on Bely. In *Petersburg*, those representing the generation of sons with terrorist intentions, Dudkin and Nikolai Apollonovich, are figured as bombs. As Dudkin's eyes catch sight of senator Ableukhov, who is hermetically enclosed in his carriage, they open wide, shine, and flash like an exploding bomb (30). And, in a terrifying nightmare dating back to Nikolai Apollonovich's childhood, the senator's son first assumes the form of his own double, Pepp Peppovich—whose first name and patronymic somehow mutate into the names of two arrested revolutionaries (380)—and then expands and explodes (304–5). At different moments, both father and son spontaneously and viscerally imagine the elder Ableukhov's destruction in a bomb blast. In *Petersburg*, the bomb's violence is no longer associated with sublime transformation but with the grotesque reduction of the individual's body to undifferentiated matter—to bloody slush.[20]

From 1905 through 1907, political violence in Russia mounted until it exceeded both the Socialist Revolutionaries' and the tsarist government's ability to contain it. Terrorism, like other social behaviors, is imitative and reciprocal, so that the Combat Organization's carefully choreographed attacks inspired pettier and more sordid acts of violence. Between October 1905 and October 1906, a total of 3,611 state officials of all ranks were killed or wounded as terrorist groupings of various political confessions proliferated throughout the Russian Empire.[21] These smaller organizations typically relied on run-of-the-mill robberies—ideologically dignified by the term "expropriations"—to fund their terrorist operations. As the historian Anna Geifman has argued, the magnitude of the violence far surpassed that of the "first wave" of revolutionary terrorism, in the 1860s and 1870s, as did the level of cultural saturation: "Whereas in the nineteenth century every act of revolutionary violence was a sensation, after 1905 terror became so widespread that many of the country's newspapers no longer bothered to publish detailed reports of every attack. Instead, they introduced special new sections dedicated exclusively to chronicling violent acts in which they printed daily lists of political assassinations and expropriations throughout the empire."[22]

Terrorism entered into the very fabric of Russian society, as children played pranks on police by outfitting watermelons as bombs, students threatened unpopular instructors with assassination, and humorous anecdotes such as the following appeared in satirical journals in the wake of a spate of revolutionary expropriations (robberies). "Due to an increase in the incidence of bank robberies, mask and costume businesses are showing large profits. A domino mask goes for sixty rubles rental, a harlequin for more than eighty. The administration intends to institute price controls in order to curb merchants' greed."[23] Newspaper chronicles, food disguised as bombs and vice versa, terrorist robbers wearing domino masks and harlequin costumes—all this constitutes the historical realia Bely imbues with symbolic significance and weaves into his modernist novel, set in the revolutionary year 1905. The cultural association of the domino mask—especially a red one—with illegal revolutionary activity explains senator Ableukhov's deeply aversive reaction to it at the Tsukatovs' ball, and his horror upon discovering that it concealed his very own son.

By late 1907, the government under Prime Minister Pëtr Stolypin had unequivocally defeated the revolution, casting a pall over public sentiment with relentless repression, epitomized by the infamous "Stolypin necktie"—the noose used to execute political criminals. Countless polemical and literary works reflected a mood of hopelessness, disillusionment, and recriminations, and Bely was particularly susceptible to these momentous shocks in public life. Directly following the revelation of Azef's treachery, a group of former Marxists turned idealist thinkers published a collection of essays, *Signposts* (*Vekhi*, 1909), taking to task Russia's radical intelligentsia for its impatient maximalism, lack of legal consciousness, and desire for the total transformation of society. Terrorism exemplified all of that, and Bely demonstratively sided with *Signposts'* authors in an article entitled "The Truth about the Russian Intelligentsia." And if the writer needed a reminder about Azef, the Russian-Jewish terrorist and double agent, Stolypin was assassinated in September, 1911, just as Bely geared up to write *Petersburg*'s first chapters. The prime minister's Russian-Jewish assassin, Dmitrii Bogrov, was suspected of working for the police.

The year of the Azef scandal was a watershed in Bely's artistic career as he embarked upon a novelistic trilogy that contemplated Russia's historical destiny at the crossroads of East and West. In 1909, he serialized the proposed trilogy's first installment, *The Silver Dove* (*Serebrianyi golub'*), and began contemplating the triptych's middle part—the future *Petersburg*. In the same year, Boris Savinkov, the leader of the SR Combat Organization, published a novella, *The Pale Steed* (*Kon' blednyi*), under the pseudonym Ropshin. Savinkov's narrator, a terrorist who was the author's transparent alter ego, set out to "unmask" revolutionary terrorism and state violence as morally equivalent. The novella followed a stream of literary works that reflected society's—and the radicals'—disappointment with the failed revolution, along with their second thoughts about political violence. But Savinkov's *Pale Steed* stood out by virtue of offering an unprecedented peephole into terrorist conspiracy, and especially into the most spectacular attacks of the period: the assassinations of Von Plehve in 1904 and of Grand Duke Sergei Romanov in 1905. Bely would later claim that he had based his intellectually sophisticated but mystically inclined and morally tormented terrorist, Dudkin, on the Savinkov of 1905.[24] In that year, however, Savinkov had not suspected Azef of treachery and bitterly defended him until Azef's guilt was proved beyond reasonable doubt.

Unmasking the Terrorist Plot in *Petersburg*

By the first decade of the twentieth century, terrorist plots in literary fiction verged on a cliché, but they had acquired a twist that foreshadowed reality: the apparent terrorist was really an agent provocateur. In Joseph Conrad's *The*

Secret Agent (1907), a crude and manipulative agent provocateur named Verloc incites his vulnerable and mentally disabled brother-in-law to commit a terrorist act in London. The indoctrinated Stevie is killed accidentally, when he trips over a tree root, detonating the bomb that was intended to destroy the Greenwich Observatory. In a far more playful and humorous vein, G. K. Chesterton's *The Man Who Was Thursday* (1908) describes the fantastic adventures of a police agent who believes he is joining a dangerous international anarchist conspiracy only to discover that its members are all in fact police agents. In both novels, the characters turn out to be puppets whose strings are pulled by virtually invisible hands for unfathomable reasons. *The Secret Agent* and *The Man Who Was Thursday* underscore the individual's lack of agency and inability to discern and comprehend the forces that shape his destiny, something that scholars have called "agency panic." While Bely may well have read both novels before embarking on *Petersburg*, his own historical experience and personal world view made such foreign literary influence somewhat superfluous.

Whereas in Conrad's *The Secret Agent*, Verloc's status as agent provocateur and the goal of the provocation are established at the beginning of the novel, in a conversation between him and the ambassador of an unnamed Eastern European state, Bely gives us no such scene. Instead, as the revolutionary terrorist Dudkin makes his way along Nevsky Prospect, strains of conversation and fragments of words come together seemingly of their own accord, but in fact at the behest of Dudkin's unconscious. "They're getting read . . ." "What, to throw a . . ." "At whom . . ." only to be suddenly overturned by a single word "provocation." "Provocation went on a spree along Nevsky. Provocation changed the meaning of all the words that were heard. Provocation had its seat within him."[25] Bely thus drops a very strong hint that Dudkin already knows that he is entangled in a disgraceful police plot, rather than a heroic terrorist plot. Like Raskolnikov in *Crime and Punishment*, Dudkin himself possesses the key to the mystery but willfully represses it.

Olga Matich has observed *Petersburg*'s affinities with the popular genre of detective novel, and there is no shortage of detectives (plainclothes surveillants) on Bely's St. Petersburg streets, which "turn people into shadows and shadows into people."[26] In the chapter entitled "Our Role," the narrator even self-parodically declares that *his* role is precisely that of an agent, and as he anticipates Senator Ableukhov's desire to investigate Dudkin, the narrator ends up instead eavesdropping on two "shadows," who are themselves police agents. It falls to the reader to decode a fragmentary and almost nonsensical conversation, identify and track the participants by their physical characteristics, and puzzle out the contours of a sinister plot in which a disaffected son will be forced to assassinate his own father. By tracking the shadows and piecing together the vital clues in the conversation, the reader realizes that the provocation plot is two-pronged: one prong involves the terrorist plot and the physical assassination of Apollon Apollonovich, and the other prong involves the sleazy Jewish journalist Neintelpfain, whose sensational stories of a menacing revolutionary Red Domino are disseminated in the *Chronicle of Events*.

Nikolai Apollonovich's unintentional self-unmasking as the Red Domino at the Tsukatovs' ball provides just the scandal that the boulevard press craves and the police have counted on, clinching the political and moral destruction of the old senator. The terrorist plot and the physical destruction of Apollon Apollonovich are rendered completely superfluous when the press—identified as "Jewish"—and the police act in cahoots, as the shadow displays unshakable confidence that "my man Neintelpfain will cause a sensation." For Bely, the word—or rather, the "paragraphs" in the *Chronicle of Events*—however debased, is still mightier than the bomb. It is no coincidence that, in *Petersburg*, the agents of the police and press provocation plot are Jewish: Bely fully subscribed to the anti-Semitic conspiracy theories of his conservative contemporaries (see Henrietta Mondry's essay in this volume).

Nikolai Lippanchenko, who in the conversation between shadows repeats "the whole thing is arranged like clockwork," was modeled closely on his historical prototype, Evno Azef, a Jew from Southern Russia. Azef was strikingly ugly and repelled many of his idealist SR comrades with his crudely pragmatic intelligence, uncouth behavior, and self-seeking materialism, which were out of place in a revolutionary milieu that prized theoretical sophistication and self-sacrifice.[27] Many former comrades subsequently recalled that, on first acquaintance, Azef struck them as "a police character." Only after their initial aversion to him did they grow to prize his unvarnished pragmatism. Although rumors of Azef's police entanglements circulated already during his student days in the 1890s, as Azef climbed in the party hierarchy and took the credit for the SR Combat Organization's sensational successes, it became taboo to countenance any accusations of treachery that were directed against him. When, for example, the SR Central Committee received an anonymous letter, in September 1905, that implicated Nikolai Tatarov and Azef as agent provocateurs, the Party proceeded to investigate, try, and condemn Tatarov to death, while Azef was left uninvestigated and untouched.[28]

Two years later, when Vladimir Burtsev finally produced the testimony of the former director of the Secret Police, Aleksei Lopukhin, as proof positive that Azef was a police agent, the shock of party members, and especially of Azef's devotees in the SR Combat Organization, verged on trauma. Both the

SR Central Committee and the party's advocacy of terrorism came under fire from rank-and-file members and from the general public: how could the Socialist Revolutionaries have elevated, venerated, and remained blind to the true nature of this enemy in their midst?

This is the psychological conflict Bely dramatizes with such stunning originality in *Petersburg*. From Dudkin's first meeting with Lippanchenko at a seedy tavern, Bely, through Dudkin's perspective, draws attention to the unmistakable markers of fakery and falseness in Lippanchenko's appearance: the rhinestone rings and dye-stained finger nails. At the same time as Lippanchenko's "oriental" (Mongol and Semitic) features, bulky and grotesque physicality, and even the sounds of his name, elicit visceral disgust in Dudkin, they exercise a sort of hypnotic fascination. By these means, Bely evoked the moral and existential threat that the agent provocateur and provocation more generally posed to the revolutionary party.

In the months and years after the revelation of Azef's double game, the image of "Azef der Grosse" (Azef the Large)—originally referring to Azef's heft but also evocative of "Azef the Great" as a consummate manipulator—proliferated in the Russian boulevard press and pulp fiction, while the biblical Judas served modernists and revolutionaries alike as a figure for the arch traitor.[29] In the chapter "Our Role," Lippanchenko's shadow spouts an unholy mix of metaphors—likening himself to a conductor who just has to swing his baton and to an artist who will not accept a salary for his work, and then boasting that "the business is set up like clockwork" (49). Dudkin shares this assessment. For him, Lippanchenko looms as a diabolical mastermind whose colossal forehead appears as a hallucination on the yellow wall paper of his room. This perception becomes especially acute when Lippanchenko forces Dudkin to betray Nikolai Ableukhov by craftily turning the charge of provocation against Dudkin himself: "That you have participated in provocation is not yet established. But I warn you, in all friendship, Aleksandr Ivanovich, my dear fellow, you've set something shady in train" (377). Lippanchenko's threat to expose Dudkin as a provocateur is all the more ironic because he uses it to make Dudkin complicit in the provocation, a complicity that ultimately drives Dudkin to such a distressing pitch of cognitive dissonance that he goes entirely mad.

The novel as a whole offers a different, diminished vision of the provocateur, and in his final scenes, Bely portrays Lippanchenko as a ruin of a man, a helpless infant, an animal viciously slaughtered, and a mounted beast. It is, therefore, crucial to realize that Lippanchenko is not the provocation plot's mastermind. Like Dudkin, Nikolai Apollonovich, Sofia Likhutina, Varvara Evgrafovna, and implicitly others, he, too, is only a blind tool, a node in the network, rather than an intentional agent. Bely and his contemporaries were very much aware that a police agent did not act on his own prerogative, but rather served a higher power—whether it was the Chief of Police or the Minister of the Interior himself. By alluding, at the beginning of the novel, to Apollon Apollonovich's ongoing feud with "Count W, the head of the ninth department" (19), Bely suggests that the senator has enemies not only among the revolutionaries, but near the apex of power. Scholars have argued that Count W stands for Count Sergei Witte, the adroit Prime Minister during the turmoil of 1905, who ultimately persuaded Tsar Nicholas II to issue the liberalizing October Manifesto, which granted Russia its first parliament, legalized political parties, and lifted censorship strictures. It was widely rumored that Witte had known in advance about the terrorist plot to assassinate his long-time adversary, von Plehve, and had not intervened to stop it.[30] Radical circles also commonly assumed that provocation was a means of settling scores and conducting intrigues within the highest echelons of the government. Bely's first readers also readily picked up on the allusion to Count W's ninth department in the surname of Lippanchenko's agent Neintelpfain (in German *neun* means "nine," and *Teil* denotes "section"), a rival fictional department.[31] Indeed, precisely Senator Ableukhov's liberal and progressive (i.e., socialist) political rivals stood to benefit most politically from the conservative senator's fall, and they are in the ascendant as the novel draws to a close. But as Bely's readers also knew, the tsar shortly reversed his liberalizing course, and Witte resigned in January 1906. As the novel's Epilogue clearly signals, the uneasy stalemate that ensued was untenable in the long run.

Unlike those who magnified the role of "Azef the Great," Bely saw the mundane operation of provocation not as the product of a single diabolical mastermind, but as a network of police agents (Lippanchenko, Morkovin) in conjunction with unscrupulous journalists (Neintelpfain) and simple dupes, like Sophia Likhutina. Bely, however, was not primarily interested in the mundane operation of anything: he was an inveterate systematizer who sought a single, all-encompassing explanation for everything. Depending on his changing sources of influence, these systems might be conspiracy theories, positing a vast Jewish-Asiatic plot against Orthodox Russia, or Rudolf Steiner's "secret" Anthroposophical doctrine (see Henrietta Mondry's and Maria Carlson's essays in this volume).

Bely wrote a portion of *Petersburg* as his interest in Anthroposophy waxed. In this intellectual context, "cerebral play" proper to Bely's characters may be understood as the machinery of provocation by which thought forms from the astral plane, theorized by Steiner, entered the physical plane as antinomies in order ceaselessly to provoke one another in an agonistic cosmic contest. Cerebral play, along with a great many other actions in the novel, is involuntary and outside the protagonists' control and consciousness. Revolutionary struggle, and especially the heroic voluntarism of revolutionary terrorism, was premised upon the notion of individual agency—of the individual's ability, through the exercise of conscious will and the performance of a single, self-sacrificial act—to destroy the corrupt old order and usher in a transformed reality. Before 1905-7, Andrei Bely clearly believed that the modernist artist possessed the heroic agency to transform the world. By 1909-10, however, Bely had come to share the agency panic of his fellow modernists, though he had not lost his zeal for unmasking.

Petersburg deals a double blow to the heroism of the revolutionary struggle by unmasking the terrorist plot as a provocation plot and denying the individual the willpower for an act of heroism, terrorism, or self-sacrifice. Rather, "our role"—the role of all human beings—is that of unwitting agents of unseen forces, be they insidious foreign conspiracies against the Motherland or energy bodies that manifest themselves through cyclical ages in which cause and effect are reversed. To paraphrase Voltaire's famous quip regarding the (non)existence of God: when it comes to *Petersburg*, if provocation had not existed, Bely would have had to invent it.

Notes

1. Vladimir Alexandrov, *Andrei Bely: The Major Symbolist Fiction* (Cambridge: Harvard University Press, 1985), 100.

2. Carola Dietze, *Die Erfindung des Terrorismus in Europa, Russland und den USA, 1858-1866* (Hamburg: Hamburger Edition HIS, 2016), 27.

3. Martin Miller, *The Foundations of Modern Terrorism: State, Society, and the Dynamics of Political Violence* (New York: Cambridge University Press, 2013), 3.

4. See Timothy Langen, "Andrei Bely's *Petersburg* and the Dynamics of Political Response," in *Just Assassins: The Culture of Terrorism in Russia*, ed. Anthony Anemone (Evanston: Northwestern University Press, 2010), 199.

5. For a microhistory of this attempt, see Claudia Verhoeven, *The Odd Man Karakozov: Imperial Russia, Modernity, and the Birth of Terrorism* (Ithaca: Cornell University Press, 2009).

6. The best English-language study of the affair is Philip Pomper's *Sergei Nechaev* (New Brunswick: Rutgers University Press, 1979).

7. Oszkar Jaszi, John Lewis, *Against the Tyrant: The Tradition and Theory of Tyrannicide* (Glencoe: Free Press, 1957).

8. Nurit Schleifman, *Undercover Agents in the Russian Revolutionary Movement: The SR Party, 1902-14* (New York: St. Martin's Press, 1988), 11.

9. Jonathan Daly, *Autocracy under Siege: Security Police and Opposition* (DeKalb: Northern Illinois University Press, 1998), 6.

10. Miller, *The Foundations of Modern Terrorism*, 102.

11. Richard Pipes, *The Degaev Affair: Terror and Treason in Tsarist Russia* (New Haven: Yale University Press, 2003), 118–19.

12. Norman Naimark, *Terrorists and Social Democrats: The Russian Revolutionary Movement under Alexander III* (Cambridge: Harvard University Press, 1983), 40.

13. See Robert Henderson, "Vladimir Burtsev and the Russian Revolutionary Emigration: Surveillance of Foreign Political Refugees in London, 1891–1905" (PhD diss., Queen Mary University of London, 2008).

14. See Barbara Melchiori, *Terrorism in the Victorian Novel* (London: Croom Helm, 1985).

15. On the topic of terrorism in Russian literature, see Lynn E. Patyk, *Written in Blood: Revolutionary Terrorism and Russian Literary Culture, 1861–1881* (Madison: University of Wisconsin Press, 2017).

16. Andrei Bely, *Petersburg*, tr. John Elsworth (London: Pushkin Press, 2009).

17. Andrei Belyi, *O Bloke: Vospominaniia, stat′i, dnevniki, rechi*, ed. A. Lavrov (Moscow: Avtograf, 1997), 102.

18. Oleg Lekmanov, *Zhizn′ Osipa Mandel′shtama* (Saint-Petersburg: Zvezda, 2003), 25, 82–86. Magnus Ljunggren, *Twelve Essays on Andrej Belyj's Petersburg* (Göteborg: Slavica Gothoburgensia, 2009), 33, 53–56. Aleksandr Sobolev, "Merezhkovskie v Parizhe (1906–1908)," *Litsa* 1 (1992), 353.

19. John Elsworth, *Andrey Bely: A Critical Study of the Novels* (Cambridge: Cambridge University Press, 1983), 107.

20. Olga Matich, "Poetics of Disgust: To Eat and Die in Petersburg," in *"Petersburg"/Petersburg: Novel and City, 1900–1921*, ed. Olga Matich (Madison: University of Wisconsin Press, 2010), 59.

21. Anna Geifman, *Thou Shalt Kill: Revolutionary Terrorism in Russia, 1894–1917* (Princeton: Princeton University Press, 1993), 14.

22. Geifman, *Thou Shalt Kill*, 22.

23. Geifman, *Thou Shalt Kill*, 265n64.

24. Andrei Belyi, *Mezhdu dvukh revoliutsii* (Chicago: Russian Language Specialties, 1966), 69–70.

25. Andrei Belyi, *Peterburg*, ed. L. Dolgopolov (Moscow: Nauka, 1981), 27–28. The translation here is my own. Cf. pages 34–35 in John Elsworth's translation.

26. Olga Matich, "Backs, Suddenlys, and Surveillance," in Matich, *"Petersburg"/Petersburg*, 33–34.

27. Anna Geifman, *Entangled in Terror: The Azef Affair and the Russian Revolution* (Wilmington: Scholarly Resources, 2000), 106.

28. Geifman, *Entangled in Terror*, 89–90.

29. Marina Mogilner, "The Russian Radical Mythology, 1881–1914: From Myth to History" (PhD diss., Rutgers University, 2000), 215.

30. Geifman, *Entangled in Terror*, 170.

31. Marietta Shaginian, "'Peterburg' Andreia Belogo" (1914), in *Andrei Belyi: Pro et Contra*, ed. A. Lavrov (Saint-Petersburg: RKhGI, 2004), 395.

Petersburg and Modern Occultism

MARIA CARLSON

At the turn of the twentieth century, Europe experienced a period of exceptional intellectual ferment, one important aspect of which was the "Modern Occult Revival." The word "occult" comes from Latin *occultus* and refers to special knowledge that is hidden or concealed from the average person. Such secret doctrines have a long history, but they have traditionally flourished underground. The late nineteenth-century Occult Revival, however, introduced a larger public to various esoteric doctrines, including spiritualism, mystery cults and religions, Theosophy, astrology, and Freemasonry.

These occult systems offered an alternative to the onslaught of modernity, to the illusion of progress, to the overwhelming burst of scientific invention, and to the prevailing philosophies of positivism and materialism. At a time when traditional religion was on the wane, occult doctrines offered to return a sense of the divine and the transcendent to people's lives. Russian modernists, highly sensitive to the call of the mystical and the spiritual, were fascinated by occultism. While Andrei Bely was familiar with a number of occult traditions, he was primarily interested in two doctrines that emerged during the Occult Revival: Theosophy and Anthroposophy. By exploring the building blocks of Bely's world view—especially since they lie outside mainstream cultural, philosophical, and religious traditions—the reader of *Petersburg* will gain new insights into the novel's artistic merits and into its many levels of meaning.[1]

Andrei Bely's modernist peers recognized the occult nature of *Petersburg* after its publication in 1913–14. The philosopher Nikolai Berdiaev identified it as an "astral novel" that was set in an "intermediate world between spirit and matter," while the literary critic Ivanov-Razumnik pointed out that "without knowing 'Theosophy' it is impossible to understand either the individual parts or the totality of the novel *Petersburg*."[2] Many things may be found in Bely's novel besides its occult content, but some knowledge of Theosophy and Anthroposophy illuminates much of what strikes the reader as startling, innovative, and opaque in *Petersburg*.

Theosophy and Anthroposophy

The word "theosophy" comes from the Greek and means the "wisdom of God." With a small "t," theosophy includes esoteric intellectual currents such as Hermeticism, Christian Kabbalism, spiritual alchemy, Rosicrucianism, and the speculative mysticism of philosophers like Jacob Boehme (1575–1624), Emmanuel Swedenborg (1688–1772), and Vladimir Solovyov (1853–1900). Aspects of small-t theosophy are found throughout Bely's literary and critical writings.

When spelled with a capital "T," however, Theosophy refers to a mystico-religio-philosophical system characterized by strong Buddhist and Gnostic elements that claims to reveal a "secret doctrine" containing the answers to the great questions of existence. It was the brain-child of a well-born Russian expatriate with an unconventional past, Elena Blavatskaia, better known as Mme. Blavatsky (1831–91). With the assistance of her American friend Colonel Henry Olcott (1832–1907), Mme. Blavatsky founded the Theosophical Society in New York City, in 1875, to spread her new doctrine. This woman of genius (or notorious charlatan, depending on one's point of view) initiated an enterprise—eventually headquartered in both London and Adyar, India—that, in its time, attracted tens of thousands of adherents worldwide. The Theosophical Society had three stated goals: 1) To form a nucleus of the universal brotherhood of humanity without distinction of race, creed, sex, caste, or color; 2) to encourage the study of comparative religion, philosophy, and science; and 3) to investigate the unexplained laws of nature and the powers latent in human beings.

Theosophy offered an alternative to materialism, rationalism, positivism, and weakening Western Christianity. It is a syncretistic doctrine, meaning that it attempts to reconcile or unite different or even opposing religious traditions, schools of philosophical thought, and cultural concepts into a single, coherent system. Theosophy thus commingles Buddhism and Hindu mysticism, Western esoteric traditions, ancient mystery religions, small-t theosophy, and other doctrines; it claims to be nothing less than the "Synthesis of Science, Religion, and Philosophy," as the subtitle of Mme. Blavatsky's foundational text, *The Secret Doctrine* (1888), indicates. Mme. Blavatsky insisted that "Esoteric philosophy reconciles all religions, strips every one of its outward, human garments, and shows the root of each to be identical with that of every other great religion."[3] Theosophy, she claimed, was a distillation of a universal esoteric tradition that highly evolved adepts in secret lodges had been jealously guarding from the uninitiated for thousands of years. Blavatsky professed herself to be those adepts' chosen messenger to humanity.

Among the Russians interested in Theosophy, one finds the philosopher Vladimir Solovyov, who exercised great intellectual influence on early Russian modernist culture, as well as that culture's many exponents: the philosopher Nikolai Berdiaev; the writers Konstantin Bal´mont, Viacheslav Ivanov, and Maksimilian Voloshin; the composer Aleksandr Skriabin; and the painters Wassily Kandinsky, Mikalojus Čiurlionis, and Nikolai Roerich. Even some prominent Marxists, notably Maxim Gorky and Anatolii Lunacharskii, flirted with Theosophy. Widespread attraction to this new occult doctrine left its mark on all the arts of the period, in Europe, Russia, and North America.

Andrei Bely initially encountered Theosophy in 1896 but began to take an interest in it only after 1903. He first heard about the charismatic leader of the Society's German Section, Dr. Rudolf Steiner (1861–1925), in 1905, from several of the "Theosophical ladies" who frequented the same Moscow Theosophical circles as Bely and his mother. The ladies had traveled abroad to hear Dr. Steiner's lectures, and they returned to praise his insights and share their lecture notes. By 1909, Bely was acquainted with Steiner's better-known Theosophical writings, although he did not meet "the Doctor" in person until May 1912.

Trained in science and philosophy, Rudolf Steiner added German philosophical idealism, organicism (the view that human beings and the universe are mutually reflecting entities), and Christian mysticism to Blavatsky's Buddhist-saturated Theosophical doctrine. Steiner was not impressed by Blavatsky's tendency toward "occult miracles"—communicating with the dead through spiritualist mediums; moving material objects through space by the power of mind alone; causing flowers, aromas, or sounds to materialize out of thin air— or by the leadership of Annie Besant (1847–1933), who succeeded Blavatsky and

Olcott to the presidency of the Theosophical Society in 1907. Still, Steiner worked for many years within the doctrinal framework of the Theosophical Society. His early works describing the structure of the cosmos became part of the Theosophical canon, and he led the Theosophical Society's large German-Austrian Section from 1902 until September 1912.

Steiner left the Theosophical Society for two reasons. First, the Doctor did not support Besant's promotion of a young Indian boy, Jiddu Krishnamurti, as an advanced spiritual entity who would serve as a "vehicle" for a messianic World Teacher (Krishnamurti himself later rejected this role). Besant's initiative caused considerable controversy among Theosophists and splintered the society's leadership. Second, Steiner's own occult thinking gradually evolved in new directions. He developed his own version of Theosophy, which he recast as a more disciplined, structured, and Christianized "spiritual science," calling it Anthroposophy.

The Anthroposophical Society was formally established in Cologne in December 1912, with an initial membership of 3,000. Most members were German and Austrian Theosophists, but among them were a number of Russians, including Andrei Bely. Having begun his work on *Petersburg* in September 1911, Bely went abroad in the spring of 1912. In May, he had his first personal audience with "the Teacher." Over the next year and a half he attended Steiner's courses while working on *Petersburg*. Bely followed the Doctor on his lecture circuit to cities all over Europe. He was also invited to join Steiner's elite and intimate Esoteric Classes. The writer completed *Petersburg* in November 1913, during this period of intense spiritual work.

When the Anthroposophical Society moved its headquarters to Dornach, Switzerland, Bely followed. In Dornach, he was among those who worked on the building of the first Goetheanum, the Anthroposophical Temple designed by Dr. Steiner. Bely left Dornach only when he was recalled to Russia for military service, in 1916. Bely's subsequent relationship with Steiner had its ups and downs, but he remained a committed Anthroposophist until his death.

Anthroposophy, as its name implies, emphasizes "knowledge of the nature of man," as opposed to Theosophy's emphasis on knowledge of the divine. It posits a spiritual world that is comprehensible to the human intellect and accessible to those who have developed their spiritual organs of perception—clairvoyance. Trained, like Steiner, as a natural scientist, Bely found himself more in agreement with the Doctor's rationalized, Christianized, more intellectual version of Theosophy than with the neo-Buddhistic, mystical, associative variant promoted by Blavatsky and Besant. Bely's preference for Anthroposophy, however, did not represent a sudden turn to a radically new ideology. In becoming an Anthroposophist, the writer simply took the next logical step in the spiritual quest that consumed his entire life.

Theosophy and Anthroposophy share a lot of common ground. Both aspire to the "synthesis of science, religion, and philosophy" as a means of giving meaning to human life; both seek to develop the human "spiritual organs" in order to achieve clairvoyance; and both accept the notions of reincarnation and karma, although Anthroposophy rid itself of Theosophy's other exotic Buddhist vocabulary. Theosophy and Anthroposophy also share one canon of esoteric works; similarly privilege the spiritual over the material; and subscribe to a Judeo-Christian moral ethic tempered by spiritual Darwinism, which posits the survival of those with the fittest spirit. Finally, both occult doctrines have the same cosmology. Anthroposophy may be viewed as a more coherent and "westernized" form of Theosophy that emphasizes Western culture's Christian element, to which Mme. Blavatsky had been hostile.

Sifting Theosophy from Anthroposophy, especially during the period when Bely worked on *Petersburg*, is not really possible, since Steiner's ideas grew from Theosophical soil. This essay uses the term "Theosophical" to describe ideas from both doctrines as they appear in *Petersburg*. Bely conceived and wrote his novel as Steiner was in the process of leaving the Theosophical Society and starting his own movement, with the result that *Petersburg* simultaneously bears the marks of Mme. Blavatsky, Annie Besant and her coauthor Charles Leadbeater, and Rudolf Steiner.

A Crash Course in Theosophical Thinking

Theosophy and Anthroposophy are complex doctrines eluding concise description. Their inherent syncretism, that is, their attempt to "systematize" all major occult systems into a single, all-encompassing "secret doctrine" of the ages, makes description even more difficult. What do we need to know to appreciate what Bely has achieved in *Petersburg*?

Theosophy and Anthroposophy are fundamentally Gnostic systems in that they posit the dualism of Spirit and Matter. The term *Gnostic* comes from the Greek *gnosis*, which means "knowledge" in the sense of spiritual insight and revelation, not reason or science. While originally applied to esoteric religions that first arose in the second century, the term is presently used for religious or philosophical systems that assume the duality of Spirit (goodness, light) and Matter (evil, darkness).

In Theosophy, Absolute Spirit—the unknowable, ineffable Divine—stands at one end, while Matter, dense and gross, stands at the other. Spirit, comprehending Itself (Divine Consciousness), begins a series of emanations out of Itself, and the further these emanations proceed from their origin in Absolute Spirit, the more material and dense they become. Spirit progressively descends into Matter over the course of many cosmic incarnations. Divine Consciousness moves from pure Spirit toward substantive, material Form (Matter). As it devolves, it creates increasingly less spiritual and more material worlds, as well as different humanities to inhabit them. After these emanations reach complete materiality, the process reverses, returning from the material to the spiritual. Absolute Spirit rolls Itself back up into Itself and rests. A single cycle occurs over vast passages of time and many cosmic incarnations. When the cycle ends, another cycle begins, and there is no end to this process. Such macrocosmic drama is also reflected at the microcosmic level in individual human beings.

Our world (Earth) and the human monads (units, entities, souls) that inhabit it are but a tiny part of this enormous cosmic cycle of world incarnations. In Theosophical cosmology, our Earth incarnation is the fourth in the current cycle of seven, having been preceded by the Saturn, Sun, and Moon incarnations. The Earth incarnation has become almost completely material, so sunk in physicality and matter that most of its inhabitants have forgotten their true origin in Spirit. This materiality conceals from people the knowledge that there are other levels of existence beyond the material. These other levels of existence nevertheless influence the progression of the Earth incarnation.

The Theosophical cosmos is built on the number seven: there are seven planetary chains (of which the Earth chain of seven globes is only one), seven rays, seven principles, seven rounds, seven root races (epochs), each with seven subraces, etc. There are also seven planes in which the world, nature, and humanity exist. They are: 1) physical, 2) astral, 3) mental, 4) intuitional (Buddhic), 5) spiritual, 6) monadic, and 7) divine. These planes, Annie Besant explains, are "concentric interpenetrating spheres, not separated from each other by distance, but by difference of constitution."[4] They are different states of consciousness. The relevant planes for understanding Bely's novel are the first two—physical and astral—since they most immediately affect human beings and human events in this, the fourth Earth incarnation. The third, mental plane is the highest one achievable, in the present incarnation, by "advanced humanity"—those enlightened individuals who have refined their spiritual organs of perception and understood the cosmic imperative. The remaining four states will be accessible in the distant future, after humanity begins the series of reincarnations that will move away from Matter and back toward Spirit.

The physical plane is one of animal desires, of the dense, visible, material, three-dimensional world in which human beings live, think, and act. The least refined of all planes, the physical plane embodies the most primitive representation and understanding of reality. The repercussions of feelings, ideas, thoughts, and actions on the physical plane, however, are felt beyond it on the astral plane, which Theosophy sometimes calls the fourth dimension of space. The astral world surrounds and interpenetrates the physical world but is invisible to most people.

The astral plane is "a perfect replica" of the physical world in astral matter.[5] It is populated not by humans, but by their auras, or etheric doubles, and by all the feelings, thoughts, fears, desires, and intentions people experience, and which emit vibrations that oscillate the astral matter and give it astral form. Theosophy calls these entities "thought-forms" or "artificial elementals." As they evolve, thought-forms change shape and color in response to changes in the ideas or emotions that generated them. Astral thought-forms do not disappear; all thought-forms that have been created since the Earth incarnation began are preserved in the Akashic Record (Record of the Astral Light), a sort of multidimensional, cosmic history of the Earth's incarnation, imprinted on the ether and accessible to those who have developed their clairvoyant potential—like Dr. Steiner, who claimed to be able to read the Akashic Record.

Annie Besant and Charles Leadbeater defined, described, and illustrated astral thought-forms in an influential book, *Thought-Forms* (1901). The book included a chart of twenty-five colors with explanations of their intellectual and emotional meanings—a primer for those occultists who had developed astral vision and wanted properly to interpret auras and elementals. Many artists were interested in and inspired by what *Thought-Forms* had to say about the mysticism of thought, color, light, sound, music, and form. Wassily Kandinsky, for example, integrated the book's ideas into his 1911 study *Concerning the Spiritual in Art* (see Olga Matich's essay in this volume). Aleksandr Skriabin designed an organ that projected colored lights when his musical compositions were played, thus synaesthetically combining color, light, and sound.

Petersburg, as Berdiaev rightly observed, takes place on the astral plane, where thought-forms exist and act. The novel is the astral expression of the thoughts and feelings that Russians experience on the physical plane of October 1905. A son is asked to liquidate his father. A mysterious intermediary brings him a bomb. The plot fizzles. A double agent is murdered. But what the reader experiences in the world of the novel is not the physical plane on which the characters live and events take place, but the astral plane on which ideas and feelings and intentions take on astral forms and live and act. These astral forms assume lives of their own in the astral matter—with consequences, it turns out, for events on the physical plane. Astral events that manifest themselves on the physical plane may appear arbitrary, incomprehensible, or absurd, but they have their own ineluctable logic on the cosmic level. They affect history.

Bely's Astral Novel

Petersburg begins with what its narrator calls "idle cerebral play" (42) precisely because that is how thought-forms are generated.[6] Mme. Blavatsky explains: "Given a certain intensity of will, and the shapes created by the mind become subjective. Hallucinations, they are called, although to their creator they are real as any visible object is to anyone else. Given a more intense and intelligent concentration of this will, and the form becomes concrete, visible, objective."[7] Senator Ableukhov has this capacity: "His cranium became the womb of mental images [*myslennye obrazy*—thought-forms], which were forthwith embodied in this spectral world" (34/44).[8] The reader learns that "every idle thought obstinately developed into a spatio-temporal image, continuing its now uncontrollable activities—outside the senator's head" (45). And the senator is not alone. His thought-form Dudkin, for example, "turned out to have idle thoughts of his own; and his idle thoughts possessed all the same qualities" (45). All of these idle thoughts "escaped and acquired solidity" (45). The senator's "idle thoughts" continue to express themselves "in the form of the senator's house, and in the form of the senator's son, who carries in his head idle thoughts of his own" (73).

Senator Ableukhov's cerebral play and idle thoughts that acquire "solidity" are rooted in the Theosophical notion of the generation of thought-forms in the astral world, which mirrors and interpenetrates the physical world. "Astral world scenery much resembles that of earth in consequence of its being largely made up of the astral duplicates of physical objects," explains Besant. The "idle thoughts," leading an existence separate from the mind that evokes them, "are living entities, with bodies of elemental essence and thoughts as the ensouling lives, and they are then called artificial elementals, or thought-forms."[9] These astral "inhabitants," it must be stressed, are not people: they are thoughts, feelings, fears, desires, and impulses of human beings on the physical plane. These nonmaterial entities assume form and force on the astral plane. Dudkin thus arises as a thought-form generated by Senator Ableukhov's fears of "the inhabitants of the islands" (27)—the workers, the revolutionaries, and their chaotic ilk—and begins an existence that corresponds to the senator's worst projected fears.

Thought-forms (or artificial elementals), when generated with sufficient intensity of will, have staying power and even a degree of independence. "If a man thinks a good or an evil thought, that thought calls into existence a corresponding form or power within the sphere of his mind, which may assume density and become living, and which may continue to live long after the physical body of the man who created it has died," writes the German Theosophist Franz Hartmann.[10] As the senator senses, with an anxious glance toward the islands (25), these thought-forms are potentially dangerous: "These elementals master us if we do not master them."[11] Last but not least, the staying power of thought-forms means that astral St. Petersburg is populated not only by "revolutionary" thought-forms generated in the heated climate of 1905, when the novel takes place, but also by thought-forms willed into existence by generations of Peterburgians—writers, musicians, bureaucrats, tsars, workers, and revolutionaries—and long surviving those who originally thought and willed them. This sequence of projections of thought-forms onto the astral plane first began with the thought forms created by Tsar Peter I himself when he first conceived of the city of Petersburg in 1703 and continued, unbroken, into the time of the novel.

A prisoner of positivism, Senator Ableukhov is not aware that he generates thought-forms. He reads Auguste Comte (158), not Blavatsky or Steiner. His positivistic inclination is underscored by the fact that both his head and his house—a traditional metaphor for the brain—are yellow. Yellow indicates intellectual capacity of the rational sort, Besant explains.[12] Bely's choice of yellow to stress Apollon Apollonovich's rationalism exemplifies the impact of Theosophy's color theory on *Petersburg*'s imagery. (For other meanings Bely attached to the color yellow, see Henrietta Mondry's and Judith Wermuth-Atkinson's essays in this volume.) The novel uses Besant's aura colors to guide the reader's response to other events as well. *Petersburg* sports the deep rose of affection, the bright red of anger, the gray-green deceit of the "malevolent mist," and the black of evil malice. Colors are important, since thought-forms (and human auras) assume an intensity of color that reveals their true nature. In the astral world, one sees things how they truly are, assuming that one has "astral sight"—the ability to see on the astral plane, since thoughts acquire visible shapes and colors in astral matter.

The positivistic senator unwittingly accesses the astral world, which can be reached through dreams, madness, intoxication, or clairvoyance. The two spaces Apollon Apollonovich observes as he is falling asleep are the physical and astral planes: "One was material (the walls of rooms and the sides of his carriage), the other was—not spiritual exactly (it was also material)"; this second space consists of "nebulous blurs," "swirling cores," lights, and bright colors (183). This is an accurate description of the illustrations of astral forms provided in Besant and Leadbeater's *Thought-Forms*. In fact, while working on *Petersburg*, in December 1912 and January 1913, Bely had a breakthrough in the practice of spiritual exercises that Steiner had assigned to him: he claimed to have experienced his first visits to the astral plane.[13]

The astral world is made of astral matter (elemental essence), which is finer than physical matter and therefore amorphous and fluid. It manifests as mists, fogs, and shadows; it continually changes shapes that appear and disappear, as human thought-impulses oscillate the elemental essence. In *Petersburg*, the word *tuman* (mist or fog) appears more than one hundred fifty times in various forms; *ten'* (shadow) appears more than sixty times. Bely's descriptions of shadows emerging from and vanishing into the St. Petersburg mist echoes Besant's description of the astral world in *Man and His Bodies*, the book Sofia Petrovna Likhutina is reading in the novel (83). Besant explains that the astral world is "full of continually changing shapes [and] vast masses of elemental essence from which continually shapes emerge and into which they again disappear."[14] "An astral entity," she writes, "will change his whole appearance with the most startling rapidity, for astral matter takes form under every impulse of thought, the life swiftly remoulding the form to give itself new expression."[15] This fluid quality of astral matter explains why characters in *Petersburg* constantly change into other people: the Semitic Mongol—the student Lipenskii—Lippanchenko—the Greek from Odessa, Mavrokordato; Shishnarfiev—Shishnarfne—Enfranshish; Voronkov—the "hallucinatory" Morkovin; the Bronze Horseman—the Dutchman—the sailor—the Bronze Guest. Malleable and fluid characters, realized metaphors, slippers and wallpaper that come alive and suitcases that reshape themselves—all are astral thought-forms that are constantly being molded and remolded by two hundred years of Russian thoughts, ideas, and emotions about St. Petersburg and its founder.

Thoughts on the physical plane become deeds on the astral plane. Steiner points out that "a lie in the physical world becomes an agent of destruction in the astral world. A lie is a murder in the astral world."[16] Nikolai Apollonovich Ableukhov thinks of snipping a vein in his father's neck with a pair of scissors (297) and his thought becomes a thought-form. Since Nikolai is the son of Apollon Apollonovich's body, and Dudkin is the "son" of the senator's cerebral play, Nikolai's astral "brother" carries out his thought, murdering Lippanchenko with a pair of scissors. Dudkin is found sitting astride Lippanchenko's corpse in the symbolic pose of the Bronze Horseman, for Dudkin is also Peter the Great's progeny—the Bronze Guest greets Dudkin as "my son" (411).

The choice of scissors is not accidental. These are symbolic scissors that cut centuries, people, and philosophies apart, and have the power to resolve antinomies when closed. Bely identified "the problem of scissors and antinomies" as a problem to be solved by modernist art and thought.[17] For him, such antinomies, or contradictions between two otherwise reasonable beliefs, included science and religion; Nietzsche and Solovyov (see Edith Clowes's essay in this volume); form and content; will and representation; consciousness and the sub/unconscious (see Judith Wermuth-Atkinson's essay in this volume); and, of course, Europe and Asia, whose clash is reflected in the title of Bely's unfinished trilogy, *East or West*, with *Petersburg* as its second installment. Dudkin, the "son" of the Bronze Guest—Peter the Westernizer—kills Lippanchenko "the Mongol" (380–81) with a pair of Bely's fateful scissors on the astral plane, perhaps in a failed attempt to resolve the antinomy of East and West.

Rudolf Steiner explains that the astral world is the inverted mirror image of the physical world, a detail reinforced by the many images of reflection, reversal, and doubling in *Petersburg*. For instance, the inconceivably huge number 1 plus 30 zeros that so frightens Nikolai Apollonovich is really a modest 30 zeros plus the single digit 1 (439–40). Immeasurable, "ethereal spaces" are no more than a dot. An explosion is an implosion. Enfranshish is Shishnarfne. Ivanov is Vonavi. The father is the son, and the son the father. Just as objects are mirror-inverted on the astral plane, so is time. Astoundingly, the astral world is the "inverse unraveling of things."[18] Everything that happens in the physical world plays in reverse in the astral world. History runs backward. Instead of cause and effect, we have effect and cause, thus making the goal, or aim, appear to be the cause, and "proving," as Steiner insists, that aim and cause are ultimately the same thing: "In the astral light the cipher 365 must be read backwards: 563. If an event unfolds before us, it is perceived in inverse sequence. In the astral world the cause comes *after* the effect, whereas on Earth, the effect follows the cause. In the astral world, the aim appears as the cause—proving that the aim and the cause are identical."[19]

Since astral history runs backward, there are several instances of reverse chronological sequences in *Petersburg*, with effects leading back to a "cause." Sofia Petrovna experiences this literally: "A segment of the recent past broke away into that gray-black night"; then "the whole of the past day broke away"; "no sooner did she try to evoke the impressions of the previous day—than the previous day broke away again"; "her years of marriage, her wedding flashed by and dropped away; a void was tearing them away and swallowing them piece by piece"; "the whole of her life flashed by, the whole of her life dropped away, as though her life had never happened" (232–33). All Sofia Petrovna hears is the clang of metal on stone, "as though there behind her back, clanging loudly against the stone, a metallic horseman had set off to chase her" (233). Sofia Petrovna's consciousness has run backward to the time of Peter and the origins of his imperial city, via a dark reference to the wretched hero of Pushkin's *Bronze Horseman*.

While in a dream state and on his own "astral journey" (316), Nikolai Apollonovich comprehends that "everything revolved the other way—revolved terribly" (320). He realizes that the sound he hears "was the calendar running backwards" (321). Time goes to zero and returns Nikolai Apollonovich to his ancient Turanian (Eastern) origins: he relives the sequence of the individual and planetary incarnations (Saturn being the first in the current cycle) and realizes that in the breast of his father, the consummate Petrine bureaucrat, beats the heart of a Mongol from the Asiatic steppes (Ab-Lai), and that he, his father's son and heir, has wasted his time on Kant and failed to understand the Mongol mission (316–21).

In another example, Shishnarfne, an artificial elemental projected onto the astral plane by Dudkin's passion for tobacco and vodka, also points out that the astral plane works in reverse. He tells Dudkin: "Our spaces [in the astral world] are not yours; everything there flows the other way . . . And a simple Ivanov there is a Japanese, for the name, read backwards, is a Japanese one: Vonavi" (401). Shishnarfne himself then becomes Enfranshish. The "Mongol" Lippanchenko, the senator with Mongol roots, the senator's son in his Bukhara dressing-gown, Shishnarfne-Enfranshish—every European façade reverses to reveal an Asiatic threat.

The hidden racial threat of the Yellow Peril in *Petersburg* reflects the realities of the Russo-Japanese War (see Henrietta Mondry's essay in this volume). The oriental cosmopolitan Shishnarfne-Enfranshish is a fount of information about the astral plane. He makes it clear that St. Petersburg is "our" capital—an astral capital whose citizens carry a shadow passport. "After all we do not live, it has to be admitted, in the visible world," he explains. "The tragedy of our situation is that, like it or not, we are in the invisible world." In short, Shishnarfne informs Dudkin, "you are left with no option but respectfully to submit your petition to the world of shadows" (399). Shishnarfne describes the city in this manner: "Petersburg doesn't have three dimensions, it has four; the fourth is subject to uncertainty and is not marked on maps at all, unless by a point, for a point is the place of contact between the plane of this existence and the spherical surface of the immense astral cosmos; so any point in the spaces of Petersburg is capable in the twinkling of an eye of throwing up a resident of this dimension" (399–400). Shishnarfne decodes the novel's Prologue for the reader: St. Petersburg "manifests itself—on maps: in the form of two concentric circles with a black point in the middle; and from this mathematical point, which possesses no dimensions, it energetically proclaims that it exists" (12). The point with no dimensions is the entryway to the fourth dimension, to the astral world.

What Does Theosophy Add to *Petersburg*?

On 11 April 1912, in a separate address to the Russians who participated in his Helsinki lecture course, Steiner spoke about the mission of the Slavic soul.[20] He explained that Eastern thought was passive and belonged to the past; Western thought was active, but it was of the present. The Slavic soul, in Steiner's view, was still a young soul, and it unfortunately felt a dangerous attraction to the East. But the Slavic soul was also highly spiritual: once it succeeded in escaping both Eastern passivity and Western materialism, it would create a new path to the spiritual future, in the Sixth Post-Atlantean Age, according to Anthroposophical cosmology. Steiner, who had learned about Vladimir Solovyov from the Russian members of the Theosophical Society, singled out the philosopher of Sophia, the Wisdom of God, as the guiding light of the Russian soul.

Steiner's view of the Slavic soul's mission corresponded to Bely's own thoughts about Russia's cultural quandary and its possible solution, not least thanks to the great importance of Solovyov's thought to early Russian modernism. For Bely, Russia's Mongol and Petrine legacies led to cultural bifurcation or at least to antinomy, and unresolved antinomy led to revolution. Since the time of Peter's reforms, thoughts of ancient Asia and modern Europe were sent into the astral plane and precipitated out on the physical plane as a destructive duality, manifest as seemingly irreconcilable antagonists in Russian culture: East vs. West, God vs. Kant, common people vs. intelligentsia, Slavophile thinker vs. Westernizer, conservative bureaucrat vs. bomb-throwing revolutionary. "Since that fraught time when the metal Horseman came hastening to the banks of the Neva, since that time, fraught with days, when he thrust his steed on to the gray Finnish granite—Russia has been split in twain; the very fates of the fatherland have been split in twain as well; suffering and weeping until the final hour—Russia has been split in twain" (131–32).

Thus, Peter's city, a dot on the map of Russia, becomes the epicenter of the crisis of culture and consciousness, of which the failed 1905 revolution is but one expression. The most intentional and rational city on earth, St. Petersburg was willed into being by Peter the Great. For Theosophists reading Bely's novel, Peter's act had significant repercussions on both physical and astral levels. Since its founding, the Russian national consciousness had molded and remolded the city's (and Russia's) astral image, populating it with strange and dangerous thought-forms. Roiling in astral St. Petersburg, the resultant thought-forms precipitated revolution onto the physical plane: this was inevitable and had its own inexorable, cosmic logic: it was the collective Karma of the Russian people.

A Theosophical reader might see Senator Ableukhov as a powerful thought-form produced by Peter I's vision for Russia. But his state uniform conceals the dangerous Turanian (319) whom Peter tried and failed to squeeze out of Russia. In Theosophy, the Turanians are the fourth of seven subraces of the Atlantean root race or epoch, which preceded our current, fifth "Aryan" epoch. Their evolution ended with the Mongolians. For Russian culture, this marks them as a force that impedes progress: Nikolai thus learns that the "Mongol business" is "not the destruction of Europe—[but] its stagnation" (319).

The senator's cerebral play produces Dudkin, a thought-form induced by fears of revolutionary terrorism transformed into an agent of destruction. Neither the senator nor Dudkin is the "real" Russia. The Bronze Guest is a thought-form produced not only by Dudkin's madness, but also by the thoughts and will of Empress Catherine II, who commissioned Tsar Peter I's equestrian statue (1782). It is also produced by Aleksandr Pushkin, who wrote that statue into his programmatic narrative poem, *The Bronze Horseman* (1833). And it is produced by the *very idea* of Petrine Russia as conceived by Peter's indomitable will and subsequently massaged by generations of Russian minds as they argued about the tsar's legacy. Alas, the Bronze Guest "destroys irrevocably" on the astral plane (288). Both the Mongols and Peter the Great have a lot to answer for in Bely's *Petersburg*.

Bely's novel does not resolve the problem of Russia's fate, but it does leave the reader with hope. First, Bely offers Anthroposophical comfort: the tall, sad, and silent White Domino who solaces Sofia Petrovna (230–32) reflects Steiner's belief that Christ would soon return in the etheric body, visible only on the astral plane, as "a living comforter" to humankind.[21] Second, in the novel's Epilogue, we see that both the senator and Dudkin are now "gone," while Nikolai Apollonovich has rejected his old self and actively undertaken to change his own Karmic path. He leaves Kant behind and seeks inspiration in the philosophy of Grigorii Skovoroda (a maternal relative of Vladimir Solovyov). Perhaps Russia, too, can change its own destructive Karma. Perhaps the Russian soul will find that third way that transcends both East and West.

The novel is more a tribute to Bely the artist than to Bely the occultist. *Petersburg* rises above the constraints of Theosophy's and Anthroposophy's cosmological and ideological systems to become a unique and provocative work of art (and philosophy!) on its own merits. Too often literary texts inspired by occult systems fail to transcend their ideologies. In the case of *Petersburg*, this is fortunately not the case.

Notes

1. This essay is based on previously published work. See Maria Carlson, *"No Religion Higher Than Truth": A History of the Theosophical Movement in Russia, 1875–1922* (Princeton: Princeton University Press, 1993); "Fashionable Occultism: Spiritualism, Theosophy, and Hermeticism in Fin-de-siècle Russia," in *The Occult in Russian and Soviet Culture*, ed. B. G. Rosenthal (Ithaca: Cornell University Press, 1997), 135–52; and "Theosophy and History in Andrei Belyi's *Peterburg*," *Russian Literature* 58.1 (2005), 29–45.

2. Nikolai Berdiaev, "Astral´nyi roman" (1916), *Sobranie sochinenii* (Paris: YMCA, 1989), 3:437. R. V. Ivanov-Razumnik, "Andrei Belyi," in *Russkaia literatura XX veka (1890–1910)*, ed. S. A. Vengerov (Moscow: Mir, 1916), 3:53.

3. H. P. Blavatsky, *Secret Doctrine* (London: Theosophical Publishing Company, 1888), 1:xx.

4. Annie Besant, *The Ancient Wisdom* (Adyar: Vasanta Press, 1977), 63.

5. Annie Besant, *Man and His Bodies* (Adyar: Theosophical Publishing House, 1975), 36.

6. Andrei Bely, *Petersburg*, tr. John Elsworth (London: Pushkin Press, 2009).

7. H. P. Blavatsky, *Isis Unveiled* (New York: J. W. Bouton, 1877), 1:62.

8. The first number in dual page references designates the original text: Andrei Belyi, *Peterburg*, ed. L. Dolgopolov (Moscow: Nauka, 1981). The second refers to John Elsworth's translation. Russian Theosophists, Bely included, translated "thought-forms" as *myslennye obrazy* or *mysle-obrazy*. The noun "thought" (*mysl´*) and its derivatives occur in *Petersburg* hundreds of times, indicating that the projection of thoughts is a major leitmotif in the novel.

9. Besant, *The Ancient Wisdom*, 65, 67.

10. Franz Hartmann, *An Adventure among the Rosicrucians* (Boston: Occult Publishing Company, 1887), 83.

11. Hartmann, *An Adventure among the Rosicrucians*, 90.

12. Annie Besant, Charles Leadbeater, *Thought-Forms* (Wheaton, IL: Theosophical Publishing House, 1971), 40.

13. See Andrei Bely's diary for January 1913, in "Dornakhskii dnevnik (Intimnyi)," at http://bdn-steiner.ru/modules.php?name=Books&go=page&pid=205.

14. Besant, *Man and His Bodies*, 39.

15. Besant, *The Ancient Wisdom*, 65.

16. Rudolf Steiner, *An Esoteric Cosmology* (Blauvelt, NY: Spiritual Science Library, 1987), 62–63.

17. Andrei Belyi, "Pochemu ia stal simvolistom" (1928), *Simvolizm kak miroponimanie* (Moscow: Respublika, 1994), 431.

18. Steiner, *Esoteric Cosmology*, 60, 59.
19. Steiner, *Esoteric Cosmology*, 59.
20. Rudolf Steiner, "Address to the Russian Participants," in *Spiritual Beings in the Heavenly Bodies and in the Kingdoms of Nature* (Hudson, NY: Anthroposophic Press, 1992), 216–29.
21. Rudolf Steiner, "The Reappearance of Christ in the Etheric" (25 January 1910), in the Rudolf Steiner Archive, http://wn.rsarchive.org/Lectures/ReapChrist/19100306p01.html.

Petersburg and Russian Nietzscheanism

EDITH W. CLOWES

The Russian modernists' romance with Friedrich Nietzsche's metaphysical anarchism began in the 1890s, when the German philosopher garnered an intense, if confused, following among the broader Russian readership. Nietzsche's moral critique and call for the "revaluation of values" offered political radicals and artistic innovators alike the intellectual gunpowder they needed to blow away the materialist, rationalist philosophical outlook dominant in previous decades.[1] The goal of this essay is to present the aspects of Nietzsche's thought in their Russian context that Andrei Bely both adopted and transmuted in *Petersburg* in order to articulate his own original view. One caveat is in order: piecing together and understanding Bely's uses of Nietzschean philosophy in *Petersburg* takes patience. As other essays in this volume show, Bely was a heterogeneous and synthetic thinker of rare complexity. Sorting out the strands of thought and theme in his oeuvre will reward readers with a more satisfying experience of the novel.

It is hard to overestimate Nietzsche's role in spurring a revolution of moral consciousness in fin-de-siècle Russia.[2] Overall, we encounter among Nietzsche's Russian readers both a new belief in the power of human agency and a radical challenge to traditional concepts of good and evil. The Nietzschean intellectual fashion among modernists, led by Zinaida Gippius and Dmitrii Merezhkovskii, meshed with various Russian strands of thought. Paramount among them were Dostoevsky's humanist religious sensibility and the apocalyptic thinking of Russia's greatest nineteenth-century philosopher, Vladimir Solovyov. Nietzsche's thought also offered an alternative to Tolstoy's ascetic, self-denying dismissal of elite culture.[3] Modernist writers—notably, Viacheslav Ivanov, Aleksandr Blok, and Andrei Bely—found particular inspiration in the tragic vision of human fate developed in Nietzsche's *The Birth of Tragedy from the Spirit of Music* (1872). They read Nietzsche's work as a welcome challenge to Christian doctrine, and in their own writings they conjured Christ anew, as a life force bringing regeneration.

The overriding goal of Bely's creative activity was to invoke the end of an intolerably stagnant present moment and to apprehend signs of the Apocalypse (see David Bethea's essay in this volume). Like many modernists, he hoped that the destruction of the current political order would unleash vital creative energies, triggering a revolution in the human condition. As a university student, Bely was smitten with Nietzsche's thought, adopting Nietzsche as a life mentor. Beginning in the fall of 1899, as Bely later recalled, he "had lived and breathed Nietzsche" as "the borderline between the end of the old and start of the new era."[4] The German philosopher proved to be a strong stimulus in the creation of *Petersburg*, particularly thanks to his conception of tragedy. Before exploring the uses of this tragic vision in *Petersburg*, it is helpful to offer an overview of the main signposts in Nietzsche's metaphysical anarchism—his philosophy of life, creativity, and art. We will focus on Nietzsche's ideas of the Dionysian and Apollinian forces and on his cherished figure of the great and good human, Zarathustra (Zoroaster)—the ancient Persian philosopher who is commonly considered to have invented the concepts of good and evil.

Bely's Nietzschean Outlook

It was Nietzsche's earliest work, *The Birth of Tragedy*, that first propelled Bely's thought beyond the confines of the scientific positivism predominant in the late nineteenth century. Moving away from the linear thinking dominant in empiricism and Hegelian philosophy, Nietzsche views time and human fate in terms of cycles of destruction and creation. New culture and new life, he believes, emerge through the death and regeneration of life force. This force takes the form of the tragic hero. Within the hero two ideas of creativity clash and form a new synthesis. One kind of creativity takes on a physically palpable shape, creates a sense of order and purpose, and is visually pleasing; the other is a hidden life force, bringing new life through horrific death and expressed through passion, madness, and violence.

In *The Birth of Tragedy*, Nietzsche argues that, in ancient Greek culture, these forces take the form of two gods, Apollo, the god of the arts, and Dionysus, the god of life. This view of human existence is essentially tragic because it foretells the destruction of everything a person or a culture cherishes. Most importantly, in Nietzsche's tragic vision, these gods engender profound mythic creation, the end goal of which is to invoke the renewal of life itself.[5]

Nietzsche describes the Dionysian element as a divine life force worshipped across the ancient world from India to Greece. Dionysus, who is popularly known as the god of wine, represents for Nietzsche not just birth and growth but also a cyclical, burgeoning life energy, both destructive and creative, suffering and ecstatic. While it can motivate tremendous world-creative acts, the Dionysian can be at times anarchic and at times tyrannical. In the human psyche, the Dionysian marks the psychological weakening of individual will and reason and is associated with states of intoxication and delirium. Seen in this way, the Dionysian force is at once chaotic and regenerative; it inspires both terror and the "blissful ecstasy that wells up from the innermost human and, indeed, nature's depths."[6]

As a source of creative energy in nature, music is the artistic medium that best conveys primal Dionysian ecstasy and terror (*The Birth of Tragedy*, 40). In Nietzsche's view, music expresses that Dionysian life force that crushes the arrogant claims of human reason. The crucial function of ancient Greek religious rituals, Nietzsche argues, was to perform music and choral chant in order to invoke the power exercised by Dionysus. Later, this ritual became the foundation of Greek tragedy—for example, in the plays of Sophocles. The worship of Dionysian ecstasy, violence, and terror gradually declined in the ancient world, in Nietzsche's account, as the power of reason gained authority. Greek analytical philosophy, Nietzsche argues, was deeply hostile to the enchantment of music at the heart of Dionysian ritual. For example, while attracted to music, the philosopher Socrates repressed its power over himself, even as he opened up an optimistic, logically ordered, scientific world view (*The Birth of Tragedy*, 106).

Apollo, for Nietzsche, is the Greek god who offered the ancient Greeks a visual, aesthetic, and rational hedge against the violent chaos of Dionysian culture; he does so through "primitive" yet order-imposing art and thought. Here the viewer experiences a heroic dream story of the human conquest of brutal demi-gods and monsters. The Apollinian dream triumphs over the terror-inspiring beat of the Dionysian musical chant. Homeric epic, Nietzsche argues, emerged as evidence of the "complete victory of Apollinian illusion" (*The Birth of Tragedy*, 43–44). With its form-, symbol-, and sense-making, the visual

Apollinian medium gives us access to the Dionysian—which, in Nietzsche's philosophy, is akin to the unconscious psyche—while also limiting its power.[7] In brief, the Apollinian permits us an illusion of control over the chaos of existence.

For Nietzsche, visual art, sculpture, and architecture are foregrounded through the Apollinian, allowing for the appearance of an individual human figure—a hero (or heroine) who is visually pleasing, represents order over chaos, has will and agency, is physically and mentally disciplined, and confronts moral choices (*The Birth of Tragedy*, 46).[8] Together, these two divine forces, the Apollinian and the Dionysian, inspired the first tragic drama, which was distinct from the "barbarian" Dionysian rites (39). While Dionysian festivals highlighted sexual license, cruelty, and extravagance, the idea of Apollo shielded ancient Greece from the worst excesses of these rites. Tragedy created an artistic world that allowed the Greek viewer to experience life's horror at a safe distance, without becoming morally despondent (59).

Greek tragedy, Nietzsche argued, had its roots in music and the tragic chorus adapted from the original Dionysian rites (64). The atmosphere engendered in the ritual invocation of Dionysus supplanted ordinary reality and left the audience in a frenzy, face to face with the power of life itself. The chorus chanted the story in dithyrambs—an improvised lyric song to honor Dionysus. In the tragic drama, now a separate art form, characters took shape out of the spoken verbal material of the chorus. In Nietzsche's view, the tragic hero combines Dionysian, violent, suffering life force with Apollinian reason, form, and visual delineation. A purely Dionysian character (Nietzsche gives the example of Hamlet) is both lethargic and lacking in will, although highly intelligent. Such a character is nauseated by coming face to face with the "essence of things": only tragic art offers respite from this existential nausea because tragedy creates distance and balances the "*sublime* as the artistic taming of the horrible, and the *comic* as the artistic discharge of the nausea of absurdity" (60).

Toward the end of his career, Nietzsche developed his own tragic idea of "the eternal return of the same." The idea of the eternal return posits that a self-aware person simply must embrace life in all its recurring ecstasy and horror. In addition, Nietzsche's later depiction of the same conflicting forces of Dionysian self-destructive passion and Apollinian self-affirming order takes the form of the philosophical-religious figure Zarathustra. He imagines Zarathustra as a teacher who synthesizes and deepens the forces of the Apollinian and Dionysian, combining them with total life affirmation that defined "the eternal return." In *Thus Spoke Zarathustra* (1883–85), Nietzsche offered a narrative of regeneration that made this work a classic of world literature and thought. Andrei Bely, in turn, embraced Zarathustra as one of his own "teachers of life."[9]

In the 1900s, the most important Nietzschean trend among Russian modernists was the conflation of Christ and Dionysus in the figure of the "crucified Dionysus," as Nietzsche himself signed his letters shortly before his descent into madness in 1890.[10] The principal Russian thinker to probe these overlapping images was Viacheslav Ivanov, who, along with Blok and Bely, offered a profound response to *The Birth of Tragedy*. In the late 1880s, while studying in Germany with the famous historian of antiquity Theodor Mommsen, Ivanov read *The Birth of Tragedy*. In response to Nietzsche, he later produced an original study that drew parallels between the ancient cults of Dionysus and the passion of Christ. In 1903, Ivanov made a brilliant debut in Paris and St. Petersburg with a series of lectures, "On the Hellenic Religion of the Suffering God." Bely attended Ivanov's lectures and read them when they appeared in book form.[11]

For Bely, Nietzsche was a forerunner of the Russian modernists and a sage who anticipated their idea of artistic practice as theurgic ritual—an invocation of the divine, vested with the power to create new life. Bely hoped to realize this ideal of god-like creativity in his own art. As he wrote in an essay: "Art is not our ultimate goal. It must be surmounted by theurgy.... We [modernists] aspire to the embodiment of Eternity by means of the transfiguration of the resurrected personality. This is a difficult and dangerous path. The theurgist must go where Nietzsche halted."[12]

Although we find the figures of Dionysus and Christ in *Petersburg*, Bely, unlike Ivanov, did not initially view Dionysus as a prototype of Christ. Instead, he saw Christ as what Dostoevsky had called an "idiot"—that is, an exception to human psychology, a beatific spirit. Only later, while seeking sacrifice and regeneration in his own spiritual life during his 1912 sojourn in Switzerland, did Bely become immersed in the idea of the crucified Dionysus. In Switzerland, Bely came to identify ever more fully with his early mentor, thanks to intense awareness that this was the place where Nietzsche had first suffered his debilitating illness.[13] In *Petersburg*, we find this dual figure in the character of Aleksandr Ivanovich Dudkin.

The question of Bely's creative identity remains to a degree unresolved. While revering Nietzsche, he also cherished a "Christ fantasy"—the son's sacrifice to the father.[14] To be sure, non-Nietzschean Christ figures are prominent in *Petersburg*. It has been argued, for instance, that the philosopher Vladimir Solovyov furnished the model for the enigmatic white figure intermittently encountered by the novel's protagonists.[15] The Anthroposophical vision of Christ articulated by Rudolf Steiner, Bely's mentor in Switzerland, also plays an important role in *Petersburg* (see Maria Carlson's essay in this volume). Here the figure of Christ becomes a regenerative force in the complex evolution of the cosmos.[16]

In *Petersburg*, Nietzschean motifs support three sets of themes—the flow of time (linear vs. cyclical); order, chaos, and meaningful regeneration; and the clash of aesthetic and ethical values in the new "revaluation of values." Bely's novel challenges the rationalist idea of time as progressing in a linear, chronological fashion. In *Petersburg*, this orderly conception of historical time is fragmented, soon giving way to temporal chaos both in the plot construction and in characters' perceptions of time. The old and new ideas of time become palpable in the novel through opposing modes of perception. In some characters, sight—especially the recurrent perception of architecture and statuary—overwhelms other senses and gives them confidence in an orderly flow of time. Other characters perceive sound—music, spoken language, and street noises—above all else, and they associate those sounds with chaos.

To explicate the weave of Nietzschean ideas of Apollinian order, Dionysian chaos, and the moral implications of Zarathustra in the fabric of Bely's novel, I will focus on *Petersburg*'s three protagonists: Senator Apollon Apollonovich Ableukhov, his son, Nikolai Apollonovich, and the revolutionary Aleksandr Ivanovich Dudkin. I will also offer some commentary on Nikolai Apollonovich's love interest, Sofia Petrovna Likhutina; his mother, Anna Petrovna Ableukhova; and the double agent Lippanchenko.

Focusing on a conspiracy to assassinate Senator Ableukhov, narrated against the historical backdrop of the general strike of October 1905, *Petersburg* is filled with the anticipation of imminent upheaval that is indeed cosmic rather than merely political. The novel both seriously invokes and parodically mocks the traditional eschatological Christian expectation of the world's destruction and rebirth. It is this ambiguous apocalyptic tonality that gives *Petersburg* added spice, as it both capitalizes on the elements of Nietzsche's tragic vision and makes fun of them. The result is a novel that, while expressing a fervent hope for the Apocalypse and the radical renewal of the human condition, humorously refuses to succumb to rituals invoking the divine or to satisfy readers' desire for such theurgical practices.

The Apollinian

The Apollinian principle of order, as Virginia Bennett argues, appears to dominate the external structures of Bely's novel, such as chapter and subchapter headings, in which the narrator seems to guide the bewildered reader. In contrast, the moral struggle that is the thematic red thread of *Petersburg* is animated by the clash of the Apollinian with the Dionysian. But while Bennett oversimplifies the revolution of 1905 as the confrontation of "the Apollinian order of the tsarist government" with "the Dionysian outbursts of the rebellious masses," the situation is actually more complex. The Apollinian leitmotif in *Petersburg* does more than merely mimic Nietzsche's ideas.[17]

The Apollinian is embodied primarily in Apollon Apollonovich Ableukhov, one of the novel's father figures. His given name and patronymic, Apollo son of Apollo, make explicit reference to the Greek god, reflecting the Russian state's westernized, "rational" order that the senator embodies. His surname, in contrast, plays humorously with Apollon Apollonovich's Mongol heritage, treated here as a force from the chaotic East. The narrator traces the Ableukhov family name to a Central Asian forebear Ablai, nicknamed Ukhov, apparently thanks to his prominent ears (*ukho* is the Russian for an ear)—a physical trait the senator inherited. His surname also contains a pun, suggesting the word *opleukha*, or a "box on the ears."

Not surprisingly, then, in his habits of mind and behavior, Apollon Apollonovich represents a comical version of the Apollinian idea. He embodies the principles of order, balance, reason, and enlightenment, though often in trivial ways. In his career, he is a lawyer and professor of the philosophy of law, further supporting the Apollinian notion of order. He wears clothing bedecked with bright ribbons and medals, recalling Nietzsche's reference to Apollo as the "shining one" (15, 44).[18] The senator loves geometry and feels most comfortable in a rationally ordered world: he is calmed by straight avenues and geometrically shaped buildings, or "parallelepipeds."

Unlike his Nietzschean model, Apollon Apollonovich is not beautiful. He is an aged, pedantic, sclerotic, ugly, and silly version of the Apollinian idea (17, 31). He is bald with large, protruding ears, and he is weak and bent of body. The god Apollo shoots arrows as a way of punishing his enemies and is characterized by Nietzsche as an arrow thrower. The senator sees the map of Petersburg in terms of the "arrows" of the city's prospects that control the masses (25). Comically, this bureaucratic Apollinian swaps sharp arrows for pencils with perfectly sharpened points (14).

Instead of using his rational powers to rule justly, Apollon Apollonovich engages in rationalizing trivialities. For example, he orders the clothing in his closet according to points of the compass (17–18). And, instead of imposing a productive order, he is frightened into isolation by the Dionysian medium of sound on the street and the visual fragmentation of passersby into synecdoches, for example, noses, eyes, and moustaches (26–27).

Significantly, Apollon Apollonovich is compared not to Apollo but to an ancient father figure, Zeus. The narrator describes him as being "in a certain sense like Zeus: from his head there emerged gods, goddesses, and genii" (45). Still, like Nietzsche's Apollinian force, Apollon Apollonovich gives visual shape to shadowy feelings, thoughts, desires, and anxieties (for another, Anthroposophical, reading of this episode, see Maria Carlson's essay in this volume). Senator Ableukhov's brain functions as "the womb of mental images, which were forthwith embodied in this spectral world" (44). For example, the senator's inchoate fear for his own safety is embodied as the revolutionary Dudkin, the "stranger with the little black moustache" (45). Now brought to life, Dudkin "continued as a *being* there and then in the yellowish expanses of the Neva" (45). In the senator's imagination, Dudkin gains agency and thereby comes into view and into play.

The Dionysian

The Dionysian thread can be found at the heart of *Petersburg*'s chaotic narrative. Bennett cleverly contrasts the "strict format, the balance, and the harmony of the external organization" of the novel with the substance of each chapter, which is a "chaotic jumble of the feelings, sensations, imaginings, and impressions of the characters," further complicated by "abrupt switches from one person to another, often going back in time to bring the reader up-to-date on characters previously left dangling." Bennett apprehends the Dionysian in snippets of street conversation, unformed sounds, the nonlinear movement of the narrative, and, perhaps most important, in Bely's rhythmic prose, which "rises at times to a frenzy." The novel's theme of revolution is expressed in Dionysian terms as well. In the cityscape, Bennett sees the "impending explosion of a cataclysm—the destructive unleashing of the Dionysian forces which will shatter the illusion of the city-mirage conjured up by Peter and his successors"; the Dionysian is embodied in the "chaotic forces of reality represented by the masses"; and, finally, the uprising appears as a natural force, a swirling wind that sweeps away old "exhausted culture."[19]

Like the Dionysus-inspired, goat-hoofed caryatid adorning the classical (Apollinian) façade of the government Establishment, directed by Apollon Apollonovich (33, 355, 447), the Dionysian element is ubiquitous in the senator's life and is embodied in a broad array of characters surrounding Apollon Apollonovich. His estranged wife, Anna Petrovna, is marked by impulsiveness and a passionate musical gift. Sofia Petrovna Likhutina, a society lady and the object of Nikolai Apollonovich's affection, sympathizes with the revolutionary cause, loves exotic, Asiatic clothing and décor, and is not averse to bucking the traditional marital order, pursuing love interests outside her marriage. The double agent Lippanchenko is impossible to pin down. At one moment, a character describes him as a Greek (and his real surname is, allegedly, Mavrokordato), while at other times he is characterized as Ukrainian, sometimes implicitly Jewish, and even Mongol (see Henrietta Mondry's essay in this volume). Through his physical features and his licentious behavior, however, Lippanchenko represents a corrupted Dionysian type—physically fleshy, visually revolting, and morally bestial.

Nikolai Apollonovich is torn between the Apollinian and the Dionysian. This "son of Apollo" and of a Dionysian mother was conceived in lust, subservience, and horror (487). Like Apollo, he is "divinely" handsome, with flaxen hair and a "marble profile," but his face, while resembling an Apollinian "ancient mask," betrays a chaotic Dionysian inner life (61–62). A student of philosophy and rational thought, Nikolai is overcome with existential anomie. He flagrantly violates the rules of high-society civility, stalking a married woman. Much more disturbing, he appears to be willing to kill his father. His associate, the revolutionary Dudkin, compares Nikolai's anomie to Dionysus's own experience of being torn to pieces (347).

To give order to his troubled inner life, Nikolai disciplines his mind by studying philosophy. He sorts through the thought of the idealist philosopher Immanuel Kant and the positivist philosopher Auguste Comte, even becoming caught up in the wordplay between the two homophonic names (157–58; see Timothy Langen's essay in this volume). However, Nikolai secretly struggles with his Dionysian spirit. He indeed suffers from the sense of being torn apart. As Magnus Ljunggren points out, while Nikolai seeks to sacrifice himself to his father, he is also susceptible to patricidal impulses. In short, he possesses an Apollinian mind and a Dionysian soul that urges him to yield himself to a "cosmic crucifixion."[20] This duality is exacerbated by the fact that Nikolai Apollonovich, much like his father, is a comical, even slapstick, version of the Nietzschean ideas he embodies. Despite his handsome appearance, he has a poorly coordinated body and waddles like a duck (290). When he visits Sofia Petrovna, she notices that Nikolai's "god-like" face recalls a mask, and that his smile looks like the mouth of a frog (85).

A difficult puzzle in Nikolai Apollonovich's persona that gives him somewhat greater depth is his strange use of Christ's words, when he encounters Sergei Sergeich Likhutin, Sofia's husband. Afraid that Nikolai may be planning patricide, Sergei Sergeich irreverently manhandles him. In response to the officer's apology, Nikolai Apollonovich awkwardly paraphrases words spoken by Jesus on Golgotha (Luke 23:33–34), "You knew not what you did" (500). Somehow, the senator's son seems to be forgiving Sergei Sergeich for roughing him up, although it is he, Nikolai, who doubly caused the situation—by breaching his friend's marital relationship and by considering patricide. Following this incident, Nikolai anxiously searches for the bomb, to get rid of it so that no one is hurt. At this point, writes Robert Mann, Nikolai veers from the Dionysian path to a different resolution, at least in Bely's world view—namely, the path of Christ.[21] Indeed, Nikolai is not the "crucified Dionysus." That role will be left to Dudkin.

If we can agree that there is tragedy in Bely's parodic yet ominous adaptation of Nietzschean ideas, then it certainly resides in the story of the revolutionary Aleksandr Dudkin. Critics have paid particular attention to Dudkin, who is susceptible to Dionysian intoxication and whose party pseudonym recalls a panpipe that drives its listeners into an orgiastic frenzy.[22] Although Dudkin is little more than a shadow for much of the novel, he gains a form of selfhood when Nikolai Apollonovich makes him aware of the deception of his party handler, the double agent Lippanchenko (334–37). Dudkin's subsequent murder of the agent provocateur is an act of revolutionary justice that turns out to be the one true tragic deed in all of *Petersburg*. Ultimately, though, despite Dudkin's goal of destroying an evil person, this murder helps no one.

Dudkin embodies both Nietzsche's concept of the Dionysian and his late self-image of the "crucified Dionysus." He also enacts many themes specific to the Russian reception of Nietzsche's ideas, such as Ivanov's fusion of Dionysus with the figure of the suffering Christ; the pronounced Nietzscheanism of some Russian Marxists; and the vulgarized Nietzscheanism of the contemporary Russian reading public. As a Dionysian, Dudkin is a chronic drunk and a chain smoker. In keeping with Nietzsche's description of the Dionysian sensibility, Dudkin's world is oriented toward sound rather than sight. He himself is hardly visible (appearing to Senator Ableukhov only through the synecdoches of eyes and a moustache) and is rather more connected to audible cues, particularly the ominous moaning chorus with its droning "u-u-u" sounds coming from the city's workers' quarters (130). Having escaped from his exile in Siberia, Dudkin now survives unregistered in St. Petersburg's political underground. He is known as the "Shadow of the Elusive One" and spends his time radicalizing young people (119).

In conversation with Nikolai Apollonovich, Dudkin says explicitly that he thinks of himself as a Nietzschean (113). By this term he invokes not so much Nietzsche's conception of the Dionysian, but rather a vulgarized notion of the

German philosopher's famous projection of the ideal human being of the future—the Superman—whom Dudkin understands as a dictatorial leader manipulating the masses to enact grand, world-shattering, historical changes. Like many of Russia's Marxist Nietzscheans, Dudkin thinks of revolutionary work as world-creative activity, with human beings in their social ambience as his material.[23] Calling himself "an underground agent" in Nikolai Apollonovich's presence, Dudkin hurries to add: "Only don't you imagine that I operate in the name of social utopias [. . .]. For us Nietzscheans the masses, disposed to rebellion and aroused by their social instincts [. . .] turn into an operational mechanism [. . .] where people (even people like you) are the keyboard, on which the fingers of the pianist [. . .] fly freely" (113). What spares Dudkin the hackneyed image of a pop-Nietzschean tyrant is a possible wordplay that transforms a pianist (пианист) into its self-ironic pun, a drunken pianist (пьянист)—a fine point missing in *Petersburg*'s English translations.[24]

True to his confused Dionysian essence, Dudkin is mentally and psychologically chaotic and has major problems following a rational line of thought. He is in a perpetual delirium induced by alcohol, tobacco, and insomnia. His thought is lost in the "surging abundance" of sensory impressions with their "ambient absurdities" that make a "substantial mess" (344).

The crucial Russian modernist Nietzschean theme embodied in Dudkin is the proximity of Christian and Dionysian sensibilities. The Dionysian revolutionary Dudkin keeps a cherished icon of St. Serafim of Sarov in his room and wears a silver cross beneath his shirt (325). He calms his delirium by standing in a crucifixion pose, pressed against the wall (122), and he reads the Book of Revelation (331), which closes the Christian Bible with a prophesy of the Apocalypse to come.

In contrast to Viacheslav Ivanov's view of Dionysus as a prefiguration of the "suffering Christ," Bely clearly favors self-denying, or *kenotic*, Christian sacrifice. This image of Dudkin as ultimately self-sacrificing is fundamentally different from the vulgarized reductive reading of Nietzsche's thought, skewing its focus to the egotistic quest for power. By the end of the novel, Dudkin will choose Christian, self-effacing *kenosis* over the pseudo-Nietzschean explosion of human social and cultural mores by a powerful, tyrannical leader.

Zarathustra

One of *Petersburg*'s riddles linking the novel to Nietzschean undercurrents is presented by Dudkin's recurrent word play featuring the absurd pair *enfranshish/ shishnarfne*. This pair of nonsense words that muddle Dudkin's brain obliquely connects to Nietzsche's figure of the life-teacher Zarathustra. Although the historical Zarathustra is credited with first articulating the moral vision of the world comprised of both good and evil, Nietzsche's imagined Zarathustra guides the world *beyond* conventional morality with its notions of good and evil.

While Bely's narrator insists that *enfranshish* is a nonsense word and nothing more, we know that little in Bely's world happens by chance. To work toward an answer, we proceed in the way that Bely constructed his poetic world—through sound and theme associations. Dudkin's phantasmagoric encounter with the Persian Shishnarfne can help us understand the shadowy but still Apollinian incarnation of state power—the equestrian statue of Peter the Great, or the Bronze Horseman. *Enfranshish* is hidden in a string of color, sound, and mood descriptions of St. Petersburg as sickly "dark saffron" (*shafran*ovyi), as well as in the "yellow-saffron" (zhëlto-*shafran*ovyi) coloration of Lippanchenko's face and of a political gathering (117, 123, 130, 510). On the other hand, the word evokes nightmarish associations with tobacco smoke and with Lippanchenko, who smokes Cuban cigars: it has been suggested that Dudkin's word *enfranshish* may have its origin in the prerevolutionary labeling of imported goods, "en franchise" (duty paid), on Lippanchenko's cigar box.[25]

This is an intriguing, but only partial solution. Like Lippanchenko, Dudkin also regularly uses an imported product—the "Persian powder" with which he kills bedbugs in his tenement flat (325). Furthermore, it is clear that *enfranshish* has magical power over Dudkin, invoking a superhuman force that acquires human form as the Young Persia activist, Shishnarfne (*enfranshish* spelled backwards), who also goes by the Russianized version of his Persian last name, Shishnarfiev (363). Keeping in Dionysian aural character, this figure arises as a sound in Dudkin's throat. The metal that will subsequently give a somewhat Apollinian (though dark, demonic) form to Dudkin's mental mirage of the Bronze Horseman can first be heard in Shishnarfne's metallic voice (394) and then as clanging of a horse's hooves in the street (185, 405).[26]

However we resolve the source and meaning of *enfranshish/shishnarfne*, this nonsense word is indirectly connected to Zarathustra, that central symbolic figure of late-Nietzschean thought. In Bely's day, the Russian spelling and pronunciation of the name of Nietzsche's thinker was "Zaratushtra." In the sound orchestration "shishnarfne" and "Zaratushtra" share a number of phonemes—/sh/, /a/, and /r/. Both Shishnarfne and Zarathustra are Persian. And true to Nietzsche's Zarathustra, Shishnarfne spurs Dudkin "beyond good and evil"—the concepts that the historical Zarathustra first invented—to commit murder. Crucial to Dudkin's decision to kill Lippanchenko is his intellectual shift from revolution as an aesthetic act—recall his self-description as a political pianist—to revolution as a moral act, a shift manifest in Dudkin's attempt to take the law into his own hands and punish a corrupt human being, even if this act of murder is doctrinally evil. For an instant, then, the Apollinian sense of clarity and determination to act combine, in Dudkin, with chaotic Dionysian life force, bringing him to the decision to get rid of a double agent who has been muddying both state order and revolutionary uprising.

Conclusion

This discussion has shown Bely's complex attitude toward Nietzsche, whom the writer revered as his life mentor, while also seeking his own voice and outlook through parody of Nietzsche's thought and its Russian iterations. In much of his early writing, Bely took Nietzsche's philosophy as a form of prophecy and strove to find its embodiment in Russian life. Through parody—understood as both stylization of and debate with the work of a literary-philosophical forebear—Bely arrived at his own outlook. Ultimately, Bely seeks but does not find an idea of the Apollinian as a force of order or a figure of the Dionysian enacting the Greek god's regenerative force. What he does regain, however, is a moral view of the world. With this observation in mind, I conclude with a brief discussion of three questions pertaining to Nietzsche and *Petersburg*. If, as many essays in the present volume show, Bely's novel often offers a complex parody of its artistic and philosophical subtexts, what is the result of that parody? What is the author's new vision? And does Bely sacrifice ethical values to aesthetic interests?

On the question of balancing ethics and aesthetics, Carol Anschuetz argues that *Petersburg* can be viewed as a radical departure from the nineteenth-century psychological novel, particularly Dostoevsky's, because "for the ethical solution offered by Dostoevsky it substitutes the aesthetic solution proposed by Nietzsche." Anschuetz further writes that, in Bely's novel, "evil is just as necessary a condition for good as destruction is for creation." Despite Christian imagery, in Anschuetz's view, Bely is no Christian writer: "In his hands the eschatological vision of Christianity—not, however, its ethic—produces what might be called the eternal return of the poetic rather than the divine word."[27] Most critics disagree with this diagnosis. Leonid Dolgopolov sees in *Petersburg* a modernist realization of art as theurgy, wherein an aesthetic philosophy transforms into ethics.[28] In my own opinion, the loss of the Dionysian force in the novel's epilogue suggests the failure of regeneration and the return to an ethical life, not in a Socratic rationalizing register but rather in Tolstoyan self-abnegating ways.[29] Mann sees *Petersburg*'s elusive White Domino as a hint at the superiority of Christian ethics over a pagan Dionysian outlook.[30] Most recently, it has been argued that Bely contributed to the Christianization of the Russian Nietzsche.[31]

Petersburg is a parody of Nietzsche's visions of destruction and renewal because the time bomb fails and because the plot falls apart and ends with an epilogue written in the register of quiet resignation. The characters themselves are puppets with relatively impoverished psychological lives who undermine the philosophical concepts they appear to embody.[32] The Apollinian is an empty shell of social and political order, except that in the end the father does the right thing by his son: Apollon Apollonovich refuses to sign an order to suppress rebellion and later decides against turning Nikolai over to the police. The son does the right thing as well, by ultimately refusing to murder his father. In any case, even before the failed assassination attempt, the senator resigns his powerful post. Dudkin, that offspring of Apollon Apollonovich's brain, is the truly tragic character in the novel. He understands that the Dionysian force by itself can only lead to ruin—it offers no principle of renewal. The new, in Bely's vision, might be said to be the reanimation of a moral consciousness that, ironically, motivates Dudkin to kill Lippanchenko—the Dionysian agent of a corrupt Apollinian political order. Consistent with its own inconclusiveness, *Petersburg*'s creative play with Nietzsche's concept of tragedy leaves us debating this knot of aesthetic and ethical questions.

Notes

1. Friedrich Nietzsche, *On the Genealogy of Morals*, tr. W. Kaufman (New York: Vintage, 1969), 34. See also Edith W. Clowes, *The Revolution of Moral Consciousness: Nietzsche in Russian Literature, 1890–1914* (DeKalb: Northern Illinois University Press, 1988), 25.

2. See Nikolai Berdiaev, "Creativity and Morality" (1916), *The Meaning of the Creative Act*, tr. D. Lowrie (New York: Harper, 1955).

3. Bernice G. Rosenthal, *New Myth, New World: From Nietzsche to Stalinism* (University Park: Penn State University Press, 2002), 19.

4. Cited in V. Bystrov, "Ideia obnovleniia mira u russkikh simvolistov," *Russkaia literatura* 3 (2003), 6. See also Clowes, *The Revolution of Moral Consciousness*, 153–54.

5. Rosenthal, *New Myth, New World*, 6–9.

6. Friedrich Nietzsche, *The Birth of Tragedy and the Case of Wagner*, tr. W. Kaufmann (New York: Vintage, 1967), 36.

7. Mary Ann Frese Witt, introduction to *Nietzsche and the Rebirth of the Tragic*, ed. M. A. Frese Witt (Madison: Fairleigh Dickinson, 2007), 23.

8. Edith W. Clowes, "Groundlessness: Nietzsche and Russian Concepts of Tragic Philosophy," in Frese Witt, *Nietzsche and the Rebirth of the Tragic*, 136.

9. Andrei Belyi, "Fridrikh Nitsshe," in *Arabeski* (Munich: Wilhelm Fink, 1969), 90.

10. Friedrich Nietzsche, *Werke*, ed. K. Schlechta (Frankfurt: Ullstein, 1984), 4:1330, 1350.
11. Clowes, *The Revolution of Moral Consciousness*, 156.
12. Andrei Belyi, "Simvolizm kak miroponimanie" ("Symbolism as a Worldview"), cited in Konstantin Mochulsky, *Andrei Bely: His Life and Works*, tr. N. Szalavitz (Ann Arbor: Ardis, 1977), 59.
13. Clowes, *The Revolution of Moral Consciousness*, 154.
14. Magnus Ljunggren, *The Dream of Rebirth: A Study of Andrej Belyj's Novel "Petersburg"* (Stockholm: Almquist and Wiksell, 1982), 55.
15. Vladimir Alexandrov, *Andrei Bely: The Major Symbolist Fiction* (Cambridge, MA: Harvard University Press, 1985), 36.
16. Alexandrov, *Andrei Bely*, 106, 116, 124.
17. Virginia Bennett, "Echoes of Friedrich Nietzsche's *The Birth of Tragedy* in Andrej Belyj's *Petersburg*," *Germano-Slavica* 3.4 (1980), 244–45.
18. Andrei Bely, *Petersburg*, tr. John Elsworth (London: Pushkin Press, 2009).
19. Bennett, "Echoes of Friedrich Nietzsche's *The Birth of Tragedy*," 246–48.
20. Ljunggren, *The Dream of Rebirth*, 37, 90.
21. Robert Mann, "Apollo and Dionysus in Andrei Belyi's *Petersburg*," *The Russian Review* 57 (1998), 522.
22. Bennett, "Echoes of Friedrich Nietzsche's *The Birth of Tragedy*," 252; Mann, "Apollo and Dionysus in Andrei Belyi's *Petersburg*," 517.
23. Clowes, *The Revolution of Moral Consciousness*, 200–23.
24. Andrei Belyi, *Peterburg*, ed. L. Dolgopolov (Moscow: Nauka, 1981), 85. See also Robert Mann, "Apollo and Dionysus in Andrei Belyi's *Petersburg*," 518.
25. See Robert Maguire and John Malmstad's annotations, in Andrei Belyi, *Petersburg*, tr. Robert Maguire and John Malmstad (Bloomington: Indiana University Press, 1978), 346–47.
26. On the Apollinian aspect of the Bronze Horseman, see Mann, "Apollo and Dionysus in Andrei Belyi's *Petersburg*," 522.
27. Carol Anschuetz, "Bely's *Petersburg* and the End of the Russian Novel," *The Russian Novel from Pushkin to Pasternak*, ed. J. Garrard (New Haven: Yale University Press, 1983), 126, 148, 151.
28. Leonid Dolgopolov, "Tvorcheskaia istoriia i istoriko-literaturnoe znachenie romana A. Belogo 'Peterburg,'" in Belyi, *Peterburg*, 538.
29. Clowes, *The Revolution of Moral Consciousness*, 171–72.
30. Mann, "Apollo and Dionysus in Andrei Belyi's *Petersburg*," 525.
31. N. Bonetskaia, "Russkii Nitsshe," *Voprosy filosofii* 7 (2013), 134.
32. Volker Klotz, *Die erzählte Stadt* (Munich: Hanser, 1969), 260.

Neo-Kantianism in *Petersburg*

TIMOTHY LANGEN

In chapter 3 of *Petersburg*, Nikolai Apollonovich Ableukhov sits down to an exquisitely awkward supper with his father, Apollon Apollonovich. Increasingly desperate for a conversation topic, he finally blurts out that he has been reading Hermann Cohen's philosophical treatise *Kant's Theory of Experience* (1881). Cohen, Nikolai explains, is "a most important representative of European Kantianism." This remark initiates the following exchange between father and son:

> "Did you say—Comteianism?"
> "Kantianism, papa . . ."
> "Kan-ti-an-ism?"
> "Yes, exactly . . ."
> "But surely Kant was refuted by Comte? It's Comte you're talking about?"
> "No, not Comte, papa, I'm talking about Kant! . . ."
> "But Kant isn't scientific . . ."
> "It's Comte who isn't scientific . . ."
> "I don't know, I don't know, old chap: in our days people didn't think like that . . ." (158)[1]

This exchange can hardly be called a philosophical discussion; it is more like a vaudeville act based on the phonetic similarity of the surnames of the philosophers Immanuel Kant and Auguste Comte. Such superficiality is indeed the point: father and son are in a sense strangers, capable of pretending to converse but not of saying anything significant to each other. Yet their creator's wide-ranging intellectual interests are often reflected in scenes just like this one—that is to say, in shards of conversation or description that seem to lead nowhere in particular. It is Andrei Bely's own interest in Neo-Kantian philosophy that the name of Hermann Cohen evokes most directly, and this essay will attempt to explain some of the context and significance of that interest.

Kantianism

Neo-Kantianism, or *Novokantianstvo*, as early readers of *Petersburg* would have found it in the Brockhaus-Efron encyclopedia (along with the moniker for the trend's representatives, *novokantiantsy*), is described there as a "highly vague term" denoting a number of German thinkers—Friedrich Albert Lange, Hermann von Helmholtz, and Otto Liebmann, among others—indebted to Kant's philosophical work.[2] Liebmann, in his *Kant and the Epigones* (1865), repeatedly exhorted his readers to go "back to Kant" as a corrective for what he saw as the shortcomings of nineteenth-century philosophy. Yet the so-called Neo-Kantians made it clear that theirs was not strictly a restorative or rearguard action intended only to undo mistakes. They wanted to build on Kant, using his principles in order to open new space for philosophy. Thus Wilhelm Windelband wrote, in 1884, that "to understand Kant meant to go beyond him."[3]

Going back to Kant—if only to move beyond him—meant, among other things, returning to epistemology; that is, to the key philosophical questions about knowledge. A major branch of philosophical inquiry, epistemology investigates such issues as what we can and cannot know; how we know things; and what it means to know something. Among Immanuel Kant's seventeenth- and eighteenth-century predecessors, the so-called rationalists—exemplified by René Descartes and G. W. Leibniz—sought the foundation of knowledge in the structure and activities of reason itself. By contrast, the so-called empiricists, above all David Hume, saw knowledge about the world as deriving from an observation of it. The distinction here is between a priori and a posteriori knowledge. The former encompasses propositions justified independently of experience, as in mathematics; the latter consists of propositions justified through experience, as in biology.

However, one particularly compelling group of propositions—metaphysical ones, concerning, for example, the existence and nature of causality, freedom, and substances that persist through changing properties—seemed to fall through the cracks. Hume, for example, argued that neither reason nor experience could justify our causal beliefs. In other words, neither type of argument can justify the thought that any particular A is the cause of some other particular B. Our reasoning cannot justify our belief in a necessary causal connection between the two since there is nothing contrary to reason in imagining that A happens and yet B does not. And while we may observe the occurrence of A and the occurrence of B, we do not observe any "causing" relation between the two. So our experience does not reveal any necessary connection of causation either. Our belief in causation is, then, left without justification by reason or experience.

Kant's solution to this dilemma began with another distinction: propositions are either analytic—that is, true by definition (e.g., "cats are animals")—or synthetic (e.g., "cats are agile," where agility is not part of the concept of cats). Analytic propositions tell us nothing about the world. The truth of "cats are animals" does not depend on how the world is; it is true even if there are no cats, or no animals for that matter. By contrast, synthetic truths do tell us something about the world—about cats, in our example. Kant thus refined the important epistemological question: Is everything we know about the world justified by experience? Are all synthetic propositions a posteriori? Or are there some propositions about the world—that is, synthetic propositions—that we can know a priori? If so, metaphysical propositions would be among them.

Kant argues that knowledge of synthetic a priori propositions *is* possible, but only to the extent that those propositions are necessary for the possibility of the coherent experience of the world. For example, we cannot justify a proposition about causality by saying that we have observed it; but we can argue that the positing of causality is necessary if we are to experience the world in any meaningful way. However, this argument—known as Kant's transcendental deduction, where "transcendental" means that the argument concerns necessary conditions of our knowledge or experience—depends on the fact of our coherent experience; and no such argument can amount to or result in knowledge of things entirely *outside of* our experience. The "thing in itself" (*ding an sich*) remains unknowable. In another key, we can speak of the distinction between phenomena, or things as they relate to our experience, and nuomena, or things or aspects of things unrelated to our experience. In this sense, Kant did not so much resolve epistemological and metaphysical questions as sharpen them in ways that spurred subsequent philosophers to overcome the limitations he had posited.

Post-Kantian Philosophy

The overcoming of Kantian thought began with J. G. Fichte, F. W. J. Schelling, G. W. F. Hegel, and other early nineteenth-century philosophers commonly grouped under the heading of German Idealism. Generally speaking, these thinkers tried to use the instruments of philosophy, including some of Kant's own concepts, to establish higher-order claims about nature, the universe, spirit, and other matters understood as metaphysical. This strain of philosophy gripped a generation of Russian thinkers in the middle of the nineteenth century, and even beyond those years it set a sort of cultural tone for what philosophy was understood to be and do. In Russia, this was also where literature came closest to philosophy, with prolonged discussions of the deepest and most seemingly abstract questions.

Other philosophers, impressed by the achievements of science (as Kant had been back in his day), countered with a strongly anti-metaphysical stance. If we want to understand how we know things, they argued, we should look not to the Kantian transcendental deduction but rather to science itself, with its back-and-forth between observation and theory. This philosophical outlook, shaping up in the mid-nineteenth century, arranged sciences hierarchically. For example, it saw biology as dependent on chemistry, which itself depended on physics. The final science was sociology, with humanity itself imagined as proceeding through stages: theological, metaphysical, and positive. This philosophical outlook was known as positivism, and readers of Bely's *Petersburg* find it invoked in the mention of the French thinker August Comte during the father-son dinnertime debate cited above. Last but not least, there existed varieties of philosophical materialism, which diverged from positivism on epistemological and metaphysical points but overlapped chronologically, and shared a tendency to valorize science. Among prominent materialists one can cite Ludwig Feuerbach and especially Karl Marx, both of whom had been significantly influenced by Hegel. However, other versions of materialism were also important—above all a scientific variety represented by Ludwig Büchner.

Neo-Kantianism

It is against this intellectual backdrop that the German philosophical movement known as Neo-Kantianism arose in the 1860s and 1870s. The new current's initial argument was in favor of a return to Immanuel Kant's transcendental idealism as a way to address epistemological concerns that both idealism and materialism had neglected, and also as a way to bridge the gap between them.

In due time, the movement split into two main branches, one associated with the University of Marburg, and the other with the University of Heidelberg (some of those invoking the second current preferred to identify it with Freiburg, Baden, or, even more generally, southwestern Germany). Hermann Cohen, Paul Natorp, and, a generation later, Ernst Cassirer were the principal representatives of the Marburg school of Neo-Kantianism. Cohen's *Kant's Theory of Experience*, which Nikolai Apollonovich mentions to his father, argues that, for Kant, synthetic a priori structures are not subjective features of individual minds, but rather necessary and, in that sense, objective. Moreover, Cohen ultimately links those structures not to psychology but rather to natural science itself. The Marburg school was thus associated, above all, with the epistemology of science, though the school's exponents wrote extensively in other fields, such as politics (often from a socialist though not Marxist perspective), law, religious ethics, philosophy of history, and, in Cassirer's case, the study of culture as a whole.

Indeed, out of the entire Neo-Kantian intellectual heritage, Cassirer's thought was perhaps most intrinsically congenial to Bely's own thinking, given its ambitious synthesis of mathematics, science, and culture. Both Bely and Cassirer were supremely interested in the phenomenon of symbolization—that is, in bringing things, sensations, or ideas to the common denominator of a sign that can then be manipulated directly. In Cassirer's view, articulated in 1910, the development of science followed the evolution through history of the ordering systems that governed these signs—the synthetic a priori realm of mathematics being the paradigm case. In his three-volume *Philosophy of Symbolic Forms*, Cassirer extended these insights into a full-blown theory of culture. However, this magnum opus was published between 1923 and 1929, too late for Bely to have read it while writing and even rewriting *Petersburg*.

The southwestern school of Neo-Kantianism, led by Wilhelm Windelband and Heinrich Rickert, shared with the Marburg philosophers a thorough grounding in Kant's work and an effort to re-philosophize and to some extent reconcile idealistic and materialistic tendencies in thought. However, they did not see the natural sciences as foundational in the same way the Marburg philosophers did; instead, for them, natural and human sciences were distinct, neither reducible to the other, and of equal significance. For Windelband, natural sciences were "nomothetic," in that they moved toward the general (thus deriving physical laws from observed phenomena). The humanities, by contrast, were seen as "idiographic," in that they strove toward specification of what was unique about an observed phenomenon. For Rickert, the human sciences ultimately grounded the rest of knowledge, because values formed the bedrock not only of ethics but of epistemology as well: every act of knowing was necessarily an act of judging (measuring, say, against a physical yardstick or against an ethical or aesthetic norm). These acts could be conceived, at bottom, as saying "yes" or "no" to a given proposition, and as belonging, finally, to the realm of the "ought" (*Sollen*), the transcendental value of truth. It was this argument in particular that captivated the young Andrei Bely.

Neo-Kantianism in Russia[4]

The European, and above all German, revival of interest in Immanuel Kant's thought came to Russia at a time when philosophy as a whole was reconstituting itself—and, to some extent, positing itself for the first time—as an autonomous academic discipline. In 1850, reacting to revolutionary events abroad, the tsarist state abolished chairs in philosophy in all Russian universities, except for the one at Dorpat (Tartu). It took more than a decade to bring back philosophy as an academic discipline in Russia. Unsurprisingly, during and even after this period philosophical ideas received their most arresting expression not in academic or other formal philosophical treatises, but in literary, journalistic, epistolary, and conversational discursive forms related only obliquely to philosophy as a university discipline. It was a distinct feature of Russian thought that the new spirit of academic professionalism was not the default mode of philosophizing: such professionalism was only one among several ways to attack the deepest philosophical problems, and it often lacked the imaginative or rhetorical boldness of those other discursive forms.

Part of the task of Russian academic philosophy in the late nineteenth century, then, was to establish how it could contribute to an already vigorous debate about the fundamental nature of knowledge, virtue, beauty, and the like. One important part of this task was to determine the distinctive rules or procedures by which such contributions could be made. One possible role for academic philosophy was perhaps to provide a common language and set of rules according to which disparate—and often dramatically stated—points of view might interact. In fact, Bely's father, a professor of mathematics at the University of Moscow, had proposed that his own discipline could play a similar role, providing a common ground and rules of engagement for other academic fields.[5]

Vladimir Solovyov's entry on Kant in the Brockhaus-Efron encyclopedia seems to express a similar view of the foundational philosopher's work as refining problems and preparing a sort of conceptual space for further inquiry and debate. "Kant's significance," wrote the Russian religious philosopher who greatly affected Bely's intellectual trajectory, "is exaggerated only by those who see in his work not the reformulation and more thorough grounding of the central questions of philosophy, but their best and all but definitive solution."[6] For Solovyov, then, the significance of Kant's influence was not in establishing a particular view or set of propositions, but rather in enabling or clarifying philosophical discourse as such. Similarly, as Nina Dmitrieva has recently put it, "among Russian Neo-Kantians, the question of the autonomy of reason found expression in the problem of the autonomy of philosophy, that is, in the recognition of the need to cleanse philosophical content of worldview-ideological and above all religious components."[7] This "cleansing" could be good or bad, depending on one's point of view. For Bely's contemporary Nikolai Berdiaev, "there were no creative Neo-Kantian traditions in Russian philosophy," and "true Russian philosophy followed a different path."[8] Be that as it may, Neo-Kantian thinking was certainly important in early twentieth-century Russian intellectual and cultural life. One major outlet was the Neo-Kantian journal *Logos* (1910–14), coedited by Russians (Fëdor Stepun, Nikolai Bubnov, Sergei Gessen) and Germans (Richard Kroner, Georg Mehlis).[9] In addition, several Russians, including the budding modernist poet Boris Pasternak, traveled to Marburg in order to study with Cohen and Natorp. More generally, many of the age's most important Russian philosophical and social thinkers—among them Pëtr Struve, Semën Frank, Pavel Novgorodtsev, and Sergei Bulgakov—as well as the generation that emerged a decade later—above all, the circle of Mikhail Bakhtin—engaged deeply the questions raised by Neo-Kantianism, even if some of them eventually moved on to entirely different philosophical outlooks.

In the context of early twentieth-century Russian intellectual life, then, Neo-Kantian philosophy meant at least two different things. For those who viewed it positively, it represented a reinvigoration of genuinely philosophical thought that never took anything for granted, never excluded any area of inquiry, and always proceeded with the greatest possible rigor. Thus, while studying with Cohen and Natorp at Marburg, Boris Pasternak was struck by the originality of their thinking, their immunity to fashionable "isms," and their thorough grounding in history.[10] But from another perspective, Neo-Kantianism seemed to represent the pedantry of Western philosophy, with its spiritless ethos of abstraction. A year prior to Berdiaev's negative assessment, his intellectual antagonist, the Marxist theorist Georgii Plekhanov, had written something remarkably similar about thinkers in the Kantian tradition: "With them, thinking is always divorced from being."[11]

Bely and Neo-Kantianism

For Andrei Bely, thinking was rarely, if ever, divorced from being. With his artistic mother and intellectual father apparently so different from and even alien to one another, Bely was attracted, from a young age, to theories of reconciliation. Such, for example, was the Nietzschean vision of tragedy as a medium for the interaction of chaotic Dionysian and ordering Apollinian energies (see Edith Clowes's essay in this volume). Such was also the philosophy of Vladimir Solovyov, which informed in many ways a number of intellectual currents in early Russian modernist culture. While at the University of Moscow, Bely studied natural sciences but sustained his literary activities and his interest in music. On 28 May 1903, he received his degree in natural sciences; the next day, his father, the mathematician Nikolai Bugaev, died. Under these circumstances, it is easy to understand how Bely would have been drawn to philosophical approaches that focused on science alongside with ethics, aesthetics, and the whole of human culture. He began to study Kant's thought deeply that same summer of 1903. Then, in the fall of 1904, he turned to the study of Neo-Kantianism. By October 1907, Cohen's and Rickert's writings were at the center of Bely's philosophical attention.[12]

The peak of Bely's enthusiasm for Neo-Kantian thought can be seen in his essays from the late 1900s—especially "The Problem of Culture," "On Scientific Dogmatism," "Criticism and Symbolism," and "The Emblematics of Meaning." He ultimately collected these writings in his critical anthology *Symbolism* (1910), whose overarching argument cast Kant's thought and Neo-Kantianism among the possible foundations for modernist theory. "If at the present moment it is possible to speak of the liberation of the spirit from age-old nightmares," Bely wrote at the beginning of "Criticism and Symbolism," "then we owe this, of course, to Kant."[13] Here, and to some extent in the other essays, we seem to be indebted to Kant for something like criticism itself. Science, Bely pointed out, was inherently inductive; it could generate principles that were valid only for the phenomena it observed. As these phenomena became more numerous and intricate, science grew increasingly subdivided. Each individual science established its own principles of validity, but none was equipped to address the form of validity as such. Psychology was limited for related reasons: it was unable to provide the universal principles that governed the phenomena it studied. Philosophy, by contrast, no longer tried to cover all the content of the individual fields of knowledge; instead it attempted to understand the *forms* of their principles.

Bely's most fully elaborated argument on this subject comes in his essay "The Emblematics of Meaning." While Bely is not entirely consistent in his terminology or mode of argumentation, his overarching point can be summarized as follows: humans come to know and understand content—of any sort—by giving it a form. Philosophical criticism examines such forms by interrogating the principles undergirding our knowledge (or apparent knowledge). These principles are independent of any content that we may observe and indeed condition our very ability to observe at all. In Bely's reading, Rickert demonstrates that these principles are governed by *value*, in the sense of a force that guides the subject's judgments. For Bely, this is where thorough philosophical investigation finally reveals that every act of cognition *necessarily* involves a contribution from the knowing subject, a judgment of "yes," an ethical valuation of knowledge as such. Creation—that is, the creation of forms and values—is in this sense prior to cognition; it is the precondition for knowing, just as the Kantian categories and a priori forms of sensible intuition are the epistemological preconditions of Kant's philosophy. It is precisely the idea of the Symbol, Bely argues, that discloses the underlying form of human creative *and* cognitive activity.[14]

In 1923, Bely lamented, with reference to his earlier self, the "disastrous consequences of an over-estimation of Neo-Kantian literature; the philosophy of Cohen, Natorp, Lask has an effect on one's feelings of the world, and produces in one a split into *hardness* and *sensuality*."[15] As John Elsworth points out, this is the split within Nikolai Apollonovich.[16] It is also represented in the split between Apollon Apollonovich and his wife, Anna Petrovna. For the Bely of 1923, Neo-Kantian thinking is a *cause* of such splits. But his view some dozen years earlier, when he was writing *Petersburg*, was more complex and shifting. He was losing his enthusiasm for Neo-Kantianism, yet he was still capable of seeing in it a vocabulary for *naming* and perhaps even *overcoming* (not just creating) the split between thinking and being or between hardness and sensuality. It is this shifting view that makes *Petersburg*'s Neo-Kantian theme highly ambiguous.[17]

Nikolai Apollonovich

One of the tools novelists can use in treating ideas is to depict characters who hold those ideas. In *Petersburg*, the bureaucrats and intellectuals who oppose Senator Ableukhov may include members of the generation of social thinkers influenced by Neo-Kantian thought. What they have in common is a commitment to forms and procedures analogous to, and in some ways founded on, the way Neo-Kantian philosophers treat questions of knowledge and value.[18] However, we learn very little about them beyond the fact that, at least within the setting of the novel, they seem unable to act very effectively. The novel's main Kantian or Neo-Kantian, then, is Nikolai Apollonovich himself, and Bely later wrote that "being a Neo-Kantian revolutionary was the tragedy of the senator's son in *Petersburg*."[19] If the youthful Andrei Bely of "Criticism and Symbolism" thought Kant could liberate the spirit, Nikolai Apollonovich Ableukhov seems to represent much the same view in *Petersburg*. The walls in his study "were lined with oak shelves, tightly packed with books, in front of which a silk curtain slipped easily on bronze rings; an attentive hand could either conceal the contents of the shelves entirely from gaze, or, alternatively, could reveal rows of black leather-bound spines, studded with inscriptions saying '*Kant*.' The study furniture was upholstered in dark green; and a bust was resplendent there . . . also of Kant, of course" (56). The Russian for "of course," in the cited passage, is *razumeetsia*—a play on *razum*, or reason, which is the primary object of Kant's critique.[20] And here is where Nikolai Apollonovich does his philosophizing: "In his room, Nikolai Apollonovich truly grew into an autonomous, self-existent centre—into a series of logical premises flowing out from that centre, which determined thought, the soul and this table right here: here he comprised the sole centre of the universe, both conceivable and inconceivable, flowing cyclically through all the aeons of time" (58). Whatever else one might make of Nikolai Apollonovich's philosophical meditations, it seems clear that they thrive in a sort of charmed space where ordinary physical reality can fade away:

> When he was deeply immersed in thought, Nikolai Apollonovich used to lock the door of his study: then it began to seem to him that both he and the study, and the objects in that study, were instantly transforming from objects of the real world into mental symbols of purely logical constructions; the space of the study merged with his desensitized body into a general chaos of being, which he called the *universe*; and Nikolai Apollonovich's consciousness, separating from his body, was directly linked to the electric lamp on the writing desk, which was called "the sun of consciousness." Behind locked doors and thinking through his system, which was being raised step by step to unity, he felt that his body was split out into the "universe," that is to say, the study; the head of this body was then transposed into the rotund glass head of the electric lamp under its flirtatious shade.
> And thus transposed, Nikolai Apollonovich became a truly creative being.
> That was why he liked locking himself in: a voice, a rustle, or the footstep of another person, transforming the *universe* into a study, and the *consciousness* into a lamp, shattered the fastidious structure of Nikolai Apollonovich's thought. (59)

This is a parodic rendering of philosophy as such, or at least Nikolai Apollonovich's version of it, which seems mainly to be an advanced apparatus for fancy daydreaming. Or, alternatively, it is philosophy diverted from its normative reason-governed route toward frankly mystical experience—perhaps in this case potentially serious, but far from Kantian or Neo-Kantian. For surely what Nikolai Apollonovich is doing—and enjoys doing—in his philosophical exertions is leaving the phenomenal world behind and getting a glimpse of the noumenal world in its place—the world of the thing-in-itself, which Kant says cannot be experienced or known directly. Judith Wermuth-Atkinson interprets this section as a "dialogue" between Neo-Kantian thought and Karl Jung's analytic psychology. As a Neo-Kantian, Nikolai Apollonovich rejects or wants to reject the notions of paradise and temptation central to Jungian theory.[21] We might also observe that, for Nikolai Apollonovich, Kantian and Neo-Kantian thought, in suspending (indefinitely) description of any "thing-in-itself," is in fact a kind of psychological torture mechanism designed to tempt the thinker into nonphilosophical "cheating," biting at the apple-in-itself and thereby casting oneself out of philosophy's Garden of Eden.

Cognition and Creation

Prone to confusion and not particularly verbally gifted, Nikolai Apollonovich would hardly be an exemplary representative for any philosophical school. If he were, he might have responded to his father's dinnertime remark about Comte along these lines: "The predominance of Comte contributed to the decline in Russia not only of philosophical thought, but of interest in philosophy as such [. . .] by reason of Comte's denial of self-observation, his lack of anything resembling a fully developed theory of knowledge, the resulting dogmatism with regard to the historically established principles of the exact sciences, and his reduction of all philosophy to the mere systematization of their conclusions."[22] These words belong to Aleksandr Vvedenskii, the pre-eminent Russian Neo-Kantian philosopher, for whom Comte represented the temptation not to reflect, not to question one's assumptions, and not to take epistemological problems seriously. Symptomatically, Vvedenskii, in one scholar's opinion, "shared certain characteristics with the Kant of modernist writers and thinkers like Andrei Bely [and] his popular lectures might have had some input into shaping the modernist Kant."[23]

It may seem odd that the ultra-conservative Senator Ableukhov takes the side of Comte in the brief philosophical exchange with his son. Apollon Apollonovich is not a philosopher, and he would no doubt disagree vehemently with many of the often progressive views of Russian positivist thinkers who followed Comte. But the senator's is not a retrospective vision, yearning to return to an idealized, pre-Petrine Russia of some two hundred years earlier. It is, on the contrary, a bureaucratic and to some extent technological dream, and the city of St. Petersburg itself is one of Apollon Apollonovich's ongoing preoccupations. The subjugation of the unruly population of St. Petersburg's islands (25) and the importation of American reaping machines (15) represent a vision of how a nation grows—a statist progressivism in which the government is the agent of positive change and must impose it upon an often resistant population. In Apollon Apollonovich's stream of consciousness, this project often seems to arise from a fear of the dark, unregulated outside space; but it is, in its own way, a utopian and willful vision echoing and pushing ever further Peter the Great's reforms—a vision hostile to epistemic doubt and underlying the creation of the city of St. Petersburg itself.

By contrast, one important feature of *Petersburg* the novel is its continuous preoccupation with the nature and limits of perception and knowledge. Here one might describe the relation of *Petersburg* to Neo-Kantianism in terms of an overlap, since epistemology is the conceptual neighborhood serving as "home turf" both for Bely's novel and for Neo-Kantian philosophy. In this neighborhood we might find the novel's many obsessive self-qualifying statements. The following passage is a representative sample: "In the greenish light of the Petersburg morning, in a protective 'or so it seems,' a quite ordinary phenomenon was also circulating before senator Ableukhov: an atmospheric phenomenon—a stream of people; people here became dumb; the streams of them, scurrying like waves breaking on the shore, thundered and roared; the ordinary ear did not register at all that this surge of people was a surge of thunder" (30). Despite Apollon Apollonovich's positivistic inclinations, he lives in a novel shot through with "or so it seems," a phrase and a sensation making one question every bit of knowledge. Thus, the reader of *Petersburg* hears much about modes and sources of knowledge—among them newspapers, prophecy, informers, memory, direct experience, hallucinations, novelistic foreshadowing—all of which can prove deceptive.

The potential deceptiveness of any apparently "known" thing is not in itself philosophically decisive in any direct sense: positivists can acknowledge the possibility of error and deception as readily as Neo-Kantians or any other philosophers. But if one keeps in mind the insistent return to epistemological questions that during Bely's time would have been associated, above all, with the Neo-Kantians, *Petersburg*'s doubt-encouraging passages take on added significance. The practical problems of verifying news sources and ensuring accurate reporting serve as reminders of larger problems of what one can know, and specifically of the fact that procedures of knowing are necessarily *constructed*—whether they are mechanical, social, or mental procedures. "The object of knowledge is thus for transcendental idealism not given, either immanently or transcendentally, but set [as a task to be performed]," Rickert insisted.[24] Bely, for his part, would say these procedures of knowing are created before any act of cognition. And this is an idea Bely associated directly with Neo-Kantianism.

It is, however, not necessarily a Neo-Kantian position in a strict sense. As Valentin Asmus has observed, in one of the first sustained discussions of Neo-Kantianism in *Petersburg*, Bely takes much further Rickert's insistence on the inherently transformational activity of the epistemological subject—in other words, of a person questioning the processes of human cognition and the knowledge about the world obtained through these cognitive processes.[25] For Rickert, the main point is that the subject necessarily contributes something, and that the subject's contribution is related to the human faculty of judgment and therefore to ethics. For Bely, the same observation moves the whole discussion in the direction of myth and mysticism. Asmus's line of criticism is especially relevant to Bely's essay collection *Symbolism*. Insofar as the modernist writer wants to represent his conclusions as a logical consequence of contemporary philosophy, Bely's idiosyncratic use of Neo-Kantian concepts compromises his own argument.

These problems are less acute in *Petersburg*, though, where Bely is not expounding a philosophical theory. Instead, he is simultaneously looking at and through this theory (along with several others). It is not only in the character of Nikolai Apollonovich that this principle operates. Rickert himself, the most important of Bely's Neo-Kantian references, is objectified in the "Day of Judgment" section of *Petersburg*'s chapter 5, when Nikolai Apollonovich presents, in a dream, his own philosophical exercise books to a Turanian guest: "Paragraph one: Kant (proof that Kant, too, was a Turanian). Paragraph two: the value, understood as nobody and nothing" (318). "Value," a crucial concept that Bely borrows from Rickert, appears to lose its value here. As Leonid Dolgopolov, the editor of the first academic edition of *Petersburg*, has pointed out, this is a parodic self-reference to Bely's former, Rickert-influenced views, which the Russian modernist had expressed earlier in his essay "The Emblematics of Meaning."[26]

And yet, to cite once more Vladimir Solovyov's verdict on Immanuel Kant, the significance of Neo-Kantianism in *Petersburg* may lie in its ability to pose problems rather than to solve them. In Bely's novel, Neo-Kantianism is partly an echo of the modernist writer's intellectual past—in terms of both his ambitions and his limitations. It is also partly an index of cold Western rationalism and an invigorating attempt to get beyond artificial philosophical barriers, an attempt that could end up recapitulating the initial problem or preparing the leap into a new, more unified mode of consciousness and being. In *Petersburg*'s ideal order, Neo-Kantianism is, in this way, a "character" like other characters: seen, seeing, heard, hearing, enclosed in a context, and striving beyond it.

Notes

1. Andrei Bely, *Petersburg*, tr. John Elsworth (London: Pushkin Press, 2009).

2. Cited in James West, "Art as Cognition in Russian Neo-Kantianism," *Studies in East European Thought* 47.3–4 (1995), 196.

3. Cited in D. G. Ritchie, "Wilhelm Windelband, *Präludien*," *Mind* 10.37 (January 1885), 135.

4. For an excellent overview, see "Neo-Kantianism, Russian," in *Routledge Encyclopedia of Philosophy*, ed. Edward Craig (London: Routledge, 1998), 6:792–97.

5. Nikolai Bugaev, *Des mathématiques, considerées comme instrument scientifique et pédagogique*, tr. M. L. L. (Paris: Gauthier-Villars, 1872).

6. Cited in West, "Art as Cognition in Russian Neo-Kantianism," 203.

7. Nina Dmitrieva, "Logon didontai, ili Neskol′ko slov o nauchnosti filosofii," in *Knigoizdatel′stvo "Musaget": Istoriia. Mify. Rezul′taty*, ed. Anna Reznichenko (Moscow: RGGU, 2014), 467–68.

8. Nikolai Berdiaev, "Philosophic Truth and Moral Truth," in *Landmarks*, tr. Marion Schwartz, ed. Boris Shragin and Albert Todd (New York: Karz Howard, 1977), 15. See also Joan Delaney Grossman, "Introduction," *Studies in East European Thought* 47.3–4 (1995), 151.

9. See Michael A. Meerson, "*Put′* against *Logos*: The Critique of Kant and Neo-Kantianism by Russian Religious Philosophers in the Beginning of the Twentieth Century," *Studies in East European Thought* 47.3–4 (1995), 225–43.

10. Pasternak, *Okhrannaia gramota*, in his *Vozdushnye puti: Proza raznykh let* (Moscow: Sovetskii pisatel′, 1982), 211.

11. George Plekhanov, *Fundamental Problems of Marxism* (New York: International Publishers, 1969), 95.

12. Aleksandr Lavrov, *Andrei Belyi v 1900-e gody* (Moscow: NLO, 1995), 305–8.

13. Andrei Belyi, "Krititsizm i simvolizm," *Simvolizm* (Moscow: Musaget, 1910), 20–30.

14. For an overview of Bely's thought, see Steven Cassedy's introduction to his translation of *Selected Essays of Andrey Bely* (Berkeley: University of California Press, 1985), 3–69. For more on Bely and Neo-Kantianism, see John Elsworth, *Andrey Bely* (Cambridge: Cambridge University Press, 1983), 14–36, and Nina Dmitrieva, *Russkoe neokantianstvo: "Marburg" v Rossii* (Moscow: Rosspen, 2007), 348–69.

15. Quoted from Elsworth, *Andrey Bely*, 95.
16. Elsworth, *Andrey Bely*, 95.
17. For an extended reading of Neo-Kantianism in *Petersburg*, see James West, "Kant, Kant, Kant: The Neo-Kantian Creative Consciousness in Bely's *Petersburg*," in *The European Foundations of Russian Modernism*, ed. Peter Barta (Lewiston: Edwin Mellen, 1991), 87–135.
18. See, for example, Andrzej Walicki's remarks on Pavel Novgorodtsev in Walicki, *Legal Philosophies of Russian Liberalism* (Notre Dame: University of Notre Dame Press, 1992), 310.
19. Andrei Belyi, *Mezhdu dvukh revoliutsii* (Leningrad: Izdatel'stvo pisatelei v Leningrade, 1934), 210.
20. Andrei Belyi, *Peterburg*, ed. L. Dolgopolov (Moscow: Nauka, 1981), 43.
21. Judith Wermuth-Atkinson, *The Red Jester: Andrei Bely's "Petersburg" as a Novel of the European Modern* (Berlin: LIT Verlag, 2012), 146–49.
22. Aleksandr Vvedenskii, "Sud'by filosofii v Rossii" (1924), cited in West, "Art as Cognition in Russian Neo-Kantianism," 201.
23. Catherine Evtuhov, "An Unexpected Source of Russian Neo-Kantianism: Alexander Vvedensky and Lobachevsky's Geometry," *Studies in East European Thought* 47.3–4 (1995), 251. See also Thomas Nemeth, "The Rise of Russian Neo-Kantianism: Vvedenskij's Early 'Critical Philosophy,'" *Studies in East European Thought* 50.2 (1998), 126.
24. Cited in Elsworth, *Andrey Bely*, 15.
25. Valentin Asmus, "Filosofiia i estetika russkogo simvolizma," *Literaturnoe nasledstvo* 27–28 (Moscow: Zhurnal'no-gazetnoe ob''edinenie, 1937), 1–53.
26. Leonid Dolgopolov, "Primechaniia," in Belyi, *Peterburg*, 670n33.

Petersburg and the Philosophy of Henri Bergson

HILARY FINK

In an outline of Andrei Bely's intellectual horizons, Steven Cassedy lists the following sources that influenced the writer's thought: G. W. F. Hegel, Arthur Schopenhauer, Friedrich Nietzsche, Edmund Husserl, the Neo-Kantian school, Henri Bergson, "and many, many others."[1] Indeed, Bely was a philosophical omnivore and a heterogeneous thinker who drew on a wide array of previous and contemporary intellectual currents, using them all in a highly idiosyncratic fashion and always to his own ends. This essay will focus on just one aspect of the intellectual context of Bely's novel *Petersburg*, Bergsonian philosophy, especially as it relates to the currents of Neo-Kantianism and Nietzscheanism also at play in the novel. But first it will be helpful to consider Henri Bergson's impact on Russian modernist culture at large, a culture that provided the immediate backdrop for Bely's art and thought.

Bergson and Russian Modernism

In the decade preceding World War I, the French philosopher Henri Bergson reached the summit of his international fame, even as his most important works—*Introduction to Metaphysics* (1903) and *Creative Evolution* (1907)—were being read all over Europe. The philosophical revolution ushered in by Bergson's interrelated concepts of intuition and duration (the latter he also called "real time") largely mirrored the revolution that had taken place in physics in the waning years of the nineteenth century, effectively calling into question the ability of science to explain reality in its entirety.[2] Beginning with the discovery of X-rays and radioactivity in 1895–96, and continuing with the development of quantum theory, the new science of physics "chipped away at the classical picture of a static universe composed of fixed and permanent atoms and molecules [. . .]. A nondeterminist physics was gradually taking shape which created significant doubts about mechanical causation and which therefore struck at the very heart of mechanistic science."[3] As a result, turn-of-the-century thinkers no longer considered reality to be a closed system of phenomena, wholly discoverable by the laws of reason and mathematics; instead, reality was increasingly seen as dynamic, in many ways mysterious, and accessible not through intellect or analysis alone but also through religion, metaphysics, and intuition. In rare moments of intuition, suggested Bergson, an individual senses (rather than tries to analyze intellectually) both the fluid movement that runs throughout the living world and one's own place within that flow. As opposed to the rational exercise of our intellect, Bergson considered intuition more of a spiritual moment of sympathetic unity with all of life. Russian modernists therefore embraced Bergsonian intuition as a direct and powerful mode of apprehending reality.

Bergson's conception of duration, or "real time," represented the time of the individual's inner life as always in flux, constantly changing, and therefore impossible to analyze mathematically or scientifically. This continuous flow of interpenetrating moments of time—the fluid movement of life—cannot be dissected and approached spatially, like individual frames of a film strip, but must be felt temporally as a continuous reel of film that produces the movie, so to speak, of our lives. Human intellect, according to Bergson, was no longer the only—or even the main—means of learning about the world. Rather, intellect had to be supplemented with intuition that provided a deeper kind of cognition, one that was capable of grasping, at once, the flow of inner duration and the constant flux of the external world. Only with the help of intuition, Bergson argued, could we achieve "spiritual harmony with the innermost quality" of all things, thereby apprehending the vital inner principle, which ensured the uniqueness of our object of perception.[4] In this sense, intuition was the privileged realm of the artist. "The intention of life," wrote Bergson, "the simple movement that runs through the lines, that binds them together and gives them significance, escapes [our eye]. This intention is just what the artist tries to regain, in placing himself back within the object by a kind of sympathy, in breaking down, by an effort of intuition, the barrier that space puts up between him and his model."[5]

Bergson thus joined the psychologists Carl Jung and Sigmund Freud, the physicist Albert Einstein, the painter Pablo Picasso, and many other contemporary artists, scientists, and philosophers in the shared exploration of the mysteries of spirit, consciousness, and creativity.

Bergson's championing of artistic intuition as a way of apprehending "the intention of life" appealed to a wide range of Russian modernists in their quest to reclaim for the individual a more intuitive, dynamic, and direct link with reality. The philosopher Nikolai Losskii, for example, found in Bergson a "favorable spirit" that was helpful in the articulation of Losskii's own theory of intuitivism.[6] The poet Osip Mandel'shtam, to take another example, hailed Bergson's thought for "having liberated" from the shackles of time "the internal connection among phenomena."[7] A latter-day modernist writer, Daniil Kharms—who listed all of Bergson's major works among the books he had, at one time or another, taken out of a library—probably used Bergson's treatise *Laughter* (1899) as a springboard for elaborating his own poetics of the absurd.[8] Last but not least, and long before Kharms, Andrei Bely had been similarly drawn to Bergsonian thought.

In fact, the writer's interest in Bergson's philosophy continued even after he became deeply involved with Rudolf Steiner's Anthroposophical doctrine (see Maria Carlson's essay in this volume), which he may have initially understood "from the point of view of Bergson."[9] *Petersburg*'s readers learn, for instance, that "a magnificently-bound book *Man and his Bodies*, by some Madame Henri Besançon, sat in splendor" on a table in Sofia Petrovna's apartment; and Bely's narrator hurries to add that "Sofia Petrovna had got things confused again: not Henri Besançon—Annie Besant" (83).[10] This humorous reference alludes simultaneously to Henri Bergson and Annie Besant, a prominent figure in the Theosophical movement, which gave rise to Anthroposophy.[11] It reads as an attempt on Bely's part to unite certain aspects of Rudolf Steiner's and Henri Bergson's philosophical systems.

Bergsonian Echoes in *Petersburg*

If Steiner's Anthroposophy, like Bergsonian thought, retained its importance in Russian intellectual life well into the 1920s, the influence of Bergson's philosophy on the Russian modernist landscape outlived that of several other competing philosophical currents, most notably Neo-Kantianism and Nietzscheanism. To be sure, Nietzsche remained of some interest to optimistic Russian terrorists: "We are all Nietzscheans," proudly proclaims Aleksandr Ivanovich Dudkin in Bely's novel as he delivers the bomb that will be used in an attempt on Senator

Ableukhov's life (113). Yet Nietzsche's vision of the heroic Superman (see Edith Clowes's essay in this volume) dimmed in Russia following the failed 1905 revolution, which Bely uses as the historical setting for the dramatic action in *Petersburg*.[12] In contrast, Bergson's philosophy continued to appeal to post-1905 Russian modernists interested less in championing the Nietzschean Superman than in discovering new modes of artistic perception by which to tap into what Bergson called the élan vital, or vital force, of existence and thereby to discover the true essence of life. And as for Immanuel Kant and his followers (see Timothy Langen's essay in this volume), they did not go far enough, for Bely and other modernists, in promoting intuition as a vital means of apprehending reality.

Taking note of this shortcoming in his 1904 essay "Criticism and Symbolism," Bely wrote: "Kant admitted to the absolute impossibility of knowing the world in its essence [. . .]. If, according to Kant, we are not capable of penetrating to the essence of things by means of inner feeling, then we are even less capable of doing so by way of thought [. . .]. And here, Kant's negative thinking may be likened to a man who has fallen into a swamp."[13] In another essay, "Circular Movement" (1912), Bely again referred to the "swamp"—which he now called the "abyss"—of Kantian "negative thinking": "Its name is contemporary philosophy, where over-refined reason—Kantian reason, in which almost nothing of Kant has remained—hurls itself into the abyss, taking with it the modernist philosopher; the modernist falls headfirst; along with him goes *The Critique of Pure Reason*, which he continues to read upside down and right to left."[14]

Bely and other Russian modernists were attracted to Bergsonian philosophy as a possible way up and out of this Kantian swamp/abyss—a way to "penetrate to the essence of things." Like Bergson, Bely sought, through his art, to break down the "barrier" between the individual and the true nature of reality, a barrier that had been erected, he believed, by the overreliance on reason. In *Petersburg*, the embodiment of reason may be found in the figure of Apollon Apollonovich Ableukhov, the one character in the novel most comfortable with the symmetry of straight lines and right angles (24–26)—that is, with the very geometry of the city founded by Peter the Great as a "window onto Europe" and thus informed by Western rationalism in both structure and mindset.

However, Apollon Apollonovich's son, Nikolai Apollonovich, is just as much an embodiment of overreliance on reason as is his father, if not more so. Introduced from the outset in rationally clear-cut opposition to his father (a young, radical revolutionary vs. an aged stalwart of established state order), he is an avid reader of Kant for most of the novel. Nikolai Apollonovich might be seen as the modernist philosopher from Bely's essay "Circular Movement." As in the essay, the novel's modernist philosopher is toppling into the abyss, largely because of his close and destructive association with Kantian reason, which, in Bely's understanding, limits human knowledge to the realm of phenomena or appearances. This idea is conveyed through the mirror imagery in *Petersburg*, especially the maze of mirrors overwhelming the costumed Nikolai Apollonovich at the Tsukatovs' ball. Indeed, it is left to Nikolai Apollonovich to turn Kant upside down in favor of more authentic sources of knowledge and reality ("Kant? Kant is forgotten," 563). By the end of the novel, Nikolai Apollonovich rejects Kant in favor of the Slavic religious thinker Grigorii Skovoroda.

In this sense, Bely might be seen to embrace Bergsonian intuition as a way to escape the abyss of the proverbial modernist philosopher through the intuitive apprehension of a type of "total unity" beyond the physical realms of time and space. For Bely, movement in art, or what Bergson might call artistic duration, represents the continuous movement of everyone and everything toward the divine. Whereas Bergson resists the presupposition of a divine Whole at the base of the ceaseless movement of duration, Bely conceives of movement in precisely such a religious, teleological framework. For Nikolai Apollonovich, to break out of the horrifying labyrinth of mirrors, with appearances eternally reflected back upon one's view, he must be able to apprehend and appreciate a larger whole, a spiritual unity that transcends the isolated self. In other words, Nikolai Apollonovich, who is at once endowed with "a godlike countenance" (443) and "condemn[s] himself to be the executioner—*in the name of an idea*" (444), must abandon his man-godhood and, like Dostoevsky's Raskolnikov and Nietzsche's Superman, discard his cerebral plans of patricide in favor of spiritual evolution and intuitive understanding of a divine whole.

Interestingly, Dudkin is the one who tries to show Nikolai Apollonovich the way out of this cerebral abyss, that same Dudkin whose "conscious 'self'" is taken over by "acute insanity" (407) when he believes he is visited in his garret by the Bronze Horseman, the mounted statue of Peter the Great come alive at night. Although Dudkin attempts to "break out" (411) of the stifling cycle of history set in motion by Peter the Great—and reminiscent of "the eternal return" of Nietzsche, whereby all of life's experiences ceaselessly repeat—he falls short of his goal. While successful in killing the double agent Lippanchenko, Dudkin still appears ridiculous at that moment, straddling the dead Lippanchenko in a mockery of the Bronze Horseman's pose. Nonetheless, it is Dudkin who chastises Nikolai Apollonovich for "poring over Kant in an unventilated room" and urges him instead to throw the tin with the ticking bomb into the Neva River (352). This would be one way for Nikolai Apollonovich to climb out of the Godless, solipsistic modernist abyss: instead of gluing his eyes to the pages of Kant, he must learn to listen to the music of what Bergson calls the "uninterrupted humming of life's depths."[15]

In his works, Bergson often employed musical metaphors for the dynamic flux of life. He compared "pure duration" to "the notes of a tune, melting, as it were, into one another."[16] Similarly, he defined intuition as that which "attained the spirit, duration, pure change."[17] Only through intuition, argued the philosopher, could one grasp the continuous movement, and music, of duration at the heart of reality. Bely shared with Bergson this philosophical vision based on the intuition of a musical type of duration as the means by which to comprehend the essence of reality. One of the central slogans of modernism, in both France and Russia, was Paul Verlaine's decree from his poem "Art poétique" (1884): "De la musique avant toute chose!" (Music before all else!) Furthermore, Russian modernists adopted Arthur Schopenhauer's belief in music as the highest art form due to its lack of any true external form, in contrast, for example, to painting and sculpture. "Music," wrote Bely, "deepens everything it touches. Music is the soul of all the arts."[18] As a result, Bely described himself as "more of a composer of language [. . .] than a writer in the usual sense of the word."[19] Music thus represented for him pure movement; the pure, inner essence that ran through all static, outer forms (see Steven Cassedy's essay in this volume). Symptomatically, in a 1903 letter praising the musicality of Bely's early literary compositions, which the writer entitled *Symphonies*, his friend and fellow modernist poet Aleksandr Blok noted that the "inner depths of music and its *lack of any external reality* suggested the notion of its noumenal quality; music explained the mystery of movement, the mystery of *existence*" (emphasis in the original).[20]

Seeking an escape in *Petersburg*, both from the horrifying nontranscendence of circular reasoning and from the artificial, intellectualized nineteenth-century construct of time as linear and spatial—represented as individual units of time, each following the next in a rational, unidirectional line—Bely turned to an alternative geometry, that of the vortex or spiral (see David Bethea's essay in this volume).[21] As *Petersburg*'s narrator observed:

> Leaves began to move sluggishly, encircling the flaps of [Nikolai Apollonovich's] coat in dry, yellow rings; but the circles narrowed, began to twist in ever more restless swirls; a golden swirl, whispering something, danced with ever greater vigour. The vortex of leaves twisted swiftly, darted here and there and, no longer swirling, ran off somehow sideways; a ribbed, red leaf moved slightly, flew forwards and lay flat. A dark network of criss-crossed branches stretched out drably, standing straight against the steely horizon; he passed into this network; and when he passed into the network, a ferocious flock of crows shot upwards and starting circling above the roof to Peter's House; the dark network began to rock; the dark network began to hum; and timorously melancholy sounds began to blend together; they merged into a single sound—the sound of

an organ voice. The atmosphere of evening thickened; once more the soul sensed that there was no present . . . (192–93)

The images here of spiraling leaves, the melancholy "hum" of the "network" of branches, and the sense of the continuous flow of time ("no present"), all point to the interconnection among music, time, and duration. Such an interconnection is vital to both Bely's and Bergson's metaphysics and is also illustrated earlier in the novel through "the sound of some other world"—"the October song" of "uuuu-uuuu-uuu" (102). Bely suggests that, within the intuitive appreciation of "uuuu-uuuu-uuu," lies the bridge between the phenomenal and noumenal worlds—the haunting notes of history, of the failed revolution of 1905, that blend seamlessly into the present, crumbling culture, already flowing into an apocalyptic future. Through this "October song," Bely highlights a Bergsonian musical duration ("the uninterrupted humming of life's depths") that offers the creative individual, with a capacity for artistic intuition, a grasp of the divine Absolute.

Petersburg between Nietzsche and Bergson

While Bely very clearly writes against Immanuel Kant in *Petersburg*, his relationship with Nietzschean thought in the novel is more complex, with Bergson serving, in my opinion, as an important component in the mix. Although I have suggested above that Bely's depiction of music could be seen as quite compatible with Bergson's notion of duration, Bely explicitly associates Friedrich Nietzsche with the power of music (and art more generally), as Bernice Rosenthal points out in her study of Nietzsche in Russian intellectual history: "Bely stated that Zarathustra was his 'manual.' He saw in Nietzsche [. . .] 'an artist of genius whose rhythms would penetrate all artistic culture.' A lover of music, Bely knew that Nietzsche had tried his hand at composing, and hoped that through the spirit of music an all-embracing new culture could be formed that would incorporate the truths of art, science, religion, and philosophy."[22]

Bely shared Nietzsche's belief in the prime importance of an artistic approach to life, which promised, for Bely, a sense of creative unity with the divine universe. The writer was also a student of the Russian religious philosopher Vladimir Solovyov, who, as Rosenthal points out, "shaped Bely's concept of the redemptive role of the poet, his conviction that religious, rather than unformulated mystical feeling, must be the basis of art . . . [a conviction] which Bely merged with a Nietzschean aestheticism."[23] In his essay "The Magic of Words" (1909), Bely described the power of the word to spark rebirth in the modernist abyss: "In periods of general decay, the new word of life is nurtured in poetry. We revel in words because we recognize the meaning of new, magical words through whose use we will increasingly be able to conjure the gloom of night hanging over us. We are still alive, but we are alive because we hold on to words."[24] Indeed, the relationship of "word" and "world" is central to *Petersburg*, whose author may be seen to create reality through the very sounds of his linguistic expression. For example, early in the novel, Aleksandr Ivanovich Dudkin incorrectly overhears a conversation taking place in the street. Although the actual word spoken is "proper," he thinks he hears "provo-cation": "Provocation was abroad on the Nevsky. Provocation changed the meaning of all the words that were heard: an innocent 'proper' it endowed with 'provo-cation'; and turned a 'tabula rasa' into the devil only knows what" (35). There is perhaps no coincidence in the fact that it is Dudkin, the self-proclaimed Nietzschean, whose use of language serves, in effect, to bring about a new world order.

While Bely was clearly drawn to Nietzsche's "spirit of music," he was dismissive of the German philosopher's theme of "the eternal return," a concept that pointed to an inexorable stasis and nontranscendence at the heart of history/human experience ("Everything becomes and recurs eternally—escape is impossible!" writes Nietzsche).[25] Incidentally, the nightmarish circularity of Pepp Peppovich Pepp and many other spherical images in *Petersburg* all but illustrate the suffocating horror of forever returning to the point where one started. As a result, Bely perhaps turned more toward Bergson when it came to the interconnection between the musicality of the ceaseless flow of uninterrupted time, intuition, and transcendence. In "The Magic of Words," he claimed that "in sound, there is recreated a new world within whose boundaries I feel myself to be the creator of reality [. . .]. With a successfully created word I can penetrate far more deeply into the essence of phenomena than I can through the process of analytic thought" (94–95). This statement finds its demonstration within the pages of *Petersburg*, itself an artistic, musical explosion on the Russian literary landscape through which Bely is able to create a new modernist reality. In the "uuuu-uuuu-uuu" of the October song of 1905, in the melancholy "organ voice" of the spiraling leaves, in the birth of the word "provocation" from "proper," the individual who possesses the capacity for artistic intuition might apprehend the "essence of phenomena"—truth that can only be created or discerned from the very sounds of the "World Orchestra"—a term used by Bely's fellow modernist Aleksandr Blok.[26]

By the end of the novel, one wonders if Nikolai Apollonovich Ableukhov might succeed where Dudkin failed. Having traded in Immanuel Kant for the Slavic religious thinker Grigorii Skovoroda, having traveled outside the artificial, deadly westernized city of Petersburg to the beginnings of civilization in Egypt, Nikolai Apollonovich may yet come to appreciate the "magic of words" that Bely associated with ancient Egypt. Bely wrote in the "Magic of Words": "Every one of the sacred hieroglyphs of ancient Egypt had a triple meaning. The first meaning went with the sound of the word, and the sound gave a designation to the hieroglyphic image (time); the second meaning went with the spatial inscription of the sound (the image), that is, with the hieroglyph itself; the third meaning was contained in a sacred number symbolizing the word" (95–96).

Although Nikolai Apollonovich is shown at the end of the novel leaning "against the side of the lifeless pyramid" in a scene suffused with apocalypticism, it is also the case that he "starts to imagine that not everything is dead; that there still are some sounds; these sounds rumble away in Cairo; a very special rumble" (563). Perhaps Nikolai Apollonovich has intuited—if only briefly—both the nature of time as an unceasing musical flow in the Bergsonian sense of duration as well as the magical nature of the word as combination of image, sound, and symbol. In Egypt he has, after all, completed his manuscript *On the Letter of Daufsekhrut*, a treatise that, significantly, deals with the topic of a father trying to teach his son. Not accidentally, Apollon Apollonovich, who in retirement acquired "the habit of forgetting absolutely everything," still remembered clearly that obscure and difficult word "Daufsekhrut" because his son "Kolenka was writing about 'Daufsekhrut'" (563).

Henri Bergson's notions of time and consciousness as an immeasurable, musical flow of ceaseless change (duration); intuition as the means by which to penetrate this flow; and the subsequent ability to intuitively grasp the essence of life were all ideas embraced by Russian modernists in their self-appointed role as creators of, and participants in, the essence of reality. Bergson joined Kant, Nietzsche, Steiner, and others as one of the many notes that contributed to the flowing symphony of *Petersburg*, a work that hums and rumbles with the music of Russian history, (r)evolution, the power of the word, and the continuous movement toward an artistically intuited and transformed world.

Notes

1. Steven Cassedy, "Bely the Thinker," in *Andrey Bely: Spirit of Symbolism*, ed. John Malmstad (Ithaca: Cornell University Press, 1987), 319.

2. R. C. Grogin, *The Bergsonian Controversy in France, 1900–1914* (Calgary: University of Calgary Press, 1988), 8–12.

3. Grogin, *The Bergsonian Controversy*, 9.

4. Henri Bergson, *The Creative Mind*, tr. M. L. Andison (New York: Citadel Press, 1992), 200.

5. Henri Bergson, *Creative Evolution*, tr. A. Mitchell (Lanham: University Press of America, 1983), 177.

6. Nikolai Losskii, *Vospominaniia: Zhizn' i filosofskii put'* (Munich: Wilhelm Fink, 1968), 127.

7. Osip Mandel´shtam, "On the Nature of the Word," *Osip Mandelstam: Critical Prose and Letters*, tr. and ed. J. G. Harris (Ann Arbor: Ardis, 1979), 117–18.

8. Daniil Kharms, *Gorlo bredit britvoiu: Sluchai, rasskazy, dnevnikovye zapisi* (Riga: Glagol, 1991), 68–69.

9. Bely's 1913 letter to Emilii Metner, Rossiiskaia Gosudarstvennaia Biblioteka, f. 167, ed. khr. 7, 3–4.

10. Andrei Bely, *Petersburg*, tr. John Elsworth (London: Pushkin Press, 2009).

11. See Robert Maguire and John Malmstad's annotations to their translation of Andrei Bely, *Petersburg* (Bloomington: Indiana University Press, 1978), 318.

12. See Bernice Glatzer Rosenthal, introduction to *Nietzsche in Russia*, ed. Bernice Glatzer Rosenthal (Princeton: Princeton University Press, 1986), 27–28.

13. Andrei Belyi, "Krititsizm i simvolizm," *Vesy* 2 (1904), 6–7.

14. Cited in Robert Maguire and John Malmstad, "*Petersburg*," in Malmstad, *Andrey Bely*, 122.

15. Bergson, *The Creative Mind*, 149–50.

16. Henri Bergson, *Time and Free Will*, tr. F. L. Pogson (New York: Macmillan, 1910), 100.

17. Bergson, *The Creative Mind*, 33–34, 149–50.

18. Andrei Belyi, "Printsip formy v estetike," in *Simvolizm* (Munich: Wilhelm Fink, 1969), 179.

19. Andrei Belyi, "O sebe kak pisatel´," in *Andrei Belyi: Problemy tvorchestva*, ed. S. Lesnevskii and A. Mikhailov (Moscow: Sovetskii pisatel´, 1988), 19–20.

20. Aleksandr Blok, *Sobranie sochinenii* (Leningrad: Khudozhestvennaia literatura, 1983), 6: 37.

21. See Maguire and Malmstad, "*Petersburg*," in Malmstad, *Andrey Bely*, 98–105.

22. Bernice Glatzer Rosenthal, *New Myth, New World: From Nietzsche to Stalinism* (University Park: Penn State University Press, 2002), 20.

23. Rosenthal, *New Myth, New World*, 39.

24. Andrei Belyi, "The Magic of Words," *Selected Essays of Andrey Bely*, tr. and ed. Steven Cassedy (Berkeley: University of California Press, 1985), 110.

25. Friedrich Nietzsche, *The Will to Power*, tr. and ed. W. Kaufman and R. J. Hollingdale (New York: Random House, 1967), 545.

26. Aleksandr Blok, "Intelligentsiia i revoliutsiia," in *Sobranie sochinenii v shesti tomakh* (Leningrad: Khudozhestvennaia literatura, 1980–83), 4:231–32.

Petersburg and the New Science of Psychology

JUDITH WERMUTH-ATKINSON

At the turn of the twentieth century, scientists and artists alike challenged the hitherto predominant materialist world view, based on Newtonian physics, which rigidly distinguished between the objective or physical realm and the subjective or psychic realm of human existence. Albert Einstein's *Special Theory of Relativity* (1905) cast doubt on the very idea that properties of matter had an objective existence independent of observation. Einstein introduced a unitary vision of reality, whose material aspects were no longer seen as separate from the psychical ones. In another domain of scientific inquiry, the same unitary approach informed the new science of psychology, whose practitioners, intent on retrieving and elucidating the secrets of the human unconscious, became both observers and participants in their patients' inner lives.

Concurrently with these scientific advances, modernist artists and thinkers mounted their own challenge to the materialist world view. Part and parcel of this effort, Andrei Bely's *Petersburg* confronted its original audience with an unprecedented narrative form. Giving the novel's readers access to hidden processes in the unconscious of its protagonists, Bely's fragmented and confusing narrative strove to approximate the workings of the human psyche, as shaped by the conditions of social and cultural modernity. This essay will examine the new science of psychology—particularly the theories of the Austrian neurologist Sigmund Freud—as an intellectual context of *Petersburg*, a context whose reconstruction gives today's readers a fuller appreciation of this Russian modernist classic.[1]

What knowledge could Bely have had of Sigmund Freud's work? By the late 1900s, psychoanalysis was a full-fledged movement in Russia, which became the first country where Freud's *Interpretation of Dreams* appeared in translation (in 1904).[2] In a 1914 essay, Freud observed: "In Russia, psychoanalysis is very generally known and widespread; almost all my writings as well as those of other advocates of analysis are translated into Russian."[3] Indeed, in 1909–11, a number of Freud's works, beginning with a volume titled *On Dreams*, became available in Russian translation under the imprint of the Psychotherapeutic Library. These publications were framed by a sustained public discussion of Freud's theories.[4] In 1911, a Russian member of Freud's Wednesday Group, Tatiana Rozenthal, published a paper on the contemporary Danish writer Karen Michaelis, pioneering the use of psychoanalysis as an interpretive tool of literary criticism and thus bridging the new science of psychology and the modernist preoccupation with the inner life of the artist and the hidden sources of creativity.[5]

Magnus Ljunggren asserts that Bely might not have read Sigmund Freud prior to writing *Petersburg*, but that Freud's ideas were in the air and Bely must have come into contact with them while working on the novel. Ljunggren points out that Russia was the first country outside German-speaking Europe where Freud's therapeutic method was adopted, with psychoanalysis influencing the circles to which Bely belonged. In 1909, psychoanalytic therapy was introduced at Moscow's University Clinic. In the same year, Bely reviewed the Russian translation of Otto Weininger's international best seller, *Sex and Character* (1903), which referred to Freud's studies. Bely also attended meetings at Moscow's Psychological Society, cofounded by his father. Furthermore, his close friends and fellow modernists Sergei Solovyov and Emilii Metner underwent Freudian therapy just as Bely was writing *Petersburg*. In 1912, Bely visited Sergei Solovyov in a psychiatric clinic and had two conversations with one of its doctors, Mikhail Lakhtin, who used Freud's ideas in his research.[6] The participation of many Russians in the psychoanalytic movement, whose ideas impacted Russian modernist culture, and the interest in psychoanalysis expressed by Bely's spiritual teacher, Rudolf Steiner, leave little doubt about the writer's familiarity with analytical psychology at the time of *Petersburg*'s creation.

The Freudian Dream of Nikolai Apollonovich

The desire to interpret dreams is perhaps as old as human civilization. However, in his first major work, *The Interpretation of Dreams* (1900), Freud endeavored to formulate a scientific understanding of dreaming, which he saw as a product of psychic activity occurring during sleep and compensating for all that was suppressed by human consciousness in the state of wakefulness. Dreaming, for Freud, "took the place of action," balancing out the psychological tensions generated by our conscious self-censorship. The life of the psyche, Freud argues, is marked by repressed wishes. Dreams act as "fulfillments of wishes in the form of dream-thoughts": while some dreams "reveal themselves without any disguise as fulfillment of wishes," others "might turn out to be a fulfilled fear," or merely "a reflection" of a memory; but regardless of how different from wakeful life the dream may be, there are "no dreams but wishful ones" (156–57).[7] Naturally, Freud's notion of the dream as the mind's play on the border of conscious and unconscious states could not fail to appeal to modernist artists in their quest for true reality beyond the confines of the visible, as testified by many affinities between Bely's narrative method in *Petersburg* and the arguments presented in Freud's *Interpretation of Dreams*.

A clear case of Bely's Freudian approach in *Petersburg* is the connection between politics and patricide, which the novel establishes in ways reminiscent of Freud's *Interpretation of Dreams*. Nikolai Apollonovich Ableukhov's involvement in a political assassination plot against his own father is underpinned by the son's troubled psychological state, centered on his feelings of resentment and anxiety regarding Senator Apollon Apollonovich Ableukhov. In chapter 5, in the section "The Day of Judgment," Nikolai Apollonovich has an elaborate dream whose narrative presentation triggers numerous associations with Freud's dream theories, and particularly with "The Dream of the Uncle with the Yellow Beard," analyzed in *The Interpretation of Dreams*. It is as if Bely wanted his audience to read Nikolai Apollonovich's dream through the Freudian lens.

Freud cites "The Dream of the Uncle" as an example of distortion—a contrast between manifest and latent content of dreams. His notion of dreaming as a wish fulfillment mechanism presupposes the existence of thoughts that underlie dreams and are revealed through psychoanalytic interpretation. Distressing, painful or fearful dreams, Freud argues, are "counter-wish-dreams [. . .] whose subject matter is the frustration of a wish or the occurrence of something clearly unwished-for." For Freud, a dream can represent a "(disguised) fulfillment of a (suppressed or repressed) wish." He thus describes the situation informing "The Dream of the Uncle." In 1897, Freud was recommended for a professorship, but he also knew that his chances were undermined by his Jewish origins. Then, a friend of his, R., shared alarming news: his own appointment had been delayed because he was Jewish. After R.'s visit, Freud dreamed: "My friend R. was my uncle. I had a great feeling of affection for him. I saw before me his face, somewhat changed. It was as though it had been drawn out lengthways. A yellow beard that surrounded it stood out especially clearly" (171).

In the ensuing interpretation of this dream, Freud proposes several reasons for seeing R. as his uncle Josef. First, since R. and his uncle had similar facial features and hair, the face in the dream was, at once, that of R. and that of Josef. Secondly, Freud's father considered Josef an idiot because of a legal problem in his past. Freud thus takes R.'s appearance as Josef to mean that, deep down, he thinks R. is an idiot. Finally, searching for the dream's purpose as a wish-fulfillment mechanism, Freud establishes a link between R. and another Jewish colleague, N., who had been waiting for a professorship as well. Freud once suggested to N. that the reason for the delay might be because N. was Jewish (like R.); but N. attributed the delay to some legal trouble in his past (as in Josef's case). Freud concludes that the dream conveyed his fear that, like R. and N., he would not be able to secure a professorship because he was Jewish. He sees the purpose of the dream as establishing reasons (idiocy, legal trouble) for the delay in his colleagues' appointments that would not apply to him: the dream suppressed Jewishness as a possible reason. As Freud did not consider himself an idiot and had no previous legal entanglements, he could keep hoping that he would receive the professorship despite being Jewish.

Let us now turn to the "The Day of Judgment" in *Petersburg*. The preceding section, "Pepp Peppovich Pepp," sets the stage by calling Nikolai "an unconscious man" (*chelovek bessoznatel'nyi*) because he, like his father, is periodically subject to a "very strange semi-somnolent condition" (*polusonnoe sostoianie*) that transports him from daily life into another dimension (234–35/314–15).[8] The narrator then describes Nikolai during one such episode, as he sits in front of the sardine-tin containing the bomb: "When his weary head bent down silently on to the desk (on to the sardine-tin), in through the open door to the corridor the bottomless infinity gazed at its own reflection, that strange thing that Nikolai Apollonovich had tried to cast off as he made the transition to the current business: to his distant astral journey, or sleep (which, we observe, is the same thing); but the open door went on gaping amongst all that was current, opening into it its own profundity, not current at all: cosmic infinity" (315). As in Freud's dream, there is a face in Nikolai's dream: "Something standing outside the door in the infinity had looked at him [. . .] some kind of head was poking through" (315). The narrator describes that dreamy vision as the "ancient Turanian" (317–18) from whom the Ableukhovs descended. In this way, Nikolai's "heredity was making itself felt; heredity was coursing into consciousness; in his sclerotic veins his heredity was beating in millions of yellow blood corpuscles" (316).

While in Freud's dream, yellow is the color of the two beards marking the kinship of R. and uncle Josef, Bely's narrator talks about "yellow blood corpuscles," pairing physiological terminology with a fantastic element, since blood corpuscles can only be white or red. I see this as a reference to Freud's interpretation of yellow as a color symbolizing an unpleasant transformation, such as when people grow old or sick (168–94). In the Ableukhovs' case, yellow may symbolize such a transformation within a family in decline—consider the "sclerotic veins" of its young scion—the kind of hereditary degeneration that preoccupied the European medical and psychiatric establishments at the turn of the twentieth century (see Henrietta Mondry's essay in this volume, discussing the racial dimension of the color yellow in *Petersburg* in relation to the European discourse of degeneration).

The most explicit allusion to Freud in Nikolai's dream is the narrator's statement that the hero's "heredity was coursing into consciousness." In "The Dream of the Uncle," Freud interpreted the affinity of R.'s and Josef's faces by drawing on the technique of composite portraiture (superimposed facial photos), devised by the British eugenicist Francis Galton to test his theory that mental and physical heredity was expressed in facial traits (172). Bely appears to be invoking the word "heredity" with reference to Freud's use of Galton, whose composite portraiture technique the writer appropriates, following Freud's cue, as a tool for building Nikolai Apollonovich's dream, as I will discuss below.

Speaking of the hero's Asiatic heredity, Bely's narrator wonders, "Was that perhaps the reason why Nikolai Apollonovich felt such sympathy [*nezhnost'*] for Buddhism?" (235/316). The word *nezhnost'*, better translated as "tender feeling," appears to be yet another allusion to Freud's "Dream of the Uncle," which insists on the dreamer's tender feeling for R./Josef. In Freud's view, that feeling belongs neither to the latent content nor to the dream-thoughts behind the dream. In reality, he had no affection for Josef, and the dream's affection for R. was exaggerated. The function of that tender feeling, Freud surmises, is to obfuscate the dream's unpleasant implication that his friend R. is an idiot. The dream thus distorted its real latent content ("a slander against R."), acting as a suppression mechanism, and suggesting that, in cases where a wish is disguised, "there must exist some inclination to put up a defense against that wish" (174–75). Digging into his childhood memories for additional clues, Freud recalled twice hearing that someone thought someday Freud would become a government minister. He concludes that, in "The Dream of the Uncle," he "mishandled"

R. and Josef because they were Jewish, while he personally identified with a government minister: "I put myself in the minister's place. Turning the tables on his Excellency with a vengeance! He refused to appoint me professor [. . .] and I retaliated in the dream by stepping into his shoes" (226). This kind of distortion, Freud argues, is also practiced in social life, in situations of power imbalance (226). As an example, he cites a political writer who, on account of censorship, "must soften and distort the expression of his opinion [. . .]. For instance he might describe a dispute between two mandarins in the Middle Kingdom, when the people he really has in mind are officials in his own country" (175–76).

Bely shows the latent content, or the real wish, of Nikolai Apollonovich's dream in a way that closely echoes Freud's analysis in "The Dream of the Uncle," including his invocation of China (the two mandarins from the Middle Kingdom) and of Galton's composite facial portraiture. On the surface level of Nikolai's dream, or the level of images, as Freud defines it, the head that appears in the doorframe changes, as in Francis Galton's superimposed photographs of different faces, from "the head of a *god* [. . .] such as can to this day be encountered among the tribes of the north-east, who have since time immemorial peopled Russia's tedious tundra," to the ancient head of Confucius or Buddha, and to Nikolai's own Kirgiz-Kaisak ancestor Ab-Lai (315–16); then to the infanticidal god Chronos-Saturn of Greco-Roman mythology; and eventually to Apollon Apollonovich Ableukhov (319–21), with whom Nikolai Apollonovich is locked in an uneven power struggle. The political implications of their power struggle recall Freud's example of distortion in social life, cited above; but the father-son antagonism in *Petersburg* has deeper psychological resonance—hence the appearance of Chronos-Saturn the devouring father in Nikolai's dream, alluding to Freud's interpretation of the Oedipus myth, discussed later in this essay.[9]

Bely refers even more directly to Francis Galton's physiognomic photography in the two sections immediately preceding "The Day of Judgment," where Nikolai's dream is narrated. In "Packets of Pencils," the old senator's face changes once he learns that his estranged wife has returned: "His aged face became younger [. . .]. Apollon Apollonovich might have reminded anyone of his son: most of all he resembled a photograph of his son taken in 1904" (308). Then, in "Pepp Peppovich Pepp," Bely's narrator repeats and reverses the same photographic comparison: "Nikolai Apollonovich now resembled the senator: most of all he resembled a photograph of the senator taken in 1860" (311). As we have seen, Nikolai's dream holds the key to the father and son's physiognomic kinship, which testifies, above all, to their Asiatic heredity and to the Asiatic nature of authority as it is exercised in their family. Like Freud, putting himself in the shoes of a government minister in "The Dream of the Uncle," Bely's young hero fully identifies with a figure of authority:

> Nikolai Apollonovich leapt up.
> An ancient, ancient head: was it Confucius or Buddha? No, it was no doubt his ancestor Ab-Lai peeping in at the door.
> A multicolored iridescent silk gown rustled and swished; for some reason Nikolai Apollonovich remembered his own Bukhara dressing gown with its iridescent peacock feathers . . . A multicolored iridescent silk gown, across whose smoky, smoky-sapphire background (and into that background) little dragons were crawling [. . .]. The worshipful Mongol entered the colorful room; and behind him wafted the winds of millennia [. . .].
> And Nikolai Apollonovich recalled: he—the old Turanian—had been embodied a multitude of times [. . .]. On Nikolai Apollonovich's face a forgotten, Mongol expression appeared; he seemed now to be a mandarin of the Middle Empire, clad in a frock coat for his passage to the West. (316–17)

The image of the mandarins from the Middle Empire represents authority exactly as it does in Freud's discussion of the political writer who fears censorship. The association of the Turanian father figure with an administrative hierarchy—"Nikolai Apollonovich rushed up to the guest—Turanian to Turanian (subordinate to master [*podchinënnyi k nachal'niku*])" (237 / 318)—echoes Freud's statement, in "The Dream of the Uncle," that a dream-like distortion occurs in social situations "when two persons are concerned, one of whom possesses a certain degree of power which the second is obliged to take into account" (175). In "The Day of Judgment," Bely thus establishes an emblematic reference to Freud's reading of the desire for authority into his dream about R./Uncle Josef. As in Freud's interpretation of "The Dream of the Uncle," the latent content of Nikolai Apollonovich's dream gives no access to his consciousness. When Nikolai awakes, he realizes that he had a horrible dream but he cannot remember it: "With a shudder, he realized that his head was lying on the sardine-tin [with the bomb]. And he jumped up: a terrible dream; but what kind? He could not remember the dream; his childhood nightmares had returned" (321).

The Patricidal Wish in the Dream of Nikolai Apollonovich

If we were to follow Freudian principles of dream analysis, as Bely appears to be doing, how would we define the latent content of Nikolai Apollonovich's dream? I think the key to the answer is hidden in the Mongol face that the sleeping Nikolai at first sees on his guest and then takes for his own, assuming a "Mongol expression" that marks him as a reincarnation of his distant Asiatic ancestor (317). The Mongol face in Nikolai's dream helps Bely articulate the connection between history, politics, and the hero's secret wish to kill his father, the senator, a connection that largely follows the Freudian model exemplified in "The Dream of the Uncle." In *Petersburg*, this Mongol face simultaneously emblematizes authority and alludes to Freud's vision of perennial intergenerational struggle. The dreaming Nikolai Apollonovich realizes that, in him, his Turanian ancestor has come back "in the flesh and blood of the Russian imperial nobility of ancient lineage, with the task of fulfilling an age-old, sacred purpose: to dislodge all foundations; in the degenerate Aryan blood the Ancient Dragon was to flare up and consume everything in its flame; the age-old East was scattering a hail of invisible bombs into our time" (317). To understand the full meaning of the Mongol face in Nikolai's dream, then, we must heed Bely's idea of the opposition between East and West in the context of Russian history.

The writer originally conceived *Petersburg* as the second part in an epic trilogy, *East or West*, contemplating Russia's historical destiny as a country that combined two opposed cultural principles, European and Asiatic. The clash of these principles became ever more evident and relevant to Bely and his modernist peers after Russia's defeat in the war with Japan (1904–5) and the failed revolution of 1905. The trilogy, however, was going to explore the workings of history not as a grand narrative of wars and revolutions but as a subjective expression of human spirit and mentality. "The depth of the soul and the surface of history are like two mirrors reflecting each other," wrote Bely in an essay. "It does not matter which of the two looks at the other [. . .]. If history has created us, then again, we appear to be our own creation in history. We create history."[10]

In the first book of the trilogy, *The Silver Dove* (1909), Bely imagined the principle of the East as the darkness, gloominess, and irrationality of passions producing senseless bloody rebellions and wanton destruction. The antithesis to the Eastern principle, for Bely, was that of the rationality of the West. The theme of the trilogy's second installment, *Petersburg*, is the clash of the two principles in one and the same individual and culture (the writer never completed his trilogy). In *Petersburg*, Bely plays on the age-old Russian apprehension of the all-conquering Mongol/Tatar East, which acquired new urgency in turn-of-the-century Russian thought thanks to the contemporary European racial discourse about the Yellow Peril, embraced by such an important intellectual precursor to Russian modernists as the philosopher Vladimir Solovyov, who proposed his own, apocalyptic version of the threat from the East—"Pan-Mongolism" (see David Bethea's and Henrietta Mondry's essays in this volume). *Petersburg* shows the Russian nobility and imperial institutions as bearers of the hereditary marks of the Mongol East, left by the country's history of Mongol domination. Bely the Europeanizer contrasted the Turanians, or the East, to the Aryans, or the West. In *Petersburg*, the ancient goal of the East is to shower modern times "with a hail of invisible bombs" (317) and to destroy the very foundations of Western culture.

"The Dream of the Uncle" is not the only text from Freud's *Interpretation of Dreams* that helps Bely structure Nikolai Apollonovich's racial nightmare: Bely also draws on Freud's "Rome Dreams." In the fourth "Rome Dream," Freud mentions the story of the Carthaginian Commander-in-Chief Hamilcar Barca, who was not able to fulfill his goal of conquering Rome and thus made his son, Hannibal, swear that he would take vengeance on the Romans (136). In a clear echo to this episode, Nikolai's dream casts Apollon Apollonovich and Nikolai Apollonovich as two military commanders hailing from the East, with the father similarly ordering his son to take vengeance on his enemies: "Apollon Apollonovich, the Emperor of China [*bogdykhan*], commanded Nikolai Apollonovich to slaughter many thousands (which was done); and in those relatively recent times, when thousands of Tamerlane's horsemen flooded over Russia, Nikolai Apollonovich came galloping from the steppes to that same Russia on his steed; later he became embodied in the blood of a Russian nobleman; and took up the same old business: just as he had slaughtered thousands then, so now he planned explosion: he planned to throw a bomb at his father; to throw a bomb at swift-flowing time itself" (238/319–20).

Freud's invocation of the legend of Hannibal served Bely in developing his own idea of the East-West opposition, since the Punic Wars between Rome and Carthage (264–146 BCE) had been fought over cultural dominance, with Hamilcar Barca and his son Hannibal representing the East in its struggle against the Western imperial power of Rome. In the quoted passage, Bely emphasizes the issue of cultural domination by identifying Apollon Apollonovich with the Chinese emperor. Yet he uses a Mongolian term for Buddhist dignitaries, *bogdykhan*, commonly denoting the Chinese emperor in colloquial Russian speech. Nikolai's dream thus establishes Senator Ableukhov as another incarnation of the Mongol face emblematic of the mentality, culture, and authority of the East, bent on a bloody conquest of the West.

We can see how Bely steadfastly constructs the real wish behind Nikolai's bizarre dream by means of a complicated chain of overlapping images, as if challenging his reader to make sense of their chaotic and senseless constellation by examining it through the lens of the Freudian interpretive method. Nikolai Apollonovich has mixed blood, Aryan and Turanian. In the dream, he identifies with his Mongol ancestor Ab-Lai and the East more generally. As in the legend of Hamilcar and Hannibal, Nikolai assumes from his father what Bely imagines to be the ancient Turanian mission to subjugate and destroy the Western civilization. Stepping out of Nikolai's dream, we realize that the same mission turns the son against his father, Senator Ableukhov, who incarnates the Russian imperial status quo. Nikolai, furthermore, harbors power ambitions of his own, given that, in the dream, he eventually merges with a figure of authority ("He seemed now to be a mandarin of the Middle Empire, clad in a frock coat for his passage to the West," 317). This allows Nikolai to take the place of a powerful official such as his father, in the same way that Freud steps into the government minister's shoes in "The Dream of the Uncle." Finally, Nikolai sees the Mongol face as both Chronos-Saturn, the father of time and devourer of his own progeny, and as Apollon Apollonovich Ableukhov: "In the first instant Nikolai Apollonovich thought that in the guise of his ancestor, Ab-Lai, Chronos had come to pay him a visit" (317); but a few paragraphs down, the narrator observes: "The wrinkled countenance, familiar to the point of horror, bent right down to him: thereupon he glanced at its ear, and—he understood, understood everything: the old Turanian [. . .] was Apollon Apollonovich [. . .]. Nikolai Apollonovich was cast down into the immeasurable by Saturn, his parent [. . .]. His father was Saturn, the cycle of time turned upon itself, and closed" (319). Bely's readers surely remembered that, in Greco-Roman mythology, a son of Chronos-Saturn can survive only by fighting and defeating his father.

Bely's use of overlapping images in Nikolai's dream reflects Freud's view that the overlapping of meanings is the most difficult but at the same time also most rewarding aspect of the interpretation of dreams.[11] In his dream, Nikolai at once takes the place of a Chinese mandarin, a god, Chronos-Saturn, Senator Ableukhov, their ancestor Ab-Lai, and a hallowed Turanian. In this way, he gains the authority that in reality belongs to his father. By dint of his family history and despite his westernized appearance and mentality, Apollon Apollonovich embodies destructive, dark, and gloomy Asiatic heredity. His social status and position as a government official similarly fuse the Russian empire's irreconcilable Eastern and Western elements. In Freud's "Dream of the Uncle," the purpose of the dream comes down to vengeance: "Turning the tables on his Excellency with vengeance. He refused to appoint me *professor*," writes Freud, "and I retaliated in the dream by stepping into his shoes" (226). The purpose of Nikolai's dream is also vengeance:

> And so with breathless, soul-searing enthusiasm the ancient Turanian, clothed for the time being in the mortal coil of an Aryan, rushed up to a pile of old

> exercise books, in which the premises of the metaphysics he had developed were sketched out; he grasped the exercise books with a mixture of embarrassment and joy; all the exercise books in front of him amounted to a single, immense undertaking—the business of his whole life (they could be compared to the sum of Apollon Apollonovich's business). The business of his life was however more than the business of *his* life: a single, immense Mongol business shone through in the notes under all points and all paragraphs: the great mission entrusted to him before his birth: the mission of destroyer. (317–18)

Nikolai Apollonovich's Aryan form is temporary: underneath the outer layer of Western civilization he remains, by virtue of heredity, an ancient Turanian, an exponent of the East, who has unconsciously devoted his life to one cause only, that of destruction. This enormous cause is defined and displayed before Nikolai in all his exercise books, which stand for his current intellectual endeavors as a rational and creative European; yet they also "shine through" with a different message, that of the chaotic, irrational, and destructive Mongol East. The same exercise books represent the sum total of Apollon Apollonovich's deeds throughout his life, as if Nikolai, while writing them, stepped into his father's shoes. In the dream, Nikolai identifies Apollon Apollonovich as "the old Turanian who once upon a time instructed him in all the rules of wisdom" (319)—a statement referring as much to the senator's European rationality and longing for order as to his hereditary Asiatic, cruel and destructive, authoritarianism. For Nikolai, to take his father's place in the dream is to bring vengeance on the senator's head by means of that same wisdom the son inherited from the father. "Paragraph four," recites Nikolai to his Turanian guest (doubling as Apollon Apollonovich) from an exercise book: "The destruction of the Aryan world by the system of values. Conclusion: the age-old Mongol business" (318).

In Freudian terms, this is a fulfillment of Nikolai's wish, or the latent content of his dream. His tender feeling (*nezhnost'*) for Buddhism (235/316), an emblem of the East, belongs to the dream's manifest content, disguising the real wish. Nikolai Apollonovich, the narrator reminds us, remains a Neo-Kantian (316)—that is, a rational adept of a European philosophical tradition (see Timothy Langen's essay in this volume). As a Neo-Kantian, he believes in Europe's immutability. In the name of that immutability, Nikolai wishes to have the authority to destroy his father as the embodiment of Russia's Mongol element. His political and cultural wish, then, is inexorably linked to patricide—a link that is of paramount importance to Freud in *The Interpretation of Dreams*. However, the Mongol mission encoded in Nikolai's Asiatic heredity does not target the East, but rather the West. By wishing, in the name of Western civilization, to destroy his father, or the Mongol element of Russia that the senator emblematizes, Nikolai Apollonovich will only uphold the Mongol cause, as Bely sees it, assuring the continuity of civilizational destruction. In other words, by killing Apollon Apollonovich, Nikolai would be killing himself. Hence the father's remark in the dream: "You planned to blow me up; and therefore everything is perishing" (320). Nikolai's partial response, "It was not you, but . . ." (320), leaves room for the dream's interpretation. The first interpretation belongs to the dreamer himself: waking up, Nikolai calls what he saw a nightmare (321). Nudging the reader, once again, to turn to Freud for ways to interpret the dream, Bely's narrator links it to Nikolai's childhood—"His childhood nightmares had returned [. . .] his age-old childhood delirium was returning" (321)—in an allusion to the theory Freud proposed in *The Interpretation of Dreams* concerning "infantile material as a source of dreams" (221).

Nikolai's Dream and *Petersburg*'s Oedipal Scenario

The main theme of *Petersburg*—patricide—also functions as an emblem of freedom. Nikolai's political and cultural wish to destroy Mongolism is suppressed (censored) in his dream, but his patricidal wish, usually suppressed in his waking life, appears completely undisguised here: "So now he planned explosion: he planned to throw a bomb at his father" (320). It is as if Bely deliberately tailored Nikolai's nightmare to Freud's theory, in *The Interpretation of Dreams*, regarding dreams about the death of loved relatives. In such dreams, Freud argues, a repressed wish could elude all censorship by the dreamer's consciousness, passing into the dream "without modification" (281–305).

Freud insisted on the hereditary nature of rivalry between fathers and sons, looking for proofs of its perennial centrality to human experience in Greco-Roman mythology. To this end, in *The Interpretation of Dreams*, he paid special attention to the infanticidal father-figure Chronos-Saturn, a symbol of inexorable time that swallowed everything it sired; and to the myth of Oedipus, which cast the same filial rivalry from the vantage point of patricidal sons (281). Rejecting the traditional interpretation of Sophocles's *Oedipus Rex* (429 BCE) as a tragedy of destiny, Freud presented the play as all about the "process of revealing" the truth—namely, that Oedipus was Laïus and Jocasta's son, and also his father's slayer. Freud then likened this "process of revealing" in *Oedipus Rex* to "the work of psychoanalysis" (281), which was all about deepening an individual's self-knowledge. As a result, the modernist artists privy to Freud's work interpreted the myth of Oedipus, following its reading in *The Interpretation of Dreams*, as a moral and intellectual quest "to escape fate and acquire self-knowledge" (199).

Modernists across Europe found in Freud's reading of patricide a powerful metaphor for their own aesthetic, philosophical, moral, and spiritual break with the past, and their struggle for the freedom of thought and creative expression. Characteristically, to proclaim his generation's liberating artistic revolt, Gustav Klimt's poster advertising the first show of the Vienna Secession movement (1897)—a group of modernist painters rebelling against Austria's authoritarian and conservative artistic establishment—featured Theseus slaying the Minotaur to free the youth of Athens from being devoured by the monster. Klimt thus used a myth echoing that of Oedipus, who freed all travelers in Thebes from another monster, the Sphynx. This larger, pan-European context helps us recreate the full meaning of Bely's recourse to Freudian imagery and vocabulary in *Petersburg* as a novel partaking in the transnational modernist revolt, the way Bely wanted it to be read by his original Russian interpretive community. In *Petersburg*, Bely discusses different aspects of patricide, turning this theme into a universal emblem with multiple functions—political, aesthetic, spiritual, and cultural. As mentioned earlier, Nikolai's dream prominently features the myth of Chronos-Saturn, effectively inscribing the son's feelings toward his father into an age-old mythical pattern whose significance Bely's contemporaries, and the author himself, understood in tandem with recent developments in the new science of psychology.

This essay has taken only one example, Nikolai Apollonovich's dream, to illustrate Bely's intellectual debt to the new science of psychology; but *Petersburg* is full of instances of readily identifiable images, notions, and allusions to Sigmund Freud and his disciples. The second installment of Bely's unfinished trilogy, *Petersburg* was meant to be a kind of landscape of the philosophy, art, literature, and science of the time, as well as a description of the frustrations and inner struggles of the contemporary human being as shaped by modernity. In turn-of-the-century Europe, patricide had become an emblem of freedom and liberation, and Bely chose to use it also to express Russia's frustration with its plight of being stuck between East and West.

Notes

1. For a more detailed treatment of this topic, see Magnus Ljunggren, *The Dream of Rebirth: The Study of Andrej Belyj's Novel "Peterburg"* (Stockholm: Almqvist and Wiksell, 1982). Judith Wermuth-Atkinson, *The Red Jester: Andrei Bely's "Petersburg" as a Novel of the*

European Modern (Berlin: LIT, 2012). For reasons of spatial economy, this essay examines only Freud's impact on Bely's artistic imagination. In my book *The Red Jester*, the reader will also find a discussion of Bely's intellectual debt to Carl Gustav Jung and other contemporary psychologists.

2. Martin Miller, *Freud and the Bolsheviks: Psychoanalysis in Imperial Russia and the Soviet Union* (New Haven: Yale University Press, 1998), 3–53, 180n13.

3. Sigmund Freud, *The History of the Psychoanalytic Movement*, Nervous and Mental Disease Monograph Series 25 (New York: Nervous and Mental Disease Publishing Company, 1917), 25.

4. Miller, *Freud and the Bolsheviks*, 27–34.

5. Miller, *Freud and the Bolsheviks*, 41. Wermuth-Atkinson, *The Red Jester*, 105.

6. Ljunggren, *The Dream of Rebirth*, 10, 32, 138. Miller, *Freud and the Bolsheviks*, 34. See also Alexander Etkind, *Eros of the Impossible: The History of Psychoanalysis in Russia*, tr. Noah and Maria Rubins (Boulder: Westview Press, 1997), 39–80.

7. Sigmund Freud, *The Interpretation of Dreams*, tr. A. A. Brill (New York: Macmillan, 1913).

8. Andrei Belyi, *Peterburg*, ed. L. Dolgopolov (Moscow: Nauka, 1981). Andrei Bely, *Petersburg*, tr. John Elsworth (London: Pushkin Press, 2009). Throughout this essay, single page references designate the novel's English translation. In dual page references, the first number designates the Russian original. While I cite John Elsworth's translation for the sake of consistency with other essays in this volume, in my book on Bely—*The Red Jester: Andrei Bely's "Petersburg" as a Novel of the European Modern*—I used David McDuff's 1995 translation, which seems to me more suitable for exemplifying my arguments.

9. We should distinguish Freud's treatment of the Oedipus myth in *The Interpretation of Dreams* from his later writings on the Oedipus complex, such as "The Dissolution of the Oedipus Complex," published in 1924.

10. Andrei Belyi, "Merezhkovskii. Trilogiia," in *Arabeski* (Moscow: Musaget, 1911), 420.

11. See the footnote text in the fifth chapter of the original German edition: Sigmund Freud, *Studienausgabe*, Vol. 2: *Die Traumdeutung*, ed. A. Mitscherlich et al. (Frankfurt: S. Fischer Verlag, 1989), 227.

Petersburg and Contemporary Racial Thought

HENRIETTA MONDRY

Andrei Bely came of age as an artist and thinker at the time when European intellectual life was haunted by anxiety about spiritual, psychological, and physical degeneration. The purported cause of this degeneration was economic and social modernity, which, according to common wisdom, wreaked havoc in the minds and bodies of European males.[1] The concurrent rise of racial thought, which imagined humanity as an agglomeration of races engaged in a Darwinian struggle for survival, exacerbated this anxiety by theorizing Christian Europeans as the Aryan race whose purported decline benefited two rivals: the Semitic race—a newly coined designator for Jews as Christian Europe's perennial Other; and the Yellow or Mongol race—a catchall concept vaguely referring to "Asians," variously defined in contrast to Europeans. Racial theorists particularly feared the contamination of the weakened Aryan race by its Jewish and Asian foes, whom they often conflated in the image of a single biological adversary bent on sapping from within the bodies and minds of the heirs to European civilization. This essay will explore the place of contemporary racial thought in Andrei Bely's *Petersburg*, a novel that partook in the pan-European discourse about biological, spiritual, and cultural decline and degeneration.[2]

Bely and the Racial Thought of His Day

Abounding in ethnic markers, *Petersburg* transforms perceived racial characteristics into symbols informing the novel's political messages. A student of anthropology during his university years, Bely always maintained that interest in sciences was an important component of his desire to create art.[3] It is with this information in mind that one must approach the topic of human biological races in *Petersburg*. In Bely's day, anthropology was a discipline that accepted race as a scientific category, and the writer drew extensively on racial science while working on his novel. At the same time, from an early age, thanks to his family upbringing, Bely was influenced by popular racialism, which thrived throughout Europe as a by-product of current anthropological theories and of the ancillary political ideology of racism.[4] Both were popularized in Russia by such international best sellers as Houston Stewart Chamberlain's *Foundations of the Nineteenth Century* (1899) and Otto Weininger's *Sex and Character* (1903).

Russian racial thought owed much to H. S. Chamberlain's terminology, taxonomy, and conspiracy theories, which capitalized on the obsessive Judeophobia of the British author's father-in-law, the German composer Richard Wagner. Among other things, Chamberlain alerted Aryans to the threat of racial contamination carried by Semites—"a mongrel race that always retains [its] mongrel character," subverting other races through miscegenation.[5] Chamberlain was read and discussed in Bely's circle.[6] Not accidentally, we find echoes of the British author's contradictory vision of race, as both fluid and immutable, in several of *Petersburg*'s personages.

Treating the moral, intellectual, and physical traits of individuals as the biologically predetermined characteristics of their respective racial groups, European intellectuals endowed the concept of race with all-inclusive meaning, as "the most significant determinant of man's past, present and future."[7] Among the races whose existence was taken for granted, the Semitic and Mongol ones provoked particular apprehension thanks to the mass westward migration of Jews after the Russian pogroms of the 1880s; the growth of the Chinese diaspora in the West; and Japan's victory in its 1904–5 war with Russia.[8] A possible alliance between China and Japan, for a future attack on the West, formed a key part of contemporary racial paranoia. In Russia, Japan's military triumph coincided with a new wave of anti-Jewish pogroms. The ambient anti-Semitism of Russian society found new fodder in the alleged connection between Japanese and Jewish interests, surmised from the fact that the Rothschild banking family had made loans to Japan, thereby stoking conspiracy theories about the Jewish quest for world domination through international finance, as foretold in *The Protocols of the Elders of Zion*—an anti-Semitic fabrication by the tsar's secret police, first published in Russia in 1903 and reissued in 1911, in the year Bely began writing *Petersburg*. This new edition of the *Protocols* was appended to the apocalyptic treatise by a notorious anti-Semite, Sergei Nilus, whose prophesy of the Antichrist's imminent reign on earth through Jewish machinations came out of a publishing house belonging to the Russian Orthodox Church.[9]

And as if this were not enough, dramatic events coinciding with Bely's work on *Petersburg* kept the Russian public focused on the "Jewish question." In September 1911, just as Bely sat down to write the novel's opening chapters, Prime Minister Pëtr Stolypin was assassinated by a Russian-Jewish terrorist, Dmitrii Bogrov, a rumored double agent embodying what Russian anti-Semites had always imagined as the simultaneous treacherousness and subversiveness of the Jews. The years 1911–13 were also marked by the Beilis Affair, so named after Kiev's Jewish resident Mendel Beilis, who was accused in March 1911 of ritually killing a Christian boy. Beilis was acquitted two years later, after a protracted and widely publicized trial. Russia's equivalent of the Dreyfus Affair, the Beilis Affair had an overtly racial character, with forensic experts and anthropologists called upon to voice their opinions on the alleged practice of ritual murder among Jews as a psychological peculiarity of their race. This historical context enhanced the apocalyptic vision of Russia's impending doom in *Petersburg*, a vision grounded in acute apprehension regarding the two perils, Yellow and Semitic, which menaced not only Russia but all of Europe.[10]

Petersburg's protagonists, Apollon Apollonovich and Nikolai Apollonovich Ableukhov, illustrate the impact of the admixture of Asiatic blood on its Aryan bearers. Although their Turkic-Mongolian antecedent converted to Christianity two centuries earlier, the senator and his son still carry physical and psychological characteristics of their Asiatic ancestors. In the novel's economy, Apollon Apollonovich's genetic code is the implicit source of his dictatorial style of governing. Similarly, Nikolai Apollonovich's ethnic origins are in part to blame for his involvement in revolutionary violence. As he dozes off in front of the bomb whose clockwork mechanism he has just set in motion, Nikolai dreams of his Asiatic ancestors because "his heredity was making itself felt; heredity was coursing into consciousness; in his sclerotic veins his heredity was beating in millions of yellow blood corpuscles" (316).[11] Both men act as incarnations of ancient Turanians—understood in *Petersburg*, following H. S. Chamberlain's usage, as Turkic and Persian peoples—on a mission to destroy the Russian Empire. (For other meanings inherent in Bely's idea of the Turanian-Aryan contrast, see Maria Carlson's essay in this volume.)[12] Nikolai's dreams reveal this unconscious call of his ancestors, a hereditary drive that materializes in his terrorist activities, linking him with other actors in the Yellow cum Semitic conspiracy, above all the crypto-Jew Lippanchenko. In his most elaborate dream, narrated in the section "The Day of Judgment" (chapter 5), Nikolai realizes that he is the current reincarnation of his Turanian ancestor come to life "in the flesh and blood of the Russian imperial nobility of ancient lineage, with the task of fulfilling an age-old, sacred purpose: to dislodge all foundations; in the degenerate Aryan blood the Ancient Dragon was to flare up and consume everything in its flame; the age-old East was scattering a hail of invisible bombs into our time" (317).

In *Petersburg*, the overlap of the Yellow Peril with the universal Jewish plot is articulated by a newspaper editor who, chatting with other guests at the Tsukatovs' ball, insists on connecting the Russo-Japanese war to "the Jews who threaten us with Mongol invasion and with sedition." The same editor sees the Jewish hand in the Chinese Boxer Rebellion and attributes all international and domestic troubles to the universal Judeo-Masonic conspiracy (205–6). The latter theory was all too familiar to Bely's contemporaries, courtesy of Russia's right-wing press, whose anti-Semitic imagination was instrumental in articulating and popularizing the main ideas of *The Protocols of the Elders of Zion*. At the same time, Russia's liberal press is treated in *Petersburg* as controlled by the Jews (240, 242, and 299). The cover of "one of those *yid* magazines," as Apollon Apollonovich puts it, caricatures the senator against the "bloody background of a burning Russia" (16). For the senator, as for the political conservatives among Bely's original readership, the journal's red cover invoked both revolutionary violence stoked by the Jews and the Russian blood spilt by the Japanese in Manchuria with help from Jewish financiers.

The novel's omnipresent and most evasive character, Lippanchenko, is a Mongol and a Semite at once, despite his nominally Ukrainian origins. Simultaneously working for the revolutionary cause and for the tsarist police, he invoked in the minds of Bely's first readers the recent scandalous revelation of the prominent Russian-Jewish revolutionary Evno Azef as a double agent (see Lynn Patyk's essay in this volume). Russian anti-Semites derived Azef's duplicitous actions from his Semitic race.[13] Bely used Azef's physical features in his description of Lippanchenko's appearance.[14] But he also made sure that Lippanchenko's physique would lend itself to a racial interpretation allowing the reader to brood over the composite fluidity of the traitor's crypto-Jewishness, evocative of current anthropological theories of race.

We find one such theory in Viktor Vorob´ëv's *Great Russians: An Essay on the Physical Type* (1902). Published during Bely's studies at Moscow University, the book addressed the influence of Mongol and Turkic peoples on Russians and Ukrainians. Vorob´ëv claimed that history and geography had conspired to leave Ukrainians with significantly more Mongol and Turkic biological traits than Russians had. He also noted that those Ukrainians who were moving up north (like Bely's Lippanchenko) were passing on some of these contaminating racial elements to Russians.[15] And as for the Semitic ingredient in the double agent's persona, the reader of Bely's day could find its explanation in the anthropological theories concerning the racial influence of the Khazars among the Slavic inhabitants of the Black Sea region.[16] A Turkic people with a state spanning today's southern Ukraine, Russia, and the Caucasus (that state had dissipated in the tenth century), the Khazars had been ruled by an elite professing Judaism—a fact that, for a racial thinker, would have been enough to justify the combination of Ukrainian, Turkic, Semitic, and Mongol elements in Lippanchenko's shifting and evasive ethnicity.

Lippanchenko's Frontal Bone and the Question of Race

While Lippanchenko is modeled on the historical character of Azef, he remains, above all, a cultural construct and, therefore, a product of Bely's racial imagination. It was as such an artifact that Lippanchenko became recognizable as a Jew in Bely's interpretive community.[17] Describing Lippanchenko's physique, his creator used markers borrowed from anthropological literature. In the subchapter "Frontal bones" (chapter 6), *Petersburg*'s narrator gives a detailed craniological description of Lippanchenko's head: "So a careful analysis of this monstrous head revealed only one thing: the head was that of a premature baby; someone's feeble brain had been prematurely encased in layers of fat and bone; at the same time as the frontal bone protruded outwards to excess in the arcs above the eyebrows (have a look at a gorilla's skull)" (368). In Bely's day, this description had definite underpinnings of racial science. The term *lobnaia kost'*— frontal bone—had been previously used with very specific connotations by the Russian anthropologist Dmitrii Anuchin. In his essay "On Certain Anomalies of the Human Skull and Especially on Their Distribution According to Races" (1880), Anuchin argued that the forehead and temple bones covered the parts of the brain responsible for abstract thinking; in pathological cases, rapid tissue growth around these bones reduced human intelligence, whereas the size and development of these bones reflected the innate intellectual abilities of races.[18] Bely knew Anuchin's work since he studied under his supervision at Moscow University in 1902–3.[19]

Describing Lippanchenko's head, Bely's narrator also mentions that it exhibits tell-tale signs of brain disintegration, "known in the vulgar parlance as softening of the brain" (368). This functions as a marker of psychopathology and madness that anchors Lippanchenko's persona in the opinion of contemporary psychiatric science that Jews are particularly prone to psychological ailments.[20] The Jews of the European imagination functioned both as a personification of mental degeneration and as a warning about this negative effect of modernity, which also threatened Christian Europeans. Finally, Lippanchenko is likened to a chimera that grows and grins like a real Mongol (380–81) on the yellow wallpaper of Dudkin's room. This image conveys the dual, Semitic and Yellow, peril carried by Lippanchenko, whose ethnic hybridity Bely pathologizes in anthropological, racial, and quasi-scientific terms as something that, in itself, presents a danger to pure-blooded Aryans.

Race and Music

Another reference to Lippanchenko's frontal bone appears in the episode where he plays violin and sings his "swansong" shortly before Dudkin murders the traitor to the revolutionary cause. "No, his frontal bone could not understand," observes Bely's narrator with respect to the performer's inability truly to comprehend the Russian music he played, for "his brow was small" (516; *lob byl malen'kii*).[21] Lippanchenko can extract sounds from his violin and can sing in a pleasant bass. But, in the narrator's opinion, he cannot grasp the meaning of the romance he is performing, for this musical genre is supposed to express the spirit of the Russian soul and this essentialist spirit is racially alien to Lippanchenko.

Bely theorized a connection between music and race in his article "Mass-Produced Culture" (1909), which distinguished between Aryan and Semitic music; for, "while culture is a process of spiritual education and growth, race is its point of departure."[22] Jews, then, are biologically incapable of understanding, let alone producing, European art and music. Their artistic production is marked by the cosmopolitan eclecticism of "mass-produced culture" devoid of national individuality. Bely's essay relied on the writings of his friend Emilii Metner, a music and literary critic, publisher, and Russian promoter of Richard Wagner's ideas about the superiority of Aryan art over its Semitic antipode.[23] Of special relevance to Lippanchenko's musical skills, and to the singing of his guest — another racially suspect and demoniac character, Shishnarfne — is Bely's quote from Metner, in "Mass-Produced Culture," that Jewish musicians "try to create affected vibrating sounds, steeped in sweet sappiness of southern passions, barbarically destroying noble European style" (77). Lippanchenko's and Shishnarfne's sweet and passionate singing falls into this Wagnerian notion of Semitic music. The nominally Persian Shishnarfne, whose fluid ethnicity is further problematized by his geographic association with the cosmopolitan and heavily Jewish city of Odessa, is implicitly assimilated to crypto-Jews like Lippanchenko by virtue of his musical performance. Shishnarfne's indeterminate origins also link him to the area around the Black and Caspian seas, suggesting to Bely's racially minded readers the presence of Mongol/Tatar (Yellow), Turanian, and Khazar (Jewish) elements in the personage's menacingly hybrid racial make-up.

To be sure, Bely's racial outlook would have carried a Wagnerian stamp even without Metner's intellectual mediation, for the writer had become interested in the art and thought of the German composer back in the university days. Among Wagner's contributions to racial thought was his critique of the sounds allegedly produced by Jewish singers, a criticism rooted in the racialization of the Jewish body in the European imagination as radically different from that of Europe's Christian (Aryan) inhabitants.[24] In *Petersburg*, there is evidence of direct borrowings from Wagner's pamphlet "Judaism in Music" (1869), whose subject matter must have acquired renewed urgency for Bely in the spring of 1912, when he attended three Wagnerian operas while writing *Petersburg* in Brussels.[25]

A case in point is the description of Shishnarfne's singing, as witnessed, significantly, by a Russian—Aleksandr Ivanovich Dudkin—upon his arrival in Lippanchenko's home. I am quoting it in my own translation: "The most important thing was the voice [...]. The voice was completely cracked, impossibly loud and sweet; and moreover: the voice had an impermissible accent. At the dawn of the twentieth century it was not done to sing like that: it was simply shameless: people in Europe do not sing that way."[26] Shishnarfne's voice here becomes a marker of race, together with his racialized singing style. In a similar fashion, Wagner's essay links what the composer imagines as Jewish speech and phonetic articulation to the alleged inability of Jews to sing in a manner pleasing to Europeans. Wagner writes: "Song is just Talk aroused to highest passion: Music is the speech of Passion. All that worked repellently upon us in [the Jew's] outward appearance and his speech, makes us take to our heels at last in his Song [...]. Very naturally, in Song—the vividest and most indisputable expression of the personal emotional-being—the peculiarity of the Jewish nature attains for us its climax of distastefulness; and on any natural hypothesis, we might hold the Jew adapted for every sphere of art, excepting that whose basis lies in Song."[27] Bely thus encodes aspects of Wagner's racial musicology into the singing and violin playing of his non-Aryan protagonists, leaving it up to the reader to detect the anti-Semitic subtext of his composite yet essentially crypto-Jewish characters.

Race, Gender, and Sexuality

The excessive sensuality of Lippanchenko's singing denotes his excessive materiality—a stock feature of Christian Europe's imaginary Jews. Lippanchenko's Jewish carnality is played out through his relationship with a female consort, Zoia Fleisch. She too is cast in unmistakably racialized terms. In keeping with the Jewish stereotypes common in Bely's day, aspects of race, gender and sexuality converge in Zoia's persona. Her appearance is described as belonging to the general "category of sultry Oriental brunettes."[28] But some clear markers—beginning with name and surname—expose Zoia Fleisch's cryptic Jewishness.

A name of Greek origin, Zoia is etymologically and phonetically related to "zoo," suggesting proximity to the animal world. This biological identifier fits the racial stereotype of the Jew as one who is closer to nature than to culture on the evolutionary scale. Zoia's surname, Fleisch, is of Germanic/Yiddish origin, and it can mean both "meat" and "flesh," further emphasizing her materiality and carnality. Christianity has traditionally defined itself as the religion of the spirit, encoding Judaism as its carnal opposite in order to explain the refusal of most Jews to embrace Christianity by their inability to see spiritual truth, an inability that consigns practitioners of Judaism to the realm of the material. This theological tradition of casting Jews as people of the flesh, whose carnality provides a didactic foil to Christianity's spiritual ideal, received a secular reinterpretation in nineteenth-century racial thought, which viewed Jews, through the Darwinian lens, as lagging behind Aryans in evolutionary terms: Jews were said to be primitively animalistic and sensual in contrast to the civilized, restrained, and cerebral Europeans.[29]

The same ideas informed the stereotype of the seductive and dangerous Jewess, extensively explored in turn-of-the-century art as a symbol of degeneration amalgamating two major threats to the European Christian male—unchecked female sexuality and racial miscegenation.[30] Like the innumerable Judiths and Salomes of fin-de-siècle painting, who lure males with sexual wiles only to destroy them, Zoia Fleisch is deceitfully seductive and, on closer examination, as repulsive as a predatory Siren. Bely's narrator shows her face changing from young and attractive to old and repellent, since what first looks like a beautiful face turns out to be an artifact produced by skillful makeup and a wig

(505–6). Zoia is one of those changelings who are particularly dangerous in the economy of Bely's novel because they elude clear definition. To unmask her, *Petersburg*'s narrator deploys stock Jewish racial markers—a large, hooked nose and black, bulging eyes (358, 506–7). In Bely's day, these imagined loci of Jewish biological difference were discussed in medical and anthropological literature as indicative of the psychological and spiritual qualities of the Semitic race.[31] Finally, the narrator's remark that Zoia's nose is akin to a hawk's beak (509) denotes her predatory nature as a sexual temptress whom we first encounter in her "habitual coquettish conversation" with a male guest.[32]

For Bely's interpretive community, Zoia's nervousness also functioned as a racial marker. Contemporary medical and anthropological sciences insisted on the hysterical predisposition of the Jews, variously attributing it to hereditary and acquired characteristics of their race, from inbreeding to unhealthy urban lifestyles.[33] Another tell-tale sign of her racial origins is Zoia's peculiar smell, which plays on the belief, still widespread in nineteenth-century popular cultures and medical literature alike, that Jews emitted a particular odor. Originating as a theological metaphor for Jewish refusal to embrace Christianity—*foetor Judaicus*, or the stench of Jewish disbelief—this notion, like many elements of Christian theology concerning the Jewish Other, became literalized in European folklore and high art. Here, the initial religious explanation of the revolting odor of the Jews as Satan's children was eventually replaced by an array of secular motivations, ranging from poor hygiene to exotic diets to racial biology.[34] Characteristically, meeting Zoia, Dudkin recoils from the bad smell that even her heavy perfume cannot hide (358, 365). Surrounding the malodorous Zoia by devils incarnate, Shishnarfne and Lippanchenko, Bely prods his reader to bridge racial biology with the more traditional, Christian religious construction of Jewishness.

Bely's probable model for such bridging can be found in the work of a fellow Russian modernist, Vasilii Rozanov, whose writings on sexuality the author of *Petersburg* read and admired. In these writings, Rozanov turned to Jews and Judaism as a positive alternative to Christian asceticism in sexual matters, grounding his racialized ideas of Jewish sensuality and keen sense of smell in Jewish religious practices. In Rozanov's writings, to be sure, the qualities ascribed to the Jews easily changed evaluative connotations, according to the writer's rhetorical needs, from positive to derogatory. Bely could thus take away from Rozanov's oeuvre the vision of the Jew as an amalgam of modern racial and ancient religious stereotypes. Like the crypto-Jews of *Petersburg*, Rozanov's Jews possessed biologically atavistic bodies emitting a smell that had to be concealed. At the same time, theirs were non-Christian bodies, whose odor signified the divine curse striking the Jews for rejecting Jesus Christ as their Savior.[35] Characteristically, during the Beilis Affair, even as Bely was hard at work on *Petersburg*, Rozanov authored a series of articles that capitalized on his ideas about Jewish carnality, sensuality, and exaggerated olfactory sensitivity to argue that the atavistic brain cells of the Semitic race could have forced Mendel Beilis to commit the crime for which he stood accused, the ritual murder of a Christian child.[36]

Pairing Zoia with Lippanchenko, Bely appeals to his readers' knowledge of medical and anthropological theories about Jewish sexuality. Zoia is driven by physical desire. In the scene preceding Lippanchenko's murder, he declines Zoia's amorous advances. This exposes Lippanchenko's masculinity as deficient. Such pairing of an oversexed Jewess with an emasculated Jewish male was part of the contemporary racial discourse that explained Jewish women's supposedly excessive sexual drive by the inability of male Jews to satisfy them.[37] Later, as Lippanchenko undresses in his bedroom, with Dudkin hiding there and watching, the narrator describes the Jew's chest in terms evocative of female breasts ("two effeminate convexities were clearly visible on his hirsute chest," 519), effectively casting his body as hermaphroditic, in a sign of biological atavism associated with Jews in racial science. Lippanchenko's body emblematizes the fear of degeneration haunting the European imagination: it brings together anti-Semitism, general racial attitudes, and misogyny to articulate its agony over the perceived decline of the Aryan male as the principal creator and guardian of Western civilization's cultural and spiritual values.[38]

The scene in the bedroom ends with the mad assassin Dudkin sitting astride Lippanchenko's corpse in a powerful trope that showcases the elimination of the emasculated and sexually ambivalent Jewish body, which is emblematic of the ongoing decline of the European cum Christian civilization. Stabbed with a pair of scissors, Lippanchenko dies like a stuck pig, recalling the standard Judeophobic association of Jews with swine.[39] In a gruesome inversion, the scene parodies the Bronze Horseman monument in St. Petersburg: instead of Peter the Great, Russia's westernizing emperor riding his stallion, Dudkin rides the slaughtered Lippanchenko in another symbol of the downfall of Western civilization.

Last but not least, we must discuss Otto Weininger's *Sex and Character* (1903) as one of Bely's major sources for racializing Jewish sexuality and gender.[40] An assimilated Viennese Jew, Weininger subscribed to current racial theories. Central to his psycho-biological notion of the relationship between the masculine and feminine elements in human nature was the dichotomy between the Jew and the Aryan. The Jew, according to *Sex and Character*, was closer to the feminine element. Bely could have found useful, for the purposes of articulating the dual Semitic/Mongol menace hovering over Western civilization, Weininger's insistence on the parallelism of Jewish and Chinese gender dynamics. Weininger saw signs of femininity in Chinese men's alleged lack of facial hair and in their customary braids. This braid found its way into *Petersburg* together with other markers of the Yellow Peril, such as "squint eyes" and yellow skin. The Ableukhovs' valet, Semenych, mentions the male braid as that feature which the Russian popular imagination finds most fascinating in "those pig-tailed Chinamen" (459)—literally, long-braided (*dlinnokosye*; Belyi, *Peterburg*, 341)—a feature that, like Lippanchenko's hermaphroditic body, feminizes a racial Other, following stock practices in the current racial discourse. Fittingly for racial anthropology, Weininger also wrote about the influence of Asian blood on Jewish biological traits, such as skin color and facial shapes. Bely's conflation of Semitic and Mongol markers in *Petersburg* both borrowed from and contributed to the contemporary European racial discourse disseminating this cultural construct along with other popular stereotypes.[41]

The Russo-Japanese War, Race, and Russian Anthropology

Russia's defeat in the war with Japan—a central element of *Petersburg*'s historical backdrop—did much to inform the racial discourse of Bely's time. In the writer's modernist milieu, this war was understood in the apocalyptic terms fusing Christian theology with racial science (see David Bethea's essay in this volume). These terms had been set by the Russian poet and philosopher Vladimir Solovyov, whose poem "Pan-Mongolism" (1894) and ultimate essay—*Three Conversations about War, Progress, and the End of World History, with a Short Story about the Antichrist* (1900)—visualized "the last days" as the clash of races ushering in Christ's Second Coming. Solovyov vividly depicted a new Mongol invasion of Europe under Japanese leadership—an "explicitly racist variant on the theme of the Yellow Peril" that helped articulate, several years after Solovyov's death, the Russian modernist understanding of the Russo-Japanese War.[42]

If Bely had ventured outside modernist culture, he would have found that Russian anthropological science reacted to the war in similarly racial terms. For example, Ivan Sikorskii's 1904 public lecture, delivered at a Red Cross fund-raising event, laid out the "Characteristics of Black, Yellow and White Races in Connection with the Question of the Russo-Japanese War." In his lecture, the eminent psychiatrist and aspiring anthropologist insisted that, "in wartime, Yellow races easily became fanatical and gave themselves to feeling and passion rather than to rationality and reason."[43] Following the racial discourse of the time, Sikorskii included the Chinese and the Mongols among the "Yellow races," raising issues typologically similar to those informing Bely's *Petersburg*. As Sikorskii wrote:

> In the past three hundred years, the Russians have engaged in a process of peaceful assimilation in Siberia, reaching the Pacific Ocean. Anthropological research on the peoples of Siberia shows that the Russians have already achieved a great deal in their biological influence: everywhere, as a result of mixed marriages, there has appeared a healthy, strong, and spiritually advanced population that has absorbed the Russian soul and the Russian national spirit [. . .]. The Japanese have suddenly and rudely interfered with this peaceful work of nature and this process of mutual cooperation, trying to roll back the gigantic wheel of history. In this war, the Russian people have heard a historical call to stand up in defence of their historical mission of pouring healthy juices into the flesh and blood, into the nerves and soul of the Mongol peoples for whom the Russians are the supreme contributing spiritual and biological force.[44]

Thinking in biological categories, and imagining Russians as carriers of superior Aryan qualities, Sikorskii and his fellow scientists justified the Russian Empire's eastward and southern expansion by the prerogatives of racial eugenics, which benefited, physically and spiritually, the colonized populations of Siberia and Central Asia. But this triumphalist logic contained the implicit threat of a reverse process, whereby the colonized races could biologically alter the Aryans, who were increasingly weakened by the negative impact of socio-economic modernity.

Bely's mentally unstable revolutionary, Aleksandr Ivanovich Dudkin, suffers from terrifying hallucinatory visions of Japanese, Tatars, Semites, Mongols, and other "oriental persons" that, fittingly, appear against the background of Jewish Cabbalistic signs (117). Dudkin's feverish visions conveyed Bely's own fears, evident in his correspondence with friends, about the Yellow/Semitic Peril as the hereditary, destructive influence of alien biology on the Russian people, imagined as paragons of Aryan virtue.[45] Bely's apprehension of the peoples of different "blood" drew, simultaneously, on contemporary racial science and on popular racial stereotypes, whose urgency grew in tandem with the multiethnic Russian Empire's deepening socio-political crisis that makes up the historical backdrop for *Petersburg*'s dramatic action.

Notes

1. I would like to thank Leonid Livak for sharing with me his own significant expertise on the subject.

2. Arkadii Bliumbaum, "Apollon i liagushka," in *Na rubezhe dvukh stoletii*, ed. V. Bagno et al. (Moscow: NLO, 2009), 70–85.

3. Andrei Belyi, *Na rubezhe dvukh stoletii*, ed. A. Lavrov (Moscow: Khudozhestvennaia literatura, 1989), 435.

4. On the thoroughly racialized and anti-Semitic outlook of Bely's father, the professor of mathematics Nikolai Bugaev, see Ilona Svetlikova, *The Moscow Pythagoreans: Mathematics, Mysticism, and Anti-Semitism in Russian Symbolism* (New York: Palgrave Macmillan, 2013), 23–32.

5. Houston Stewart Chamberlain, *Foundations of the Nineteenth Century*, tr. John Lees (New York: Howard Fertig, 1977), 367, 389.

6. Ilona Svetlikova, "Kant-semit i Kant-ariets u Belogo," *Novoe literaturnoe obozrenie* 93 (2008), 62–98.

7. Douglas A. Lorimer, *Colour, Class and the Victorians* (Leicester: Leicester University Press, 1978), 14.

8. Daniel Renshaw, "Prejudice and Paranoia: A Comparative Study of Antisemitism and Sinophobia in Turn-of-the-Century Britain," *Patterns of Prejudice* 50.1 (2016), 44.

9. Sergei Nilus, *Bliz griadushchii antikhrist i tsarstvo diavola na zemle* (Moscow: Tipografiia Sviato-Troitskoi Sergievoi Lavry, 1911).

10. Henrietta Mondry, *Vasily Rozanov and the Body of Russian Literature* (Bloomington: Slavica, 2010), 22–50.

11. Andrei Bely, *Petersburg*, tr. John Elsworth (London: Pushkin Press, 2009).

12. Vladimir Toporov, "O evraziiskoi perspektive romana Andreia Belogo *Peterburg*," in *Peterburgskii tekst v russkoi literature* (Saint-Petersburg: Iskusstvo, 2003), 488–519.

13. Vasilii Rozanov, *Sakharna* (Moscow: Respublika, 1998), 21, 120.

14. Leonid Dolgopolov, *Andrei Belyi i ego roman "Peterburg"* (Moscow: Sovetskii pisatel', 1988), 273.

15. Viktor Vorob'ev, "Velikorussy: ocherk fizicheskogo tipa," in *Russkaia rasovaia teoriia do 1917 goda*, ed. V. Avdeev (Moscow: Feri-V, 2002), 163–94.

16. Vadim Rossman, "Prizraki XIX veka: 'zheltaia opasnost'' i evreiskii zagovor v evropeiskikh stsenariiakh zakata Evropy," *Paralleli* 2–3 (2003), 11–52.

17. Lev Vygotskii, "Literaturnye zametki," *Novyi put'* 47 (1916), 28–32.

18. Avdeev, "Predislovie," *Russkaia rasovaia teoriia*, 20.

19. Belyi, *Na rubezhe dvukh stoletii*, 421–32.

20. Sander Gilman, *The Jew's Body* (New York: Routledge, 1991), 55–76; *Difference and Pathology: Stereotypes of Sexuality, Race, and Madness* (Ithaca: Cornell University Press, 1985), 155–62.

21. Andrei Belyi, *Peterburg*, ed. L. Dolgopolov (Moscow: Nauka, 1981), 383.

22. Andrei Belyi, "Shtempelevannaia kul'tura," *Vesy* 9 (1909), 77.

23. Mikhail Bezrodnyi, "O 'iudoboiazni' Andreia Belogo," *Novoe literaturnoe obozrenie* 28 (1997), 100–25. Magnus Ljunggren, "*Peterburg*—An Anti-Semitic Novel," in *Twelve Essays on Andrej Belyj's "Peterburg"* (Göteborg: Göteborgs Universitet, 2009), 63–72. Monika

Spivak, "Buldukov il' Buldoier . . . razberis'!," in *Andrei Belyi—mistik i sovetskii pisatel'* (Moscow: RGGU, 2006), 324–34.

24. Gilman, *The Jew's Body*, 10–13.

25. Bely to Aleksandr Blok (14.V.1912), in their *Perepiska, 1903–1919*, ed. A. Lavrov (Moscow: Progress-Pleiada, 2001), 455.

26. Belyi, *Peterburg*, 267; cf. page 359 in John Elsworth's translation.

27. Richard Wagner, "Judaism in Music," in *Prose Works*, tr. W. A. Ellis (London: Kegan Paul, 1894), 3:82.

28. Belyi, *Peterburg*, 269 (my translation); cf. page 361 in John Elsworth's translation.

29. Gilman, *The Jew's Body*, 38, 235. Gilman, *Difference and Pathology*, 151–62.

30. Bram Dijkstra, *Idols of Perversity: Fantasies of Feminine Evil in Fin-de-Siècle Culture* (Oxford: Oxford University Press, 1986), 277, 386–401.

31. Umberto Eco, ed., *On Ugliness* (London: Harvill, 2007), 269. Sander Gilman, *Creating Beauty to Cure the Soul: Race and Psychology in the Shaping of Aesthetic Surgery* (Durham: Duke University Press, 1998), 60.

32. Belyi, *Peterburg*, 267 (my translation); cf. page 358 in John Elsworth's translation.

33. Henrietta Mondry, *Exemplary Bodies: Constructing the Jew in Russian Culture* (Boston: Academic Studies Press, 2009), 34–36.

34. Leonid Livak, *The Jewish Persona in the European Imagination: A Case of Russian Literature* (Stanford: Stanford University Press, 2010), 93–97.

35. Vasilii Rozanov, *Opavshie list'ia*, in his *Izbrannoe* (Munich: Neimanis, 1970), 169.

36. Vasilii Rozanov, "Oboniatel'noe i osiazatel'noe otnoshenie evreev k krovi," in *Sakharna*, 276–341.

37. Sander Gilman, *Freud, Race, and Gender* (Princeton: Princeton University Press, 1993), 77.

38. Dijkstra, *Idols of Perversity*, 209.

39. Isaiah Shachar, *The Judensau: A Medieval Anti-Jewish Motif and Its History* (London: The Warburg Institute, 1974).

40. Bezrodnyi, "O 'iudoboiazni' Andreia Belogo," 90.

41. Spivak, "Buldukov il' Buldoier," 330.

42. Milan Hauner, *What Is Asia to Us? Russia's Asian Heartland Yesterday and Today* (Routledge: London, 2013), 112.

43. Ivan Sikorskii, "Kharakteristika chernoi, zheltoi i beloi ras v sviazi s voprosami russko-iaponskoi voiny," in Avdeev, *Russkaia rasovaia teoriia*, 298.

44. Sikorskii, "Kharakteristika chernoi," 301–2.

45. Ljunggren, "*Peterburg*—an Anti-Semitic Novel," 63–72.

Petersburg as Apocalyptic Fiction

DAVID M. BETHEA

Certain literary works, among them Andrei Bely's *Petersburg*, can be usefully described as "apocalyptic fictions" because they are *about the End*. By this I mean the end of history after the Second Coming of Christ, which brings about the final judgment of humanity in order to separate the righteous, who will live forever—first in Christ's millennial kingdom on earth and then in paradise—from the sinful, who will perish in the fires of hell, as prophesied in the conclusion to the Christian Bible, known as the Book of Revelation, or the Apocalypse of John. For the purposes of this essay, I will refer to works of fiction as "apocalyptic" when they: (1) invite the reader to interpret current events through the prism of Revelation; (2) create an intentional confusion, one that cuts across the grain of narrative verisimilitude, by introducing a character who comes from a temporality *beyond* and who presents a revelatory message to other characters still trapped *in history*; and (3) use as the primary means of moving their stories forward the apocalyptic images of horse and train (iron horse). This essay will explore how the idea of the Apocalypse, which is central to Christian eschatology—a branch of theology concerned with the final destiny of humankind—is embedded in the language and narrative of Andrei Bely's *Petersburg* and in the thought patterns of the novel's characters.[1]

Andrei Bely and Russian Modernist Apocalypticism

Between the early 1890s and the aftermath of the October 1917 Bolshevik coup, Russia witnessed an unprecedented explosion of apocalyptic literary fiction, painting, music, and philosophical speculation, most of it emanating from modernist circles. In the early 1900s, such different poets and thinkers as Viacheslav Ivanov, Dmitrii Merezhkovskii, Aleksandr Blok, and Andrei Bely agreed that the end of the world and Christ's millennial kingdom on earth were imminent.[2] Bely worked this urgent apocalyptic expectation into his art and into the legend of his life. Casting himself as a Christ figure—Revelation's "white horseman" and offspring of "Woman Clothed with the Sun," inaugurating the millennial era—Boris Bugaev took the penname of Andrei Bely, or Andrew the White, for eschatological reasons, thanks to the Greek root meaning of Andrei ("courageous") and the apocalyptic symbolism of the white color in the Bible. A crucial source of Bely's apocalypticism was the work of the religious thinker Vladimir Solovyov, whose impact on early Russian modernists rivaled that of Friedrich Nietzsche (see Edith Clowes's essay in this volume). Both philosophers died in 1900—a coincidence Russian modernists interpreted as a watershed auguring the era of radical change prophesied by Solovyov and Nietzsche.

Solovyov's thought had many appealing aspects for Bely's impressionable and speculative mind. Among them was the philosopher's interpretation of the hidden movement and meaning of history. In his quasi-Platonic dialogue *Three Conversations about War, Progress, and the End of World History* (1900)—containing "The Short Tale of the Antichrist," which dramatizes the Apocalypse of John by bringing it closer to contemporary life—Solovyov offers his eschatological account of what history has in store for the twentieth century as a time of "last great wars, civil strife, and revolutions." His narrative anticipates an era marked by a Japanese-led emergence of "Pan-Mongolism"—a unified Asiatic assault on Russia and Europe.[3] In "The Short Tale of the Antichrist," this new Mongol invasion results in a racially destructive intermingling of blood (see Henrietta Mondry's essay in this volume); an ultimate loss of faith; and conditions fertile for the appearance of a Superman, as Nietzsche predicted. From this point on, Solovyov's narrative follows the Book of Revelation since the Superman, whose eloquent genius deceives and captivates humanity, is none other than the Antichrist.[4] As he spreads his reign across the world, the Antichrist sees his supremacy challenged by a multi-denominational group of faithful Christians that makes its way into the desert to await the End. Ultimately, as foretold in the Bible, the Antichrist and his armies are swallowed up by a lake of fire, and the faithful are rewarded by the vision of Christ's Second Coming in the transfigured city of Jerusalem, where He will reign for a thousand years.

Many ideas and images from *Three Conversations* made their way into *Petersburg*. In fact, Bely's novel can be read as his own tale about the Antichrist, a dialogue with the Revelation of John mediated by Solovyov's thought. In *Petersburg*, Bely offers a russified version of the last book of the Bible, casting Peter the Great—the novel's Bronze Horseman—as the Antichrist. Furthermore, Bely's apocalyptic summons to the end of history heeds Solovyov's cue that in the times of social and political turmoil one has to read the signs carefully in order to glimpse the watermark of divine intentionality in destructive human actions. Mention of the Bronze Horseman, whose role in *Petersburg* is crucial, brings us to Bely's modernist repositioning of Pushkin's eponymous narrative poem, which tells the sad tale of an ordinary man's unequal battle with the city of Peter and its totemic spirit.

In Pushkin's *Bronze Horseman* (1833), St. Petersburg's equestrian statue of Russia's greatest tsar and the city's founder comes to life in order to chase down and punish the poem's hero, Evgenii, for disobedience. What in Pushkin's poem is still implicit becomes explicit in Bely's novel: the horse and rider are *apocalyptic*—they signal judgment, retribution, and the end of time. For Bely and his Russian modernist peers, the horse image was a convenient, visually compelling meeting place for chivalric, folkloric, and religious traditions, all of which used the horse to symbolize the passage and shape of historical time in general and of times of crisis in particular. It is difficult to find a Russian modernist poet or prose writer who did not at some point write a piece centering on a horseman of doom, usually linked to Peter the Great as a russified version of the biblical horsemen of the Apocalypse.

Before entering the fraught world of *Petersburg*, we need to pose another question of context: How did Bely, with his modernist, myth-building leanings, imagine the *shape* of historical time? How did he *figure* history's meaning in this time of crisis? Like their Irish counterpart, W. B. Yeats, both Andrei Bely and Aleksandr Blok were intrigued by the form of the spiral. It is quite possible that they saw historical time in general and their individual artistic trajectories not in linear but rather in helical or conical terms. Near the end of his life, Blok spoke of his literary oeuvre as a spiral, each loop representing a specific work.[5] A few years earlier, Bely similarly cast his own literary activity in terms of spiralate development.[6] Where does this spiralate conception of time come from?

The spiral of history, most often associated with Hegelian dialectic and the Romantic period, entered Western thought as a marriage of the Neoplatonic circular conception of time, wherein everything is bound endlessly to repeat itself (the conception informing Nietzsche's vision of history as the eternal return), and its Christian theological alternative (most famously articulated by Saint Augustine), which views history as a linear movement toward the End. It is difficult to say precisely where Bely found his image of the spiral as a metaphor for historical time. It is possible that the idea came to him from Rudolph Steiner's Anthroposophical doctrine, which Bely studied concurrently to writing *Petersburg* (see Maria Carlson's essay in this volume). What makes this possibility particularly compelling is the fact that Steiner's elaborate schematization of universal history recalled certain aspects of Solovyov's historical vision, by virtue of their common sources in Christian theology.[7]

But regardless of the specific provenance of the spiral as Bely's metaphor for historical time, there is evidence that, while working on *Petersburg*, he had this geometrical form in mind for representing history in the novel.[8] Consider two articles he wrote in 1912—"The Line, the Circle, the Spiral" and "Circular Movement." Many symbols central to *Petersburg* appear here in passing. In both articles, Bely insists that, as cognitive models for understanding our position in the time-space of history, the line, viewed as an evolutionary series of moments, and the circle, viewed as an endless turning in place that opposes qualitative change, are only half-truths. The former is a perspective too mired in the here and now; the latter—too disengaged, abstract, and "motionless." Only when these perspectives are conflated, only when progress through time is reconciled with the stasis of eternity, will the apocalyptic revelation and humanity's deliverance from history ensue. In Nietzsche's notion of the eternal return, Bely argues, excessive emphasis on circularity was the source of the philosopher's madness, trapping him in a vicious circle. Bely's articles urge their readers, who are also the future readers of his novel-in-progress, to overcome the tragedy of the circle. All of world culture, he exclaims in "Circular Movement," has been possessed by circularity, and what is needed is a new metaphysical compass and walking stick: "We should have understood that the path [Nietzsche] described was a spiral, yet we hastened to enclose our line [. . .]. Let us *once again* take up our staffs and—upward, upward! But this time along the spiral."[9]

It seems almost fated that Bely, always obsessed with the revelatory power of language, would transpose his metaphysical figurations to the act of artistic creation itself, to the novel he was then writing. And so he does. In the same article he compares the form of a book to the shape of a spiral: "A book is indeed a four-dimensional being [. . .]. The fourth dimension, intersecting three-dimensionality, describes, as it were, a cube in the shape of a booklet in octavo, where the page is a plane, and the line—time in its most linear form. The transition of one line [to the next], forming the plane of the page, is a joining of circular movement to straightforward movement: from line to line the eye describes a circle. The joining of page to page, which combines circular movement with movement along a line, forms a spiral. The truth of a book is spiralate; the truth of a book is the eternal change of changeless positions."[10]

This is perhaps as close as the reader comes to actually witnessing Bely's mind in the act of modernist border-crossing, in the acrobatic leap from philosophy to aesthetics. It is also a suitable point for making our own leap from the novel's intellectual context to the text itself.

Apocalypticism in *Petersburg*'s Narrative Structure

Bely saw St. Petersburg as the symbolic center of the continuous generational strife sparked by the reforms of Peter the Great—a paradoxical figure in the Russian cultural imagination by virtue of his willingness to combine paternal authoritarianism with youthful rebelliousness. According to Bely, this generational strife came to a head in the revolution of 1905, which supplies the background to *Petersburg*. The novel begins as the tale of a father figure, Apollon Apollonovich Ableukhov, a state official threatened by a political crisis shaking the Russian empire to its foundations. In his personal life, Apollon Apollonovich's obsession with order and regimentation brings about the breakup of his marriage and estrangement from his son Nikolai Apollonovich. In his professional life, the senator's passion for bureaucratic order sires an offspring very much its opposite—the counterforce of strikes, subversion, anarchism, and revolution.

Petersburg's other son figure, the terrorist Aleksandr Ivanovich Dudkin, a Nietzschean and an alcoholic with a mystical, apocalyptic mindset, works to undermine the tsarist state embodied by Apollon Apollonovich. In a fit of spite following a failed romance, Nikolai Apollonovich offers his services to Dudkin's party and is unwittingly drawn into an assassination plot against his own father. Dudkin is unaware that the bomb he brings Nikolai for safekeeping is meant for Senator Ableukhov, making Nikolai a potential patricide. When Dudkin finally discovers that he and Nikolai have been manipulated by the agent provocateur Lippanchenko, *Petersburg*'s other father figure, he rebels against his own party. Soon thereafter, the spirit of Peter the Great—the novel's ultimate paternal model—appears in the doorway of Dudkin's flat, in the guise of the Bronze Horseman, and pours his destructive essence into the delirious terrorist. Less than twenty-four hours before the mad Dudkin slaughters Lippanchenko under the guidance of the Bronze Horseman, an explosion goes off at the Ableukhovs: the impulsive Nikolai, again acting out of spite against his father, has set the bomb's clockwork mechanism in motion and, having come to his senses, failed to locate the explosive device in the family mansion. Fortunately, the explosion only frightens Apollon Apollonovich, who has just resigned from his official position and reunited with his estranged wife.

With this partial plot summary in mind, let us take a closer look at how Bely's apocalypticism—specifically, his view of history as spiraling toward an end—is inscribed in the novel's narrative structure. Logic dictates that we start with Apollon Apollonovich, who seems to be the prime mover of the plot. Every action that moves the novel forward in terms of narrative time and space is attributable—that is, *returns*—to Apollon Apollonovich's repressive nature. The bomb-carrying Dudkin first appears in response to Apollon Apollonovich's urge to bind what he perceives as inchoate Russian space outside central St. Petersburg with the pinching lines of his administrative intellect. From Dudkin's appearance soon issue the fuzzy shapes of the double agents Lippanchenko and Morkovin, and the subplot associated with them. Apollon Apollonovich recalls Dudkin's face as that of the terrifying stranger whom he recently glimpsed on the way to work and who had once visited the senator's son in their own home. The memory of these two encounters links the novel's terrorist subplot to the domestic subplot, closing the circle at the end of chapter 1, when Apollon Apollonovich *returns* home from the office and Nikolai Apollonovich, in red domino costume, leaves to terrorize Sofia Petrovna Likhutina. Nikolai Apollonovich's desire to avenge himself on Sofia Petrovna by donning the red domino, which echoes his dual role as a terrorist and a romantic clown, is generated by his sexual ambivalence, which again has its origin in his father's repressive nature. And to close the circuit once more, Nikolai Apollonovich made his fateful promise to the revolutionary party in the wake of his disastrous affair with Sofia Petrovna. In a word, everything in the narrative is interconnected, and all the interconnections, if pieced together, ostensibly lead back to Senator Ableukhov.

What emerges from this glance at *Petersburg*'s opening is a dramatic rhythm. Each chapter in the novel proceeds toward and ends with a narrative "bang" that closes one circle of action while adumbrating the explosion that will end the story at large. This echo of the bomb-to-come is usually associated with death or retribution in some form and with significant mention of the Book of Revelation and its apocalyptic symbolism. *Petersburg*'s composition resembles a series of expanding circles—a figure mentioned in the Prologue (12)—whose center is Senator Ableukhov and whose outer circle is the exploding bomb at the end of chapter 8.[11] However, in the eyes of the novel's characters, these circles lead back to the repressive nature of the senator and forward to death, revolution, and the exploding bomb. "And one such escaping thought of the stranger's was the thought that he, the stranger, existed in fact," comments the narrator as the senator reflects about Dudkin, "This thought ran back from the Nevsky into the senator's brain [. . .]. And so the circle was closed" (45). This image of violent and senseless recurrence has led commentators to conclude that Bely's overall design is circular and ironic, that the Apocalypse in *Petersburg* consists exclusively in negative judgment, a death sentence passed on the city and its inhabitants. But this view overlooks Bely's teleological—end-goal oriented—thinking and his concurrent effort to "transvalue evil into something closer to good."[12] So the questions to be answered by Bely's readers are these: *How* might these circles take on depth, become a spiral with a way out? And how might they rise out of the notion of the Apocalypse as only an end? After all, the biblical Apocalypse is an end that brings a new beginning, realizing the theological promise of Christ's millennial kingdom on earth.

In his essay on "Circular Movement," cited above, Bely argues that a flat page can acquire additional dimensions when pierced with a certain understanding. What appears at each level of perception (character, narrator, reader) as a vicious circle of death, revolution, and fallen historical time can change its shape if one admits the possibility that there are greater forces orchestrating human affairs. This accounts for the grotesque deflation and distancing in the depiction of *Petersburg*'s characters, and for the narrator's conspiratorial efforts to implicate the reader in the circle of terror: what is "real" is not the rounded portrait of a hero but the thoughts that, appearing to have originated in his brain, take on a life of their own. Everything that seems playful and idle (73–74)—the senator's thoughts, the narrator's chatter—is anything but, and Bely's irony is directed precisely at those who read the novel thinking they are situated safely beyond its chaos and contaminating traces. For Bely the only way out of the circle—the "madness"—of history and into the spiral is to remain *open* to the intrusion of the fourth dimension into the three-dimensional realm of habitual cognition—to intuit, as it were, the fingers of one's author turning the pages of the book that is one's life. *Petersburg* as its author imagined it is not just another work of art or instance of verbal pyrotechnics; it is a supreme act of modernist theurgy.

To read Bely's novel in this way is to see immediately that Apollon Apollonovich is not truly at the center of the novel's plot. Standing behind or above him is the shadowy presence of a more ominous father figure and the plot's true originator—the Bronze Horseman. Bely does not attempt, in terms of a strict narrative causality, to identify the Horseman's origins as prior to those of Apollon Apollonovich. These origins, while alluded to elliptically, are of another order, lying, as it were, *beyond* the boundaries of the printed page. The epiphany-like moments when the Bronze Horseman moves into action do not really make him a character in the story. Quite the opposite, his role is to remove the story of the senator from its narrative time. Peter's equestrian figure embodies the End that appears, anachronistically, when various characters, still caught in the middle of their story, are forced to confront turning points that they are in no position to understand. The Bronze Horseman is a symbolic prime mover, the genuine author of the chaos. No amount of psychological realism can adequately account for the causal link that exists between his invisible (yet real) influence and the marionette-like actions of the lesser characters. To claim that he is a projection of the characters' anxiety and madness is to reverse Bely's equation, for the characters are functions of the Bronze Horseman, not vice versa. And in the sense that death and the end of world history cannot be narrated but must be shown as a threshold of some sort, the Horseman seems to wait, all-powerful, beyond the edge of the story, intermittently crossing its threshold for the sole purpose of reminding others of the ultimate threshold that is his meaning.

Apocalypticism as a Stylistic Problem in *Petersburg*

If Bely had simply written about the Apocalypse, instead of offering his version of it, there would be little difference between his prose and that of many Russian modernists. But his entry into the world of eschatological thinking was not through the portal marked "theme." Bely conceived *Petersburg* as a kind of linguistic echo chamber, where meaning originated in sound. As he had previously theorized in his article "The Magic of Words," any revelation or "piercing" of time begins at the fundamental level of language, in the interplay of sound and sense.[13]

For instance, *Petersburg*'s Prologue introduces, in numerous guises, the Russian prefix *pro-*, denoting "motion through," which then becomes perhaps the most important semantic field in the novel. Already in chapter 1, we find densely planted evidence of this sound-sense reverberation as we follow Apollon Apollonovich's forward movement from home to office. The hero proceeds through the physical space ("*pro*stranstvo") of his household and the streets ("*pro*spekty"), and through the metaphysical space of his dreams of portioning out and controlling Russia. He "strode through [*pro*shestvoval] into the study" (12/14); "passed through [*pro*shël] into the dining room" (12/14); "strode through [*pro*shestvoval] for his coffee" (12/15); "walked out [*pro*shël von] of the room" (17/20); "went striding past [*pro*shestvoval mimo] servant-boys"

(17/21).[14] This movement forward through time and space reaches its apogee in the senator's musings as he speeds to his office in the carriage: "He wanted the carriage to fly onwards [*pro*letela], the Prospects [*pro*spekty] to come flying to meet them—Prospect after Prospect [za *pro*spektom *pro*spekt] [...] he wanted the whole earth, compressed by Prospects [*pro*spektami], in its lineal cosmic course to intersect with the immeasurable in accordance with a rectilinear law; he wanted a network of parallel Prospects [*pro*spektov], intersected by a network of Prospects [*pro*spektov], to spread out into the abysses of interstellar space in planes of squares and cubes" (21/26).

All of this protrusion of one man's physical and intellectual energies into the surrounding world is futile, however. Apollon Apollonovich is simply the agent of a larger divine—or for the time being demonic—dispensation. He is *not* in control, as is soon made clear when the intellectually piercing *pro*- of his gaze encounters the anarchic expansion of Dudkin's eyes at, significantly, a crosswalk (*perekrëstok*) on Nevsky Prospect (25–26/31–32). This is the lowest level of piercing in the novel. Bely seems to be saying that our attempts to control our inner and outer worlds through intellect alone do not lead to deeper understanding and resolution. Instead, they generate the antipodal image of expanding circles (i.e., the bomb) and of a world reeling out of control (the "*provokatsiia*" [provocation] of terrorist acts). In this regard, it is not surprising that Apollon Apollonovich and Lippanchenko, the two father figures who in purest grotesque fashion embody the Western and Eastern principles here at war, are the least susceptible to the presence of the Bronze Horseman. And just as the senator's piercing intellect will be undone by the expanding circles of the bomb, so will the double agent's rounded belly be ripped open by Dudkin's scissors.

The next level of piercing is connected with the Bronze Horseman, whose character unites a conscious return to the atmosphere of Pushkin's eponymous poem and an obvious allusion to a horseman of the Apocalypse. The silhouette of the steed and its master coalesce for Bely into one potent image—the outstretched ("*prostërtaia*") arm of Peter's equestrian monument pointing, like the hand of fate, the way into the future. This outstretched arm, *prostërtaia ruka*, normally appearing in verb form ("stretching out [*pro*stiraia] his heavy, verdigris-encrusted hand the same enigmatic Horseman..." 99/131), constitutes a sort of magnet for all manner of *pro*-prefixed verbs, which seem to gather in the narrative vicinity of the Horseman and even, one might say, to assemble his contour around the imperious arm. There are many instances of this, a number coming at climactic moments at the ends of chapters, but for the sake of brevity I shall mention only the first. In the section entitled "So it is always," which serves as the first chapter's emotional climax, Nikolai puts on the red domino and sets out to terrorize Sofia:

> Over the empty streets of Petersburg barely-lit amorphous forms were flying by [*pro*letali...]. A patch of phosphorescence [a leitmotif associated with the Bronze Horseman] floated [*pro*nosilos´]—nebulous and deathly—across the sky; the sky was shot through [*pro*tumanilas´] with a misty, phosphorescent brilliance; and it made the roofs and chimneys glisten [*pro*blistali]. The green waters of the Moika flowed [*pro*tekali] past there [...]. On the bright background of the bright building, a cuirassier of Her Majesty was passing slowly by [*pro*khodil]; he had a gleaming golden helmet.
>
> And a silver dove raised [ras*pro*stër] its wings above that helmet.
>
> Nikolai Apollonovich, shaven and scented, was making his way [*pro*biralsia] along the Moika wrapped in furs [...].
>
> A sheaf of light flew past [*pro*letel]: a black carriage from the royal court [flew past—*pro*letela]: it bore [*pro*nesla] its bright-red, as though bloodshot, lamps past the bright cavities of that self-same house; on the black current of the Moika the lamps played and glittered [*pro*igrali i *pro*blistali]; the ghostly outline of a servant's tricorn and the outline of a flapping overcoat flew by [*pro*leteli] with the light [...].
>
> Up above—vague outlines spread [*pro*stirali] their ragged grieving arms across the sky. (53–54/69–71)

The ultimate intrusion of this symbol into the narrative comes at the end of chapters 6 and 7. In the first instance, Dudkin is visited by the Bronze Horseman, who turns white hot ("*pro*kalias´"), flows over ("*pro*tëk") his victim, and pours ("*pro*lilsia") himself into Dudkin's veins (307/412). In the second, he is directed by the Horseman's outstretched arm ("*pro*stërtaia ruka") to Lippanchenko's bedroom, where, after committing the murder, Dudkin ends up in the pose of his apocalyptic father figure: "This man had seated himself astride the dead body; he was clutching a pair of scissors in his hand; this hand was stretched out [*pro*stër]" (386/520).

The highest level of penetration, however, does not belong to the Bronze Horseman. As Apollon Apollonovich is the stalking-horse of a higher order, which in this context points to the Antichrist whose reign is about to begin, so is the Bronze Horseman part of a higher order still, one whose function is to turn personal and national endings into new beginnings. Consider the Ableukhov coat of arms, which features a unicorn goring ("*pro*bodaiushchii") a knight (19/23). Here too we find the prefix *pro-* with all of its connotations. A unicorn is a traditional emblem of Christ.[15] But in the symbolic economy of *Petersburg* the unicorn ties together in one image the apocalyptic white horse and the instrument of death. Each level of penetration has brought the reader closer to the central equine image. Apollon Apollonovich, surrounded physically by the walls of his carriage and metaphysically by the walls of his logic, is separated from his horses but driven by them; the Bronze Horseman, still a human figure who straddles the roles of autocrat and rebel, father and son, holds the steed's reins as he points the way; and the unicorn, purged of human frailties, has merged with the steed itself.

Thus, for Bely, the unicorn is another, higher version of the Bronze Horseman: the coppery steed has become white and the penetrating arm has become the horn. This horn, like all of Bely's symbols, has more than one meaning. Its apocalyptic resonance extends beyond its function as an instrument of death: against the backdrop of the Book of Revelation, the horn becomes the archangel's trumpet announcing the Apocalypse. It produces both the sound—the language of the End that is the New Beginning—and the image of the physical cross on which the characters must die, at least figuratively, in order to be reborn on the tree of life.

The ways in which Bely inscribes this highest level of penetrating sound and sense in *Petersburg*'s narrative are too numerous to detail here. Suffice it to say that the novel's many factory chimneys and schooner stacks (*truby*); smoking pipes (*trubki*), including those of the Bronze Horseman and Flying Dutchman; gramophone speakers (both *truby* and *roga*); hunters' horns (*roga*); and flourishing trumpets (*truby*) fall within this semantic field, defined roughly as announcement of the revelation at hand. Equally significant are the novel's multiple invocations of horned or tusked beasts—rhinoceros (*nosorog*), bull (*byk*), wild boar (*kaban*), and deer (*olen'*). These animals serve as parodic surrogates for the unicorn (*edinorog*), hints of a metaphysical penetration beyond a brute physical one. Here, no doubt, Bely was playing with his own real surname—Bugaev comes from the Ukrainian for bull (*bugai*)—which he replaced early on with the pseudonym Bely (White), the color signifying purity of intention, unity of being, and apocalypticism.

If Dudkin comes to assume, on a parodic level, the equestrian pose of his apocalyptic maker, then so does Nikolai Apollonovich, in his masquerade disguise, become a debased version of the unicorn. At the ball, his father, the senator, perceives the approach of the red domino as that of "a creature with a single horn" that "emerged from the masks and Capuchins to throw itself upon the little knight, with its horn it broke the knight's luminous emanation" (163/218). The transfiguring horn of the mythical beast is more powerful than the little knight's sword of logic. But Nikolai Apollonovich, as an agent of the unicorn, does not understand his purpose; indeed, he too senses that he is being gored by a higher force even as he does his goring. The repeated nursery rhyme that represents the call of his origins catches the young hero in a familiar pose:

Дурачок, простачок,
Коленька танцует:
Он надел колпачок –
На коне гарцует. (120–21, 224, 330)

Silly laddie, simple chap,
Little Nicky's dancing:
On his head a dunce's cap,
On a horse he's prancing. (160–61, 300, 444)

Although Bely's intention is clearly to deflate his split and imperfect hero, the combination of equine image and pointed object protruding from the head (the dunce-cap) resurrects unmistakably the symbol of the unicorn and its spiritual harmony. Thus the penetration of this symbol into the flat and circular narrative inhabited by his characters is another, perhaps ultimate, means by which Bely gives additional dimensions to his text.

It is at a point such as this, when one recognizes the similarity within the difference, and the essential seriousness within the parody, that the various linguistic seams of Bely's prose are brought most vividly to the fore. The fine line dividing sound from sound, sense from sense, suddenly materializes. The reader of this apocalyptic fiction must be able to apprehend *both* points of view, the lower and the higher, Nikolai's and the unicorn's, simultaneously. The various phonetic, morphological, and semantic borders are thereby made palpable even as we are urged to cross them, to see that Nikolai *is* the unicorn when of course he is not, and to look back at the text from *the other side,* where the long hidden mystery has at last been made manifest, or revealed, in an allusion to the root meaning of the Greek word Apocalypse (*Apokalūpto*). From one angle, the plot brings no resolution: Dudkin kills an excessively Eastern father figure, who is compromised in his eyes; Nikolai Apollonovich mentally murders his excessively Western father, whose social standing is compromised even before the bomb goes off. From another, more privileged vantage, however, the death and chaos *are* necessary, as steps toward the final explosion of the revolution, the millenarian reign of the Antichrist, the Second Coming, and the divine judgment and the end of time.

Conclusion

There exists a higher movement inscribed within the lower movement of Bely's narrative. The fact, however, is that *Petersburg* can still be read *either* way: its narrative shape can be seen as circular and senseless—the end everyone keeps returning to is simply that, one leading nowhere; or as spiralate and open, which is to say, only *through* the End can we make a genuine New Beginning. It all depends on who and where the guiding intelligence is. Lest we forget, *Petersburg* is an *apocalyptic* fiction: it is about the end of the road. Its idea of space-time relations cannot be stretched out indefinitely, but must be collapsed toward a world picture implying closure. Yet even St. Petersburg, this ultimate threshold city and dark parody of the paradisiac New Jerusalem prophesied in the Book of Revelation as Christ's seat after the Second Coming, holds in its explosive center the seeds of spiritual regeneration.

They are found on those very *thresholds* that transform narrative time, in Mikhail Bakhtin's words, into "the fourth dimension of space."[16] The Russian word *porog* (threshold) conceals the *rog* (horn) on which *Petersburg*'s various characters are gored as they pass into the fourth dimension or it passes into them. Bely is conscious of this wordplay; he employs it often in important contexts as the primary semantic source for all the other threshold images. The end thus makes its presence felt whether we observe Nikolai Apollonovich, clad in his domino, at the threshold of Sofia Petrovna's apartment; or the Christ-like White Domino that meets Sofia Petrovna as she crosses the threshold and leaves the Tsukatovs' ball; or the encounter between father and son, in the presence of the unicorn, at the threshold of their home; or the Bronze Horseman as he passes over the threshold into Dudkin's room; or Lippanchenko's hesitation as he crosses the threshold to his bedroom and the death awaiting him there.

Perhaps one concluding quotation will bring home how persistently Bely sought to incorporate all these meanings—worldly chaos, otherworldly order, and the *limen* where the one enters the other—at the sacred center, the word, where his art began:

> The Prospects spread out [*pro*stërlis′ *pro*spekty . . .]
>
> The Admiralty thrust out [*pro*dvinulo] the eight columns of its aspect: a glimpse of pink [*pro*rozovelo] and it vanished [. . .].
>
> Apollon Apollonovich Ableukhov, who had just seen [*pro*vodivshii] the young girl to her home, was now hastening to the threshold [k *porogu*] of the yellow house. [. . .]

Then Apollon Apollonovich heard behind him the rumble of a cab [*pro*lëtka] [...]. The senator saw: there, over the seat—an old-fashioned and misshapen [u*rod*livyi] young man [...].

The eyes of that unpleasant young man [...] stopped still in a gaze full of horror. [...] It was the gaze of his subordinates as they looked at him, it was the gaze of the hybrid race as it passed by [*pro*khodiashchii ubliudochnyi *rod*...]. And the number on [the cab's] badge could be glimpsed: nineteen hundred and five [...].

Nikolai Apollonovich jumped out of the cab [*pro*lëtka] [...].

Above the gryphons [depicted on the walls of the porch] the Ableukhov coat of arms was hewn into the stone; this coat of arms depicted a knight with long plumes and rococo curls, impaled [*pro*nizannogo] by a unicorn [edino*rog*om]; a crazy thought passed through [*pro*shla] Nikolai Apollonovich Ableukhov's mind [...]. Apollon Apollonovich, who lived [*pro*zhivaiushchii] beyond the threshold [za *porogom*] of that embossed door, was himself the impaled [*pro*bodaemyi] knight; and after that thought another flitted by, quite nebulously [*pro*temnitsia ...]. The ancient family crest was addressed to all the Ableukhovs; he too, Nikolai Apollonovich, was also one impaled [*pro*bodaem]—impaled by whom [no kem *pro*bodaem]? (215–17/289–91)

In the year 1905, in the city of St. Petersburg, a father (*rod*itel´—parent) and a son (u*rod*livyi iunosha, ubliudochnyi *rod*—a misshapen young man, a mongrel breed) cross paths. The unexpected, unwanted meeting produces the psychic equivalent of a small electrical storm, and the sparks that fly raise the question of the ultimate why, the origin, the birth (*rod, rozhd*enie) of this conflict. The answer is of course "by Christ," by the point of His logos—divine reason and creative order—though Bely leaves this unsaid.

Such constant crossing of borders is meant to suggest not lateral, but vertical movement. In *Petersburg*, the various levels of meaning and interpretation—literal, allegorical, moral, and now anagogical (in other words, concerned with the afterlife)—show forth in an elusive verbal staircase. It is Bely's way of verbalizing the impossible: the outside from within, the end from the middle. For him, the city of Peter is not simply a window to the West, as it was for its founder, but a window to the beyond. Each epiphany in *Petersburg* is a small-scale template of the cosmic revelation at hand. The bomb is the final such template, but even it, considering the consequences, is a grotesque parody of the end that Bely felt was bearing down on his generation. Indeed, the apocalyptic End and the New Beginning that lay beyond these personal endings could not be narrated or incorporated into a story unfolding over time.

In *Petersburg*, then, the much desired step beyond "Finis" exists by implication, or symbolization, as Bely would put it. The spiral of Euclidean geometry is open-ended, yet Bely insists that that which has a point of origin must also, in some fourth-dimensional space and time inaccessible to human figuration, have a point of destination. Bely brings his modernist generation closer to the threshold of pure verticality than ever before. In the end, his time was not the ultimate apocalyptic border he hoped and feared it was, and his identification of revolution with revelation was not borne out in the years ahead. Be that as it may, Bely's apocalypticism has its own literary-historical vindication. *Petersburg* can still be seen as a uniquely Russian eschatological reworking of the Apocalypse of John, a swansong to the most mythologized of Russian cities, whose end had been prophesied virtually from the time of its foundation.

Notes

1. This essay is an abridged version of the *Petersburg* chapter in David M. Bethea, *The Shape of Apocalypse in Modern Russian Fiction* (Princeton: Princeton University Press, 1989), 105–44.

2. Andrei Belyi, "Apokalipsis v russkoi poezii," in *Lug zelenyi* (New York: Johnson Reprint, 1967), 246; *Na rubezhe dvukh stoletii* (Letchworth: Bradda Reprint, 1966), 486. Aleksandr Blok, *Zapisnye knizhki*, ed. V. Orlov (Moscow: IKhL, 1965), 169. Dmitrii Merezhkovskii, *Tolstoi i Dostoevskii* (Saint-Petersburg: Mir iskusstva, 1901–2), 528.

3. Vladimir Solov'ev, *Tri razgovora o voine, progresse i kontse vsemirnoi istorii* (New York: Chekhov, 1954), 193.

4. Solov'ev, *Tri razgovora*, 199–200.

5. N. Pavlovich, "Vospominaniia ob Aleksandre Bloke," in *Blokovskii sbornik* 1, ed. Iu. Lotman et al. (Tartu: Tartuskii Gosudarstvennyi Universitet, 1964), 487.

6. Leonid Dolgopolov, "Dopolneniia," in Andrei Belyi, *Peterburg*, ed. L. Dolgopolov (Moscow: Nauka, 1981), 520.

7. John Elsworth, *Andrey Bely: A Critical Study of the Novels* (Cambridge: Cambridge University Press, 1983), 38–45.

8. Robert Maguire and John Malmstad, "*Petersburg*," in *Andrey Bely: Spirit of Symbolism*, ed. John Malmstad (Ithaca: Cornell University Press, 1987), 97.

9. Andrei Belyi, "Krugovoe dvizhenie," *Trudy i dni* 4–5 (1912), 68.

10. Belyi, "Krugovoe dvizhenie," 58.

11. Andrei Bely, *Petersburg*, tr. John Elsworth (London: Pushkin Press, 2009).

12. Vladimir Alexandrov, *Andrei Bely: The Major Symbolist Fiction* (Cambridge, MA: Harvard University Press, 1985), 131.

13. Andrei Belyi, *Simvolizm* (Munich: Wilhelm Fink, 1969), 429–48.

14. The first number in dual page references designates the original text: Andrei

Belyi, *Petersburg*, ed. L. Dolgopolov (Moscow: Nauka, 1981). The second refers to the English translation by John Elsworth.

    15. See Maria Carlson, "The Ableukhov Coat of Arms," in Malmstad, *Andrey Bely*, 160–67.

    16. Mikhail Bakhtin, "Forms of Time and of the Chronotope in the Novel," in his *The Dialogic Imagination*, ed. Michael Holquist, tr. Caryl Emerson and Michael Holquist (Austin: University of Texas Press, 1981), 84.

Part Two

The Aesthetic Context

Petersburg and Music in Modernist Theory and Literature

STEVEN CASSEDY

To trust Andrei Bely's own account (which is to trust a lot), *Petersburg* got its start in pure sound, specifically the sound /ū/, which came to the author one day as if out of nowhere, followed by a motif from Tchaikovsky's opera, *The Queen of Spades* (1890), in turn followed by the visual image of Senator Ableukhov's carriage.[1] Even if this story is not literally true, there is no doubt that it is highly unconventional. Ideas come to writers in any number of ways, and many writers wax creative when they tell about the inspirations for their works, but it would be difficult to find another example of an account like this: My novel started out as a vowel sound.

Bely went on to make that sound a recurrent theme in the novel, where it is said to ring out in the night, without an identifiable source, as if from another world. "*Uuuu-uuuu-uuuu*," we read in chapter 2, "that was how it sounded in those spaces; that sound—was it a sound? If it was a sound, then it was certainly the sound of some other world" (102).[2]

As for the phrase from *The Queen of Spades*, this opera briefly shows up in the novel, just before and after the scandalous scene of the Red Domino. The first time, it is about the music, "the divine, entrancing, marvelous harmonies of a certain opera." Sofia Petrovna sings a phrase, which is rendered like this:

"'Tatam: tam, tam! . . . Tatatam: tam, tam! . . .'" (169)—immediately recognizable to opera buffs as the opening phrase in Scene 20, set by the Winter Canal. The second time, it is about Liza, a character in Tchaikovsky's opera whom Sofia Petrovna recalls, passing the canal, and with whom she identifies (172–73).

It turns out that music had a great deal to do not only with the initial moment of inspiration for Bely's *Petersburg*, but also with the entire conception and design of the novel. Bely wrote *Petersburg* at a time when the cultural world, in Russia and in Western Europe, was alive with a modernist movement to establish the supremacy of music among the arts and to integrate music into literary works. Bely, ever the cultural sponge, eagerly soaked up everything associated with this movement and, synthesizer and systematizer that he was, sought to devise grand theories that accorded to music an almost divine status.

As with almost any cultural movement, there is theory and practice. Theory comes not only from practitioners but from philosophers, critics, and various other sorts of commentators. Practitioners do not always supply theory. When they do, their practices do not always match or successfully embody their theories. Bely was a theorist and a practitioner, so it makes sense first to look at both the broad context in which his theories arose and the theories that he elaborated. Then we will look at the works, *Petersburg* above all, in which Bely sought to realize those theories.

The Sources of Modernist Ideas about Music

If we are wondering where and when music began to assert itself as the supreme mode of artistic expression, we could do worse than to say the German-speaking lands in the decade of the 1810s. Here are some landmarks: The year 1810 saw the publication of E. T. A. Hoffmann's groundbreaking review of Beethoven's Fifth Symphony. Hoffmann offered up not only an analysis and assessment of the symphony but a full-blown theory of musical romanticism. It might surprise some readers today to learn that not only Beethoven, but Haydn and Mozart before him, were considered romantic composers. Music, Hoffmann claimed, was the most romantic of the arts, and instrumental music must be placed at the summit of all music because it is as removed as possible from both language and the world we apprehend through our senses. Romantic music, of the sort we hear in Beethoven's Fifth Symphony, exemplifies the possibilities of this supreme art form because of its grandeur. Thus we see an upward trajectory from Haydn through Mozart to Beethoven: "Beethoven's music sets in motion terror, fear, horror, pain and awakens the infinite yearning that is the essence of romanticism."[3] Hoffmann repeatedly refers to "the infinite" to describe what romantic music is capable of evoking.

The decade of the 1810s in German philosophy produced two important hierarchies of the arts that were essentially identical except for the forms placed in the top and penultimate positions. In his *Lectures on Aesthetics* (delivered in 1818–29, published in book form in 1835), G. W. F. Hegel arranged the art forms from bottom to top in what he regarded as a move from externality to increasing inwardness and subjectivity, from "the sensuous element" (*das sinnliche Element*, that which is experienced through the senses) to the subjection of that sensuous element to "the spirit and its representations." Hegel's hierarchy was this: architecture, sculpture, painting, music, and, at the top, poetry. He even classified the final three arts as "romantic," owing to their heightened level of subjectivity. For Hegel, poetry stands atop music because of "the power with which it subordinates the sensuous element, from which music and painting had begun to liberate art, to Spirit and its representations." Put slightly differently: the sound element of music is sensuous; it is the entirety of what we experience in music. In poetry, by contrast, sound, meaningless in and for itself, is subordinate to the meaning of the word, the word being understood as an "articulated sound."[4]

At the same time that Hegel was delivering his lectures, Arthur Schopenhauer, in *The World as Will and Representation* (1818), gave the same hierarchy but with the order of music and poetry flipped. Schopenhauer's view of the nature and function of art was not entirely different from Hegel's. The end of all the arts, as he saw it, was "the representation of the Ideas." Differences among the various art forms had to do with the "level of objectification of the Will" to which the Idea to be represented belongs (*Will* being a kind of supreme, dark force in Schopenhauer's world). Thus, the material corresponding to each art form more or less successfully objectifies the Will and more or less successfully represents the Idea. For Schopenhauer, music is in a class entirely its own. More than the other fine arts, it has the capacity to give us access to the world's deepest secrets. The "imitative relation" of music to the world is "a very intimate, infinitely true, and accurately striking one, because it is instantaneously comprehensible to everyone." The other fine arts "speak only of shadows, while [music] speaks of essence."[5] Thus, where Hegel saw the sensuous nature of sound in music as a barrier on the path to Spirit (a pinnacle term for him), Schopenhauer regarded sound, in the absence of words, as capable of giving freer access to Ideas (a pinnacle term for *him*). Schopenhauer's view became the orthodox one in the lineage that led from him to the host of figures that Bely and so many of his contemporaries embraced at the century's turn.

Far and away the most significant figure in that lineage was Richard Wagner, the German opera composer who gave us, among others, *Lohengrin* (1850), *Tristan and Isolde* (composed in 1857–59, first performed in 1865), and the colossal four-part cycle *The Ring of the Nibelung* (composed in 1848–74, first performed as a cycle in 1876). A year after he had begun work on the *Ring* cycle, Wagner discovered Schopenhauer and read *The World as Will and Representation*. Then, notwithstanding the great length of this work, he read it again three times, within a year. Reflecting on his first encounter with Schopenhauer's work years later, Wagner wrote of "the significant conception of music" that he had found there.[6] What precise impact the reading of Schopenhauer had on Wagner's artistic practice is difficult to say. Even if we cannot find a direct connection between the ideas Wagner found in *The World as Will and Representation* and the operas that he wrote, it was certainly part of the composer's story that Schopenhauer had somehow shaped those operas.

What about artistic practice? If we are speaking of the legacy of Wagner for modernism, three features stand out. The first is the concept of the *Gesammtkunstwerk* (as Wagner spelled it, with an extra *m*) or "total artwork." Wagner described this dream object in extremely grandiose terms in an essay titled "The Artwork of the Future" (1849). The *total* in "total artwork" meant, in part, the joining together of the various individual art forms. But to Wagner it meant much more: "The great total artwork [*Gesammtkunstwerk*]," he wrote, "which has to embrace each one of these art forms, in order all the more certainly to use each as a means, in order to destroy it in the name of the common goal of *all*, namely the unconditioned, immediate representation of perfected human nature—[the artist] recognizes this total artwork not as the arbitrarily possible deed of the individual, but as the necessarily conceivable common work of man of the future."[7] In practical terms, this would mean that, in an opera, words and music would no longer be separate elements awkwardly stitched together. Instead, they would be organically joined. Thus, no longer would the composer create a melodic line for the voices and then write an orchestral score that would do nothing more than undergird the melodic line by providing suitable harmonies. Orchestra and voice would be interwoven in ways never heard before. And, given that the voice is the vehicle for the libretto, words would blend with the music as organically as voices and instruments. Naturally, given that opera is *theater*, and therefore spectacle, the visual element would be integral to the whole as well.

The second feature is Wagner's use of what came to be called, by others, "leitmotifs" (*Leitmotive* in German—literally, "leading motifs"). Much has been made of these short, recurrent musical phrases and the functions they served in some of Wagner's operas. In many accounts, each leitmotif signifies a character, object, or idea in the drama, so that every time we hear it, we are meant to be reminded of the character, object, or idea. Catalogues of leitmotifs and their meanings have been published for the *Ring* cycle, *Tristan and Isolde*, and other operas. Wagner himself, while certainly acknowledging that he used recurrent motifs in his operas, firmly denied a simplistic, one-for-one correlation between phrase and identifiable referent. But, whether or not each time we hear the four-note phrase that opens the overture to *Tristan* we think—"Ah, Longing and Desire!"—we certainly are aware throughout the opera that we have heard this simple phrase dozens of times. In theory, this means that each time we hear it, we are brought back to earlier instances of it in other contexts, so that a kind of network forms, transcending the linear temporal progress of the opera, in which diverse moments of the long work are joined together.

The third element is a cyclical structure—of a sort. The plot of *The Ring of the Nibelung* revolves around a ring of gold that confers upon its owner the power to rule the world. The opening scene of the first opera, *Das Rheingold*, reveals a trio of maidens swimming in the Rhine and singing about the magic gold that may be fashioned into The Ring. The orchestra plays a rippling major chord, meant to be suggestive of the flowing water. In the final scene of *Götterdämmerung* (Twilight of the gods), the fourth and final opera of the cycle, the ring is returned to the Rhine, where we find, once again, the Rhine maidens. The orchestra briefly plays music virtually identical to that in the opening of *Das Rheingold*, and the maidens sing the same melody line as in that opening. Anna Russell, an English comedian who performed a satirical analysis of the *Ring* cycle in the 1950s and 1960s, singing and accompanying herself on the piano, would come to the bit in the final scene and close her show by exclaiming, in a high-pitched hoot, "You're exactly where you started, twenty hours ago!" Whether the recurrence of an initial theme at the end of a long work constitutes cyclical structure is for Wagner's listeners to decide. But recurrence is a consistent feature of not only the *Ring* cycle but other operas that include leitmotifs, and at the very least we can say that there is a kind of self-reflexivity or folding-back-on-itself in these works.

And then there is Friedrich Nietzsche. When the twenty-six-year-old professor of philology published *The Birth of Tragedy from the Spirit of Music*, in 1872, he could hardly have known what an impact this salad of ideas thrown together from Schopenhauer and Wagner would eventually have on the artistic world of Europe, a generation later. If, in his distinction between the orgiastic and irrational Dionysian, on one side, and the contemplative and rational Apollinian, on the other, Nietzsche tilted toward the former and lamented the life-denying impulse of the latter (while admittedly recognizing its place in a necessary tension between the two), it is no surprise that *music* had something essential to do with the vital force of the irrational. Neither Schopenhauer nor Wagner had used the terms "Dionysian" and "Apollinian," but both of course had emphasized the primacy of music, and Wagner had even elaborated a cultural-historical model that Nietzsche followed: for him the West's crowning cultural achievements, where the ideal of the *Gesammtkunstwerk* came closest to being realized, were the tragedies of Aeschylus. Nietzsche would later repudiate Wagner and recognize his own early essay for what it was—a piece of juvenilia—but that didn't stop several generations of artists and intellectuals from jumping on the Nietzsche bandwagon (see Edith Clowes's essay in this volume).

A cult following developed around Wagner's music in the last decades of the nineteenth century, especially among literary folk. Nowhere in the literary world, at first, was sentiment as fervent as in France, where modernism elevated Wagner to an almost divine status. Of course, it was a matter not simply of admiration for Wagner's music but also of applying the master's ideas and practice to the literary arts. Charles Baudelaire had praised Wagner's music as early as 1861, in a review of *Tannhäuser*. Édouard Dujardin, who would become known as an originator of the stream of consciousness technique in fiction, founded a journal, *La Revue wagnérienne* (1885–88), dedicated to the study and celebration of Wagner's works. Paul Verlaine, in his verse manifesto "Art poétique" (1874), had called for "music before all else" ("De la musique avant toute chose") in poetry, specifying how to achieve this end: through odd-number rhyme schemes, imprecise language, nuance over direct statement, and "beautiful eyes behind veils." In 1886, in an essay on what he regarded as a crisis in poetic language, Stéphane Mallarmé spoke of how "Music rejoins Verse in order to form, ever since Wagner, Poetry."[8] Mallarmé's language was famously elliptical and oblique, but in this statement he is clearly referring to an amalgamation of art forms, with an emphasis on the element of music in poetry. A year earlier, he had written a poetic tribute to Wagner, in the form of a sonnet, and a kind of homage in prose to the German composer as well, titled "Richard Wagner, Reverie of a French Poet."[9] The theme in the prose piece, as best one can make it out through Mallarmé's crabbed language, was the marriage of music and drama.

Bely and Musical Modernism before *Petersburg*

In *Word and Music in the Novels of Andrey Bely*, Ada Steinberg, before examining Bely's musical devices, offered an account of the writer's background in music and in the movement that sought to marry music to the other arts. Like Nietzsche and Wagner before him, Bely fell under the spell of Schopenhauer and then, like Nietzsche, fell under the spell of Wagner. What set Bely apart from most contemporary modernists who got caught up in the Wagnerism craze was that he had more than a superficial understanding of music apart from Wagner and the campaign to join the various art forms together. By way of evidence, Steinberg reproduces a lengthy list of scholarly works on music that Bely cited in the notes to one of his theoretical essays published in the collection *Symbolism* (1910).[10] There is no doubt that the list is impressive and that it reveals a certain level of knowledge about music as an art form, but it is quite possible Bely had not read them all cover to cover.

Yet it is clear that Bely's knowledge exceeded what we find in many of his contemporaries who were passionately devoted to a fusion of music with literature. For one thing, his mother was a talented classical pianist, so some of his musical education took place at home. For another, as Steinberg relates (37–43), Bely frequented a couple of musical salons, where he was exposed to the latest in contemporary music, both Russian and non-Russian. Thus, apart from his theoretical knowledge, he had some acquaintance with actual contemporary musical styles. The odd thing, however (as Steinberg explains), is that first of all, Bely seems to have been unaware of some of the more radical musical experiments occurring during the first two decades of the twentieth century, even in Russia itself, and second, his musical tastes were quite conservative. As Steinberg puts it, "he despised all innovators in music" (42).

In his theoretical writings, Bely treated music much as Wagner and Nietzsche had done before him. Music appears as one of the art forms, enjoying the same pinnacle status as in Schopenhauer. Bely expresses all this with a minimum of reference to any actual properties of music. For example, in an early essay titled "Symbolism as a World View" (1903), Bely establishes a key principle of his own system of thought, namely the primacy of symbols. He doesn't offer a definition of symbols, but he suggests that they allow us contact with some sort of "other." "The entire essence of a man is grasped not through events, but through *symbols of the other*," he writes. "Music ideally expresses the symbol," he continues, "and for this reason the symbol is always musical. The transition from criticism to symbolism is unavoidably accompanied by an awakening of the spirit of music." Just exactly what the twenty-three-year-old poet meant by "transition from criticism to symbolism" is not clear, but what is clear is that music occupies a position of supremacy, owing to its capacity to put us into contact with other worlds. "What existed before time and what will exist in the future—this is the province of the symbol," he wrote exultantly. "Music gushes forth from the symbol. Music passes right by consciousness without stopping. He who is not musical understands nothing."[11]

A few years after "Symbolism as a World View," Bely wrote an odd little essay titled "The Principle of Form in Aesthetics," in which he reasserted Schopenhauer's hierarchy of the arts, without mentioning Schopenhauer, but with a "scientific" basis. The idea was to discover a set of laws that would provide a logical basis for the way in which each art form manifests itself concretely. Music, he says, presents us with "a purely ideal space." Once again the connection with symbols appears: "If art is symbolic, then the purpose of its images must be to combine the ideal and the eternal in the elements of the final product. But the images evoked by music are already perfect and complete." As in Schopenhauer, the distinctive feature of music appears to be its removal from concretion. "Time is the form of inner sense, and this is why music, which is a purely temporal form, expresses symbols that appear especially profound to us. Music deepens everything it touches. It is the very soul of all the arts."[12] In the second half of the essay, Bely decides to use an analogy from chemistry, specifically the law of conservation of energy, to reinforce his point about the art forms. With a set of impressive-looking equations, he arrives at the judgment that, to push the analogy (as he sees it) to its logical conclusion, music is equivalent to the gaseous state of matter.[13] It would certainly be a great mistake to claim that this judgment enhances anyone's understanding of music or its primacy among the various art forms, but it does show the strength both of Bely's belief in that primacy and of his belief that music is organically (chemically, to use his metaphor) connected with the other arts.

During the same decade when he was coming up with theoretical speculations about the nature of music and its relation to the other arts, Bely was busy in practice, experimenting with the integration of music into literature. Most prominent in this regard were the four verbal *Symphonies* he wrote between 1902 and 1908. It's hard to know what to make of these literary compositions beyond the obvious—namely, that they represent conscious attempts to create verbal artworks that are somehow "musical." Ada Steinberg lists (36) the musical devices that Bely employed in the *Symphonies*: "intricate verbal orchestration"; "repetition of sounds and verbal leitmotifs"; attachment of leitmotifs both to characters and to physical aspects of the settings; "collisions of the verbal-musical motifs," to represent "clashes between the characters"; and "extreme figurativeness," leading to "unexpected associations" and therefore "polyphony." Quite a few other scholars have taken a stab at explaining the musical dimension of the *Symphonies* too, some offering detailed analyses of the musical devices in one or more of these compositions. Bely used devices modeled on various musical structures—for example, ABA form (two discrete sections, with the first one repeated at the end); recurrence, through the use of leitmotifs; and cyclicity, as in Wagner's *Ring*.[14] The *Third Symphony*, in fact, is subtitled *The Return* and includes as a plot device the hero's fear of being caught in an endless cycle of reincarnations. Roger Keys, in a study of Bely's fiction, correctly identifies this as an obvious reference to Nietzsche's notion of the eternal return.[15] Keys takes a skeptical view of Bely's experiments, saying that, though the author spent much of his energy theorizing, "he had no firm ideas about what he was actually doing when he wrote his first four prose symphonies" (115). Keys nonetheless published a translation of *The Dramatic Symphony* (Bely's second), which affords the English-speaking reader a sense of what a symphony in prose looks and sounds like.[16]

The typographical dimension of the *Symphonies* is worth pointing out. The first two are arrayed on the page in short, numbered units, generally one to two short sentences each. The third and fourth are similarly laid out, but without actual numbers. One might say that the visual impression of the layout is in some way suggestive of a musical score. Or one might simply say that, apart from the visual impression, the organization of these works into short segments is suggestive of musical phrases. In any case, whatever one's judgment about the success of Bely's experiments with musical form in language (I tend to side with the skeptics), it is safe to say that none of even Bely's most passionate admirers would claim that the *Symphonies* represent his finest literary-artistic achievements.

Musicalizing literary art must of necessity involve sound quality. A number of years after he had written *Petersburg*, Bely published a fanciful work about sound in language, titled *Glossolalia* (speaking in tongues). His aim in this "poem about sound" was to demonstrate that the sounds of language carried their own meaning independently of the words in which they occurred. During the years leading up to the composition of *Petersburg* Bely consciously exploited what he regarded as the properties of the individual sounds of Russian in his literary compositions. Ada Steinberg gives a lengthy presentation of what she terms "vowel orchestration" and "consonantal orchestration" in Bely's works (47–134); and a number of other scholars have written about musical devices that Bely used in his poetry and prose.[17]

Music and *Petersburg*

Anyone who had read Bely's *Symphonies* and then picked up *Petersburg* when it first came out would have experienced, flipping through the novel's pages, a sense of recognition on first sight. Long stretches of text, starting just a few pages into the first chapter, are organized into short segments of one to three lines each. Bits of dialogue appear as sequences of short utterances with nothing to identify the speakers or, for that matter, the physical setting. In the original Russian edition, these sequences of short utterances often appear in groups a half-dozen lines long, separated from each other by lines of dots, as between untitled subsections within a chapter of a conventional work of prose, or as between separate items in a collection of short, untitled, lyrical poems. From the typographical standpoint, this work no more looks like a novel than the *Symphonies* looked like short stories. If the typography in the *Symphonies* visually suggested a musical score, or, at the very least, suggested an organization as if into musical phrases, then the same must have been true for the reader first seeing the text of *Petersburg*.

The reader would also immediately have noticed how un-novel-like Bely's new book was in other ways as well. The plotline is difficult to follow, in no small part because of elements that interrupt the flow of conventional "novelistic" prose—those mysterious bits of dialogue, for example. The narrative voice is inconsistent, or, rather, there are several narrative voices, and we have trouble figuring out which one(s) to follow and trust. From time to time, often in a passage set in from the margin more than a normal paragraph indentation and for no immediately apparent reason, a voice will emerge (25) to offer up a lyrical passage about, say, the Flying Dutchman (an obvious reference to the opera of that title by Wagner). At other times, a first-person narrator will poke his head through the curtain to mimic the German romantic story-tellers of a century earlier by offering accounts of his personal relations with the characters in the novel. Phrases are short, like the individual musical phrases in many actual musical compositions. The language seems to operate on a level other than the purely semantic, drawing attention to itself instead of "disappearing" once its meaning has been conveyed. Many of the author's short phrases, when read aloud, have a rhythmic lilt to them, underscoring the sonorous dimension of the language. On the basis of these initial impressions, a reader might hasten to conclude, "Goodness, there's a sort of 'musical' organization to this text!"

What is more, the narrative features what can only be classified as leitmotifs: "idle cerebral play," "Apollon Apollonovich Ableukhov suffered from dilation of the heart," "Anna Petrovna used to play Chopin (not Schumann)," "he was in charge of provisions somewhere out there," "*Uuuu-uuuu-uuuu*," "destroy(s) irrevocably." These are leitmotifs not simply because they're repeated but because the repetition is at least partly an end in itself. We don't need to be reminded that Sergei Likhutin "was in charge of provisions somewhere out there." Nor do we need to be told repeatedly of Apollon Apollonovich's dilation of the heart and of Anna Petrovna's preference for Chopin over Schumann. "Idle cerebral play" is an important theme but one that can be impressed upon us without the obsessive repetition of the phrase. So it would be safe to say, at least in a metaphorical sense, that these phrases serve a musical purpose—not, of course, that they literally carry a set of pitches and are meant to be sung, but that they recall earlier instances of themselves, as do recurring musical motifs, in a way that passes beyond the conventional communicative function of literary prose.

And Bely was fond of exploiting sound in its own right. "*Uuuu*" as a leitmotif is only one example. Ada Steinberg has shown how the sound /ū/ (which, remember, Bely claimed was the source of the novel) is pervasive in *Petersburg*'s original Russian text. The name Able*u*khov, with its own accented /ū/ sound, she shows, occurs in passages that are heavy with this same vowel. Steinberg lists numerous passages illustrating the prominence of other vowel as well as consonant sounds.

As in an actual opera by Wagner, leitmotifs serve to link disparate moments and thus to work against the linear organization we experience as we read (or listen to) the work in its proper order. I mentioned earlier that Wagner's *Ring* has cyclical structure in that the end of the final opera replicates the beginning of the first. Bely had experimented with cyclicity, at least as a plot device, in his *Third Symphony: The Return*. It would be inaccurate to characterize the structure of *Petersburg* as cyclical in any strict sense of the term. What would "cyclical" mean, as applied to a literary work? One might think of a novel contemporaneous to Bely's *Petersburg* that carries a strong suggestion of cyclicity: Marcel Proust's *In Search of Lost Time* (published, in seven volumes, between 1913 and 1927). Since the novel recounts the hero's epic quest to become an artist who will create a literary work of art from the materials of his own life, and since the conclusion of the novel presents a chain of experiences that presumably set the stage for the hero to accomplish his goal, readers experience a strong temptation to regard the work they have just finished reading as the fruit of the quest described in that work, though many Proust scholars think this is not the case. Hence the sense that the next step is to go back and start reading the whole thing all over again; or, as the aforementioned English performer Anna Russell might have put it, had she decided to do one of her comedy routines on Proust instead of Wagner, "You're headed back exactly where you started, three thousand pages ago!"

Nothing quite this obvious is present in *Petersburg*. And yet, at the end, there are a number of hints that a circle is being closed, among them the actual phrase, "The circle is closed," though in a context where its meaning is a bit mysterious (495). In chapter 8, Anna Petrovna returns, and we are brought back to the early pages of the novel with her piano playing. Then this: "He [Nikolai Apollonovich] sank down with relief into an armchair; at that moment the pealing roulades filled the silence again; that's how it used to be before: roulades would come pealing from there; nine years ago; and ten years ago: Anna Petrovna used to play Chopin (not Schumann). And now it seemed to him that there hadn't been any events, since everything could be explained so simply . . . yes, there had been no events" (547). To be sure, there is an explanation for the claim that "there had been no events" (the bomb had not gone off), but the context suggests that everything that had occurred between the era when Anna Petrovna used to play Chopin and the present has been erased, as if the leitmotif about "Chopin (not Schumann)" here, at the end, and the same leitmotif at the very beginning had come together, squeezing out all the intervening text. That last place we see Nikolai is Nazareth. We might say that this name calls to mind Jesus and, therefore, the Christian apocalyptic idea of resurrection and a Second Coming—another suggestion of cyclicity (see David Bethea's essay in this volume).

The obvious question that looms large for readers, specialists or nonspecialists, is whether the devices that a modernist author like Andrei Bely regards as "musical" really function in such a way that, at least to a certain extent, we experience the literary work in which they appear as we would experience a work of music—and, if so, (a) whether we are aware of experiencing the work in this way, and (b) whether we needed to be *told* to experience it in this way. If we needed to be told, it means the modernist author is giving us an assignment beyond what we were accustomed to in more conventional fiction: Be puzzled by what you are reading, then study my theories before you read my literary works (or have someone else explain them to you), and then experience my works in accordance with those theories. But an assignment of this sort is perfectly in keeping with the period in which Bely lived and wrote. Painters asked viewers to step forward, step back, wonder what they were looking at, and find out by what theory the painting worked (see Olga Matich's essay in this volume). Composers asked listeners to push through the experience of hearing dissonant sound combinations presented in novel structures and wonder by what theory the sounds they were hearing should actually be considered music. Literary artists threw strange and difficult new forms at their readers, challenging those readers not only to comprehend but to ask fundamental questions about the art form they were experiencing. Sculptors took things that were not art (a men's urinal, for example) and put them in the exhibition halls of museums, challenging viewers to find a theory that might define the boundary separating art objects from non-art objects.

One thing you can say in all instances: passivity is no longer an option. We have an arduous job to do when we encounter a modernist work of art—or we can decide it is just not worth the effort. To a reader who is neither Russian nor a contemporary of Bely, *Petersburg* presents a formidable challenge even apart from the array of strange artistic devices. The translators of the most widely read English version, before John Elsworth published his in 2009, thought it necessary to include more than sixty pages of notes at the end of the book, so that we would not founder in a sea of topical references and arcane allusions.[18] But once we get past these, there still remains a forbidding array of experimental formal features that cry out for explanation. Bely's most fervent proponents always cherish the hope that significant numbers of readers will rise to the challenge.

Notes

1. Vladimir Alexandrov, *Andrei Bely: The Major Symbolist Fiction* (Cambridge, MA: Harvard University Press, 1985), 121–22. "Iz literaturnogo nasledstva Andreia Belogo," *Literaturnoe nasledstvo* 27–28 (1937), 453–54.

2. Andrei Bely, *Petersburg*, tr. John Elsworth (London: Pushkin Press, 2009).

3. E. T. A. Hoffmann, *Schriften zur Musik: Aufsätze und Rezensionen*, ed. F. Schnapp (Darmstadt: Wissenschaftliche Buchgesellschaft, 1978), 36.

4. G. W. F. Hegel, *Werke*, ed. E. Moldenhauer and K. M. Michel (Frankfurt: Suhrkamp, 1970), 13:122.

5. Arthur Schopenhauer, *Sämtliche Werke*, ed. W. F. von Löhneysen (Stuttgart: Cotta, 1963), 1:297, 357–59.

6. Richard Wagner, *Mein Leben*, ed. M. Gregor-Dellin (Munich: List, 1969), 522.

7. Richard Wagner, *Gesammelte Schriften und Briefe*, ed. J. Kapp (Leipzig: Hesse und Becker, 1914), 10:67.

8. Stéphane Mallarmé, "Crise de vers," in *Œuvres complètes*, ed. H. Mondor and G. Jean-Aubry (Paris: Gallimard, 1945), 365.

9. Mallarmé, "Richard Wagner, Rêverie d'un poëte français," in *Œuvres complètes*, 541–46.

10. Ada Steinberg, *Word and Music in the Novels of Andrey Bely* (Cambridge: Cambridge University Press, 1982), 256n174.

11. *Selected Essays of Andrey Bely*, tr. and ed. Steven Cassedy (Berkeley: University of California Press), 77–76.

12. *Selected Essays of Andrey Bely*, 208.

13. *Selected Essays of Andrey Bely*, 219.

14. Boris Christa, "Music as Model and Ideal in Andrej Belyj's Poetic Theory and Practice," *Russian Literature* 4 (1976), 395–413. V. Gloshka, "Muzykal´nye osnovy

tvorchestva Andreia Belogo," *Zbornik pedagogickej fakulty v Banskej Bystrici* 17 (1969), 189–206. Gerald Janecek, "Literature as Music: Symphonic Form in Andrei Belyi's *Fourth Symphony*," *Canadian-American Slavic Studies* 8.4 (1974), 501–12.

15. Roger Keys, *The Reluctant Modernist: Andrei Belyi and the Development of Russian Fiction, 1902–1914* (Oxford: Oxford University Press, 1996), 132.

16. Andrey Bely, *The Dramatic Symphony*, tr. Roger and Angela Keys; Bely, *The Forms of Art*, tr. John Elsworth (Edinburgh: Polygon, 1986).

17. Christa, "Music as Model and Ideal," 395–413; Gloshka, "Muzykal'nye osnovy," 189–206; Gerald Janecek, "Literature as Music," 501–12; "Rhythm in Prose: The Special Case of Bely," in his *Andrey Bely: A Critical Review* (Lexington: University of Kentucky Press, 1978), 86–102.

18. Andrei Bely, *Petersburg*, tr. Robert A. Maguire and John E. Malmstad (Bloomington: Indiana University Press, 1978).

Russian Modernist Theatricality and *Life-Creation* in *Petersburg*

COLLEEN MCQUILLEN

Russian modernists rebelled against the utilitarian aesthetic doctrine dominant among the country's intelligentsia in the mid- to late nineteenth century. This doctrine held that art was responsible for documenting everyday life in service of political commentary and social critique, and it privileged the material world because it was verifiable and measurable. In contrast, modernists viewed material reality as an illusion, subjective and impermanent, and therefore sought to explore the world of the ineffable. Because they also considered the language used to describe material reality inadequate for conveying the hidden essence of life, they searched for innovative approaches to creative expression, which stimulated a range of experiments in artistic theory and practice.

Modernism's departure from naturalistic representation released an exuberant spirit that overflowed the confines of art to influence its creators' way of life. Theater, with its customs of stylizing physical appearance by means of costumes and makeup, offered a suitable metaphor for this new attitude toward living as an aesthetic project. Theater also embodied the principle of contingency informing the modernist vision of the world. An actor's stage role is temporary and can be played by many other actors, thus symbolizing the impermanent relationship between appearance and essence, between illusory reality and life's hidden truth. The practices, imagery, and idiom of theater—what this essay calls *theatricality*—were hallmarks of Russian modernist culture. Masquerade was another such hallmark. Related to theater in its use of costumes and decorated venues, masquerade was a stock modernist metaphor describing the performative approach to life. As such, the masquerade motif figured prominently in Russian modernist poetry and prose.

This chapter aims to contextualize Andrei Bely's *Petersburg* in Russian modernism's embrace of performance practices and metaphors, and to explain how the imagery and vocabulary of theater and masquerade expressed the modernist world view and sensibility.

Theater and Theatricality

In Russian theater, as in literature and visual arts, turn-of-the-century innovators undertook bold experiments with form and style. New approaches to dramatic script writing and staging accompanied structural changes to the institution of the theater. In 1882, Tsar Alexander III abolished the state monopoly on public theatrical productions, opening the way to private commercial theaters and less formal performance spaces, such as cabarets and intimate "laboratory" environments. The newfound independence freed Russian theater from the monarchy's aesthetic traditionalism and eased state censorship. These changes allowed Russians to join the international movement away from conventions of imitative theatrical representation, a movement spearheaded by such theorists and practitioners of dramatic arts as Richard Wagner, Friedrich Nietzsche, Georg Fuchs, Adolph Appia, Edward Gordon Craig, and Max Reinhardt.

A number of Russian dramatists now looked back in time for alternatives to conventional mimetic practices that privileged easily understood situations and clear meaning, as well as scenery and sets reproducing the material conditions of life. Bely and a fellow modernist, Viacheslav Ivanov, praised the theatrical and spiritual appeal of communal experience in pagan rituals and medieval mystery plays (based on Christian liturgy and usually performed outdoors). Bely advocated for the resurrection of ancient theater's mystical function, which brought together performance art and lived spiritual experience. He even began composing his own mystery play, *He Who Has Come* (*Prishedshii*, 1898–99), but never completed it. For Ivanov, the chorus of ancient Greek drama presented a model for dissolving the boundary between performers and audience. Friedrich Nietzsche had introduced that principle in *The Birth of Tragedy from the Spirit of Music* (1872), which exerted a strong influence on modernist theoreticians of theater across Europe. (On Nietzsche's place in Bely's art and thought, see Edith Clowes's essay in this volume.)

While Ivanov and Bely initially expressed the view that theater should unite audience and performers in a religious-mystical experience, Bely abandoned the hope of transforming theater into a spiritual rite in his 1908 essay "Theater and Contemporary Drama." Barbara Henry argues that such attempts to use the physical medium of theater for communicating metaphysical content failed for a reason: abstraction belongs to the realm of literature.[1] However, Bely's exhortation to blur the boundary between performer and audience, art and life, resonated with the practice of "life-creation" (*zhiznetvorchestvo*)—a Russian modernist term denoting aesthetically meaningful behavior in everyday life, discussed later in this essay. Removing the proverbial footlights to merge life with art remained a guiding principle of Russian modernist culture, which celebrated theatricality as a performative mode of social existence outside theater walls.

In the first decades of the twentieth century, various theater directors proposed different approaches to negotiating the relationship between life and art. Konstantin Stanislavsky insisted on psychological realism when staging dramatic works by Anton Chekhov and Maxim Gorky, whose writing styles differed markedly from Bely's. Stanislavsky called for actors to enter their roles fully and inhabit their characters in order to produce a performance compelling in its verisimilitude. His naturalistic method aimed at making the audience forget it is watching theater, although he believed in keeping stagecraft separate from quotidian life. While Stanislavsky's system of actor training strove to make art utterly lifelike, two other influential Russian stage directors, Vsevolod Meyerhold and Nikolai Evreinov, concurrently proposed revolutionary changes to the style and purpose of theater.

Meyerhold held that theatrical performances needed to exaggerate the artistry of stagecraft in order to distinguish them from life, thus overcoming the nineteenth century's fidelity to naturalistic representation. Following the English director Edward Gordon Craig, Meyerhold sought to make theater more self-consciously artificial by putting marionettes and puppets on stage alongside human actors. In his watershed productions of Aleksandr Blok's *The Puppet Show* (1906) and Vladimir Mayakovsky's *Vladimir Mayakovsky: A Tragedy* (1913), the director used cardboard figures as surrogates for human actors. In *The Puppet Show*, Meyerhold also used cardboard props to drive home his rejection of verisimilitude: one of the characters, a knight, wore a cardboard helmet and carried a cardboard sword. According to Meyerhold, the use of such anti-naturalistic props on stage conferred upon the performance true artistry, while naturalistic props produced a dull imitation of life.[2]

For these reasons, Meyerhold appreciated the Italian theatrical tradition of commedia dell'arte, which experienced a pan-European revival at the turn of the twentieth century.[3] Commedia dell'arte denotes a type of improvisational theatrical performance with a fixed set of stock characters easily identifiable by their personalities, dispositions, costumes, and consistent relationships. For example, Harlequin's costume has always been the same jester's outfit no matter who performs his role or where. His name is synonymous with the brightly colored diamond pattern decorating his costume, so that, as a character, he is closely identified with his appearance. In Russia, Harlequin, Columbine, and Pierrot were arguably the most popular commedia characters, thanks in part to Blok's *The Puppet Show*.[4] Meyerhold saw in this heavily stylized Italian acting tradition the potential for transporting viewers to the world of invention and play.

The Puppet Show was a *succès de scandale*: many audience members disapproved of the avant-garde drama, and Bely went so far as to call the play blasphemous.[5] His harsh response, however, came in reaction to the play's mythopoetic dramatization of Bely's real-life romantic infatuation with Blok's wife, Liubov' Mendeleeva, a dramatization that mocked both poets' mystical aspirations, rooted in the thought of the Russian religious philosopher Vladimir Solovyov. Several years later, in *Petersburg*, Bely produced his own fictionalized account of this romantic triangle. In an echo of Bely's love for Blok's wife, the novel's young hero, Nikolai Apollonovich Ableukhov, is enamored of his friend's wife, Sofia Petrovna Likhutina. As part of his masquerade costume, Nikolai wears a red domino and a black half-mask, just like the ones Bely donned during his lovesick days.[6] For other modernist writers, too, art and life became intertwined through romance, as I will show in my discussion of life-creation.

The commedia dell'arte figures in Russian modernist dramaturgy were part of a larger trend of embedding performances within theatrical plots, the most common manifestation of which was the "play within a play," as in Chekhov's *The Seagull* (1895). Other types of self-conscious performance motifs within plays included masquerades (Leonid Andreev, *Black Maskers*, 1908) and circuses (Andreev's *He Who Gets Slapped*, 1915). As a strategy for dismantling the "fourth wall" between the stage and the audience, the play-within-a-play and other embedded forms of performance addressed the theme of acting, reminding the audience that the live actors on stage were engaged in producing dramatic art.

Modernists saw artistic creativity not as an alternative to reality but as a way to uncover those aspects of reality that had been obfuscated by the nineteenth-century conventions of artistic verisimilitude. In addition to commedia dell'arte, then, other types of anti-naturalistic stage performance—pantomime, vaudeville, and cabaret routines—enjoyed increasing popularity among Russia's artistic avant-garde because they did not copy daily life but rather celebrated creative imagination.[7] The director and playwright Nikolai Evreinov called this style of stagecraft conditional (*uslovnyi*): unlike realistic theater that, in Evreinov's assessment, merely reproduced quotidian life, conditional theater made explicit the artistic rules, or conditions, of the theatrical game. The masks worn by commedia dell'arte actors were both a catalyst and a metaphor for "conditional theater" precisely because the characters existed nowhere but in the world of make-believe, thereby emphasizing art's rootedness in imagination.[8]

Theater that makes explicit its own principles and processes is one possible definition of theatricality. Another understanding, popularized by Evreinov, relates to the *theatricalization* of life. Evreinov's brand of theatricality insists on the inherently performative nature of social behavior as an innate instinct governing human interactions. Evreinov encouraged all adults, not only actors, to release their child-like impulse to play and thereby transform their everyday existence, revitalizing their passion for life. Transforming life into art was not an escapist fantasy but rather a realization of one's self. As the manager of a St. Petersburg cabaret, The Crooked Mirror (1910–18), Evreinov introduced strategies to disrupt the art-life dichotomy: performers would leave the stage to walk among the audience, and stagehands would become part of the show. In his personal life, too, Evreinov clouded the distinction between play and reality. For example, he organized impromptu theatrical performances and masquerade parties at the apartment of modernist writer Fëdor Sologub. More generally, masquerades and costume balls enjoyed wide popularity in fin-de-siècle St. Petersburg, giving ordinary citizens the opportunity to participate in the kind of theatricalized play that Evreinov advocated, and which had been reserved for members of the nobility throughout much of the nineteenth century.[9]

From its inception in the 1890s, Russian modernist culture embraced aesthetically meaningful practices in which appearance and behavior were guided by the goal of transforming life into a work of art. Russian modernist circles, starting with the World of Art (in whose eponymous journal Bely debuted as a critic), actively chose distinctive styles of clothing, hair, and accessories as ways to express their world view. Sergei Diaghilev, whose dress style was legendary, went on to become the impresario of the Ballets Russes company, renowned for its lavish costumes. Diaghilev's fellow World of Art members—Lev Bakst, Aleksandr Benois, Konstantin Somov, and Sergei Sudeikin—applied their talents as painters and illustrators to costume and set design for the Ballets Russes and other stage productions. Like Diaghilev and his model, Oscar Wilde, they embraced refined dress and devoted what was considered excessive attention to physical appearance. While it is common today to use clothing and appearance to create a distinctive public persona, doing so at the turn of the twentieth century passed for eccentric or provocative behavior. In no case was this truer than for the Russian modernist writers and artists known as the Futurists, who came of age aesthetically in the 1910s and whose rebellious personal style was a form of public spectacle. (On the kinship of *Petersburg*'s visual aesthetic to that of the Futurists, see Olga Matich's essay in this volume.)

The Practice of Life-Creation

Many modernist writers, Bely among them, fashioned their appearance and comportment—facial expressions, manners, gestures, gait, declamatory reading style—as demonstratively theatrical.[10] The aesthetic project of these verbal artists involved the fusion of writing with life practice.[11] In the 1920s, the poet Vladislav Khodasevich, by then a veteran of Russian modernist culture, coined a neologism denoting that culture's programmatic merger of art and life—*zhiznetvorchestvo*, or life-creation. For Khodasevich, modernism was more than an aesthetic movement, for it strove "to find the fusion of life and art, a kind of philosopher's stone" amalgamating life and artistic expression.[12] Khodasevich's choice of metaphor was highly relevant, since alchemists had endowed the philosopher's stone, a mythical substance capable of transforming base metals into gold, with the power to animate matter. Giving life to inanimate matter was indeed part of the ethos of life-creation. Modernists saw the myth of Pygmalion and Galatea as emblematic of the theurgic principle that gave humankind the power of godlike creativity.[13] The sculptor Pygmalion fashioned his ideal woman, Galatea, in the form of a statue and then fell in love with his marble creation. In response to his amorous entreaties, Aphrodite brought Galatea to life. By envisioning themselves as theurgists, modernists such as Bely and Blok laid claim to the divine ability to transform art into life and life into art.

In practice, life-creation was rife with tragic consequences, from cruel manipulation to broken lives and suicides. Khodasevich recounts the tragedy of Nina Petrovskaia, whose ill-fated romances with her fellow modernist writers Andrei Bely and Valery Briusov informed the plot of Briusov's novel *The Fiery Angel* (1907–8). Petrovskaia viewed her own heartbreak through the lens of *The Fiery Angel*'s tragic heroine, Renata. While recognizing herself as the prototype of Briusov's protagonist, she turned Renata into her muse, appropriating the character's fictional fate as a blueprint for her own behavior in life.[14] While Petrovskaia inspired Briusov to imagine a literary heroine on whom she then modeled her everyday conduct, Blok and Bely drew artistic inspiration from their own romantic triangle, which broke Blok's marriage and sent Bely to the brink of suicide. In addition to living their three-way relationship, they depicted it in poetry and prose, following the stock commedia dell'arte plot involving Pierrot (Blok), Harlequin (Bely), and Columbine (Mendeleeva).

During the years of Petrovskaia's romantic pursuit of Bely, 1904–5, the latter was immersed in mystical ideas informing his personal mythmaking. At the root of his metaphysical project was a belief in humankind's theurgic power. Bely spearheaded a group of modernists: the Argonauts, named after the mythical band of heroes who ventured in search of the Golden Fleece. While the Argonauts of Greek mythology were on a quest for a material object, Bely's group yearned for a transcendental journey requiring new myths to map out humanity's salvation. Bely believed in the Argonauts' projective power to realize "world-transforming goals"—that is, to transform ideas into reality. The Argonauts wanted nothing less than "the re-creation of the world following an ideal model that arose in [the artist's] consciousness."[15]

The Russian religious philosopher Vladimir Solovyov influenced the Argonauts' ideas about the apocalyptic end and rebirth of the world, including an outline of their role as artists in the regeneration of humankind (see David Bethea's essay in this volume). Bely's mythmaking thus included his self-portrayal as a Christ-like savior and his search for the reincarnation of divine Sophia (God's wisdom) in the shape of an earthly woman, as prophesied by Solovyov. The writer's penname reflected this self-stylization: at the turn of the century, his mystical experience was steeped in apocalyptic expectations symbolized by the color white, which Bely's circle associated with the exploration of the divine essence of life, including the search for the earthly incarnation of Sophia the Wise and the urgent anticipation of the Second Coming of Christ.[16]

This mystical mindset informed Bely's life-creating relationship with Blok's wife. Besides emotional torment, the romantic triangle's painful unraveling, in 1906, brought its participants bitter disenchantment with dearly held mystical notions. Blok parodied them in *The Puppet Show*, deeply offending Bely, who then offered his own commedia dell'arte version of their common search for Sophia's earthly incarnation. In *Petersburg*, Sophia the Wise becomes the not-so-bright Sofia Petrovna. In a sign of betrayed hope, Bely's alter ego, Nikolai Apollonovich, wears Harlequin's color red rather than the white inscribed in the writer's penname. In *Petersburg*, the color white becomes ambiguous. It both conveys Bely's eschatological mindset—Christ in white roams the city (230–32, 243, 382–84), his Second Coming suggesting the imminence of the Apocalypse—and parodies the mystical exaltation of Bely's youth in the tragicomic commedia figure of Pierrot the unfortunate lover (usually dressed in a white costume), played in *Petersburg* by Sofia's husband, Sergei Sergeich Likhutin (263–64, 429–30).[17]

Although the life-creating plot Bely acted out in tandem with Blok and Mendeleeva made him skeptical of the Argonauts' mystical pretentions, the writer's penchant for esotericism—a broad term denoting occult doctrines that investigate life's mysteries and their meaning—never fully disappeared.[18] When, in the 1910s, he embraced Anthroposophy (see Maria Carlson's essay in this volume), Rudolf Steiner's occult doctrine appealed to Bely, as did Solovyov's thought and Argonaut mythology, by its insistence on humankind's divine power to shape its own earthly life as a way to achieve higher spiritual goals. The same belief inspired another esoteric thinker Bely appreciated—Nikolai Fëdorov. One of the implications of the extreme creative potential that Fëdorov and Solovyov postulated was the attainability of human immortality. Fëdorov called such a revolutionary realization of humanity's creative power "projectivism." Irina Paperno defines projectivism as "concern with advancing coherent plans of action that would endow human thought with objective reality and send the world forth on the road to the practical realization of Christian ideals."[19] In other words, humankind can shape its spiritual and physical futures through the force of concentrated thought.

The esoteric thinking that circulated in Russia at the start of the twentieth century shared with the modernist program of life-creation the principle that humans could shape themselves and their world. They differed, though, in the expected scope and magnitude of the outcomes. Life-creation emphasized the transformative power of the artist to dissolve the boundary separating art and life by aestheticizing one's appearance and stylizing one's behavior. Life-creation was a practice: it was intentional and meaningful behavior taking place in earthly life. In contrast, Solovyov and Fëdorov echoed Friedrich Nietzsche's thought, speculating about humankind's ability to transcend its limits by overcoming death and the fetters of material existence. In *Petersburg*, the theme of humanity's theurgic power finds expression in the creative force of "cerebral play." Apollon Apollonovich engages in an act of creation similar to that of the novel's author: his thought becomes materialized—Aleksandr Ivanovich Dudkin, the narrator tells us, is a product of the senator's imagination (73–74).

The Theatricality of St. Petersburg

The main character of Bely's novel is arguably the city of St. Petersburg. While readers tend to focus on the theatrical idiom as it relates to human figures, some scholars have likened the city to a performance stage. Yuri Lotman has identified the cityscape of St. Petersburg as a theatricalized space in which every person simultaneously performs and observes others performing.[20] St.

Petersburg itself, Lotman argues, acts the part of a European metropolis adorned with mask-like baroque façades designed by French and Italian architects. Furthermore, as the seat of the 1905 and 1917 revolutions, and of the Bolshevik coup, St. Petersburg linked the outdoor spectacle of mass protest and conflict with political change. Katerina Clark has elaborated on the political aspect of the performance metaphor, noting that, "theater provided the charter myth of revolution, not theater up on a stage that an audience watched passively, but theater as a construct for a totalizing experience."[21] Viewing all aspects of life as theatrical meant that even politics could be directed according to a master script; a visionary political "director" like Lenin could produce revolutionary change in the theater of life.

Commenting on his production of Mikhail Lermontov's drama *Masquerade* (1835), which premiered in February 1917 in Petrograd (St. Petersburg's new name since the war's outbreak in 1914), Vsevolod Meyerhold observed that the dominos and half-masks of the Venetian carnival tradition in his staging seemed to presage catastrophe, as they did for the Republic of Venice at eighteenth-century masquerade balls.[22] The domino is a robe-like garment that fully covers the wearer's body. While the style hails from Europe, Russians adopted the custom of wearing the monochromatic cloak as a disguise at masquerades and costume balls. The color of the domino was traditionally black, conferring upon the wearer an aura of mystery and danger. The half-mask, also usually black and worn together with the domino, covered the top half of the face, leaving openings for the wearer's eyes. The mask covered the cheeks and bridge of the nose, thereby obscuring facial features. Strings threaded through the left and right sides of the mask were tied behind the wearer's head in order to secure the disguise.

As mentioned above, for Meyerhold, the domino and half mask created an appropriately ominous atmosphere presaging the collapse of the Russian Empire. His comments echo the symbolism of Nikolai Apollonovich's red domino and half-mask in *Petersburg*, as they are harbingers of socio-political crisis. Meyerhold's likening of St. Petersburg to Venice was part of a long cultural tradition in Russia. In the eighteenth century, visiting Venetian actors put on commedia dell'arte performances in one of St. Petersburg's parks, known as Mars Field. The location regained its explicit connection to the Italian folk theater during the years 1916–19, when the modernist cabaret Players' Rest (*Prival komediantov*) took up residence in a basement on Mars Field.[23] The World of Art painter Sergei Sudeikin decorated the cabaret with frescoes of commedia dell'arte masks. In one fresco, Sudeikin depicted Meyerhold as the director's alter ego, Dr. Dapertutto, in a domino-like Venetian *bauta* (described below), thereby evoking a web of relevant cultural associations. Meyerhold adopted the pseudonym Dr. Dapertutto for his work as the editor of the theater journal *Love of Three Oranges*, which took its title from the first theatrical success of the eighteenth-century Venetian commedia dell'arte master Carlo Gozzi.

The bauta that clothes the fresco's Dapertutto-Meyerhold was the same kind of garment the actress Valentina Verigina recalled wearing while roaming the streets of St. Petersburg with other performers after the 1906 production of Blok's *The Puppet Show*. Verigina wrote, "We walked around the spectral city, across canals and along the fantastical bridges of the Venice of the North, and we ourselves probably seemed like specters, we resembled the Venetian bautas of the past."[24] The word *bauta* originally referred to a mask with a beak-like protuberance, which allowed the wearer to breathe, eat, and speak without having to remove it. Such masks were worn during the annual Venetian Carnival, an Italian version of the mardi gras celebrations. Because the mask was usually worn together with a hooded cloak or cape and a triangular hat, the term bauta eventually came to signify the entire costume. Some versions of the bauta affixed to the hat a piece of lace, which would cover the wearer's face. The bauta is the Italian equivalent of the costume Nikolai Apollonovich wears to the Tsukatovs' ball in *Petersburg*: a half-mask and a domino. In her recollections cited above, Verigina called St. Petersburg "The Venice of the North," recalling Meyerhold's linkage of the two cities. She noted how St. Petersburg's misty fogs recall those of Venice—an atmospheric condition that can play tricks on the eyes to produce illusions.[25] Characterizing the city as "spectral" and her cohort as "specters," Verigina partook in the longstanding Russian tradition of casting St. Petersburg as a haunting cityscape and a place of fantastical occurrences. In *Petersburg*, the mysterious figure of the Red Domino troubling the city plays into the metropolis's mythology.

The Tsukatovs' Ball in *Petersburg*

The historical context Bely evokes in *Petersburg*—Russia's defeat in its war with Japan and the revolutionary turmoil of 1905—foregrounds a terrorist conspiracy inspired by the concurrent resurgence of political violence in the country (see Lynn Patyk's essay in this volume). The mood of anxiety gripping the imperial capital is embodied by the Red Domino, whose alleged antics are detailed in the press. The newspaper column "Chronicle of Events" calls the Red Domino haunting the city an "exceedingly enigmatic occurrence" and a "very strange sight," bemoaning the resultant "consternation" among the inhabitants (76). The public initially accepts the disturbing reports of the Domino as true, but it turns out that the accounts were inspired by a single prank. Nikolai Apollonovich donned his masquerade attire when delivering to Sofia Petrovna an invitation to a romantic tryst at an upcoming masked ball. Omitting her assumption that the domino was Nikolai, Sofia relayed her alarm to the journalist Neintelpfain, who went on to unscrupulously stoke public anxiety with tall tales about the Red Domino.

Because of the state of alarm incited by the press, Nikolai Apollonovich creates quite a stir when he arrives at the Tsukatovs' ball wearing a red domino made of satin and a black half-mask. He also wears an artificial beard made of black lace to cover the bottom half of his face. Some guests already at the ball wear fancy dress, not masquerade costumes, but there is a rumor that disguise-wearing guests—"the masks"—would come to enliven the event (208). Upon arriving, Nikolai is initially mistaken for one of these invited entertainers. However, when a statesman asks the new guest if he is a masker, he receives no response. Nikolai's reticence fuels suspicions and prompts a young military cadet to implore the guest to identify himself. His entreaty comes in the form of four lines of verse:

Кто вы, кто вы, гость суровый,
Роковое домино?
Посмотрите—в плащ багровый
Запахнулося оно (157).[26]

Who are you, somber visitor,
Fateful domino?
See—the cloak of crimson
Wraps him head to toe. (210)

As Leonid Dolgopolov points out, these verses closely echo Bely's 1908 poems "Masquerade" ("Maskarad") and "Holiday" ("Prazdnik").[27] The poem "Masquerade" features a demonic figure in a red satin domino delivering the message of death to the hostess and then running through an emptied ballroom with a bloody sword. In "Holiday," a mysterious crimson Domino appears in a dance hall and is implored to reveal his identity in words that closely echo the lines from the aforementioned poem in *Petersburg*.

Nikolai Apollonovich's arrival causes confusion among the guests, but only one—his father, the senator—finds the blood-red domino alarming to such an extent that he experiences heart palpitations. The narrator explains that, "the red colour was, of course, an emblem of the chaos that was destroying Russia," hence the fear it instilled in the senior statesman (218). The symbolic association of Nikolai's red domino with an existential menace to imperial Russia is accentuated at the ball when Sofia hands Nikolai the letter "inviting [him] to throw a bomb" at his father (225). Nikolai Apollonovich's domino and half-mask thus convey a threat to public order. The mask and the domino also signal the effacement of identity: they conceal the wearer's face and body, refusing to posit an alternative identity, as would a character costume or some other recognizable uniform or style of dress. Such negation of a readable identity breaks the universal social pact of transparency in public and, by this token, suggests antisocial, possibly menacing intentions. Edgar Allan Poe's story "The Masque of the Red Death" (1842), to which *Petersburg* alludes, equates the red domino and half-mask with the ominously silent figure of death. The scene at the Tsukatovs' likewise connects the domino to death through the symbolism of the awaited maskers' costumes. The maskers are dressed as capuchins, members of a Catholic order who wear black hooded robes resembling the cloak-like domino. Their face-covering hoods are embroidered with the morbid imagery of skulls and crossbones, signaling their association with death.

Nikolai unwittingly reveals his own identity at the ball when he raises the half-mask in order to read the letter that Sofia hands to him. This unmasking presages his inability to renounce his love for father and fatherland, and his crush on Sofia. His romantic feelings for her prompt Nikolai to read the letter in the hope that it is an invitation to an amorous dalliance. Nikolai's wish for love stymies his caution, and he shows that he cannot put the concealment of his identity above all else, which is a necessity for a terrorist. According to a notorious Russian theoretician of political terror, Sergei Nechaev, true revolutionaries must renounce their individual identities and personal attachments for the sake of their cause (see Lynn Patyk's essay in this volume).

When she delivers the note to Nikolai, Sofia is dressed as Madame Pompadour, the mistress of the eighteenth-century French king Louis XV. Rumored to have seduced the king at a masquerade, Madame Pompadour emblematized the tradition of romantic intrigue associated with costume balls. Both in real life and in literary representations of masquerades, individuals found that disguising their identity was liberating and offered an opportunity for extra-marital or otherwise taboo romantic liaisons. Sofia's hair is styled voluminously and powdered gray, which is in keeping with the eighteenth-century custom of wearing elaborate powdered wigs. Early twentieth-century St. Petersburg witnessed a renewed interest in this old custom as an organizing theme for costume balls, dubbed "powdered balls," or *bals poudrés*, because guests wore powdered wigs in the eighteenth-century style.[28] Significantly, Sofia fully identifies with Madame

Pompadour; she is no longer the wife of Sergei Likhutin, who warns her against going to the event without his permission. The theme of betrayal introduced in the main plotline of Nikolai Apollonovich as a potential terrorist and patricide resounds in a new key for the Likhutins as the theme of marital infidelity.

The imagery of costume and disguise also appears in the novel in relation to national identity, which is in turn portrayed as influencing political allegiances. The novel's first chapter reveals that the Ableukhov family descended from the Kirghiz-Kaisak Horde. When Nikolai dresses in a Bukharan robe, Tatar slippers, and a skullcap at home, his conspicuously foreign garments allude to his Asiatic heritage, as if to imply that he may not be a loyal and true-blooded Russian. The potential for treason imputed by Nikolai's non-Russian clothing is mirrored in the head terrorist Lippanchenko's yellow garment: the color alludes to racial anxieties about a perceived threat from Asia in the wake of the Russo-Japanese War (see Henrietta Mondry's essay in this volume). Lippanchenko is also referred to as "a hunch-backed yellow Pierrot," a phrase linking the commedia dell'arte tradition and the larger theatrical idiom to terrorist role-play (419). One of the radicals in Lippanchenko's cell, who brings Nikolai Apollonovich the bomb for the future terrorist plot, has multiple aliases that function as forms of disguise. Born Aleksei Alekseich Pogorelsky, this revolutionary carries a false passport bearing the name of Andrei Andreich Gorelsky, yet he also favors the moniker Aleksandr Ivanovich Dudkin.

Although these examples show that the novel's terrorist-provocateurs adopt various forms of disguise, and this self-masking aligns them with the theatrical idiom pervading Russian modernist culture, it is important to note that their pragmatic need for concealing identity differs from the artistic play of modernist life-creation. Unlike terrorists, for whom the impersonation of others was a practical matter of concealing their true identity, modernist artists stylized their real-life appearances and behaviors to establish an art-life continuum.

Conclusion

This essay has discussed the ways that the practices and idioms of theater in Russian modernist culture expressed new attitudes toward art and life that were emerging at the start of the twentieth century. The principles of transformation and transfiguration at the heart of dramatic acting, commedia dell'arte spinoffs, masquerades, life-creation, and religiously inspired eschatological ideas highlight a fundamental shift in attitudes toward the concept of reality. Many Russian modernist theorists and practitioners of dramatic arts, as well as writers like Bely, rejected an exclusively positivist world view and embraced the idea that life's truth could be fully revealed only through creative practices. The modernist belief that the richness of existence need not be confirmed by empirical evidence or accord with physical appearance aligned with other conceptual shifts of the period, such as Einstein's theory of relativity. In Russian modernist culture, Einstein's principle of contingency found expression in the idiom of theater. In Bely's *Petersburg*, it took shape in the related leitmotifs of masks and masquerade disguise.

Notes

1. Barbara Henry, "Theatricality, Anti-Theatricality and Cabaret in Russian Modernism," in *Russian Literature, Modernism and the Visual Arts*, ed. Catriona Kelly and Stephen Lovell (Cambridge: Cambridge University Press, 2000), 152.

2. Vsevolod Meierkhol'd, "Balagan," in *Stat'i, pis'ma, rechi, besedy* (Moscow: Iskusstvo, 1968), 219.

3. Douglas Clayton, *Pierrot in Petrograd: The Commedia dell'arte / Balagan in Twentieth-Century Russian Theatre and Drama* (Montreal: McGill-Queen's University Press, 1993). Catriona Kelly, *Petrushka: The Russian Carnival Puppet Theatre* (Cambridge: Cambridge University Press, 1990). Andrew Wachtel, *Petrushka: Sources and Contexts* (Evanston: Northwestern University Press, 1998).

4. See an illustrated history of the play's first staging: http://petersburg.berkeley.edu/cameron/cameron_front.html.

5. Cameron Wiggins, "The Enchanted Masquerade: Alexander Blok's *The Puppet Show* from the Stage to the Streets," in *"Petersburg"/Peteisburg: Novel and City, 1900–1921*, ed. Olga Matich (Madison: University of Wisconsin Press, 2010), 175.

6. Andrei Belyi, *Vospominaniia o Bloke* (Moscow: Respublika, 1995), 243. Vladislav Khodasevich, "Andrei Belyi," in *Nekropol'. Literatura i vlast'. Pis'ma B. A. Sadovskomu* (Moscow: SS, 1996), 58–59.

7. Spencer Golub, "The Silver Age, 1905–1917," in *A History of Russian Theatre*, ed. Robert Leach and Victor Borovsky (Cambridge: Cambridge University Press, 1999), 289.

8. Clayton, *Pierrot in Petrograd*, 7. Katerina Clark, *Petersburg, Crucible of Cultural Revolution* (Cambridge: Harvard University Press, 1998), 105–6.

9. See Colleen McQuillen, *The Modernist Masquerade: Stylizing Life, Literature, and Costumes in Russia* (Madison: University of Wisconsin Press, 2013).

10. Liudmila Levitskaia, "Litso, maska, maskarad v russkoi khudozhestvennoi kul'ture nachala XX veka," *Iskusstvoznanie* 1 (2001), 425.

11. Olga Matich, *Erotic Utopia: The Decadent Imagination in Russia's Fin de Siècle* (Madison: University of Wisconsin Press, 2005), 6.

12. Vladislav Khodasevich, "Konets Renaty," in *Nekropol'* (Paris: YMCA-Press, 1976), 8.

13. See Irene Masing-Delic, "Creating the Living Work of Art: The Symbolist Pygmalion and His Antecedents," in *Creating Life: The Aesthetic Utopia of Russian Modernism*, ed. Irina Paperno and Joan Grossman (Stanford: Stanford University Press, 1994), 51–82.

14. See Joan Grossman, "Valery Briusov and Nina Petrovskaia: Clashing Models of Life in Art," in Paperno and Grossman, *Creating Life*, 122–50.

15. Alexander Lavrov, "Andrei Bely and the Argonauts' Mythmaking," in Paperno and Grossman, *Creating Life*, 86.

16. Andrei Belyi, *Na rubezhe dvukh stoletii*, ed. A. Lavrov (Moscow: Khudozhestvennaia literatura, 1989), 358–59.

17. Andrei Bely, *Petersburg*, tr. John Elsworth (London: Pushkin Press, 2009).

18. Lavrov, "Andrei Bely and the Argonauts' Mythmaking," 104.

19. Paperno, "Introduction," in Paperno and Grossman, *Creating Life*, 6.

20. Iurii Lotman, "Simvolika Peterburga i problemy semiotiki goroda," in *Istoriia i tipologiia russkoi kul′tury* (Saint-Petersburg: Iskusstvo, 2002), 216.

21. Clark, *Petersburg, Crucible of Cultural Revolution*, 75.

22. See Anna Lisa Crone, "'Balaganchik,' 'Maskarad' and *Poema bez geroia*: Meierkhol′dian Expressions of the Artist's Crisis in Twentieth-Century Russia," *Canadian Slavonic Papers* 36 (1994), 330.

23. Clayton, *Pierrot in Petrograd*, 87.

24. Valentina Verigina, *Vospominaniia*, ed. S. Tsimbal and T. Lanina (Leningrad: Iskusstvo, 1974), 112.

25. See Vladimir Toporov, "Italiia v Peterburge," in *Italiia i slavianskii mir: Sovetsko-ital′ianskii simpozium in honorem professore Ettore Lo Gatto* (Moscow: AN SSSR, 1990), 68.

26. Andrei Belyi, *Peterburg*, ed. L. Dolgopolov (Moscow: Nauka, 1981).

27. Leonid Dolgopolov, "Primechaniia," in Belyi, *Peterburg*, 664n24.

28. McQuillen, *The Modernist Masquerade*, 181–82.

Petersburg and Modernist Painting with Words

OLGA MATICH

Andrei Bely was eleven when his mother took him to the Impressionist exhibit in Moscow (1891), where he was "bewildered" by one of Claude Monet's famous *Haystacks*. He recalled: "Stopping in front of the enjoyable motley spot, the disgraceful 'haystack' that had caused such a sensation, I got very upset that I could not share [other people's] outrage [. . .]; to tell the truth, I liked the French Impressionists, because they were multicolored and the colors ran into my eyes, but I concealed my impression, remembering it; later, more than once, I would reminisce about that strange, yet not unpleasant experience."[1] Bely's memory of Monet's "haystack" evokes one of *Petersburg*'s frequent painterly images — spots — of which there are at least eighty-five. The way Bely depicted his childhood perception of the Monet "spot" may be compared to Apollon Apollonovich's astral vision at night: "Flashes, gleams, nebulous blurs, dancing in all the colours of the rainbow and emerging from swirling cores" (183).[2]

Petersburg is Russian literature's foremost inter-art text, what Richard Wagner titled *Gesammtkunstwerk*, or total artwork, meaning synthesis of the arts (see Steven Cassedy's essay in this volume). The commingling of different art forms was a salient feature of modernist writing. The ways in which *Petersburg* renders visual images by means of verbal language will be my focus. This essay will examine how Bely's word-pictures, often in motion, make the reader *see* his painting with words and the affiliation of these word-pictures with actual works of art. I will also discuss how Bely correlated the spatial and verbal arts in his theoretical writing and consider the affinities between his aesthetic theories and those of Wassily Kandinsky, who is often called the first abstract painter.

Bely and Painting

Bely proclaimed music the highest art form in his first important theoretical essay, "Forms of Art" (1902), arguing that verbal art should aspire to music. "Every art form," he wrote, "has reality as its starting point and music, pure motion, as its final point. [. . .] The essence of motion is understood through music." Why? Because music transcends time and space.[3] Yet Bely turned as much, if not more, to visual images in *Petersburg*. He even created striking illustrations depicting the novel's characters and revealing the writer's acumen for representing motion and his desire to supplement, or perhaps explicate, the novel by means of the visual.

Already in "Forms of Art," Bely claimed that "the *ability to see* [was] the ability to understand *eternal* meaning" (104); and he named fragmentation and dissolution of form as instances of this ability. Both would later characterize *Petersburg*'s modernist aesthetic. The writer returned to the importance of the ability to see more than once. Discussing *Letters to a Painter* (1907) by the German chemist Wilhelm Ostwald, Bely quoted his maxim that "the painter must learn how to see in new ways in order to convey nature artistically, and that he must force his eye [. . .] to see only forms and colors regardless of what they represented in reality."[4] Transcendence of apparent reality for Bely had to do with visual representation.

"Forms of Art" appeared in the journal *The World of Art* (*Mir iskusstva*). Around the same time, Bely became acquainted with several painters from the eponymous modernist group: Leon Bakst, Aleksandr Benois, Konstantin Somov, and Mstislav Dobuzhinsky.[5] Benois's initial series of illustrations (1904–12) for Pushkin's narrative poem *The Bronze Horseman* likely influenced Bely's vision of Petersburg.[6] The commedia dell'arte characters from Somov's drawings and paintings may have inspired the masquerade imagery in Bely's novel (see Colleen McQuillen's essay in this volume).[7] Dobuzhinsky's *October Idyll* (1905), referencing the revolution of 1905 and depicting a large spot of blood oozing down a wall, likely also made it into *Petersburg*, especially into Nikolai's fantasy of the sticky "redness dripping" (442) on the wall in his father's bedroom, after he imagines the explosion.[8]

During his 1906 stay in Munich, Bely became fascinated by the Renaissance artists Matthias Grünewald and Albrecht Dürer, whose paintings he studied in the Old Pinakothek Museum. In Munich Bely also familiarized himself with German and Austrian modernist painters (the Secessionists), but wrote about them dismissively. Predictably, in Paris he was drawn to Impressionism, associating his 1906 stay there with the Impressionists' "new optics," which "defended people from the chaos that corroded their eyes. [...] Only in Paris *impression* served as the artist's self-defense against the bourgeoisie; [...] Manet fended it off by means of a new system of eyeglasses."[9] Bely thus came to consider Impressionism as a great new aesthetic. Among its painters, he singled out Claude Monet, Pierre-Auguste Renoir, Edgar Degas, and the post-Impressionist Paul Cezanne. Initially, he saw the French capital through Impressionist optics. Yet the city ushered him out, in 1907, with Pointillism—an artistic method of creating images by means of small spots of color that form a pattern—which Bely described as "the eye's effort to record the medley of smoke, dust and the fog's moisture."[10] The Impressionist and post-Impressionist dissolution of the object of representation, including by dots and fragmented light, found its way into *Petersburg*.

Following *Petersburg*'s publication, the Russian modernist philosopher Nikolai Berdiaev labeled it a Cubist novel, even though, to my knowledge, Bely himself first referenced Cubism as an art movement only later. His initial perception of Cubism seems to have been inspired by a 1911 trip to North Africa. Recalling this trip, Bely described Arab white houses as "cube-like," suggesting retroactively that the Egyptian experience had opened his eyes to "the outlines of Cubism," which was then emerging in Moscow. "Futurist Moscow," he wrote, "with its Cubist turn [...] prepared the new epoch."[11] It was shortly after his return to Russia that Bely began writing *Petersburg*, where cubes serve as a leitmotif. Even though the famous Moscow art collector Sergei Shchukin, whom Bely knew personally, had a whole room of Pablo Picasso paintings (his art collection was open to the public once a week), we do not know whether Bely visited it. Apparently, his only written reference to Picasso, an ironic one at that, was in his 1926 novel *Moscow under Siege*.

Metaphor, Metamorphosis, and Visuality

Images in *Petersburg* are made visible by means of truly remarkable modernist language. Bely writes about verbal image-making in "The Meaning of Art" (1910), claiming that the conversion of spatial art into language is accomplished through figures of speech: metaphor—the substitution of one image or concept for another, premised on resemblance; simile—a comparison that uses the preposition "like" or "as"; synecdoche—substituting a part for the whole or vice versa; metonymy—the affiliation of unrelated objects or concepts through contiguity; and hyperbole—exaggeration.[12] That metaphor engages sight more often than sound is already implied in Aristotle's famous definition of metaphor, in *The Rhetoric*, as bringing something before the eyes. In one scholar's estimate, "it is no exaggeration to say that the primary virtue of metaphor for Aristotle is the ability to set something vividly before the eyes of the audience."[13] This is precisely what happens in *Petersburg*. Already in his 1907 essay "The City," Bely evokes a sinister living organism that "transforms the city-dweller into a shadow: the shadow, however, does not suspect that it is spectral."[14] *Petersburg* is powered by visual metaphors, which we may describe as modernist verbal painting by means of shifting points of view, displacement, and colors that make things spectral.

One of the novel's characteristic features is the morphing of visual images into new figurations that create a continuum. Here is how Bely defines such a sequence: "As images undergo various shifts, one and the same process of vivid depiction appears to us either as simile, synecdoche, metonymy, or metaphor."[15] The underlying suggestion of Bely's claim is that verbal images are subject to metamorphosis, or transmutation, notably taking place in time and space. For Bely, metaphor and its related figures of speech undergird visual, sometimes visionary, shape-shifting—a process proper to verbal art and becoming part of the visual arts only with the advent of modernism. It was cinema (of which Bely was an early fan) that became the primary medium of such visual metamorphosis in time.

The city's and characters' recurring transmutation in *Petersburg* is typically rendered by means of images that we may call baroque. Here I employ the term transhistorically, beyond the eponymous seventeenth-century artistic style, to speak about imagery characterized by excess, affect, grotesqueness, irregularity, and dissolution of form. Perhaps the multiple transmutations of the phrase "all-at-once" (suddenly) in Bely's novel, described by the narrator as a notorious word that interrupts everything, are *Petersburg*'s most unexpected example of metamorphosis:

> Your "all-at-once" creeps up behind your back, though sometimes it precedes your entry into a room; in the first case you are terribly disconcerted: an unpleasant feeling develops in your back, as though a host of invisible forces had come thronging into your back, as through an open door. [. . .]
>
> Sometimes it happens that someone else's "all-at-once" peeps at you from over the shoulder of the person you're talking to, trying to snuggle up to your own "all-at-once." [. . .]

Your "all-at-once" feeds on your cerebral play; it loves to gobble up everything vile in your thoughts, like a dog; as it becomes bloated, you melt like a candle. [. . .] "All-at-once," sated with vileness of all varieties, like a well-fed but invisible dog, starts to precede you everywhere, creating in the detached observer the impression that you are veiled from view by a black cloud, invisible to the eye: that is your hairy "all-at-once." (50–51)

Besides the remarkable linguistic displacement of nominalizing an adverb—*vdrug* in the Russian original—the passage represents "all-at-once" from different spatial perspectives that signify motion, creating a verbal picture that evokes a Cubist painting. The embodiment of a part of speech referencing time spatializes it by endowing time with an invisible, or unseen, mass that penetrates the body; then follows the metamorphosis of "all-at-once" into a dog that devours thoughts produced by cerebral play; and, finally, into a cloud. "All-at-once" keeps changing shape, transforming one materialized metaphor into another and rendering the invisible verbally visible. The passage sets in motion a grotesque chain of metamorphoses underscoring the mutability of form: nothing is immune to metamorphosis, including parts of speech that represent time.

Next, a decidedly surreal portrait of Nikolai Apollonovich undergoing metamorphosis foreshadows by a decade French Surrealism's striving to fuse dream and reality by representing the human unconscious through unexpected, distorted images: "A feverish poison penetrated his brain, poured unseen from his eyes in a cloud of flame, entwining him in clinging blood-red velvet: as though he now looked at everything with a charred face out of flames that seared his body" (212). Another visually striking example of metamorphosis in *Petersburg* is the transformation of the Nevsky Prospect crowd, described initially as beards, mustaches, and chins (parts of the body instead of wholes). The crowd then mutates into slimy, oozing fish eggs, with the sidewalk becoming a caviar sandwich field; next, it morphs into an equally grotesque metaphor of a giant myriapod crawling along the city streets; finally, the metamorphic chain returns to the crowd—to various kinds of headwear worn by those in the crowd (342–43). The excessive baroque and surreal metamorphoses are put before our eyes. The first is a detached view of body parts; the second dissolves the crowd into organic slime; the third transforms it into a surreal giant insect; and the fourth returns to parts. This painterly metamorphosis, what we could call animated painting, engages three different visual sensibilities and conceptual references, with the third representing the hardening of unbounded viscosity into a centipede that portends apocalyptic destruction, but the word-picture returns from the brink to fragments of real life.

Petersburg also engages historical sources of metamorphosis from Greek mythology. The narrator tells us that Dudkin emerges from Apollon Apollonovich's head in a moment of "cerebral play": "His cranium became the womb of mental images, which were forthwith embodied in this spectral world. [. . .] Every idle thought obstinately developed into a spatio-temporal image, continuing its now uncontrollable activities—outside the senator's head. Apollon Apollonovich was in a certain sense like Zeus: from his head there emerged gods, goddesses and genii. [. . .] One such genius (the stranger with the little black moustache), arising as an image, continued as a *being* there and then in the yellowish expanses of the Neva" (44–45). That being is the revolutionary Aleksandr Ivanovich Dudkin. Metamorphosis is here premised not only on Bely's modernist image-making, but also on the relationship between thought and its materialization, which the narrator calls "cerebral play"—*Petersburg*'s metaphor of creativity that inspires its "forms of art." Just as Athena springs from Zeus's head in Greek myth,[16] cerebral play engenders the narrator's and characters' "thought forms" that come to life. The power of metamorphosis, inscribed in cerebral play, fuels Bely's imagination, including the break with traditional image-making.

Rudolf Steiner's Anthroposophy was among the sources of *Petersburg*'s "thought forms" (see Maria Carlson's essay in this volume). Steiner used the figure of metamorphosis to represent spiritual transformation. While living at Steiner's commune in Dornach, Switzerland, Bely made multiple illustrations of his meditation exercises that spatialized the temporal aspect of meditation. Steiner's intellectual rival, the Theosophist Annie Besant, called such images "thought forms." These were representations of mental, emotional, and spiritual states of heightened consciousness, illustrated in Besant and Charles Leadbeater's influential 1901 book, *Thought Forms*.[17] Bely described the characters of *Petersburg* as "thought forms" that had not yet reached consciousness, adding that the novel, its revolutionary setting and content were merely the "conventional dress of thought forms" that we may also affiliate with cerebral play. "My whole novel," concluded Bely, "depicts the unconscious life of crippled thought forms by means of symbols of time and place."[18] Chapter 1 ends with the narrator telling us that Senator Ableukhov's idle cerebral play produces not only the shadowy stranger Dudkin, but also his son Nikolai and the Ableukhov house, and that the author hangs their *pictures* everywhere, and even though he should take them down, he will not; for "he has sufficient right not to do so" (73), the narrator insists, suggesting the pictorial nature of the novel's characters.

These and similar examples of metamorphosis raise the question of whether verbal language, because it inscribes time, is a better medium for rendering this sort of pictorial representation than actual painting. If we seek a painterly analog of Bely's grotesque fantasy of Nevsky Prospect, we could turn to Hieronymus Bosch,[19] whose art Bely saw in Belgium and Germany while working on *Petersburg*, or to the twentieth-century Surrealists. Bely described Bosch's paintings as strangely evocative of modernist "chimera-makers"—that is, artists conjuring radically distorted vision.[20] I am, of course, not suggesting that Bosch's artistic brush is similar to Bely's, but their apocalyptic affinities and interchange of human into animal forms reveal a similar metamorphic energy, foreshadowing the Surrealist aesthetic.

Ekphrasis

But can we discuss *Petersburg* in relation to actual paintings or ekphrases (the verbal representation of a visual work of art)? The novel contains a possible reference to a contemporary painting without naming it—Dobuzhinsky's *Barbershop Window* (1906), which depicts wax hairdresser dolls. Compare Nikolai Apollonovich's description as "a hairdresser's dummy: the pale, waxen figure of a handsome man with an unpleasant, timid smile on lips that extended all the way to his ears" (124). Another, clearer reference to a visual artifact can be found in chapter 5, when Nikolai Apollonovich runs away from the equestran statue of Peter the Great (288), evoking Aleksandr Benois's illustration for an episode in Pushkin's *Bronze Horseman*, wherein the galloping horseman chases his victim.[21]

What may be described as a striking quasi ekphrasis of *Petersburg*'s metallic horseman helps the reader *see* the visual depiction of the novel's equestrian statue galloping through the city streets and finally crashing into Dudkin's garret: "The Metallic Guest, glowing beneath the moon with thousand-degree heat, now sat before him, scorching, crimson-red; now, fired right through, he turned a blinding white and released on to Aleksandr Ivanovich, as he bent before him, a searing torrent; in utter delirium Aleksandr Ivanovich trembled in the hundred-ton embrace: the Bronze Horseman was infused into his veins" (412). The phantasmagoric transformation of the Horseman is perhaps *Petersburg*'s most extravagant metamorphosis, one that may be described as neobaroque in contrast to the Neoclassical aesthetic of the original equestrian sculpture. This pertains especially to the Horseman melting and flowing into Dudkin's veins in metals, a horrific image of transmutation.

Another baroque sculptural image is that of the caryatid located on the government building from where it observes the crowd down below. Once again, the quasi ekphrasis transmutes the bearded caryatid through metamorphosis:

"The muscular arms on those elbows [. . .] would straighten; and the chiseled skull would jerk up wildly; the mouth would fly open in an echoing roar; [. . .] the street would be swathed in steam; [. . .] this ancient sculpture would collapse on to the street in a hail of stones, describing in the air a rushing, blinding arc; and in blood-stained fragments it would settle on the frightened bowler hats that passed here—deathly, unvaried, sedate" (356–57). Auguring revolution, the classical caryatid turns into a despairing baroque sculpture. Its bellowing mouth may be paired with Nikolai Apollonovich's tormented mouth as he contemplates patricide. If we consider Bely's drawing of Nikolai Apollonovich, it evokes the black and white lithograph of proto-Expressionist Edvard Munch's famed *Scream*.[22] The shouting figure is set against a blood-red sky in the painted version. In *Petersburg*, Nikolai's wide open mouth gapes at the morning sky, then turns into a bloody red column dancing among blood-red spots. Even though Nikolai's mouth is closed in Bely's drawing, his serpentine body, exuding fear and anxiety, and the thick pen strokes that envelop it are remarkably similar to Munch's lithograph. Bely's desire, perhaps even his need to draw his hero's affect, reveals the importance of the visual in the novel.

But only one painting is subject to true ekphrasis in Bely's novel: "Above the piano," observes the narrator, surveying the Ableukhovs' house, "hung a reduced copy of David's picture *The Distribution of the Eagle Standards*. The picture depicted the great Emperor in a wreath and a robe of purple and ermine; the Emperor Napoleon was stretching out his hand to a plumed gathering of marshals; his other hand was clutching a metal staff; on the top of the staff was perched a heavy eagle" (20). This painting is placed in a room characterized by cold luster, mirrors, encrusted tables, cupids, and copies of Pompeian frescoes, which, however, are not depicted. The seemingly routine ekphrasis of Jacques-Louis David's famous painting (1810) suggests Bely's disinterest in Neoclassical art, standing in stark contrast to *Petersburg*'s decidedly modernist, or what may be described as neobaroque, representation. The function of the ekphrasis is its reinforcement of the senator's alignment with state power as well as his desire for order that, in turn, may be aligned with Neoclassical art.

The other artist named in *Petersburg* is Katsushika Hokusai, whose landscapes of Mount Fujiyama adorn the walls of Sofia Petrovna's apartment, decorated in the Japanese style fashionable at the turn of the century, which also became a key ingredient of Art Nouveau and Impressionism. Hokusai's drawings, writes Bely, lack the illusion of three-dimensional perspective, and except for the alcove from behind which Sofia Petrovna appears in a pink kimono, the apartment is described as lacking perspective as well. While there are no ekphrases of Hokusai's prints in *Petersburg*, Bely admired Japanese art, writing in 1908 that "Edouard Manet resurrected it in his work, and Aubrey Beardsley recreated our century by means of the Japanese."[23] Bely's most extensive discussion of Japanese art appears in his last book, *Gogol's Artistry* (*Masterstvo Gogolia*, 1934), which is as much about his own work as it is about Gogol's. The book's translator, Christopher Colbath, perceptively writes that "Bely's main concern is the juxtaposition of Renaissance (Western) perspective with its Japanese (Eastern) counterpart."[24] Japanese perspective, says Bely in *Gogol's Artistry*, is characterized by displacement: "If you sit before an easel, you see one perspective. If you run and your head turns—to the side, slantwise, upward—you see another. This other is the kind rendered by Japanese painters" (157). Curiously, the statement may also be applied to Cubism and to visual representation in *Petersburg*.

Cubist *Petersburg*

In 1914, Nikolai Berdiaev wrote that Bely "may be called a Cubist in literature," because "*Petersburg* revealed the same process of flattening and fragmentation of cosmic life as a Picasso painting. Word crystals were atomized in his wonderful, nightmarish verbal collocations."[25] Describing his visit to Shchukin's art gallery, Berdiaev wrote that Picasso evoked feelings of terror, associated with the breakup of the cosmos. He then links Cubism to the Theosophical/Anthroposophical notion of the astral body and to the "quest for geometry, the skeleton of the objective world"—a reference to non-Euclidian geometry associated with Albert Einstein's theory of the fourth dimension, which influenced early Cubists.

Two years later, Berdiaev wrote a review of *Petersburg*, titled "An Astral Novel," in which he developed his earlier ideas: "All firmly established boundaries between objects disappear. The very shapes of people are decrystallized and atomized, firm boundaries separating one person from another, and from the objects of the surrounding world, are lost. The firmness, the limitedness, the crystallization of our fleshly world dissolve. A man morphs into another man, an object morphs into another object, the physical plane [morphs] into an astral plane, the cerebral process—into an existential process."[26] Berdiaev called Bely the only important Futurist in Russian literature, referring to the most recent modernist current in Russian poetry and painting, often used at the time as a synonym of Cubism.[27] Nowhere, however, did he actually describe what made *Petersburg* a Cubist or a Futurist novel.

What are the Cubist attributes of *Petersburg*? In the first place, fragmented representation, especially in the case of images that visualize the expansion of the body and its fragmentation. As in Cubist painting, objects and human form are dismembered. A bomb is the motor of the novel's plot, with Nikolai Apollonovich imagining that he is a bomb, bursting and shattering the space around him. Bely's description of his creative process in 1911, the year he began writing *Petersburg*, says it best: "My creative work is a bomb that I throw; life inside me is a bomb that has been thrown at me; a bomb striking a bomb—showers of shrapnel [. . .] the shrapnel fragments of my work are the forms of art; shrapnel of the seen—images of necessity that explode my life."[28]

Like Cubist painting, *Petersburg* confounds planar and perspectival shifts that present its characters and spaces from different vantage points. The novel engages geometry, naming cubes, cones, circles, and spherical shapes of all sorts, squares, parallelepipeds, and pyramids. Here is Senator Ableukhov's vision of Nevsky Prospect and the city—from below at eye level, from above, and from a distance:

> Inspiration took possession of the senator's soul every time his lacquered cube cut through the Nevsky like an arrow: there, outside the window, the numbering of the houses could be seen; and circulation took place; there in the distance, far, far away, on bright days a golden spire gleamed blindingly [. . .].
>
> The statesman suddenly expanded in all directions from the black cube of the carriage and began to hover above it; he wanted the carriage to fly onwards, the Prospects to come flying to meet them—Prospect after Prospect, he wanted the whole spherical surface of the planet to be embraced, as though by the coils of a snake, by the gray-black cubes of houses; he wanted the whole earth, compressed by Prospects [. . .] to intersect with the immeasurable in accordance with a rectilinear law. [. . .]
>
> He would give himself over for long periods to the unreflecting contemplation of: pyramids, triangles, parallelepipeds, cubes, trapezoids. (25–26)

Even though the senator represents rationalism, conservatism, and state bureaucracy, he is also the subject of the author's verbal and narrative experiments, including with geometric forms and perspectival shifts associated with Cubist painting.

The modernist critic Viktor Shklovskii likened Bely's prose to the "disintegration of form in a Cubist painting," referring specifically to the "swarm"—one of Bely's favorite metaphoric images.[29] This image appears already in the novel's Prologue, when the narrator, locating Petersburg on the map of Russia, observes that "from this mathematical point, which possesses no dimensions, it [the city] energetically proclaims that it exists: from there, from that said point, swarms of printed books issue in a torrent" (12). The word-picture suggests Cubist image-making as well as the swarm and its swirling lines that demonstrate chaos.

Despite his predilection for geometric shapes, Senator Ableukhov fears the zigzag because it represents unexpected threat. In the remarkable illustration Bely drew of Apollon Apollonovich recoiling in fear from his son, after the actual explosion, their behavior is depicted by means of zigzag-like motion.[30] The drawing reveals Bely's ability not only to see, but also to picture motion and emotion, which are often linked in the novel. The illustration, moreover, may be interpreted as a metaphor of the novel's zigzag that we first see when Dudkin, with the bomb wrapped in a bundle, stumbles and performs an anxious zigzag with his elbow. Apollon Apollonovich, for whom the bomb is intended, later observes the same zigzag motion, signifying possible rupture, when their paths cross on the Nevsky.

Considered in visual terms, the intersection of line and circle that characterizes the Cubist geometry of *Petersburg* is readily reducible to an abstract image. It already appears in the Prologue, which introduces lines and dots in motion. The Prologue at first emphasizes the rectilinearity of Nevsky Prospect, juxtaposed to its function as the space of public "circulation"; the Prologue ends by proclaiming that Petersburg exists only on maps—in the form of two concentric circles with a black point in the middle, from where, as we know, "swarms of printed books issue in a torrent" (11–12).

Wassily Kandinsky: Aesthetic Theory and Practice

Besides Cubism, *Petersburg*'s visual poetics echo other modernist practices just as much, if not more. Bely's views on art perhaps have the greatest affinity to those of Wassily Kandinsky, starting with their shared experience of the Monet *Haystack* at the Impressionist exhibit in Moscow. In his memoirs, Kandinsky wrote that the Monet "impressed itself ineradicably on [his] memory, always hovering quite unexpectedly before [his] eyes down to the last detail"; though on seeing the painting, he did not recognize the haystack of which the catalog "informed [him]."[31] Bely and Kandinsky shared a synesthetic sensibility (fusion of the senses), considering music the highest art form to which all arts should aspire. In his most influential critical piece, "On the Spiritual in Art" (1911), Kandinsky—who apparently had colored hearing, the absence of which Bely considered a defect in verbal and visual artists—described the ways in which colors and abstract shapes, channeling the "sounding cosmos," were expressions of an "inner sound."[32] He also claimed that "the psychological power of color [called] forth the vibrations of the soul" (157). Kandinsky's *Compositions* (a musical term), painted during his Expressionist Munich period (1911–14), exemplify these claims. The spiraling architecture of *Composition VII* (1913), often considered the pinnacle of the painter's prewar work, intertwines music, color, and spatialized, swirling motion of abstract shapes, conveying modernist apocalyptic anxiety that was all too familiar to Bely.[33]

Petersburg's rich color palette, sometimes linked to sound, is dominated by various shades of green, red, yellow, gray, black, and blue that often carry esoteric meanings. Bely first developed a theory of color in his essay "Sacred Colors" (1903); but his most expansive discussion of color, replete with statistics and asserting the power of synesthesia, is to be found in *Gogol's Artistry*.

Like Bely, Kandinsky was invested in Anthroposophy—a source of their shared interest in the dissolution of the object. In his mystical and apocalyptically tinged "On the Spiritual in Art," Kandinsky wrote that new art—by which he meant his own brand of modernism—marked the "coming Epoch of the Great Spiritual" (219), with the abstract aesthetic conveying the "inner sound" and the cosmic laws of astral space. What has been described as Kandinsky's "sounding cosmos"[34] exists in the fourth dimension as a spiritual, not mathematical concept. A spatial concept of infinity and unboundedness, the fourth dimension became a popular notion in European mystical and occult thought at the beginning of the twentieth century. And while Berdiaev associated *Petersburg*'s astral sphere with Cubism, the novel's astral bodies also represented Bely's "occult turn" toward Anthroposophy during his work on the novel.

A striking example is the verbal picture of Dudkin's enigmatic visitor Shishnarfne/Enfranshish, an inhabitant of the fourth dimension that we may associate with the sounding cosmos. As the visitor leaned on the windowsill in Dudkin's room, his

> black outline was becoming ever finer, more ethereal; it seemed to be a sheet of dark, black paper, stuck firmly on the window frame [. . .].
>
> Into this room had come a portly young man possessing three dimensions; leaning against the window he had turned into nothing but an outline (and moreover—of two dimensions); then: he had become a thin layer of black soot [. . .]. What was happening here was the dissolution of matter itself; this matter had been transformed entirely, without residue, into a sonic substance, clattering deafeningly—only where? It seemed to Aleksandr Ivanovich that it was clattering inside himself. [. . .]
>
> A jabbering came out of Aleksandr Ivanovich . . . "Petersburg doesn't have three dimensions, it has four; the fourth is subject to uncertainty and is not marked on maps at all, unless by a point, for a point is the place of contact

between the plane of this existence and the spherical surface of the immense astral cosmos; [. . .] so a moment before I was there—among the points situated on the windowsill, and now I have appeared [. . .] out of the point of your larynx." (397–400)

This point exists in the astral sphere, unlike the one on the map, whence "issue swarms of printed books" in the novel's Prologue. The dissolution of Shishnarfne's body reflects not only Bely's immersion in the occult, but also his impulse toward the dissolution of form. Shishnarfne's body transmutes into a contour, then lines, and finally a point, or sounding substance that emerges from Dudkin's own throat. The process recalls Bely's obsession with metamorphosis, here taking place in the fourth dimension that collapses time and space and three-dimensional perspective.

Returning to Monet's *Haystack*, Bely perceived it as a "spot" that, in *Petersburg*, represents the eponymous city: "From the Finnish marshes the city will show you the place of its demented settlement with a red, red spot: and that spot is to be seen in silence from afar against the sombre night. As you wander the length of our far-flung land, you will see from afar a spot of red blood that stands out against the sombre night" (64). The image could be used to describe an abstract Kandinsky painting. The red spot is part of a long passage that plays with shifts in point of view: first a close-up of Petersburg, then a view from a great distance (quoted here), finally a median view. All three represent the mobility of the narrator's gaze, what Bely elsewhere described as the "product of the gaze" that "constructs the experience of seeing."[35] Spots, after all, are everywhere in *Petersburg* and in Kandinsky's paintings, one of which is actually titled *Painting with Red Spot* (1914).[36] Kandinsky's claim that "painting is a thundering collision of different worlds destined in and through conflict to create the new world called the work" applies to Bely's novel, its cosmic collisions and multiple red spots. So does Kandinsky's association of a "work of art" with "the music of the spheres."[37] And like "inner necessity," Kandinsky's key term for the source of artistic creativity—the "sounding cosmos"—evokes Bely's self-description as an exploding bomb that produces "images of necessity" informing his writing.[38]

Extravagant transmutation in time and space is represented in the novel by means of motion, recalling Kandinsky's paintings. The question remains how successfully the two artists exceeded the boundaries of their chosen medium. I think *Petersburg*'s depiction of the city and its inhabitants from different vantage points transcends the temporality of the verbal medium. Kandinsky's abstract

Compositions, likewise, transcend space by presenting images from different perspectives simultaneously, compelling the viewer to examine them, up close, one after another (in other words, over time). We may conclude that Bely and Kandinsky each created a *Gesammtkunstwerk* that synthesizes art forms and fuses time and space in modernist terms.

I have made several references to the baroque not as a historically specific artistic style but as a transhistorical sensibility. But the historical Baroque's mutability, the relationship of time, space, and motion in Baroque painting are proper to Bely's novel as well. In fact, Bely's own term, "asymmetrical Baroque," coined in *Gogol's Artistry* (7), is particularly applicable to *Petersburg*. Contrary to the Russian imperial capital's architectural history—from Baroque to Neoclassicism—*Petersburg* may be described as a modernist turn to the Baroque. The novel's temporality, labyrinthine spatiality, and grotesque bodies evoke Baroque metamorphosis. The Nevsky Prospect crowd, Nikolai Apollonovich's and the caryatid's bellowing lacerated mouths, and the Bronze Horseman melting into Dudkin's veins all conjure up surreal Baroque terror.

I have used the epithet surreal instead of Surrealist self-consciously in describing some of *Petersburg*'s images. Instead of referencing Surrealism, these images in *Petersburg* prefigure it. The lackluster ekphrasis of David's Neoclassicist painting, discussed above, stands in stark contrast to the occasional Cubist vision of Senator Ableukhov. In his early essays, Bely prefigured the Russian Futurist focus on the liberation of the Word from its traditional boundaries. The novel's Cubist dimension corresponds to the emergence of Futurism in Russia at the time of the novel's writing. Even though Bely did not reference contemporary Cubist and Expressionist artists in his critical writing or memoirs, we may conclude that *Petersburg* is not only a synthesis of the arts but also of the history of art movements, ranging from the seventeenth-century Baroque, revived by some modernists at the turn of the twentieth century, to an array of other modernist practices.

Notes

1. Andrei Belyi, *Na rubezhe dvukh stoletii*, ed. A. Lavrov (Moscow: Khudozhestvennaia literatura, 1989), 300–1. See Claude Monet's *Haystack* at http://www.webexhibits.org/colorart/dh.html.

2. Andrei Bely, *Petersburg*, tr. John Elsworth (London: Pushkin Press, 2009).

3. Andrei Belyi, "Formy iskusstva," in *Simvolizm kak miroponimanie*, ed. L. Sugai (Moscow: Respublika, 1994), 100–103.

4. Andrei Belyi, "Problema kul'tury" (1910), in *Simvolizm kak miroponimanie*, 24.

5. For a survey of Russian modernist painting, see John Bowlt, "Art," in *The Cambridge Companion to Modern Russian Culture*, ed. N. Rzhevsky (Cambridge: Cambridge University Press, 2012), 213–49.

6. See Benois's *Bronze Horseman* series at http://ppt-online.org/52371. See also S. S. Hoisington, "*Mednyi vsadnik* through the Eyes of Alexander Benois," *Russian Literature* 28.4 (1990), 479–506. Megan Swift, "The Petersburg Sublime: Alexander Benois and the *Bronze Horseman* Series," *Germano-Slavica* 17 (2009–10), 3–24.

7. See Konstantin Somov's paintings and drawings at http://gallerix.ru/album/Somov.

8. See *October Idyll* at http://petersburg.berkeley.edu/bely/city.html.

9. Andrei Belyi, *Mezhdu dvukh revoliutsii*, ed. A. Lavrov (Moscow: Khudozhestvennaia literatura, 1990), 135.

10. Belyi, *Mezhdu dvukh revoliutsii*, 170.

11. Belyi, *Mezhdu dvukh revoliutsii*, 412.

12. Andrei Belyi, "Smysl iskusstva," in *Simvolizm kak miroponimanie*, 121.

13. Richard Moran, "Artifice and Persuasion: The Work of Metaphor in the *Rhetoric*," in *Essays on Aristotle's Rhetoric*, ed. A. O. Rorty (Berkeley: University of California Press, 1996), 392.

14. Andrei Belyi, "Gorod," in *Kritika, estetika, teoriia simvolizma* (Moscow: Iskusstvo, 1994), 2:324.

15. Andrei Belyi, "Magiia slov," in *Simvolizm kak miroponimanie*, 140.

16. See https://en.wikipedia.org/wiki/Athena#/media/File:Amphora_birth_Athena_Louvre_F32.jpg.

17. See Bely's drawings and some visual examples from *Thought Forms* at http://petersburg.berkeley.edu/bely/city.html.

18. Bely to R. V. Ivanov-Razumnik (December 1913), in "Dopolneniia," Andrei Belyi, *Peterburg*, ed. L. Dolgopolov (Moscow: Nauka, 1981), 516.

19. See https://www.khanacademy.org/humanities/renaissance-reformation/northern/hieronymus-bosch/a/bosch-the-garden-of-earthly-delights.

20. Bely to Aleksandr Blok (4.IV.1912), in their *Perepiska 1903–1919*, ed. A. Lavrov (Moscow: Progress-Pleiada, 2001), 448.

21. See Dobuzhinsky's and Benois's drawings at http://petersburg.berkeley.edu/bely/city.html.

22. See both drawings at http://stpetersburg.berkeley.edu/bely/characters.html.

23. Andrei Belyi, "Pesn' zhizni," in *Kritika, estetika, teoriia simvolizma*, 52.

24. Andrei Bely, *Gogol's Artistry*, tr. Christopher Colbath (Evanston: Northwestern University Press, 2009), xxxv.

25. Nikolai Berdiaev, "Pikasso" (1914), in *Sud'ba Rossii: Krizis iskusstva* (Moscow: Kanon, 2004), 275.

26. Nikolai Berdiaev, "Astral'nyi roman" (1916), in *Sud'ba Rossii*, 281. See the essay's English translation: www.berdyaev.com/berdiaev/berd_lib/1916_233.html.

27. Called Cubo-Futurism in Russian painting.
28. Andrei Belyi, "Iskusstvo," in *Kritika, estetika, teoriia simvolizma*, 200.
29. Viktor Shklovskii, "Khod konia," in *Gamburgskii schet*, ed. A. Galushkin and A. Chudakov (Moscow: Sovetskii pisatel´, 1990), 148.
30. See http://stpetersburg.berkeley.edu/bely/bomb.html.
31. Kandinsky, "Reminiscences," in *Complete Writings on Art*, ed. K. Lindsay and P. Vergo (New York: Da Capo Press, 1994), 363.
32. "On the Spiritual in Art," in *Kandinsky: Complete Writings on Art*, 147–218.
33. See http://www.wassilykandinsky.net/work-36.php.
34. See Sixten Ringbom, *The Sounding Cosmos: A Study in the Spiritualism of Kandinsky and the Genesis of Abstract Painting*. Acta Academiae Aboensis, Series A, 38.2 (1970).
35. Belyi, *Nachalo veka*, ed. A. Lavrov (Moscow: Khudozhestvennaia literatura, 1990), 146.
36. See https://www.wikiart.org/en/wassily-kandinsky/painting-with-red-spot-1914.
37. Kandinsky, "Reminiscences," in *Complete Writings on Art*, 373.
38. See Olga Matich, "Bely, Kandinsky, and the Impulse to Abstraction," in *"Petersburg"/Petersburg: Novel and City*, ed. Olga Matich (Madison: University of Wisconsin Press, 2010), 83–120.

Petersburg and Urbanism in the Modernist Novel

TARAS KOZNARSKY

As the dominant literary genre in nineteenth-century Europe, the novel is largely a city creature. The modernist novel is more than that—it emerged from an epoch of unprecedented urban growth and intensification of urban life. The modernist novel, then, is an urban genre that bears the signs of the metropolitan psychological condition, characterized by Georg Simmel as an incessant barrage of outer and inner stimuli.[1]

Throughout the nineteenth century, novelists reveled in the use of urban settings that provided a great variety of physical and social spaces and venues for their characters' pursuits and encounters, collisions and escapes. Self-styled realist and naturalist novels approached urban settings as fieldwork for examining the human condition and the complexities of the socio-economic environment. The protagonists of Honoré de Balzac, Gustave Flaubert, Émile Zola, and Guy de Maupassant move into and through Paris in search of knowledge and self-realization, seduced by the city's material wealth, comforts, power, and prestige. The Victorian London of Charles Dickens unfolds through pubs and offices, mansions and grimy streets—a vast urban labyrinth where Oliver Twist flees his foes and Nicholas Nickleby pursues his fortunes. Fëdor Dostoevsky's inhuman, socially denigrating and alienating St. Petersburg exacerbates the sufferings of his heroes in *Crime and Punishment* (1866) and *The Idiot* (1868), leading to mental disintegration, violence and crime.

By the last decades of the nineteenth century, the great age of the novel was over, its philosophical and aesthetic positivism increasingly out of sync with the new reality and out of tune with the essence of human existence in the modern age. The modernist sensibility, so effectively conveyed by Edvard Munch's iconic painting *The Scream* (1893),[2] contrasted with its predecessors in a way that Malcolm Bradbury summarized astutely, if awkwardly: "Realism humanizes, naturalism scientizes, but modernism pluralizes, and surrealizes."[3]

Among early Russian modernists, Andrei Bely most actively contributed to the creative dismantling of the novel as a form and method of representation. In his four experimental works, which the author called symphonies (1902–8), Bely attempted to render the flux of reality in ways akin to music (see Steven Cassedy's essay in this volume). Abandoning traditional characters and linear narrative altogether, the writer situated his new syncretic genre between poetry and prose, building each verbal symphony as a sequence of visually and acoustically orchestrated, numbered fragments, organized into larger moods and tied together by a network of recurrent and shifting leitmotifs. The goal was to discover, through the perceptions of material reality, the points of connection and access to the higher world. These symphonies were conceived as part of the larger modernist quest for the spiritual transformation of humanity.[4] Not surprisingly, Bely's most successful and striking symphonic sections occur in the city of Moscow, which provides rich material for approximating the discordant, spatially diverse, chaotic movement of modern life.

In search of a literary form adequate to his intellectual and spiritual quest, Bely turned to the novelistic genre. He envisioned *The Silver Dove* (1909) as the first installment of a monumental and personal trilogy, *East or West*. Compared to the bold experimentation of the symphonies, *The Silver Dove* is something of a throwback to traditional narrative form. The novel chronicles the trip of an educated urbanite to a village—the mystical heart of Russia, turned chthonic and vile—where the protagonist meets a violent end. Here Bely not only reflects on the mysteries of the Russian soul but refines his handling of various linguistic and stylistic registers while elaborating the protean figure of a narrator who mediates between the rural and archaic collective ethos of Russian peasants and the exalted and tormented mind of a poet, philosopher, and philologist whose natural habitat is the modern urban metropolis.

This novelistic detour into the national depths of Russia led Bely back to the city. In *Petersburg*, the second installment of his ultimately unrealized trilogy, the writer reenacted the theme of the civilizational crisis and mystical destiny of Russia on the grand stage of the imperial capital. *Petersburg* has been described as the first modernist city novel, foreshadowing such works as James Joyce's *Ulysses* (1922), John Dos Passos's *Manhattan Transfer* (1925), and Alfred Döblin's *Berlin Alexanderplatz* (1929).[5] To be sure, the disjointed, shocking, and disorienting city emerged in European literature as early as 1857, in Charles Baudelaire's poetic collection *The Flowers of Evil*, whose narrator conveys his experience of Paris's dream-like scenery, swarming crowds, shattering noises, tormenting urges, and ghastly and spectral street encounters. While we also find examples of urban settings and sensibilities that anticipate those of modernism in the early works of Arthur Conan Doyle, Knut Hamsun, Joseph Conrad, G. K. Chesterton, and E. M. Forster, Bely was the first to make the city a central force of novelistic creation. No novel bears the name of a city in its title as convincingly as *Petersburg*.

Urbanism and the Modernist Novel

A brief scan of iconic city novels reveals *Petersburg*'s deep affinity with the transformations of urban space and experience in modernist prose. In *Ulysses*, the narrator's imaginary return to the Dublin of his youth generates or simulates, with the help of *Thom's Official Directory* for 1904, a startlingly encyclopedic and nostalgically cherished urban panorama that rivals the importance of the characters traversing it.[6] Yet Joyce's "flexible, plural assemblage" of an urban space is and is not about Dublin: it refracts urban and artistic practices of Paris, Zurich, and Trieste, wresting Dublin (and Irishness) from the "nightmare of history."[7] The seemingly boundless spaciousness in *Ulysses* results not from emphasis on a comprehensive charting of the urban area of Dublin, a 370,000-strong "second city of the British Empire" (after the five-million strong mammoth of London, then the largest metropolis in the world).[8] A port and a retail and distillery center, ridden with poverty and dominated by tenements, Dublin occupied a compact territory of barely fifteen square kilometers.[9] In his mental remapping of the city, Joyce ensured the microscopic precision of personal physical details of Dublin but did not set out to provide an encompassing social, spatial, or cultural portrait of the city itself. Rather, he focused on the interior space of Dublin—in the mind of his protagonist—where the local and geographic realia, psychological and physiological states, and universal cultural and mythical realms are woven into an infinitely unfolding single day (Bloomsday), generating an illusion of immensity.

In *Berlin Alexanderplatz*, Döblin's German metropolis emerges as a vast panorama of montaged discourses: speeches and stories; advertisements; scientific and statistical passages; the narrator's intrusions; snippets of high and popular culture; details of daily life and urban operations. These are placed into an almost mechanical universe, where living creatures, organic processes and inorganic forces interact, coexist, coalesce, and collide.[10] The fate of the novel's protagonist, Franz Biberkopf, is predetermined from the moment he leaves prison, entering Berlin's network of social relations and urban urges and instincts. The protagonist seems almost secondary to the city and its busy, fast-paced, transitory life, scrupulously investigated by the narrator who is, at once, a sociologist, an economist, a psychiatrist, an urbanist, a reporter, and a preacher. In the Golden Twenties of the Weimar Republic—the novel's time frame—Berlin doubled its population from two to four million, supplanting Paris as the center of European creative life. Yet this ambitious city—defined by media and entertainment, commodities and consumption, politics and statistics—lacked a sense of tradition and history, compared, for example, to imperial Vienna.[11] Last but not least, Alexanderplatz, the focus of Döblin's novel and a major square turned construction site for an underground transportation system, epitomized both the dream and the nightmare of a modern Babylon where mobility, efficiency, and rationality met dehumanizing mechanization, poverty, and crime.[12]

In Dos Passos's *Manhattan Transfer*, the city emerges as the only constant fixture of novelistic reality, in which characters are purposely made secondary to their urban environment, in a kind of mega-machine that processes a steady flow of human raw material.[13] Not unlike Döblin's Alexanderplatz, Manhattan towers over the travails and destinies of a rapid succession of characters as an expansive and dynamic urban panorama that stretches over two decades and includes nonnarrative and visual fragments—facts, slogans, inscriptions, invoices, etc.—and snippets of popular culture side by side with symbolic and biblical allusions.

Bely's *Petersburg* foreshadowed these modernist novels in its portrayal of the city as an environment, a force, a text, a nightmare, and a collective self with a first-person vantage point. Perhaps *Petersburg*'s fragmented urban panorama is not as materially dense or precise as Joyce's or Döblin's, and topography in *Petersburg*, at times rendered with remarkable vividness, is neither comprehensive nor necessarily verisimilar. Yet Bely's cityscape is deliberate and guided by the novel's main principle, which the author described to an enthusiastic reader:

> My entire novel depicts in symbols of space and time the subconscious life of crippled thought-forms [. . .]. My *Petersburg* is essentially an instantly recorded

subconscious life of people, torn from their elemental nature by consciousness [. . .]. The true location of the novel's action is the soul of some person not featured here, and who is exhausted by cerebral work, while the novel's dramatis personae are thought-forms that haven't reached the threshold of consciousness, as it were. Daily reality, "Petersburg," provocation and revolution unfolding somewhere against the novel's backdrop are but conventional garbs for these thought-forms. The novel could be titled "Cerebral Play."[14]

If *Petersburg* is all about cerebral play, what, then, is the city of St. Petersburg in the novel? As in *Ulysses*, Bely's city is a predominantly inner, mental space. However, in *Petersburg*, unlike in Joyce's novel, mental emanations incessantly invade and physically implant themselves in urban reality, suffusing it and squeezing this reality back into the minds of characters and into their fourth—astral—dimension. The city's physical space emerges as a splendid and imposing metropolitan core threatened by the impoverished islands, which seethe with hatred and encroach on the imperial capital from the hazy suburban distance. The abstract mental St. Petersburg expands from Senator Ableukhov's cranium along the straight lines of well-ordered boulevards, striving to encompass and rationalize the vast Russian empire and even the planet at large. The astral St. Petersburg expands still further, into the immeasurable fourth dimension. Every place here can serve as a portal for shadowy beings, or thought-forms (see Maria Carlson's essay in this volume); while city dwellers may be summoned, at any moment, and issued a passport into the other world. The textual St. Petersburg is equally expansive, encompassing a vast array of citations and allusions remolded by Bely's "fire of dissonance," as he once put it in a letter to Aleksandr Blok, to form the leitmotifs that define the novel's narrative fabric and its ineluctable "Petersburg-ness."[15]

The City as Text in Bely's *Petersburg*

In the Prologue, St. Petersburg emerges as a point of thought, an idea from which the metropolis is ushered into reality, becoming a power that underpins the ultimately unstable edifice of the Russian Empire. Unfolding into a rational grid of public spaces, the city emplaces itself on the abstract plane of a map with the dotted circular symbol referencing the imperial capital (11–12).[16] The Prologue serves as an overture showcasing the novel's main reality-generating mechanism: cerebral play. In the first chapter, the reader is treated to the exuberant emergence of Senator Ableukhov's house out of his own head, a process fusing material—even physiological—and abstract, geometric dimensions.

The same chapter documents the appearance of the terrorist Dudkin as a materialization of Apollon Apollonovich's terror at the sight of a city crowd. The chapter concludes with the narrator's revealing commentary on the principle of construction and proliferation of the novel's shadowy nightmarish world:

> Cerebral play is only a mask; beneath this mask proceeds the invasion of the brain by forces unknown to us: and what if Apollon Apollonovich is woven from our brain—he will still be able to terrify with another startling existence that attacks at night. Apollon Apollonovich is endowed with the attributes of this existence; and with the attributes of this existence all his cerebral play is endowed too.
>
> Once his brain has erupted in the mysterious stranger, that stranger exists—exists in fact: he will not vanish from the Petersburg Prospects, as long as the senator exists with thoughts of this kind, because thought, too, exists.
>
> So let our stranger be a real stranger! And let my stranger's two shadows be real shadows! (74)

Petersburg creates a complex system of relationships between a real world that dissolves into ephemera and mental perceptions of this world that acquire material aspect. In Bely's novel, physical reality and human beings are derivations of thoughts and perceptions, as if someone were "poking fun" at the world, imagining it and forcing that imagination to materialize, yet in the end becoming fully dependent on the specters of his own making.[17]

The urban space of Bely's St. Petersburg is simultaneously real and fantastic. Some streets and locations are markedly concrete and verisimilar—for example, the Winter Canal. Others, even though presented in great detail, are pure inventions, such as the Likhutins' apartment building or the edifice with the bearded caryatid, where the senator's Establishment is housed. Leonid Dolgopolov points out several instances of spatially impossible itineraries in the novel, qualifying Bely's map of St. Petersburg as based on "the principle of topographic contamination."[18] Yet the unique specificity and individuality of Bely's cityscape is never in doubt. Topographic contamination supports the novel's fluid textuality, partaking in the multilayered production of what has been called "the Petersburg text of Russian literature," a concept first elaborated by the literary historian Vladimir Toporov and briefly discussed in Leonid Livak's introduction to this volume.[19]

Informing Bely's novel with a rich tradition of the city's literary representation, "the Petersburg text" is characterized by the inner cohesion of its constituent narratives authored by Pushkin, Gogol, Dostoevsky, and many others. Yet, where do these constituent texts cohere but in the minds of readers and writers consuming and generating them? To a significant degree, then, "the Petersburg text" is a brilliantly realized cerebral play of Vladimir Toporov, whose mind was "trained" by the cerebral play of Bely's *Petersburg*. Russian modernism, after all, did much to impart a sense of unity to the motley legacy of nineteenth- and twentieth-century Russian literature.[20] *Petersburg* is, indeed, a veritable encyclopedia of the "Petersburg text of Russian literature." Bely's diverse repertory of text-generating devices includes stylistic and narrative mimicking, prolific borrowing, and parodic appropriation from other authors.[21] As Donald Fanger observes,

> [*Petersburg*'s] tempo is Dostoevskian, as are many of the squalid indoor settings. But the street scenes are Gogolian, one of the sub-plots Tolstoyan [the senator and his wife], and a series of ubiquitous Pushkinian motifs are condensed into a central scene [Dudkin's madness], which is a reprise of the tragic crux of *The Bronze Horseman*, staged in terms that recall the confrontation of Ivan Karamazov with his devil. The element of literary pastiche is thus strong. And it serves, along with a host of musical, poetic, legendary, and historical associations, to add an anomalous dignity, a kind of bizarre portentousness, to the cartoon-like banalities of the story and the disconcerting flippancies of the protean narrative voice.[22]

The simultaneity of empirical and literary layers in Bely's urban space constitutes the unique mosaic identity of St. Petersburg, its soul and its "text"—the latter through a peculiar symbiosis of real and virtual worlds. Thus, in Robert Alter's judgment, *Petersburg* "calls to our attention a certain correlation between the modern city as a construct of human design and technology and the modern novel as an inventive assemblage of self-conscious, sometimes iconoclastic, artifices."[23] Take Nevsky Prospect, one of the central loci of the novel's cerebral play. To describe this street, Bely appeals to our knowledge of Gogol's Petersburg tales. His narrator employs a metonymical sequence of grotesquely perambulating side-whiskers, moustaches, hats, sleeves, smiles, feet, and noses (26, 340, 343–44, 433) familiar to us from Gogol's 1835 stories "Nevsky Prospect" and "The Nose." Such intertextual contamination transforms Bely's Nevsky Prospect into a protean site where the physical, mental, literary, and astral dimensions fuse, invade, and amplify one another, never losing connection to their original locus—the city of St. Petersburg, which incessantly barrages the mind with cerebral play, as underscored by the repeated use of the adjective *peterburgskii*, derived from the city's name.

Bely's purposeful use of this adjective, not necessary for the sake of mimesis, makes the city both hyper-real and strange as Petersburg is imprinted into its own weather and atmosphere, urban space and architecture, inhabitants and infrastructure. Petersburg also partakes in larger geographic networks. The "angry note of '*u*'," marking the Russian pronunciation of the city's name, becomes a sound of revolutionary unrest that grips Russia and "reaches an unusual strength and clarity: "*uuuu-uuuu-uuu*" rings out quietly in the suburban fields of Moscow, Petersburg, Saratov" (102). The city barrages the mind with its many names, nicknames and doubles: Petersburg, a western modern metropolis; Saint-Petersburg, providential and saintly city; Peter, a familiar place (11); Peterburkh/Piterburkh, a low-class locale;[24] Palmyra, an elegant and exotic capital (451); Teheran, the city's chtonic and oriental double; Gehenna, a site of infernal annihilation (64, 272). This naming interface ties together Petersburg's origins and destiny, its glorious emergence and disintegration, foreshadowed in the narrator's prophesy of the battle between West and East, order and chaos—in the vast expanse where Russia the Bronze Horse will take the ultimate leap over history: "There will be a great disturbance; the earth shall fly apart; the mountains themselves shall collapse from the great quake; and the native plains shall be covered with hills from the quake. On the hills will stand Nizhnii, Vladimir and Uglich. But Petersburg will sink" (132).

The effect of cerebral play on *Petersburg*'s urbanism is twofold. First, it persistently dislocates the city from reliable empirical reality onto the plane of the mind, which generates, absorbs, and recycles thoughts, willfully and even violently ushering them into reality. Such a fusion of empirical and mental processes contributes to the sense of the immensity of St. Petersburg. The city is, at once, a dot on the map; a nearly invisible, abstract point of thought; and a two-million strong metropolis, the world's fifth largest in Bely's day. That metropolis expands even farther, through its porous space, into the fourth dimension—the astral cosmos that, in turn, intrudes into the life of the city. Yet, unlike Joyce's witty play with elevation into other dimensions—Leopold Bloom's Elijah-like assent-departure from a pub; his mental leap into the starry sky; Stephen Dedalus's call to Edenville—astral encounters in *Petersburg* are always catastrophic and annihilating.

In *Petersburg*, cerebral play emphasizes the process of the concurrent creation of the city and the novel. The city, we read in the Prologue, "not only seems, but truly manifests itself—on maps: in the form of two concentric circles with a black point in the middle; and from this mathematical point, which possesses no dimensions, it energetically proclaims that it exists: from there, from that said point, swarms of printed books issue in a torrent; from this invisible point with great momentum issue circulars" (12). Here John Elsworth's translation of the novel departs from the Russian of the original, which can be rendered into English as follows: "The swarm of the printed book issues in a torrent; from this invisible point with great momentum issues the circular" (*nesëtsia potokom roi otpechatannoi knigi; nesëtsia iz etoi nevidimoi tochki stremitel'no tsirkuliar* [Belyi, *Peterburg*, 10]). That printed book is most probably Bely's novel, visualized as some astral-typographical "mass" emerging from the infinite plane of thought (and from a physical page), rapidly crashing onto and enveloping the vision, mind and space of its reader, *preceding* the government circular and preempting any rational prescription. The city created by Tsar Peter I's decree originated in government circulars and orders; whereas Peter's reforms, symbolized by his city, begat modern Russian literature. But in Bely's *Petersburg*, literature asserts its primacy in creating the mythologized city of Peter, which has its own "text" in the Russian literary tradition.

Foreshadowing Joyce's practice, Bely enhances his urban novel's fictional space with vast networks of quotations, pastiches, and parodies that provide schemata of characters' relationships, actions, and fates.[25] In *Ulysses*, the central Homeric intertextual scaffolding imparts coherence to the novel's structure and a degree of elegance and epic grandeur to Dublin, leading Stephen Dedalus and the reader out of the nightmare of history. In Bely's novel, the "Petersburg text of Russian literature" enters the city by means of cerebral play and leads the characters and readers alike straight *into* the nightmare of history. This nightmare is epitomized in *Petersburg* by the leitmotif of the bomb: it encompasses, on one hand, the material "sardine-tin of terrible import" that contains the ticking mechanism and intensifies the pace of the novel, and, on the other hand, the mental bomb of the impending, tactile terror of madness and disintegration, implanted in characters by the invisible trajectories of incessant cerebral play.

If the material bomb only damages the Ableukhovs' house, psychological explosive devices maim or destroy several characters—Apollon Apollonovich; his son, Nikolai; the revolutionary Aleksandr Ivanovich Dudkin; and Sergei Sergeich Likhutin, the husband of Nikolai's romantic interest Sofia Petrovna. Even Lippanchenko's grisly death is accompanied by an acute premonition and then the physiological-cosmogonic sensation of an expanding, exploding body thrust into the planetary realm (520). In the end, the novel's St. Petersburg as a material implementation of an idea and the novel itself as a work impregnated with the "Petersburg text of Russian literature" together emerge as bomb-like bodies that cannot prevent centrifugal annihilating forces from spilling back into the world, culture, and society. As the novel celebrates the city's emergence from its pages, it also sings of St. Petersburg's long prophesied demise in imminent apocalyptic calamities (see David Bethea's essay in this volume).

Even among the most ambivalent modernist explorations of the Russian imperial capital, *Petersburg* stands out by virtue of its focus on cataclysmic architecture and apocalyptic design. Should we be surprised, then, by Bely's desire to proceed from *Petersburg* to the final, positive part of his projected trilogy, *East or West*, under the tentative title *The Invisible City*? Can we actually imagine what kind of an urban space this invisible city could have been? All we know is that in his unrealized novel Bely wanted to reveal, in an Anthroposophical key, the mystical inner life of the human spirit liberated from lowly discrepancies and reunited with the universe.[26]

Urbanism and Abstraction as Narrative Problems

Great modernist novels reach beyond the boundaries of the genre, becoming works "that are no longer novels" because they turn "theory into a novel."[27] Marcel Proust's saga, *In Search of Lost Time* (1913–27), unfolds as a theory of narrated time; *Ulysses* playfully engages with Aristotelian theory; and *Berlin Alexanderplatz* opens up the space of the novel to include scientific—physical, economic, and biological—discourse. Modernist novels reject the positivism of nineteenth-century realist conventions by placing "the mind's adventures where the old form used to situate material action."[28] Engaging the mind with urban space, the narrators of *Ulysses* and *Berlin Alexanderplatz* transform mimetic representations of urban settings into dynamic assemblages of empirical details and fragments of memories, mental processes, scientific theories, and cultural artifacts—to accompany the mind's adventures in the city. As a result, Döblin's Berlin and Joyce's Dublin sport an illusory depth of existence that is at once individual and universal, inscribing these cities into the urban networks of modernist cultural production. Furthermore, as the modernist novel discovers the "stream of consciousness" narrative technique, urban assemblages become further fused with the wandering mind.

Petersburg is no exception to this general trend in transnational modernist culture. It is indeed a pioneering work by virtue of being among the first literary narratives to explore the stream of consciousness technique (see Violeta Sotirova's essay in this volume). Yet Bely's narrative consciousness is not easy to pin down or classify—it is surely not identical to the narrator or any character in *Petersburg*. The mental force behind the flow of the narrative seems to operate on a different level. Robert Alter describes the workings of the narrative mind in *Petersburg*: "Bely's very self-consciousness about the operations of the mind leads him technically not to a verbal simulation of the movement of consciousness, as in Joyce and Woolf, but rather to a narratorial overview, sometimes visually descriptive in character, of the workings of consciousness, a kind of hidden camera that pokes into the cranium [. . .] to follow, often in a manifestly visual fashion, the swirling progression of images and ideas going on in the brain."[29] Such a method, Alter suggests, contributes to the spectral irreality of the city in the novel, its "problematic relationship with both human community and individual consciousness," and its intrinsic resistance "to comprehensive observation."[30] These observations are related to the notion of cerebral play, but we can push Alter's striking metaphor still further.

What could a camera poking into a cranium reveal? Wrinkles of gray matter straightening into an elegant staircase in the Ableukhovs' house as it materializes out of the senator's head in a vividly portrayed process (45–47)? The swirling pictures that fuse retinal images of objects delivered to the visual cortex, with some colored swirls of emotions, as Bely's own drawings might suggest?[31] Colorful darkness? Or some levitating abstract geometric figures and schemes from which thoughts originate? What would a city look like on the inside of the cranium through a hidden camera? What forms could Bely's "invisible city" have taken, had he realized his plans for the *East or West* trilogy, other than a spaceship in the form of the Anthroposophical temple, the Goetheanum, which the writer helped build in the Swiss town of Dornach during World War I? Of course, we can only speculate. One thing, however, seems certain enough. Bely's aesthetic evolved in the direction of abstraction (see Olga Matich's essay in this volume) as a result of his intellectual and artistic crisis of 1913, at a critical juncture in the history of Russian modernist culture, which saw an explosion in cognate poetic and painterly experiments between 1912 and 1915. Bely's crisis expressed itself in the writer's momentary abandonment of the verbal medium for the sake of other forms of creative expression, such as eurhythmics and drawing, which, he thought, better channeled his spiritual progression.[32]

From the time *Petersburg* was serialized, in 1913–14, attempts have been made to explain the novel's qualities by aligning it with concurrent modernist practices in visual arts. Nikolai Berdiaev's assessment of Bely as a "Cubist in literature" gained some traction, drawing attention to the fragmentation, even pulverization of the world in *Petersburg*, and to the bursting of boundaries between objects and the physical, mental, and astral processes in the novel.[33] Berdiaev's striking characterization of Bely, on the same occasion, as "the only true, major Futurist in Russian literature" also seems less extravagant today. More recently, scholars have linked *Petersburg*'s visual aesthetic and its author's artistic philosophy to those of the Russian modernist painters Pavel Filonov and Wassily Kandinsky, highlighting certain salient aspects of the novel, but without offering a fully convincing explanation of the shapes, movements, and evolutions of

Petersburg's thought-forms.[34] I think that, to appreciate Bely's experimental aesthetics, one should widen our frame of reference to other modernist practices. Of these, for example, Kazimir Malevich's pictorial and architectural "pure forms," which, according to the painter, could be discovered in "the fourth dimension" by "the intuitive reason" of artists (1915), exhibit significant affinities with Bely's philosophy of art by virtue of envisioning a path toward humankind's new creative and spiritual capacities. Pavel Filonov's striving to create "biologically made paintings" that capture the entirety of visible and invisible predicates of chosen subjects also promise interesting connections with the cerebral play of Bely's novelistic narrative.

Naturally, abstraction differs from one artistic medium to another, but it always emphasizes art's departure from material reality, distilling artistic language in a given medium to its most fundamental elements. In music, abstraction is associated with the modernist composer Arnold Schoenberg's dismantling of tonal harmony, reordering the relationship between the notes, and establishing new rules of musical progression. In visual arts, abstraction meant the rejection of the figurative representation of external reality, with a shift of focus to the most fundamental elements of painting: color and form. In Russian verse, concurrently to Bely's work on *Petersburg*, the "transrational" poets Velimir Khlebnikov and Aleksei Kruchënykh sought the primeval magical energies of pure sounds, liberated from conventional verbal signification. Can there be abstraction in the medium of the novel—a literary narrative form most dependent on figurative representation? Can there be a "transrational" novel, and what would this mean for the modernist artistic preoccupation with urbanism?

In *Petersburg*, Bely clearly contemplates this theoretical issue. Other contributors to this volume (Steven Cassedy, Olga Matich) are certainly right to insist on *Petersburg*'s status as a *Gesammtkunstwerk*, or a total work of art that strives to fuse visual, acoustic, musical, and narrative dimensions of creative expression. Such syncretism and intermediality constitute *Petersburg*'s revolutionary contribution to the general history of the novelistic genre and to the development of the modernist urban narrative in particular. Bely's synthetic artistic method allows him to move well beyond the novel's generic conventions. The acoustic texture and rhythmical patterns of *Petersburg*'s language, as well as the novel's network of leitmotifs, challenge traditional means of narrative development and characterization. Bely's striving for abstract representation oscillates between the verbal and visual economy of dots, lines, and geometric figures. The visual effects of organic forms are much more difficult to render precisely in words: this explains the fact that the writer's most common device of abstraction is the figure of a swarm.[35] In *Petersburg*, Bely applies elements of visual abstraction both to human characters and to the city as the novel's protagonist, thereby approximating the existence of all his heroes, animate and inanimate, within the fluid realm of thought-forms.

As Bely moved on to other projects, the invisible city he meant to describe in the ultimate part of his novelistic trilogy remained just that. In 1917, he wrote *Glossolalia*, an experimental poem and an aesthetic-philosophical treatise pushing past the representational limits of narrative genres into the cosmogonic time of pure phonic action and ritual movement (dance, gesticulation). In *Glossolalia*—whose main characters are tongue, larynx, lips, and teeth—narrative action and space are turned inward, merging into acoustic substance and becoming a mystical swarm of sounds that burst in the human mind and mouth, the latter functioning as both an articulatory apparatus and a cosmic temple. Like visual forms in *Petersburg*, the drawings accompanying Bely's poem—triangles, circles, stylized human figures, whirling gestures, and sound-making charts—oscillate between the geometric and organic forms of abstraction.

Bely's *Petersburg* has remained the benchmark of the modernist urban novel by virtue of pioneering this genre and producing what may be its most radical realization. An exact contemporary of Proust's *In Search of Lost Time*, the first volume of which appeared in 1913, and a precursor of Joyce's *Ulysses*, *Petersburg* never gained the international recognition of its modernist counterparts. And yet, a hundred years since its appearance, Bely's novel resonates ever stronger with our current cultural concerns, tapping with its cerebral play—the theory of the novel and the theory of the city—into the civilizational tensions, intellectual quests, and creative anxieties of the twenty-first century.

Notes

1. *Simmel on Culture*, ed. D. Frisby and M. Featherstone (London: Sage, 1997), 175.
2. See Edvard Munch's *Scream* at http://stpetersburg.berkeley.edu/bely/characters.html. For a discussion of *The Scream* in connection to Bely's art, see Olga Matich's essay in this volume.
3. Malcolm Bradbury, "The Cities of Modernism," in *Modernism 1890–1930*, ed. Malcolm Bradbury and James Farlane (Atlantic Highlands, NJ: Humanities Press, 1978), 99.
4. Aleksandr Lavrov, "U istokov tvorchestva Andreia Belogo," in Andrei Belyi, *Simfonii* (Leningrad: Khudozhestvennaia literatura, 1991), 7.
5. Peter Barta, *Bely, Joyce, and Döblin: Peripatetics in the City Novel* (Gainesville: University Press of Florida, 1996), 19.
6. Heyward Ehrlich, "James Joyce's Four-Gated City of Modernisms," in *Joyce and the City: The Significance of Place*, ed. Michael Begnal (Syracuse: Syracuse University Press, 2002), 14.

7. Ehrlich, "James Joyce's Four-Gated City of Modernisms," 4–5.

8. See chart 21 in *Vseobshchii geograficheskii i statisticheskii karmannyi atlas*, third edition (Saint-Petersburg: Gikman i Marks, 1908).

9. Joseph Brady, "Dublin: A City of Contrasts," in *Voices on Joyce*, ed. Anne Fogarty and Fran O'Rourke (Dublin: University College Dublin Press, 2015), 77.

10. Nina Pavlova, "Epicheskoe nachalo v romanakh Al′freda Dioblina," in Alfred Döblin, *Berlin Aleksandrplats*, tr. I. Altukhova et al. (Moscow: Nauka, 2011), 489–90.

11. See Anne Fuchs, "Short Prose around 1900," in *The Cambridge Companion to the Literature of Berlin*, ed. Andrew Webber (Cambridge: Cambridge University Press, 2017), 71.

12. See Carolin Duttlinger, "Modernist Writing and Visual Culture," in Webber, *The Cambridge Companion to the Literature of Berlin*, 105–8.

13. James Lane, "*Manhattan Transfer* as a Gateway to the 1920s," *The Centennial Review* 16.3 (1972), 293. Heinz Ickstadt, "Province and Metropolis in the Literature of the American Twenties," *Arbeiten aus Anglistik und Amerikanistik* 8.2 (1983), 125.

14. Letter to R. V. Ivanov-Razumnik (December 1913), "Dopolneniia," in Andrei Belyi, *Peterburg*, ed. L. Dolgopolov (Moscow: Nauka, 1981), 516.

15. Andrei Bely to Aleksandr Blok (6.I.1903), in their *Perepiska 1903–1919*, ed. A. Lavrov (Moscow: Progress-Pleiada, 2001), 25.

16. Andrei Bely, *Petersburg*, tr. John Elsworth (London: Pushkin Press, 2009).

17. Leonid Dolgopolov, "Tvorcheskaia istoriia i istoriko-literaturnoe znachenie romana A. Belogo 'Peterburg,'" in Belyi, *Peterburg*, 571. For a detailed discussion of the fictional and real dimensions of St. Petersburg in the novel, see http://stpetersburg.berkeley.edu/.

18. Dolgopolov, "Tvorcheskaia istoriia," 609–16.

19. Vladimir Toporov, "Peterburg i 'peterburgskii tekst russkoi literatury,'" in *Peterburgskii tekst russkoi literatury* (Saint-Petersburg: Iskusstvo-SPb, 2003), 7–65. See also Vladimir Markovich and Wolf Schmid, eds., *Sushchestvuet li peterburgskii tekst?* (Saint-Petersburg: Sankt-Peterburgskii universitet, 2005).

20. Zara Mints, "Peterburgskii tekst i russkii simvolizm," in *Poetika russkogo simvolizma* (Saint-Petersburg: Iskusstvo-SPb, 2004), 103–15.

21. Ivan Iakovlev, "Parodiia kak intertekstual′naia lingvisticheskaia kategoriia," *Vestnik gosudarstvennogo universiteta im. N. A. Nekrasova. Lingvistika* 2 (2011), 206–10. Nadezhda Pustygina, "Tsitatnost′ v romane Andreia Belogo *Peterburg*," *Trudy po russkoi i slavianskoi filologii* 28 (1977), 80–97.

22. Donald Fanger, "The City of Russian Modernist Fiction," in Bradbury and Farlane, *Modernism*, 470.

23. Robert Alter, *Imagined Cities: Urban Experience and the Language of the Novel* (New Haven: Yale University Press, 2005), 101.

24. This folk form of the city's name is not rendered in the novel's English translations. See Belyi, *Peterburg*, 103–4, 220, 228.

25. Lena Szilard, "Andrei Belyi i Dzheims Dzhois (k postanovke voprosa)," *Studia Slavica Academiae Scientiarum Hungaricae* 25 (1979), 409.

26. Leonid Dolgopolov, *Andrei Belyi i ego roman "Peterburg"* (Leningrad: Sovetskii pisatel', 1988), 228.

27. Michael Wood, "The Modernist Novel in Europe," in *Oxford Handbook of Modernisms*, ed. Peter Brooker et al. (Oxford: Oxford University Press, 2010), 109–10.

28. Wood, "The Modernist Novel in Europe," 110.

29. Alter, *Imagined Cities*, 87.

30. Alter, *Imagined Cities*, 91, 94.

31. See Bely's drawings at: http://stpetersburg.berkeley.edu/bely/city.html.

32. See Monika Spivak, "Andrei Belyi v 1913 godu: v poiskakh al'ternativy slovu," in *1913: Slovo kak takovoe. K iubileinomu godu russkogo futurizma*, ed. Jean-Philippe Jaccard and Annick Morard (Saint-Petersburg: Evropeiskii universitet, 2015), 181–93.

33. Nikolai Berdiaev, "Pikasso" (1914) and "Astral'nyi roman" (1916), in *Sud'ba Rossii: Krizis iskusstva* (Moscow: Kanon, 2004), 275, 281.

34. Derek Maus, "Space, Time, and Things Made 'Strange': Andrei Belyi, Pavel Filonov, and Theory of Forms," in *Studies in Slavic Cultures*, ed. Helena Goscilo and Michael Brewer (Pittsburgh: Department of Slavic Languages and Literatures, University of Pittsburgh, 2000), 75–102. Olga Matich, "Bely, Kandinsky, and Avant-Garde Aesthetics," in *"Petersburg"/Petersburg: Novel and City, 1900–1921*, ed. Olga Matich (Madison: University of Wisconsin Press, 2010), 83–120.

35. Olga Matich, "Introduction," in *"Petersburg"/Petersburg*, 8.

Petersburg and the Problem of Consciousness in Modernist Fiction

VIOLETA SOTIROVA

"Let us record the atoms as they fall upon the mind in the order in which they fall," wrote Virginia Woolf in 1919, "Let us trace the patterns, however disconnected and incoherent in appearance, which each sight or incident scores upon the consciousness."[1] Woolf's plea was made in an attempt to free the writer of fiction from the tyranny of earlier traditions, nineteenth-century realism in particular. What stands out in her statement is the focus on consciousness and on the immediacy of experience, capturing accurately both the endeavor and the achievement of the modernist novel, which "manifested a general tendency to centre narrative in the consciousness of its characters, and to *create* those characters through the representation of their subjective thoughts and feelings."[2] This essay will examine the representation of consciousness in *Petersburg* against the backdrop of contemporary Anglo-American literary fiction. My goal is to locate Bely's novelistic project in the transnational modernist effort to revolutionize narrative techniques and, by so doing, to furnish a more faithful—modernists would say more realistic—account of human experience than had been made possible by nineteenth-century artistic doctrines and practices.

Consciousness as a Modernist Artistic Problem

The focus on character consciousness and the refraction of the narrative through someone's consciousness are among the defining features of the modernist novel. For one critic, commenting on James Joyce's opening in *A Portrait of the Artist as a Young Man* (1914–15), "the words seem to be said and heard directly from life itself [. . .]. Gone is any welcoming narrator, any clear or 'objective' descriptions—any proper beginning."[3] This parallel between the new novelistic language and life as we really experience it recalls Woolf's argument in "Modern Fiction" that life is not like the ordered and coherent depictions we find in nineteenth-century fiction that calls itself realist. The modernist novel does away with the controlling narrator who can instill this order in a work of art and instead allows the free-flowing consciousness of characters to dominate the narrative, thus infusing it with chaos and incoherence.

The subjective experience of literary characters, which we glean through the representation of their consciousness, is the primary concern of many modernist writers. But this subjective turn in modernist fiction was not without its literary precedents; and it did not happen in a cultural vacuum. The orientation toward narrative subjectivity burgeoned in nineteenth-century novels that presented information from a character's vantage point or filtered it though a hero's consciousness—a practice known today as free indirect style. In the Anglo-American tradition, Jane Austen is credited with pioneering free indirect style, which became the dominant narrative technique in her oeuvre. The effects of free indirect style are particularly evident in Austen's *Emma* (1815), where a character-oriented point of view governs the whole narrative, allowing for all the ironies of a protagonist's limited perspective to be experienced by readers as they occur. But nineteenth-century authors, although making use of free indirect style, often juxtaposed it with an omniscient and controlling narrator who delivered the ultimate truth of the narrative and was an arbiter of justice. Modernist writers, then, radicalized the various techniques of narrative subjectivity that their predecessors had begun to develop.

The European cultural climate informing this refocusing of the novelistic narrative was complex, and it would be reductive to single out one particular event or phenomenon. But it is certainly not an accident that the spike in modernist interest in narrative subjectivity coincided with the epistemological turn—a shift in our understanding of the basis of knowledge—occurring at the turn of the twentieth century. This epistemological turn concerned the renunciation of natural science as the paradigmatic form of truth statement dominant in the nineteenth century and on which literary fiction of the period had modeled itself.[4] This unsettling of the ultimate authority of natural science and empirical observation came with new types of scientific inquiry that looked past what was readily visible in the natural world. This refocusing also brought in its wake doubts about the scientific observer's position. Albert Einstein's theory of relativity and quantum physics undermined the universal validity of physical laws, making the human observer part of any scientific problem. The "recognition of epistemological limitation" sapped the positivist belief in science's ultimate claim on truth because it showed science as a construction of the human mind rather than a reflection of the world.[5]

Occurring parallel to the scientific revolution, the modernist revolution in art undermined any notion of ultimate truth that could be sought in a work of literature and vouchsafed by an authoritative figure such as the narrator. A parallel development in philosophy informing modernist literary practice was Henri Bergson's idea of the subjective experience of time (see Hilary Fink's essay in this volume). Bergson's concept of *durée*, or the individual experience of time, captured the uniqueness of individual consciousness. Bergson opposed his *durée* (duration) to what he called "clock time," the kind of mechanical temporal divisions imposed on the progression of time by the human intellect. In Bergson's theory, the experience of time constituted consciousness. This experience, or consciousness, was indivisible and agglomerative, uniquely individual and impossible to capture as linear progression or logical development. For one critic, "Bergson's notion of *durée* was a major influence on the cultural climate from which the stream-of-consciousness novel emerged."[6]

The philosophical and cultural underpinnings of modernist literature can help illuminate one of its most striking characteristics—its stylistic dismantling of form. Nowhere is this revolution in form more evident than in the representation of character consciousness. Motivated by an aesthetic belief in capturing the minute details of the phenomena of consciousness and embedded in a critical program seeking to subvert written conventions, the modernist representations of consciousness dismantle syntax and grammar and push literary language toward the extreme incoherence of orality and inner speech. While the central technique for the representation of consciousness, free indirect style, was used by earlier writers, its linguistic makeup becomes, in modernist literary fiction, more mimetic of the free associative leaps and referential opacities of private thought. Alongside it, the most experimental modernist works of Woolf and Joyce frequently deploy the interior monologue—an even more direct and inchoate mode of capturing the stream of consciousness.

Petersburg in the Transnational Modernist Canon

Positioning *Petersburg* within the transnational modernist canon is all the more important because, while it is often likened to the artistic achievement and significance of Joyce's *Ulysses*, Bely's modernist masterpiece actually predates and foreshadows Joyce's magnum opus. As in *Ulysses*, the city in Bely's novel becomes a literary protagonist in its own right (see Taras Koznarsky's essay in this volume). The haunting descriptions of St. Petersburg account for much of the critical agreement that *Petersburg*'s modernist provenance is "evident in the mood of anxiety and alienation that permeates the entire work and that arises out of the awareness of impending catastrophe."[7] Furthermore, as in *Ulysses*, a great part of *Petersburg*'s narrative is devoted to the thoughts and consciousness of heroes whose characterization radically diverges from the practice of the psychological novel by the self-styled realists of the nineteenth century. Thus, Hart's study of *Petersburg*'s narrative *I* emphasizes the novel's modernism by commenting on the fact that it lacks the definitive closure typical of nineteenth-century novels.[8] Keys sees *Petersburg* as a modernist narrative because he finds there "distinctive and, to a large extent, novel qualities held in common by a substantial group of works written during the period." Foremost among these qualities is narrative point of view, or the relationship between the novel's implied author, narrator, and characters.[9] However, while his modernist classification of the novel relies on many insightful comments about *Petersburg*—the lack of an objective, authoritative viewpoint; the ambiguity inherent in all statements, characters, and events; the relativity of all knowledge and cognition in the novel's chaotic universe—Keys avoids stylistic and narratological analysis that could clarify for us the representation of point of view in *Petersburg*.[10]

In her linguistic analysis of point of view in *Petersburg*, Simmons insists on the significance of "non-authoritarian narration" in the novel, which strikes her as parodic because "nothing or no one remains knowable or comprehensible," yet her main focus is on the different types of discourse presentation rather than their specifically modernist quality.[11] Although acknowledging that "one is hard pressed to line up enough convincing examples to make a case for the *Russian modernist novel* in a time marked by aversion for this genre among Russian art's movers and shakers," Livak still singles out *Petersburg* as one of two examples "in which Russian literature comes the closest to laying claim to its own 'modernist novel.'"[12] *Petersburg*'s qualities as a "philological novel" that "explores language—phonemes, morphemes, syllables, syntactic rhythm, page graphics—as a reality-generating medium," along with the fact that the novel "mocks positivist assumptions by showing the world as a linguistic illusion originating in the psyche," are the factors that most pervasively align it with transnational modernism.[13]

As mentioned above, critics have identified *Petersburg* as a counterpart to Joyce's *Ulysses*. In an article tellingly entitled "The Russian Joyce," Cornwell reviews pronouncements to this effect, starting with Vladimir Nabokov's 1965 declaration: "My greatest masterpieces of twentieth century prose are in this order: Joyce's *Ulysses*, Kafka's *Transformation* [or *The Metamorphosis*], Belyi's *Petersburg*, and the first half of Proust's fairy tale *In Search of Lost Time*."[14] Cornwell traces the critical rapprochement of Bely and Joyce back to a 1932 note in the Parisian journal *The New Review*, written by the Russian-born Irish modernist poet and translator George Reavey. Two years later, Bely obituaries—one in the Moscow newspaper *Izvestiia* (signed, among others, by Boris Pasternak), another in *The Times* of London—again compared the two authors. Writing in *The Times*, the émigré critic Gleb Struve suggested that Bely's "verbal and stylistic innovation [. . .] may be said to have anticipated [. . .] the experiments of Mr James Joyce."[15] More recent criticism locates the similarity between Bely and Joyce in shared thematic concerns, such as "the father-son, husband-wife complexes," as well as "on a mythic level, a common cult of Hellenism, parodies of Nietzsche," and "cultural provocation."[16] For Woronzoff, "Joyce's use of epiphany and Belyj's use of the aesthetic symbol" are "of central importance to the organisational patterns of *Ulysses* and *Petersburg*."[17]

Given Joyce's iconic status in the transnational modernist canon, to claim that Bely anticipated his achievement, and that there are many lines of comparison between *Petersburg* and *Ulysses*, is a powerful argument in favor of reevaluating Russian modernism's often obfuscated role in the larger history of modernist art and thought. Given also that the most significant achievement of Anglo-American modernism lies in the linguistic dexterity with which consciousness is represented in Anglophone modernist fiction, what follows is an exploration of Bely's technique of consciousness representation, with special attention to the figure of *Petersburg*'s narrator.

The Representation of Consciousness in *Petersburg*

At the time when Bely wrote *Petersburg*, free indirect style—the third person technique transcribing the thoughts, feelings and perceptions of characters, while still retaining the narratorial past tense—had been well established in the Russian literary tradition, where we find it in the writings of Tolstoy and Dostoevsky. However, Tolstoy still represents the extreme states of consciousness, when a character undergoes a crisis or is in a state of distress, through a grammatically coherent form of free indirect style, usually with some intervening narratorial explanation. Bely, in contrast, sacrifices grammatical coherence in order to capture the immediacy and the impact of the experience on a character's ability to articulate it verbally. Compare two passages, the first from Tolstoy's story "Master and Man" (1895), and the second from Bely's *Petersburg*:

> No sooner had Vasilii Andreich sprung clear than the horse found its feet again and plunged ahead. It gave a couple of leaps, let out another neigh and disappeared from sight, trailing the sackcloth and breeching behind and leaving Vasilii Andreich alone in the snowdrift. Vasilii Andreich dashed after it, but the snow was so deep and his fur coats so heavy that with every step he sank in over his knees and after running some twenty yards he was out of breath and stopped. What will become of it all? He thought. The coppice, the wethers, the leasehold, my shop and taverns, my metal-roofed house and barn, my son and heir? What's going on? It just can't be true! And for some reason he remembered the wormwood tossing in the wind which he had twice passed and experienced such a feeling of terror that he did not believe that this was actually happening to him. He thought it must be all a dream and tried to wake up, but there was no other waking world. It was real snow which lashed his face and settled on him and numbed his right hand whose glove he had lost; and this was a real wilderness, this place where he was now alone, like the wormwood, waiting for death, inevitable, swift and pointless.[18]

> He returned to his reading.
> "The necessary material in the form of a bomb with a clockwork mechanism has been conveyed to you in advance in a package . . ." Nikolai Apollonovich found an objection to this sentence: no, it hadn't been conveyed, it hadn't been conveyed! And having found an objection, he felt something akin to hope that it was all a joke . . . A bomb? . . . He didn't have a bomb?! . . . But, but—no!! . . .
> In a package?!
> Then everything came back to him: the conversation, the package, the suspicious visitor, the September day, and all the rest. (247)[19]

Both passages depict characters in a state of horror. Tolstoy's protagonist, however, is still able to think in coherent sentences in his free direct discourse, or interior monologue: "What will become of it all? He thought. The coppice, the wethers, the leasehold, my shop and taverns, my metal-roofed house and barn, my son and heir? What's going on? It just can't be true!" Likewise, Tolstoy's narrator blends the hero's inner states and thoughts into his own, third person discourse in free indirect style, while maintaining grammatical stability: "It was real snow which lashed his face and settled on him and numbed his right hand whose glove he had lost; and this was a real wilderness, this place where he was now alone, like the wormwood, waiting for death, inevitable, swift and pointless." The characteristic markers of free indirect style are prominent in Tolstoy's representation of consciousness—the strings of clauses and phrases coordinated with "and," the adverb "now" referring to the character's present moment, the evaluative and emotive language—but the syntax and grammar still comply with the standards of written language.

In contrast, the thought patterns and feelings of Bely's hero are traced in such a way that Nikolai Apollonovich's initial incredulity and gradual realization (he already has the bomb intended for killing his father) are captured in real time. Woolf's "record[ing of] the atoms as they fall upon the mind" is here brought to perfection. The narratorial depiction of the hero's inner state, or *psychonarration*—"Nikolai Apollonovich found an objection to this sentence"—presents nonverbal aspects of character consciousness. The ensuing fragments ("no, it hadn't been conveyed, it hadn't been conveyed!"; "A bomb? . . . He didn't have a bomb?! . . . But, but—no!! . . .") follow the inner dialogue that the character conducts with himself, using the technique of free indirect style. The grammatical fragmentation, although not as extreme as Joyce's free associative leaps, is strikingly mimetic of the flow of thoughts and sensations as they occur in the human mind. This more extreme mimeticism (from the Greek "imitation") is characteristic of the modernist experiments with consciousness presentation. It involves a verbatim transcription of the stream of consciousness without any linguistic editing. On occasion, it pushes the discourse beyond easy comprehension. The phrase "In a package?" is graphically separated from the framing monologue by interlinear spaces, highlighting the pauses in the character's thought process and the halted and somewhat delayed realization of the truth. This graphic manipulation of print also plays an important part in the depiction of Nikolai Apollonovich's inspection and activation of the bomb:

> Just as before a tin can full of greasy sardines was still standing on the desk (he had once made himself sick by eating too many sardines and had since stopped eating them); a sardine-tin like any other: shiny, with rounded edges . . .
> No—no—no!
> Not just a sardine-tin, but a sardine-tin of terrible import!
> [. . .] a fussy little hair-spring measuring seconds had set off on its circular gallop, right up to the moment (that moment was not far off now)—to the moment, the moment, when . . .
> —the sardine-tin's terrible import would suddenly distend hideously; in a trice it would start to expand beyond measure; and then, and then: the sardine-tin would fly apart . . .

> —streams of that terrible import would promptly hurtle out in circles, tearing the table to pieces with a tempestuous roar: something would burst in him with a crash, and his body— would be blown to pieces too [. . .]
>
> —in a hundredth of a second all that would come about: in a hundredth of a second the walls would collapse, and the terrible import, expanding, expanding, expanding, would be hanging in the air in a mess of splinters, blood and stone. (312–13)

We can feel the character's distress more strongly because his stream of consciousness is again captured in real time: the multiple instances of negation reflecting his lack of comprehension and inability to accept the consequences of his rash actions, his projections into the narrative future through the future-in-the-past modal marker "would"—all align us with Nikolai Apollonovich's experience as it unfolds. The indentation of paragraphs iconically represents the thoughts as they dart through the hero's consciousness, signaling perhaps their disordered nature. The thoughts falter at the horror of the outcome of Nikolai's hideous act: "and then, and then"; "right up to the moment (that moment was not far off now)—to the moment, the moment, when . . ." The incomplete grammatical structures mirror the inability of the character to conceive of the consequences and his inability and resistance to articulate them.

Bely is particularly skilled at transcribing the delirious states that invade Nikolai Apollonovich's consciousness as he struggles to comprehend the horror of patricide, which he is expected to commit:

> And he jumped up: a terrible dream . . . But what kind? He could not remember the dream; his childhood nightmares had returned: Pepp Peppovich Pepp, swelling up from a little ball into a colossus, had evidently fallen quiet there for the time being—in the sardine-tin; his age-old childhood delirium was returning, because
>
> > —Pepp Peppovich Pepp, this little ball of terrible import, was quite simply a bomb belonging to the party: it was ticking away there inaudibly with its hairspring and its hands; Pepp Peppovich Pepp would expand, expand, expand. And Pepp Peppovich Pepp would burst: everything would burst . . . (321)

The mixing up of childhood nightmares and characteristically alliterative names conveys some of the psychological regression that Nikolai Apollonovich is experiencing under the acute stress of his ordeal (see Judith Wermuth-Atkinson's essay in this volume). But in a manner similar to Joyce's opening in *A Portrait of the Artist as a Young Man,* Bely also evokes the perceptions of a child through the linguistic construction of this passage in free indirect style. The repetitions—"Pepp Peppovich Pepp would expand, expand, expand. And Pepp Peppovich Pepp would burst: everything would burst . . ."—resound with childhood naïveté and linguistic immaturity, as does Joyce's "Once upon a time and a very good time it was there was a moocow coming down along the road and this moocow that was coming down along the road met a nicens little boy named baby tuckoo . . . [. . .] He was baby tuckoo. The moocow came down the road where Betty Byrne lived . . ."[20] What is remarkable about Bely's passage cited above is not just his mastery of free indirect style, but the psychological dimension achieved in the presentation of his character's consciousness—the propensity of the mind to regress into infantile states when confronted by extreme stress. A further layer of literary effects is added through the juxtaposition and clash of the serious and the naïve, the political and the infantile, which produce the characteristically polyphonic spirit of the novel.

The mimetic quality of Bely's free indirect style is also visible in the frequent, sometimes excessive, repetitions that pervade the representation of character consciousness. Consider the following passages from *Petersburg,* where they are separated by two pages:

> Nikolai Apollonovich, dumbstruck by the letter, had raced past the merry *contredanse* a quarter-of-an-hour before the senator. How he had made his exit from the house he had no recollection. He came to his senses in a state of utter prostration in front of the Tsukatovs' entrance; he went on standing there in a clinging dark dream, in the clinging dark dampness, mechanically counting the number of carriages standing there, mechanically following the movements of someone tall and sad who was supervising public order: this was the district constable. [. . .]
>
> Quite naturally Nikolai Apollonovich moved off too in a clinging dark dream, in the clinging dark dampness, through which the rusty blur of a streetlamp glimmered obstinately: into that blurred light from the mist above, over the streetlamp's point, the caryatid at the entrance tumbled lifelessly, and in that blur of light a piece of the neighbouring house protruded [. . .]
>
> But no sooner had Nikolai Apollonovich moved off, than he noticed without concern that his legs were completely missing: there were some flaccid appendages floundering senselessly in a puddle; he tried in vain to gain control of those appendages: the flaccid appendages would not obey him; to look at they had all the outward appearance of legs, but he could not feel his legs (he had no legs). (243)

And now Nikolai Apollonovich kept trying to seize hold of appearances: there was the caryatid at the entrance; a caryatid like any other . . . And—no, no! It was not like any other caryatid—he had never seen anything of the sort: hanging there above the flame. And there was the little house: a little black house like any other.

No, no, no!

The house was not straightforward, just as nothing here was straightforward [. . .]

And his legs here—legs like any others . . . No, no! They weren't legs—but utterly unfamiliar flaccid appendages dangling idly. (245)

In the first passage, the narrator's discourse that describes the character's actions is saturated with the character's own perceptions, so that even this typically external report of action sounds more like character experience. The repeated prepositional phrases "in a clinging dark dream, in the clinging dark dampness" capture Nikolai Apollonovich's confused state and create a symbolic link between his inner state and the outside world. Their exact repetition across two paragraphs contributes to the sense that the hero's emotional experience governs the narration, as well as the representation of his consciousness in free indirect style. Both passages, although a couple of pages apart, are connected through a number of repetitions revolving around the protagonist's immediate perceptions of his surroundings: the caryatid, the house. The second time his perceptual focus falls on these objects, they are both presented as disfigured. In this way, Nikolai's disturbed thoughts are reflected through the disturbed perception of the caryatid and the house and through the disjointed syntax. Nikolai's inner turmoil is further enhanced through his sensation, portrayed in free indirect style, of his legs as "flaccid appendages." Once again, Bely's psychological depth in the use of free indirect style replaces the coherent and polished style of written prose. Repetition is characteristic of the modernist endeavor to represent consciousness in a verisimilar way, for as D. H. Lawrence put it, "the emotional mind [. . .] is not logical. [. . .] [It] makes curious swoops and circles. It touches the points of pain or interest, then sweeps away again in a cycle, coils round and again approaches the point of pain or interest. There is a curious spiral rhythm, and the mind approaches again and again the point of concern, repeats itself, goes back, destroys the time-sequence entirely, so that time ceases to exist."[21]

The repetition in Bely's portrayal of Nikolai's disturbed state signals the familiarity of the perceived objects (in that his mind keeps returning to them) and highlights the protagonist's acute shock, which makes these objects appear strange and disfigured. Repetition as the most rudimentary form of cohesion questions the stylistic stability of the prose, but its incantatory quality creates extreme mimeticism in the representation of consciousness. This mimeticism is further felt in the referentially opaque language that is one of the stylistic hallmarks of modernism: "All the time Nikolai Apollonovich tried not to think, tried not to understand: thinking, understanding—what *understanding* could there be of *that*; *that—just arrived, overwhelmed you, and roared*; if you thought about it—you'd go straight and throw yourself through a hole in the ice . . . What could you think? There was nothing to think here . . . because *that . . . that . . .* What was that?" (244). Again, repetition and incoherent syntax capture the disjointed nature of Nikolai's thoughts in the face of the order to blow up his father. But a further linguistic detail capturing his turmoil is the demonstrative pronoun "that," which has a distancing effect and expresses the hero's inability to articulate the hideousness of what is expected of him.

The demonstrative "that," together with the third person neuter pronoun "it," does double duty here: it signals the familiarity of the reference to the character—the fact that he does not have to articulate it to himself because he knows the referent; but it also signals the inarticulable nature of the referent. Even Nikolai cannot quite comprehend what "that" is. In terms of readerly effect, however, this use of an ambiguous pronominal reference that is familiar to the character, but not necessarily to the reader, creates a lacuna in meaning. While in this particular context, we can infer that Nikolai's thoughts flip from the packet to the bomb to the order to explode it, in other contexts the ambiguity of pronominal reference can only be resolved post factum, if at all: "It was the same as ever: *they* were keeping watch on Aleksandr Ivanovich . . . It had started like this: once, when he was returning home, he had seen a stranger coming down the stairs, who had said to him: 'You are linked with Him . . . '" (387). Although we have already witnessed some of the delusions that Aleksandr Ivanovich Dudkin experiences, it is not clear to the reader at this point, when Dudkin returns home after visiting Lippanchenko, who "they" refers to. It is not clear to Dudkin himself, but we only find this out later.

The text's semantic lacuna created by the referentially opaque pronoun has a multi-layered effect. On an immediate textual level it suggests Dudkin's unstable perceptual experiences, his paranoia and hallucinations. On the level of narrative style it underlines Bely's hyperrealism in the representation of character consciousness, a hyperrealism that creates difficulties with comprehension and processing for the reader. This technique is part of the modernist aesthetic, wherein "the opacity and relativity of deictic reference are recruited as part of a general strategy" marked by "the deliberate courting of difficulty."[22] To his credit, Bely foreshadows such opaque uses of deictic reference as are found, for example, in Katherine Mansfield's opening sentence in "*Feuille d'album*": "He really was an impossible person." Here both the referent of the pronoun "he" and the thinking consciousness behind this evaluation, which turns out to be a collective consciousness, are only revealed later in the text.[23]

The representation of consciousness in *Petersburg*, then, can be aligned with techniques practiced by Anglo-American modernist writers. Although Bely does not take his style to the extremes to which Joyce does it in *Ulysses*, his syntactic discontinuities, the pervasive use of repetition and opaque references are still features of modernist style, and by extension of free indirect style. These techniques help with the transcription of consciousness in its unorganized, spontaneous and immediate, and sometimes extreme, states. Rather than position modernism as anti-realist, they contribute to a hyperrealist quality that in itself can result in opacity.

In line with other modernist writers, such as D. H. Lawrence, Virginia Woolf, and Katherine Mansfield, Bely potentially transgresses the boundaries of realism in the dialogic interconnections that he creates across different characters' minds. One of the illusions of nineteenth-century realism is that the boundaries of individual consciousness are impenetrable. The stability of this belief is questioned and undermined by the modernist dialogic juxtaposition of different consciousnesses and by their portrayal as permeable and interconnected.

One of the parallels between *Petersburg* and *Ulysses*, suggested by Cornwell, is in the thematic focus on a father-son relationship.[24] Although, of course, both novels treat this theme differently, the dialogic links that are present in *Ulysses* between the experiences of Leopold Bloom and Stephen Dedalus create a subliminal connection between the two characters' minds and suggest indirectly Bloom's attachment to Stephen. In *Petersburg*, the complexity of Nikolai and Apollon Apollonovich's relationship, with all its political and Oedipal undertones (see Judith Wermuth-Atkinson's essay in this volume), is not only inscribed in the development of the surface plot, in Nikolai's oscillating attitude toward his father when presented with the extreme task of patricide, but also more subtly in the representation of each character's consciousness. Consider two passages from *Petersburg*:

> Evenly, slowly, languidly the cab trotted past the grenadier; evenly, slowly, languidly Nikolai Apollonovich bounced past the grenadier as well. The bright morning gleaming with sparks from the Neva, turned all its water into an abyss of burnished gold; the funnel of a hooting steamer hurtled into the abyss of burnished gold; he saw a gaunt figure on the pavement quicken its belated step, as it skipped across the stones — a gaunt figure, which . . . which he recognised: it was Apollon Apollonovich. (289)

> Apollon Apollonovich Ableukhov, who had seen the young girl to her home, was now hastening to the threshold of the yellow house; the Admiralty had just thrust at him the eight columns of its aspect; the black-and-white striped sentry-box was now behind and to his left; he was now walking along the Embankment, contemplating, out on the Neva, the abyss of burnished gold into which the funnel of the hooting steamer had just hurtled. (290)

As these excerpts demonstrate, both characters' perceptions focus on the same elements of their surroundings. At this moment, both father and son know about the assassination plot; both are terrified and disgusted by it. The description of the Neva as "an abyss of burnished gold" resonates with the feelings of both characters. More important, this description is embedded in the represented perception of each of them in the two extracts. The repetitions in the first cited passage strongly evoke Nikolai's consciousness; in the second passage, the repeated use of the past progressive in combination with the present-time deictic "now" ("was now hastening," "was now behind and to his left," "was now walking"), combined with other spatial deictic words, orientates the perspective toward the experiential perception of Apollon Apollonovich. The fact that they both perceive the river as an abyss and qualify this abyss with the same metaphor creates a strong resonance across their minds. This subtle dialogic relationship is an indirect hint at a connection that exists between the two characters and runs deeper than they may realize.

Even more striking is the fact that Apollon Apollonovich's and Nikolai's consciousnesses reverberate with the same experiences and sensations in the face of a critical situation. Compare the following excerpts from *Petersburg*:

> All the time Nikolai Apollonovich tried not to think, tried not to understand: thinking, understanding—what *understanding* could there be of *that*; *that—just arrived, overwhelmed you, and roared*; if you thought about it—you'd go straight and throw yourself through a hole in the ice . . . What could you think? There was nothing to think here . . . because *that* . . . *that* . . . What was that?
>
> No, here no one was capable of thought. (244)

> And now Nikolai Apollonovich kept trying to seize hold of appearances: there was the caryatid at the entrance; a caryatid like any other . . . And—no, no! It was not like any other caryatid—he had never seen anything of the sort: hanging there above the flame. And there was the little house: a little black house like any other.
>
> No, no, no!

> The house was not straightforward, just as nothing here was straightforward: everything in him was dislodged, disrupted; he was dislodged from himself; and from somewhere (no idea where), where he had never been, he was watching! (245)

> Apollon Apollonovich saw: there, a caryatid at an entrance; a caryatid like any other. But—no, no! It was not like any other caryatid—he had never seen anything of the sort in his life: hanging there in the mist. There was the side of a house; a house-side like any other, just a house-side, a stone one. But—no, no: it wasn't straightforward, just as nothing here was straightforward: everything in him was dislodged, disrupted; he was dislodged from himself and was now muttering senselessly into the midnight murk [. . .]
>
> Apollon Apollonovich found it hard to believe that *that* could be quite so simple. (253)

In the pair of examples cited earlier, with both Nikolai and Apollon Apollonovich contemplating the Neva, the characters occupied the same spatial location and could plausibly observe the same "abyss of burnished gold" on the river. But in the excerpts quoted above, there is no such spatial and temporal continuity between the protagonists' experiences. They are observing the same elements of their surroundings, but at different points in time. However, they both share the same subjective and distorted perceptions. There is a more interesting and less obvious connection, then, between Nikolai's consciousness and that of his father. Although a few pages apart, Nikolai's extreme sensation that "everything in him was dislodged, disrupted: he was dislodged from himself," is exactly mirrored in the representation of his father's consciousness, a mirroring that strikes the reader as odd. The exact repetition in the articulation of the characters' experiences in relation to the murder plot surpasses the logical boundaries of individual consciousness and suggests a continuation and transparency between their minds that creates a dialogic link. Although neither Nikolai nor Apollon Apollonovich would admit to such a strong subliminal connection between them, Bely inscribes it in the narrative by creating obvious echoes across the representations of their conscious and unconscious thoughts using free indirect style.

Conclusion

As *Petersburg* amply demonstrates, Bely shares with other modernist writers the quest for interrogating the boundaries of human consciousness and the possibilities that language offers for transcribing it. His dialogic use of free indirect style belongs to the transnational modernist tradition, with similar instances of dialogic interrelatedness found in the portrayal of character consciousness by D. H. Lawrence, Virginia Woolf, James Joyce, and Katherine Mansfield. These instances can be viewed as the modernist attempt to expose the artifice of fiction and, by extension, of character consciousness to which no one apart from the experiencing self should have access. But it is also possible to interpret these dialogic links across characters' minds as a positive attempt to suggest the deep connections that exist between human beings, especially if the characters' relationship is significant in the narrative.

This more metaphysical outlook on the representation of dialogic consciousness in the modernist novel is, as I have argued elsewhere, mirrored in Martin Heidegger's existential philosophy, which views people as relational beings, and in Henri Bergson's understanding of human intuition as an epistemological stance—a mode of knowledge that is as valid as cerebral intellectual analysis.[25] That twentieth-century philosophers and artists alike might be trying to represent the human subject as relational, in spite of the common critical understanding of modernism as an artistic movement that deconstructs human subjectivity and exposes the individual's alienation from herself, is not just a coincidence. It can perhaps be explained as a reaction to the chaotic and fragmented existence of the modern individual, a reaction that suggests subliminally a deeply rooted human longing for dialogue and community.

Notes

1. Virginia Woolf, "Modern Fiction," in *The Common Reader*, ed. A. McNeillie (London: Vintage, 2003), 1:150.

2. David Lodge, *Consciousness and the Novel* (London: Secker and Warburg, 2002), 57.

3. Jesse Matz, *The Modern Novel: A Short Introduction* (Oxford: Blackwell, 2004), 2.

4. Michael Bell, "The Metaphysics of Modernism," in *The Cambridge Companion to Modernism*, ed. Michael Levenson (Cambridge: Cambridge University Press, 2008), 11.

5. Bell, "The Metaphysics of Modernism," 11.

6. Anne Fernihough, "Consciousness as a Stream," in *The Cambridge Companion to the Modernist Novel*, ed. Morag Shiach (Cambridge: Cambridge University Press, 2007), 68.

7. Robert Russell, "The Modernist Tradition," in *The Cambridge Companion to the Classic Russian Novel*, ed. Malcolm Jones and Robin Miller (Cambridge: Cambridge University Press, 1998), 215. See also Maria Carlson, "Theosophy and History in Andrei Belyi's *Peterburg*: Life in the Astral City," *Russian Literature* 58.1 (2005), 34.

8. P. R. Hart, "The Ironic 'I' in *Peterburg*," *Russian Literature* 48.1 (2000), 33–45.

9. Roger Keys, *The Reluctant Modernist: Andrei Belyi and the Development of Russian Fiction 1902–1914* (Oxford: Clarendon Press, 1996), 10.

10. Keys, *The Reluctant Modernist*, 228–31.

11. Cynthia Simmons, "Non-Authoritarian Discourse in *Peterburg*," *Russian Literature* 27.4 (1990), 498.

12. Leonid Livak, "Russian Modernism and the Novel," in *A History of the Modernist Novel*, ed. Gregory Castle (Cambridge: Cambridge University Press, 2015), 131.

13. Livak, "Russian Modernism and the Novel," 125.

14. Vladimir Nabokov, *Strong Opinions* (New York: Vintage, 1990), 57.

15. Cited in Neil Cornwell, "The Russian Joyce," *James Joyce Broadsheet* 13 (1984), 2.

16. Cornwell, "The Russian Joyce," 2.

17. Alexander Woronzoff, *Andrej Belyj's "Petersburg," James Joyce's "Ulysses," and the Symbolist Movement* (Berne: Peter Lang, 1982), viii.

18. Leo Tolstoy, *Master and Man and Other Stories*, tr. Paul Foote (London: Penguin, 1977), 117–18.

19. Andrei Bely, *Petersburg*, tr. John Elsworth (London: Pushkin Press, 2009).

20. James Joyce, *A Portrait of the Artist as a Young Man* (London: Penguin, 1966), 7.

21. D. H. Lawrence, introduction to G. Verga, *Cavalleria Rusticana*, tr. D. H. Lawrence (London: Jonathan Cape, 1932), 26.

22. S. M. Adamson, "Literary Language," in *The Cambridge History of the English Language*, ed. Suzanne Romaine (Cambridge: Cambridge University Press, 1999), 4:647, 675.

23. Katherine Mansfield, *Selected Stories* (Oxford: Oxford University Press, 1981), 171.

24. Cornwell, "The Russian Joyce," 2.

25. Violeta Sotirova, *Consciousness in Modernist Fiction: A Stylistic Study* (Basingstoke: Palgrave, 2013).

Part Three

Aids for Reading and Studying *Petersburg*

An Annotated Synopsis of *Petersburg*'s First Edition (1913)

LEONID LIVAK

The purpose of this synopsis is to guide the reader through the often discouraging maze of Andrei Bely's novel, including its many logical inconsistencies, complex chronology, and deliberately disjointed narrative style. The synopsis also outlines the differences between *Petersburg*'s original, 1913 edition and its subsequent, significantly altered redactions. The plot of a novel as rife with unwitting logical gaps and intentional ellipses as *Petersburg* cannot be adequately conveyed in a traditional, linear narrative summary, since such a summary would inevitably impose a unifying and reductive interpretation on Bely's magnum opus, glossing over its irreconcilable contradictions, unduly simplifying its calculated difficulty, and obfuscating Bely's overriding modernist concern with the way a story is narrated (often at the expense of the story itself). I have, therefore, adopted an unorthodox format, splitting the novel into numbered episodes. While the synopsis faithfully follows *Petersburg*'s chapter and section divisions, the division of each section into numbered episodes is my own and informed by my experience of teaching the novel in the college classroom, where this synopsis was originally developed and tested as a reading and study aid.

At first glance, such a format may strike the reader as no less confusing than *Petersburg*'s plot, which the synopsis endeavors to trace. Yet this approach holds several advantages to more traditional plot summaries. It allows for the cross-referencing of related episodes throughout the novel, whose narrative is anything but linear. For example, the following parenthetical reference in Chapter II—(see I:40–41)—invites the reader to correlate the corresponding episode in that chapter to episodes 40 and 41 in Chapter I (with Roman numerals indicating chapter numbers and Arabic numerals representing episode numbers). This cross-referencing enables readers to go back and forth in the text, gaining a fuller understanding of particular events and making sense of seemingly unrelated but mutually informing occurrences. In its present form, the synopsis also leaves room for annotation as an additional tool for readers of *Petersburg*: it incorporates explanations of the novel's chronology; discussions of logical inconsistencies; and comparisons of *Petersburg*'s published version with early drafts that shed light on Bely's often obscure intentions.

Last but not least, this synopsis is not meant to be read in a linear fashion from beginning to end. Anyone trying to do so will see that it is by no means a work-around to reading a difficult modernist novel. Instead, the synopsis is designed to facilitate a meaningful experience of reading *Petersburg*. No reader, however well-prepared, can tackle this novel without repeatedly having to stop and ask: "What just happened?" or "Where did this come from?" or "Haven't I seen this somewhere before?" The present synopsis is designed to answer such questions: its system of cross-references and annotations lets the reader consult the synopsis at any point in the story and link any given episode, incident, or detail in the narrative to the network of related episodes, incidents, and details. In the process, it should be possible to situate specific events in the novel's overall chronology and to come to terms with *Petersburg*'s logical contradictions.

The synopsis cites *Petersburg*'s often puzzling section headings from John Elsworth's translation of the novel. For reasons of spatial economy, the following system of abbreviations is used throughout the synopsis:

1913   The novel's first edition. All page references to Andrei Bely, Petersburg, tr. John Elsworth (London: Pushkin Press, 2009).

1922   The novel's second edition. All page references to Andrei Bely, *Petersburg*, tr. Robert Maguire and John Malmstad (Bloomington: Indiana University Press, 1978).

1928   The novel's third edition (untranslated). All page references to Andrei Belyi, *Peterburg*, in *Sochineniia v dvukh tomakh*, vol. 2 (Moscow: Khudozhestvennaia literatura, 1990).

A.A.   Senator Apollon Apollonovich Ableukhov.

N.A.   Nikolai Apollonovich Ableukhov, a university student and A.A.'s son.

A.P.   Anna Petrovna Ableukhova, the estranged wife of A.A.
S.P.   Sofia Petrovna Likhutina, N.A.'s unrequited love and the wife of S.S.
S.S.   Sergei Sergeich Likhutin, an army officer and S.P.'s husband.
A.I.   Aleksandr Ivanovich Dudkin, a revolutionary terrorist and N.A.'s acquaintance.
V.E.   Varvara Evgrafovna Solovyova, a political radical and S.P.'s acquaintance.
L.   Nikolai Stepanych Lippanchenko, a revolutionary terrorist and police agent.
Z.Z.   Zoia Zakharovna Fleisch, L.'s consort.

Prologue

1. A discourse on St. Petersburg

Chapter I (30 September 1905)[1]

Apollon Apollonovich Ableukhov
1. A.A.'s ancestry
2. In the morning, a servant and a cook discuss a newly arrived letter from A.P.
3. A.A. works in his study. At 9:30, he takes his morning coffee in the dining room

In short, he was the head of a certain Establishment
4. A description of A.A.'s professional activity and social standing

North-East
5. At morning coffee, A.A. jokes with his valet
6. A.A. dresses, preparing to leave for his office. A survey of his system for shelving clothes

Grocer, grow, sir
7. Waiting for the carriage, A.A. reads his morning mail but does not open A.P.'s letter, writing on it: "Return to sender" (1913:20; this detail is excised in 1922/1928)
8. Servants gossip about A.A.'s dismissal of A.P.'s letter (1913:21; excised in 1922/1928)
9. On the way to the carriage, A.A. asks the valet about N.A.'s routine and

learns that yesterday N.A. was waiting for a costumier. Joking with the valet, A.A. leaves home

The carriage flew off into the mist

10. At 10:00,[2] A.A. gets into his carriage and departs

Squares, parallelepipeds, cubes

11. A.A. rides across central Petersburg

The inhabitants of the islands astound you

12. A stranger leaves a tenement building on Vasil'evskii Island,[3] carrying a package
13. The stranger crosses a bridge into central Petersburg

Catching sight of him, they opened wide, they shone, they flashed

14. Riding along Nevsky Prospect, A.A. sees the stranger and is deeply shocked by his gaze
15. A.A. arrives at the Establishment and jokes with a doorman

Two poorly dressed girl-students . . .

16. Shocked by the chance encounter with A.A., the stranger rushes across Petersburg
17. He is beset by street rumors about an assassination plot against A.A.

You hold your tongue! . . .

18. The stranger enters a restaurant and drinks vodka, waiting for someone
19. Another patron vainly tries to join him. The stranger hears snippets of conversations

The desk stood there

20. At the Establishment, A.A. walks toward his office and speaks with his secretary
21. A.A. enters his office, while realizing that he has seen the stranger before

He had seen the man of uncertain status[4]

22. A.A. recalls once seeing the stranger at home: he visited N.A.

Strange qualities

23. A.A. works in his office. Meanwhile, his brain engages in spontaneous "cerebral play"
24. A.A. thus sees his house, where a servant is going upstairs and across several rooms (see I:32)

Our role

25. Outside the restaurant, where the stranger is drinking vodka (see I:18–19), two police agents are discussing an imminent event. They mention a promise made by N.A.
26. One of the police agents enters the restaurant

And the face, moreover, had a glossy shine

27. The agent speaks with the unsuspecting stranger. They are L. and A.I., respectively
28. L. asks A.I. to take the package (see I:12) to N.A., along with a letter from L.[5]

What costumier might that be?

29. A description of N.A.'s living quarters at the Ableukhovs' family home
30. A precis of family history: two and a half years ago, A.P. left A.A., going abroad with a lover. The event coincided with the beginning of N.A.'s emotional and spiritual crisis
31. At noon, at home, N.A. intends to examine closely a newly arrived letter, written in verse and signed "An ardent soul." Instead, he gets engrossed in a book
32. A servant arrives at N.A.'s door (see I:24) to announce a visitor. N.A. thinks it is a delivery from his costumier (see I:9) and walks out to meet the visitor
33. A cardboard box containing a red domino and a black mask appears in N.A.'s room. He tries them on

A sodden autumn

34. A flashback to another day in September. N.A. returns to the bridge where he once almost committed suicide over unrequited love (see II:7), but decided instead to "give a terrible promise to a certain reckless Party" (1913:61; excised in 1922/1928)[6]
35. The flashback continues. On his way from the bridge, N.A. runs into S.S. and accompanies him to his domicile but is not invited to come in. Both try to avoid a sensitive topic

Apollon Apollonovich remembered

36. An explanation of A.A.'s place and importance at the Establishment
37. Working in his office, A.A. comes to the conclusion that his son is a scoundrel

Cold fingers

38. A.A. returns home from the Establishment (see II:17)
39. A.A. describes the stranger to a servant, learning that A.I. once visited N.A., but that was "quite a while ago" (1913:68; excised in 1922/1928)[7]

So it is always

40. In the evening, presumably of September 30 (see II:20–21), N.A. waits on the dark landing by the door to the apartment where he is no longer welcome (see I:35)

41. A woman arrives and is about to enter the apartment. N.A. appears before her wearing his red domino and black mask. The woman is frightened, N.A. runs away

You will never forget him!
42. A narrative digression on "cerebral play" as the source of everything we see in Chapter I

Chapter II (30 September–4 October 1905)[8]

The chronicle of events
1. Newspaper reports, dated October 1–4, about the Red Domino roaming the city streets
2. The reports are invented by the journalist Neintelpfain. His acquaintance was frightened by the Red Domino on the evening of September 30 (see I:40–41) and told the journalist about the incident that same evening

Sofia Petrovna Likhutina
3. The victim of the Red Domino is S.P. A description of her persona and apartment

Sofia Petrovna's visitors
4. A description of the regular guests in S.P.'s home

The officer: Sergei Sergeich Likhutin
5. A description of S.P.'s husband, S.S. (see I:35), and of her regular guest L. (see I:25–28)

The handsome, elegant best man
6. A flashback to S.P.'s romance with N.A., begun two and a half years ago, following her marriage[9]

The red clown
7. The flashback continues. The story of S.P.'s and N.A.'s breakup, during which she called him a "red clown" and he attempted suicide, subsequently making "a certain fatal decision" (see I:34)[10]
8. S.P. told everything to S.S., who wrote to N.A, asking him to refrain from future visits (see I:35)

A cad, a cad, a cad
9. "In those bitter days of early October" (1913:89). S.P. is tormented by the Red Domino incident (see I:40–41), which took place "a few days earlier" (1913:90). The incident is retold from her vantage point with new details: the Red Domino left behind an invitation to a masquerade
10. S.P. goes to the masquerade, accompanied by Neintelpfain (see II:2). Catching sight of the Red Domino, she reveals the incident to the

journalist, who subsequently invents more stories about the Red Domino for the *Chronicle of Events* (see II:1)[11]

An utterly smoke-ridden face (**September 30**)

11. A.I. pays a visit to N.A., bringing the package along (see I:28)
12. A.I. reminds N.A. about his two-month-old promise to help the Party (1913:98; the chronological marker is excised in 1922/1928)

Quarrels on the street became more frequent

13. Growing political turmoil across Russia in October 1905

My beloved Delvig calls me (**September 30**)

14. A.A. at the Establishment (see I:21–23, 36–37). Recalling a deceased minister, his friend and mentor, A.A. reflects on his own mortality

Meanwhile the conversation was continued

15. A.I. gives N.A. the package for safekeeping. Both think this is the extent of the promised service
16. While N.A. is in his study, hiding the package in his desk, A.I. sees the red domino and black mask (1913:107; excised in 1922/1928). N.A., visibly embarrassed, hides the costume[12]
17. Conversing with N.A. by a window, A.I. sees A.A. return from the office (see I:38–39)

The walls were snow, not walls![13]

18. Having arrived home, A.A. proceeds to his study

A certain person

19. N.A. and A.I. continue their conversation. A.A. enters his son's living quarters[14]
20. While A.A. converses with A.I., N.A. retires to the next room and puts on the red domino, hiding it under an overcoat (1913:124–25; excised in 1922/1928)
21. A.I. and N.A. leave the Ableukhov family house together.[15] A.A. thinks about A.I.

He sallied forth all right[16]

22. A description of Petersburg crowds and revolutionary ferment

Flight

23. A.I. walks home across the city
24. A digression about Russia's imminent Apocalypse

Styopka

25. Styopka, a peasant sectarian, arrives in Petersburg, moving in with the caretaker of A.I.'s apartment building
26. A.I. stops by the caretaker's lodge to talk to Styopka about politics and the end of the world

27. A.I. invites Styopka to come up to his room, where they discuss the Apocalypse

Chapter III (4–5 October 1905)

A ceremony (**October 5**)[17]
1. Early morning. Preparing for an official ceremony, A.A. sees N.A., who has spent a sleepless night
2. Last night (October 4), N.A. came home late, in a panic, followed by police agents (see III:14–15)
3. A.A. leaves for the imperial court. The reception is accompanied by a parade

To the meeting[18] (**October 4**)
4. V.E. visits S.P., asking her to give N.A. a letter at tomorrow's ball, hosted by the Tsukatov family. S.P. recognizes L.'s handwriting on the envelope
5. V.E. takes S.P. to a political rally. Leaving S.P.'s apartment building, they run into L.

Noble, elegant and pale
6. On their way to the rally, the women see N.A. walking his dog. N.A. notices them too
7. V.E., infatuated with N.A. (see IV:1–3), whispers the verses she composed about him[19]

Comte—Comte—Comte
8. Evening.[20] A.A. and N.A. dine together. N.A. has just returned from his walk (see III:6)[21]
9. A flashback to the father's relationship with his son, when N.A. was a young boy
10. Their philosophical discussion continues after dinner. A.A. enquires about A.I., ruining the conversation
11. N.A. wants to surprise S.P. on her way from the rally. He knows where she is because he saw her with V.E. It has been over two hours since their encounter (1916:164; excised in 1922/1928)

The meeting[22]
12. V.E. and S.P. are at the political rally, described satirically with anti-Semitic overtones
13. S.P. leaves the meeting when a Cossack detachment arrives to disperse the crowd

Tatam: tam, tam
14. On the way home, S.P. runs into N.A. in his red domino and black mask. He tries to frighten her but slips and falls, eliciting her mockery
15. N.A. hurries away in a cab, followed by police detectives (see III:2)

Shadows
16. L. learns from a police agent that the identity of the Red Domino has been discovered—it is N.A.
17. L. is not surprised by the news because the journalist Neintelpfain (see II:2, 10) is his agent
18. L. demands that the police leave N.A. alone for the sake of an operation in progress

A mad dog had howled
19. S.P. comes home and tells S.S. about N.A. as her Red Domino stalker
20. In her bedroom, S.P. reads L.'s letter to N.A. (see III:4) and decides to use it as a weapon of revenge
21. S.S. asks his wife not to go tomorrow to the Tsukatovs' ball; she refuses to comply; they quarrel

The senator's second space (**the night of October 4–5**)
22. A.A. readies himself for bed and falls asleep. In his sleep, he hears N.A. return home (see III:2, 15)
23. A.A. is awakened by the noise of the front door shutting behind N.A.

Chapter IV (5–6 October 1905)

The Summer Garden (**October 5**)
1. Late morning (see III:1). N.A. goes to the Summer Garden for a rendezvous. He has been summoned there by a letter delivered the same morning and signed "S"
2. He expects to see S.P. Instead, he encounters V.E. (Solovyova), the author of the letter in verse, signed "An ardent soul," which he received on September 30 (see I:31)
3. Disappointed, N.A. leaves without listening to V.E.'s confession of love

Madame Farnois
4. That same morning, S.P. wakes up late. She turns away visitors all day long. In the evening, she receives her costume for the ball at the Tsukatovs'.

Petersburg vanished into the night
5. That same evening, A.P., newly arrived from abroad, visits the Ableukhov family home, but her husband and son are out

244 Part Three / Aids for Reading and Studying *Petersburg*

Tip-tap went their slippers
6. Guests are arriving at the Tsukatovs' ball
7. The ball commences

Dancing to the end[23]
8. The ball's hostess converses with the anti-Semitic editor of a conservative newspaper
9. A precis of the life of Nikolai Petrovich Tsukatov, the ball's host

The ball
10. The hostess organizes discussions; the host oversees the dancing. A.A. is expected

As though someone were weeping
11. N.A. appears at the ball, wearing his red domino and black mask

A small withered figure
12. N.A. runs into the newly arrived A.A., who does not recognize his son. The Red Domino causes A.A.'s heart seizure
13. Masked entertainers arrive at the ball

Pompadour
14. S.P. dresses and leaves for the ball despite her husband's last-ditch attempt to stop her

The hand of fate (**the night of October 5–6**)
15. S.P., dressed as Madame Pompadour, dances with the Red Domino. N.A. does not recognize her
16. S.P. gives N.A. the letter from L. (see I:28; III:4, 20)

Apollon Apollonovich[24]
17. A.A. recovers from his heart seizure and converses with the hostess and other guests
18. A.A. is distracted by a police agent who informs him that N.A. is the Red Domino

Uproar
19. N.A., in a secluded corner, lifts his face mask and reads L.'s letter
20. The letter shocks him. N.A. leaves the ball, forgetting to lower his mask. Other guests recognize him as the Red Domino

But what if? . . .
21. S.P. finally realizes that L.'s letter orders A.A.'s assassination by the bomb N.A. keeps in his desk (see II:15–16)[25]
22. L. shows up at the ball. He knows that S.P. has read the letter and blackmails her, looking for sexual favors. S.P. is frightened and lost

The white domino (**October 6**)[26]
23. The guests are leaving the ball. S.P. notices "someone tall and sad" in a

white domino. Mistaking the White Domino for her husband, S.P. lets him walk her out to safety
24. S.P. realizes that her companion is Christ. He finds her a cab and sees her off

She forgot what had happened
25. S.P. rides home across nocturnal Petersburg
26. Upon her arrival, S.P. is not let into her apartment. At the door, she hears strange noises and the sound of a falling human body (see IV:39)

Alarm
27. At the ball, A.A. is conversing with other guests. A police agent, Morkovin, informs him that the Red Domino is his son (see IV:18)
28. Shocked by the news, A.A. sees N.A. reading L.'s letter (see IV:19; excised in 1922/1928)
29. A.A. overhears scandalous gossip about his family.[27] He leaves the ball in a hurry

The letter
30. N.A. runs out of the ball (see IV:20). At the entrance to the Tsukatovs' house he sees "the tall and sad one" (see IV:23–24) and mistakes him for a police constable
31. N.A. rereads the letter asking him to kill A.A. as a way of fulfilling his promise to the Party, "made in the summer"
32. N.A. recalls the "September day" on which he received a "suspicious visitor" (see II:11–16), finally realizing that A.I.'s package, presently stored in his desk, contains a bomb
33. Agent Morkovin (see IV:18, 27) accosts N.A., insisting that they should have a chat

A companion
34. A.A. leaves the ball (see IV:29). Noticing Morkovin in the street (see IV:18, 27, 33), he does not get into his carriage
35. A.A. follows Morkovin, for whom he has further questions, and learns about the assassination plot
36. A.A. walks home alone across nocturnal Petersburg

Out of his mind
37. After S.P. leaves for the ball (see IV:14), S.S. gets ready to hang himself
38. He hears S.P. arrive but does not open the door (see IV:26) as he attempts to hang himself

What next?
39. The ceiling collapses under his weight and S.S. falls (see IV:26) without killing himself

246   Part Three / Aids for Reading and Studying *Petersburg*

40. He tries to conceal the traces of the failed suicide and runs to open the door for S.P.
41. S.P. finds the rope and realizes what has happened. A scene of reconciliation follows

Man-in-the-street
42. A.A. walks across Petersburg (see IV:36), contemplating his existential solitude
43. He sees an adolescent girl, followed by a stalker. A.A. offers to walk the girl home
44. Having accompanied her, A.A. notices daybreak over the city

Chapter V (6 October 1905)

The gent
1. N.A. and Morkovin walk through nocturnal Petersburg (see IV:33). The Flying Dutchman and Peter the Great are walking in front of them
2. Both pairs enter a restaurant. A series of restaurant scenes

A glass of vodka
3. Morkovin and N.A. talk and drink vodka. Next to them, the Flying Dutchman and Peter the Great do likewise
4. Morkovin introduces himself as a police agent privy to N.A.'s role in the impending assassination

I destroy irrevocably
5. Morkovin then tells N.A. that he is a double agent working for the Party
6. As they leave the restaurant, Morkovin threatens to arrest N.A. should he back out of the assassination plot
7. Walking home, N.A. contemplates the mounted statue of Peter the Great
8. Realizing that he must kill his father, the laughing N.A. runs away from the Bronze Horseman

Gryphons
9. N.A. gets into a cab and rides home. On the way, he passes A.A. (see IV:44). They see each other
10. Father and son meet at the entrance to their home

As red as any flame
11. An awkward scene between A.A. and N.A. in the entrance hall and on the stairs
12. A.A. retires to his quarters as N.A. learns from the valet about his mother's return from abroad (see IV:5)

A bad sign
13. Going to his room, N.A. runs into A.A., who is waiting to invite him for a serious talk after N.A. has changed from his ball attire

By the table
14. N.A. tells the valet to inform A.A. about A.P.'s return
15. N.A. thinks about the bomb

Packets of pencils
16. The valet finds A.A. in his study and informs him about A.P.'s return
17. N.A. goes to his father's study for the serious talk. But instead of the Red Domino scandal, they discuss A.P.'s return
18. A.A. abruptly interrupts the conversation, accusing his son of dishonorable conduct. The insulted N.A. rushes out

Pepp Peppovich Pepp
19. At his desk, N.A. sets the bomb's timer in motion
20. He falls asleep in front of the ticking bomb

The Day of Judgement[28]
21. N.A.'s dream
22. N.A. wakes up with his head on the ticking bomb. He adds several hours to the timer

Chapter VI (6–7 October 1905)

Retrieving the thread of his being
1. On the same morning (October 6), A.I. wakes up in his room. Feverish, he gets dressed and goes out

The staircase
2. A.I. recalls that the night before he rushed up the stairs, running from a black outline that was chasing him

And, tearing free, he ran
3. Descending the stairs, A.I. runs into N.A.
4. N.A. refuses to fulfill his promise to the Party and accuses A.I. of dishonorable conduct. A.I. struggles to grasp the matter. Their conversation continues in the street

The street
5. A.I. learns, ostensibly for the first time, about the task N.A. has been given by the Party

A helping hand
6. A.I. and N.A. walk together, discussing the situation
7. A.I. suspects all this is a political provocation and decides to consult with L.

Nevsky Prospect
8. A description of the crowd on Nevsky Prospect, where A.I. and N.A. are now walking

Dionysus
9. N.A. admits to having set the bomb's timer is motion. A.I. advises him to throw the bomb into the Neva River. N.A. takes his leave

Revelation
10. A.I. recalls that he forgot to give N.A. the letter from L. (see I:28) when delivering the bomb for safekeeping (see II:15); he also recalls that he then asked a Party comrade, V.E., to pass the letter on to N.A. (see III:4)
11. N.A. returns to resume their conversation. They part again. N.A. intends to throw the bomb into the river

The caryatid
12. A description of political disturbances and of the caryatid on the façade of the Establishment headed by A.A.
13. A.A. leaves home in a carriage. The carriage is stalled by a crowd of political demonstrators (see VII:7, 27).

Get off me, Tom
14. A.I. pays a visit to L. but only sees Z.Z. and a French guest there
15. Listening to their conversation, A.I. also hears the singing of a neighbor — a Persian named Shishnarfiev. L. arrives home

Frontal bones
16. While L. is with the Frenchman in his study, A.I. converses with Z.Z.
17. A.I. learns from the conversation that L. is besieged by strange rumors

A bad business . . .
18. A.I. thinks about his dealings with L. and observes him through an open door
19. In the study, A.I. discusses with L. the predicament in which N.A. finds himself. L. insists that N.A. is an agent provocateur

Again the sad and sorrowful one
20. On the way home, A.I. catches sight of "someone tall and sad" (see IV:23–24, 30)

Matvei Morzhov
21. As A.I. nears his building, his paranoia worsens. He is afraid of being followed

A lifeless beam of light fell through the window
22. Entering his building, A.I. runs into a stranger waiting for him on the stairs. The man, whose singing A.I. heard on his visit to L., presents himself as Shishnarfne rather than Shishnarfiev (see VI:15). Shishnarfne accompanies A.I. to his room

Petersburg
23. Styopka (see II:25–27) is in A.I.'s room, reading a breviary. Recognizing a demon in Shishnarfne, he immediately leaves
24. Conversing with Shishnarfne, A.I. decides that his guest is a dangerous hallucination called Enfranshish (Shishnarfne read backwards). In a panic, he leaves the room, running up to the loft of his tenement building

The loft
25. From the loft, A.I. hears singing in the caretaker's lodge, along with city noises
26. The Bronze Horseman leaves his pedestal and rides across Petersburg
27. Having calmed down, A.I. returns to his room

Why this had happened . . .
28. After reflecting on his own psychological state, A.I. comes to the conclusion that L. is a traitor. He decides to do something about it

The guest
29. The Bronze Horseman enters A.I.'s room and possesses him

Scissors (October 7)
30. In the morning, Styopka wakes up a delirious A.I. and claims they did not see each other the night before (see VI:23)
31. Outside, A.I. tries to buy a knife but, because of his agitated state, they agree to sell him only a pair of scissors

Chapter VII (6–8 October 1905)

The immeasurable (October 6)
1. Having parted with A.I. on Nevsky Prospect (see VI:11), N.A. recollects his morning (see V:22; VII:11) up to the moment when he ran into A.I. (see VI:3)
2. N.A. remembers his childhood and the way his father taught him dancing

Cranes
3. With N.A. still standing on Nevsky Prospect, the crowd hears the cry of cranes and watches them fly over the city
4. Feeling as if someone "has drawn around his soul a penetrating circle of redemption and has stepped into his soul," N.A. catches sight of a "sad and dear" figure (see IV:23, 30; VI:20)

I'm just walking here . . . not getting in anyone's way . . .
5. N.A. rushes home to get rid of the bomb by throwing it into the Neva
6. The "sad" figure follows and accosts N.A., turning out to be S.S.

The conversation continued
7. Telling N.A. that he has been looking for him all morning, S.S. forces

N.A. to accompany him for a serious talk. They run into a crowd of demonstrators (see VI:13; VII:27)

The plan

8. While accompanying S.S., N.A. fantasizes about blowing up his own father

The Establishment

9. A description of the Establishment headed by A.A.

His games are over

10. A.A.'s impending promotion and entire career are compromised by the Red Domino scandal

Charcoal tablets

11. A description of A.A.'s and his valet's morning (October 6).[29] At 8:30, A.A. hears a door slam and learns from the valet that N.A. has left the house (see V:22; VI:3; VII:1). Ten minutes earlier, the valet saw N.A. watching A.A. through a peephole
12. Emotionally shaken and having aged overnight, A.A. decides not to go to work
13. At 10:00, a visitor comes to see N.A.[30] After a short wait, he departs, leaving a note

I know what I'm doing

14. At 10:00, A.A. takes his morning coffee unshaven and undressed. At 11:30, instead of going to the Establishment, he begins to dust the books in his study
15. An official from the Establishment pays A.A. a visit

You will wander like a madman

16. On the first day of a nationwide strike,[31] A.A. is expected at the Establishment, but he does not go to work
17. The Establishment's assistant director arrives at A.A.'s home (see VII:15) with an order requiring his approval, but A.A. refuses to sign the document, writing his letter of resignation instead
18. The assistant director returns to the Establishment with the news of A.A.'s resignation

A reptile

19. N.A. and S.S. arrive at the Likhutins'. S.S. forces the frightened N.A. to enter

Pitch darkness

20. Overcoming his resistance, S.S. drags N.A. into his flat and, once there, into the study

Man-in-the-street

21. Writing the letter of resignation, A.A. thinks of his estranged wife and their future life together

22. A.A. wanders into N.A.'s living quarters. His attention is drawn to the ticking object in an unlocked desk drawer. A.A. takes the strange object with him for further examination

He failed to explain himself properly

23. N.A. thinks that S.S. wants to beat him up. S.P. is watching them through a peephole
24. At 2:30, A.A. is writing in his study (excised in 1922/1928)
25. S.S. explains to N.A. that their talk does not concern S.P., but rather the terrorist plot. S.S. has learned about the plot from S.P. (see IV:41), who knows about it from L.'s letter (see III:20; IV:21–22).
26. Having assured S.S. that he has no intention of carrying out the terrorist act, N.A. leaves
27. A.A. works in his study, prepares to leave home, and rides away in his carriage. The carriage is stalled by a crowd of demonstrators (see VI:13; VII:7). A.A. gets out and continues on foot[32]

A little game of patience (**October 7**)

28. In the evening, L. and Z.Z. play a game of patience, drink tea, and converse after dinner. Z.Z. is vainly enquiring about the reasons for L.'s troubles with the Party

Inexpressible meanings

29. A "small black figure" (A.I.) creeps toward L.'s house, peeking into the living room

Swansong

30. L. plays his violin
31. A.I. tries to get into the bedroom through a window, makes noise, and hides from the alerted L.
32. L. returns to the living room as A.I. slips into the bedroom and lies in wait

A perspective[33]

33. L. retires to his bedroom with a lit candle, causing an interplay of light and shadows

Cockroaches

34. L. squashes cockroaches, locks the door, undresses, blows out the candle, and notices A.I.
35. L. attempts to run out, but the door is locked. A.I. stabs him with scissors (see VI:31)
36. In the morning (October 8), they find the mad A.I. astride L.'s corpse, clutching the scissors in his outstretched hand, in the pose of the Bronze Horseman

Chapter VIII (6–7 October 1905)

But first . . . (October 6)
1. A.P. spends the day in her hotel room
2. A.A. arrives at the hotel on foot (see VI:13; VII:27). They meet for the first time in two and a half years (see I:30)

Nodding over a pile of objects . . .
3. N.A. returns home (see VII:26) and looks for the bomb, but cannot find it in his desk (see VII:22)
4. The valet invites N.A. to meet his newly arrived mother

The servants were astonished
5. A.A. and A.P. ride home from the hotel (see VIII:2)
6. Their arrival is narrated from a servant's viewpoint
7. A.A. and A.P. enter, walk across the house, and ask the valet to call for N.A. (see VIII:4)

Utter absurdity
8. N.A. rushes to meet his mother, thinking about the lost bomb

Mama
9. Mother and son are reunited after a hiatus of two and a half years
10. N.A.'s emotional response to A.P.'s return surprises and reassures A.A.

And a roulade pealed out
11. N.A. returns to his quarters and decides that S.S., who waited there for him in the morning (see VII:13), found the bomb and took it away[34]

The watermelon is a vegetable
12. The reunited family has its first dinner together since A.P.'s departure. A.A. and N.A. converse after dinner
13. A.A. and A.P. play a game of patience and make plans for the future
14. N.A. accompanies A.P. to her hotel after seeing A.A. for the last time, as the narrator informs us[35]

Clockwork
15. N.A. returns home and spends a sleepless night[36] in search of the ticking bomb
16. The bomb explodes at dawn (October 7), in A.A.'s office, without harming anyone[37]
17. N.A. runs into his father's bedroom. Upon seeing his son, A.A. flees from N.A. into the lavatory
18. The feverish N.A. loses consciousness. During his illness, A.A. foils a police investigation and moves to the countryside
19. A.P. accompanies her son abroad for medical treatment. In the summer of 1906, she returns to live with A.A.

Epilogue

1. N.A. lives in North Africa, studying the civilization of ancient Egypt
2. A.A. lives in the country, writing his memoirs
3. His parents read N.A.'s letter informing them about his academic monograph and travels
4. In 1913, N.A. lives on the country estate of his deceased parents, having abandoned his longstanding interest in foreign thought for Russian philosophical and mystical traditions

Notes

1. I.10: " . . . the year was nineteen hundred and five" (1913:24; excised in 1922/1928); I.12: "It was the last day of September" (1913:27/1922:12/1928:19).

2. I.3: "At ten o'clock he, an old man, would leave for the Establishment" (1913:15; excised in 1922/1928).

3. In early drafts, the stranger, like A.A., leaves home at 10 a.m. ("Knizhnaia 'Nekrasovskaia' redaktsiia dvukh pervykh glav romana 'Peterburg,'" in Andrei Belyi, *Peterburg*, ed. L. Dolgopolov [Moscow: Nauka, 1981], 462). Originally, then, Bely meant to synchronize their movements in time and in space (see their encounters on September 30, in the street [I:14] and in A.A.'s home [II:17–21]).

4. The sections *He had seen the man of uncertain status* and *Strange qualities* are excised in the 1922/1928 editions, which integrate both sections' abridged contents into *The desk stood there*.

5. A.I. forgets about the letter when dropping off the package (II:11–16). He will ask a Party comrade, V.E., to take it to N.A. (VI:10). V.E. will pass the letter on to S.P. (III:4), who will hand it to N.A. at the Tsukatovs' ball (IV:16).

6. He made the promise two months before the first day of action in the novel (II:12, 1913:98; excised in 1922/1928).

7. The excision partially addresses a contradiction: in the next chapter, A.I.'s visit to N.A. coincides with A.A.'s return home from the Establishment (II:17–21). A.I.'s previous visit to N.A. was two months earlier, as mentioned in the scene of their September 30 meeting (II:12, 1913:98; excised in 1922/1928).

8. Since the last report is from October 4, the newspaper carrying it appeared, at the earliest, on that day.

9. Note the chronological coincidence between A.P.'s extramarital affair and N.A.'s crisis (I:30).

10. The breakup takes place two months (II:12) before the time when the novel's action is set, in mid-summer 1905.

11. A logical inconsistency. Earlier in the chapter (II:2), S.P. told the journalist "that she had just encountered some kind of red domino in the unlit doorway" (1913:77–78/1922:38/1928:44). The masquerade could hardly have taken place that same evening

(September 30) since the invitation said: "I shall expect you at the masquerade—such-and-such a place, such-and-such a date" (1913:91/1922:46/1928:53), rather than "tonight."

12. A logical inconsistency. If N.A. receives the costume on the morning of September 30 (I:32–33), before A.I.'s visit on the same day, he has no reason to be embarrassed since their meeting precedes the evening incident by the door of S.P.'s apartment (I:40–41) and the subsequent newspaper gossip about the Red Domino (II:1). Excising the detail from the later editions, Bely does not fix the problem. The section *An utterly smoke-ridden face* begins with N.A. going out to meet a visitor (II:11). This seems to continue the plotline interrupted in I:32 because N.A. mistakes his surprise guest, A.I., for another visitor he is expecting (1913:93), presumably the costumier. But if A.I. comes before the costumier, then the presence of the newly delivered domino in I:33 makes no sense, even after Bely removes its mention from II:16.

13. This section is excised in the 1922/1928 editions, which incorporate its shortened contents into the previous section.

14. In this section, the narrator twice mentions that A.A.'s encounter with A.I. on Nevsky Prospect (I:14) took place the day before—i.e., on September 29 (1913:117, 126; excised in 1922/1928). This contradicts the novel's general chronology: the encounter takes place "on the last day of September" (1913:27/1922:12/1928:19); N.A. later recalls (IV:32) receiving the package from A.I. on a "September day" (1913:247/1922:128/1928:131). Both events thus took place on September 30, as did A.A.'s second meeting with A.I. at the Ableukhovs', hours after their first encounter on the street. Excising this temporal marker in the later editions, Bely removes the chronological inconsistency.

15. N.A. is headed to S.P.'s apartment building in order to appear before her as the Red Domino and deliver an invitation to a masquerade (see I:40–41; II:9).

16. In the 1922/1928 editions, this section is abridged and renamed *The strike*.

17. The ceremony attended by A.A. (III:1–3) may have been either of the two receptions held at the imperial court on 5 October 1905—one to mark the ratification of the Russo-Japanese peace treaty and the other to celebrate the name day of the heir to the throne (S. Grechishkin, L. Dolgopolov, A. Lavrov, "Primechaniia," in Andrei Belyi, *Peterburg*, ed. L. Dolgopolov [Kiev: Dnipro, 1990], 660n7).

18. In 1922/1928, this section is called *At the meeting*.

19. A hint at the authorship of the versified letter N.A. received on the morning of September 30 (I:31).

20. N.A. greets A.A.: "Good evening, papa!" (1913:155; excised in 1922/1928).

21. A.A.'s exchange with N.A.: "'From the University? . . . ' 'No, I went for a walk . . . '" (1913:156; excised in 1922/1928).

22. This section is excised in the 1922/1928 editions for political reasons. Since Bely wanted the novel to sell in Soviet Russia, the satirical depiction of a revolutionary rally had to be removed.

23. This section is excised in the 1922/1928 editions, which incorporate its abridged contents into the adjoining sections.

24. This section is excised in the 1922/1928 editions, which incorporate its abridged contents into the preceding section.

25. A logical inconsistency. S.P. learns from the letter that the bomb is "already lying in [N.A.'s] desk" (1913:225/1922:115/1928:119). However, having written the letter before A.I. gave the bomb to N.A. (see I:28; III:4; VI:10), L. could not have known where exactly N.A. would hide the bomb.

26. This section is excised in the 1922/1928 editions, which incorporate its abridged contents into the preceding section. S.P.'s departure from the ball takes place after midnight—that is, on October 6: she receives her costume "just before ten" (IV:4; 1913:196/1922:101/1928:105), leaving soon thereafter; S.S. prepares his suicide "two hours" after her departure (1913:258/1922:133/1928:137); S.P., returning home, hears his failed suicide attempt (IV:25–26, 37–38).

27. The rumors follow N.A.'s precipitous departure with his mask upraised (see IV:20).

28. In the 1928 edition, the section is renamed *Judgement*, thus playing down religious connotations objectionable to Soviet censors.

29. "It was the morning after the evening at the Tsukatovs'," following A.A.'s "unsuccessful attempt to have things out with his son" (1913:458; both temporal markers are excised in 1922/1928).

30. It is S.S., who spends the morning looking for N.A. (see VII:7). Episode VII:13 is excised in 1922/1928.

31. This detail supports the novel's chronology: the general strike began on 6 October 1905.

32. Episodes VII:24 and VII:27 are excised in 1922/1928. Episode VII:27 contains a reference to episode VI:13 ("We saw this in the previous chapter," 1913:504). Judging by this parenthetical remark, Bely was keenly aware of the complexity of the novel's plot, and this awareness may have driven him to make some "simplifying" cuts in *Petersburg*'s later editions.

33. The section is excised in the 1922/1928 editions, which incorporate its abridged contents into the preceding section.

34. The section contains a semi-jocular chronological marker both clarifying and obscuring the correlation of N.A.'s and A.I.'s plot lines. The narrator mentions A.I.'s meeting with L. on October 6 (see VI:14–19): "At this very time, we remind the reader, Aleksandr Ivanovich Dudkin was indeed having things out in the cottage with the late Lippanchenko" (1913:547/1922:280/1928:279). Of course, at this time, the double agent had more than twenty-four hours to go before becoming "the late Lippanchenko."

35. A logical inconsistency. N.A. will see his father again after the explosion (see VIII:17).

36. At this time, on the night of October 6–7, the Bronze Horseman possesses A.I. (see VI:29).

37. That morning (October 7), A.I. buys the pair of scissors he will use to kill L. on the night of October 7–8, almost twenty-four hours after the explosion at the Ableukhovs'.

This chronology contains a possible logical inconsistency: L. should have learned about the plot's failure from the evening newspapers; yet he is seemingly unconcerned, spending a quiet evening with Z.Z.

Recommended Critical Literature in English

General

Alexandrov, Vladimir. *Andrei Bely: The Major Symbolist Fiction.* Cambridge, MA: Harvard University Press, 1985. Chapter 3: "*Petersburg.*"

Cooke, Olga, ed. *Andrey Bely's "Petersburg": A Centennial Celebration.* Brighton, MA: Academic Studies Press, 2017.

Elsworth, John. *Andrey Bely: A Critical Study of the Novels.* Cambridge: Cambridge University Press, 1983. Chapter 4: "*Petersburg.*"

Keys, Roger. *The Reluctant Modernist: Andrei Belyi and the Development of Russian Fiction, 1902–1914.* Oxford: Clarendon Press, 1996. Chapter 20: "A 'Perspectiveless' Novel? *Petersburg.*"

Ljunggren, Magnus. *The Dream of Rebirth: A Study of Andrej Belyj's Novel "Petersburg."* Stockholm: Almqvist & Wiksell International, 1982.

Maguire, Robert, and John Malmstad. "Petersburg," in *Andrey Bely: Spirit of Symbolism*, ed. J. Malmstad. Ithaca: Cornell University Press, 1987.

Matich, Olga, ed. *"Petersburg" / Petersburg: Novel and City, 1900–1921.* Madison: University of Wisconsin Press, 2010.

Matich, Olga, ed. *Mapping Petersburg.* http://petersburg.berkeley.edu/index.html.

Wermuth-Atkinson, Judith. *The Red Jester: Andrei Bely's "Petersburg" as a Novel of the European Modern*. Zurich: LIT Verlag, 2012.

Case Studies

Alter, Robert. *Imagined Cities: Urban Experience and the Language of the Novel*. New Haven: Yale University Press, 2005. Chapter 5: "Bely: Phantasmatic City."

Anschuetz, Carol. "Bely's *Petersburg* and the End of the Russian Novel," in *The Russian Novel from Pushkin to Pasternak*, ed. J. Garrard. New Haven: Yale University Press, 1983.

Berman, Marshall. *All That Is Solid Melts into Air: The Experience of Modernity*. New York: Penguin Books, 1988. Chapter IV.3: "Biely's *Petersburg*: The Shadow Passport."

Bethea, David. *The Shape of Apocalypse in Modern Russian Fiction*. Princeton: Princeton University Press, 1989. Chapter 2: "*Petersburg*: The Apocalyptic Horseman, the Unicorn, and the Verticality of Narrative."

Carlson, Maria. "Theosophy and History in Andrei Belyi's *Peterburg*: Life in the Astral City." *Russian Literature* 58.1 (2005): 29–45.

Cioran, Samuel. *The Apocalyptic Symbolism of Andrej Belyj*. The Hague: Mouton, 1973. Chapter 7: "The Urban Apocalypse."

Crone, Anna Lisa, and Jennifer Day. *My Petersburg / Myself: Mental Architecture and Imaginative Space in Modern Russian Letters*. Bloomington: Slavica, 2004. Chapters 2 and 3.

Hartmann-Flyer, Helene. "The Time Bomb," in *Andrey Bely: A Critical Review*, ed. G. Janecek. Lexington: University Press of Kentucky, 1978.

Lachmann, Renate. *Memory and Literature: Intertextuality in Russian Modernism*. Minneapolis: University of Minnesota Press, 1997. Chapter II.3: "Intertextuality and the Constitution of Meaning: Bely's *Petersburg* and 'Other' Texts."

Langen, Timothy. *The Stony Dance: Unity and Gesture in Andrey Bely's "Petersburg."* Evanston: Northwestern University Press, 2005.

Ljunggren, Magnus. *Twelve Essays on Andrej Belyj's Petersburg*. Göteborg: Acta Universitatis Gothoburgensis, 2009.

Steinberg, Ada. *Word and Music in the Novels of Andrey Bely*. Cambridge: Cambridge University Press, 1982. Chapters 4 and 5.

Contributors

David M. Bethea is Vilas Research Professor Emeritus at the University of Wisconsin–Madison. He is the author of numerous monographs and edited volumes on nineteenth- and twentieth-century Russian literature. Among his books are *Khodasevich: His Life and Art* (1986); *The Shape of Apocalypse in Modern Russian Fiction* (1989); *Joseph Brodsky and the Creation of Exile* (1994); *Realizing Metaphors: Alexander Pushkin and the Life of the Poet* (1998); *The Superstitious Muse: Thinking Russian Literature Mythopoetically* (2009). He is currently researching the role of Charles Darwin's ideas in the Russian cultural imagination.

Maria Carlson is a professor emerita of Slavic languages and literatures and director emerita of the Center for Russian and East European Studies at the University of Kansas. The winner of several national research, teaching, and service awards, she works on Russian cultural and intellectual history, speculative philosophies and occultism, and Slavic folklore. Among Carlson's many publications is the book *"No Religion Higher than Truth": A History of the Theosophical Movement in Russia, 1875–1922* (1993). Her current research engages, among other topics, Andrei Bely's theory of Symbolism as a world view.

Steven Cassedy is Distinguished Professor of Literature, Emeritus, at the University of California, San Diego. He has published extensively on Russian literature, Russian critical and literary theory, and Russian religious thought. Cassedy has also written on general aesthetics, music, Yiddish literature, Jewish-American culture, and American social history. His latest book is *Connected: How Trains, Genes, Pineapples, Piano Keys, and a Few Disasters Transformed Americans at the Dawn of the Twentieth Century* (2014).

Edith W. Clowes holds the Brown-Forman Chair in the Humanities at the University of Virginia, where she teaches in the Department of Slavic Languages and Literatures. Her primary research interests span the interactions between literature, philosophy, religion, utopian thought, and imaginary geography. She has authored and edited numerous books, including, most recently, *Fiction's*

Overcoat: Russian Literary Culture and the Question of Philosophy (2004) and *Russia on the Edge: Imagined Geographies and Post-Soviet Identity* (2011).

John Elsworth is a professor emeritus at the University of Manchester. He taught for twenty-three years at the University of East Anglia in Norwich and has held visiting posts at the University of Virginia and the University of California at Berkeley. His research is focused on Russian modernist literature and culture. Among Elsworth's publications are two monographs on Andrei Bely's life and work—*Andrey Bely* (1972) and *Andrey Bely: A Critical Study of the Novels* (1983)—as well as English translations of Bely's first two novels, *The Silver Dove* (2000) and *Petersburg* (2009).

Hilary Fink has taught Russian literature at Yale University and Smith College and is currently a lecturer in the Commonwealth Honors College at the University of Massachusetts, Amherst. Author of *Bergson and Russian Modernism, 1900–1930* (1999), Fink is presently working on a comparative study of Russian and Western Existentialism.

Taras Koznarsky is an associate professor at the University of Toronto, where he teaches Ukrainian, Russian, and comparative Slavic literature and culture. His research focuses on Ukrainian-Russian literary relations in the nineteenth century, modernism in European visual arts, and the imaginative construction of cities, with special attention to the city of Kyiv/Kiev in Ukrainian, Russian, Jewish, and Polish cultures. Koznarsky's recent publications explore the figure of Bohdan Khmelnytsky in the Ukrainian historical imagination and the place of the Beilis ritual murder trial (Kiev, 1913) in contemporary Russian pulp fiction.

Tim Langen is an associate professor of Russian at the University of Missouri, Columbia, where he teaches Russian literature, language, and cultural history. He is author of *The Stony Dance: Unity and Gesture in Andrey Bely's "Petersburg"* (2005). In addition to Bely, his research interests include Russian intellectual history of the late nineteenth and early twentieth centuries as well as the writings of Nikolai Gogol, Viacheslav Ivanov, and Sigizmund Krzhizhanovskii.

Leonid Livak is a professor in the Department of Slavic Languages and Literatures and the Center for Jewish Studies at the University of Toronto. His research interests include Russian and transnational modernism, literature and exile, Russian-French and Russian-Jewish cultural relations. His books include *How It Was Done in Paris: Russian Emigre Literature and French Modernism* (2003); *The Jewish Persona in the European Imagination: A Case of Russian Literature* (2010); and

Russian Emigres in the Intellectual and Literary Life of Interwar France (2010). His new monograph, *In Search of Russian Modernism*, is forthcoming in 2018.

Olga Matich is a professor emerita of Russian literature and culture at the University of California, Berkeley. She has written extensively about early Russian modernism, Andrei Bely, Russian painting, and Russian emigration. Among her books are a scholarly monograph, *Erotic Utopia: The Decadent Imagination in Russia's Fin de Siècle* (2005); an edited volume, *"Petersburg"/Petersburg: Novel and City, 1900–1921* (2010); and a memoir, *The Notes of a Russian American: Family Chronicles and Chance Encounters* (in Russian, 2016). Matich directs the digital project *Mapping Petersburg* (http://petersburg.berkeley.edu/index.html).

Colleen McQuillen is an associate professor in the Department of Slavic and Baltic Languages and Literatures at the University of Illinois in Chicago, where she teaches courses in Russian literature and visual and material culture. She has published articles on theatricality and costume balls in Russia that have appeared in *Clothing Cultures*, *Fashion Theory*, *The Russian Review*, *Teoriia mody*, and *Twentieth-Century Literary Criticism*. She is the author of *The Modernist Masquerade: Stylizing Life, Literature and Costumes in Russia* (2013).

Henrietta Mondry is a professor in the Department of Global, Cultural, and Language Studies at the University of Canterbury, Christchurch, and a fellow of the Royal Society of New Zealand. She has published widely on the representation and cultural history of race, gender, and sexuality, and she has pioneered work on intersections of body politics and the discourses of species in Russian culture. Her recent books include *Exemplary Bodies: Constructing the Jew in Russian Culture* (2009), *Vasily Rozanov and the Body of Russian Literature* (2010), and *Political Animals: Representing Dogs in Modern Russian Culture* (2015).

Lynn Ellen Patyk is an assistant professor at Dartmouth College. She is the author of *Written in Blood: Revolutionary Terrorism and Russian Literary Culture: 1861–1881* (2017). Her articles on terrorism and literature, as well as on the history of terrorism, have appeared in *Slavic Review*, *The Russian Review*, *Jahrbücher für Geschichte Osteuropas*, and *Kritika*. She is currently at work on a book-length project that investigates the role of provocation in Russian history, politics, and culture.

Violeta Sotirova is an associate professor in stylistics at the University of Nottingham. Her research focuses on the linguistic representation of consciousness in narrative and on the stylistic practices of modernism, notably the authorial revisions and stylistic development in the prose of D. H. Lawrence and Virginia Woolf. She is the author of *D. H. Lawrence and Narrative Viewpoint*

(2011) and *Consciousness in Modernist Fiction* (2013). She has also edited *The Bloomsbury Companion to Stylistics* (2016).

Judith Wermuth-Atkinson received her PhD from Columbia University, where she has taught courses on world literature, philosophy, and aesthetics. She has also studied and taught at Ludwig-Maximillian University in Munich and at Kliment Ohridsky University in Sofia. Her primary areas of scholarly interest are comparative literary, cultural, and religious studies, with a special focus on early twentieth-century European art and thought, as reflected in her book *The Red Jester: "Petersburg" as a Novel of the European Modern* (2012). In addition to her academic work, Wermuth-Atkinson has published books of creative nonfiction.

Index

Ableukhov, Apollon Apollonovich (character), 8, 118, 142; apocalypticism and, 142–46, 151; the Apollinian and, 75–77, 83; astral plane and, 61–65; cerebral play and, 61, 67, 191, 206–8, 212, 238; character synopsis and, 237–53; Comte and, 95–96; consciousness and, 95–98; Cubism and, 196, 199; Freudian Dreams and, 115–21; influences of Greek mythology, 75–79, 191; Neo-Kantianism and, 93–96; terrorism and, 45–51; thought-forms and, 62, 67, 77

Ableukhov, Nikolai Apollonovich (character): apocalypticism and, 142–43, 147, 150–51; astral plane and, 63, 67; Bergson, Henri and, 103–7; character synopsis and, 237–53; consciousness and, 223–29; Freudian Dream and, 112–19; heroism and, 114–17, 149, 174–77, 193; love interests, 75, 78–79; masquerade and, 181–82; Neo-Kantianism and, 39, 67, 89, 93–95, 97, 103–4, 120; Oedipus myth and, 121–22; patricide and, 116–22, 142, 183, 223, 250; revolutionary terrorism and, 45, 50, 183, 210

Absolute Spirit, 58–59. *See also* the Divine

abstraction, 173, 211–14. *See also Petersburg* (Bely)

agent provocateur, 42, 45, 47–50, 79, 183, 248. *See also* terrorism

Akashic Record, 60

Alexander II (Tsar), 41, 44

Alexander III (Tsar), 44, 172
Alexandrov, Vladimir, 19
Alter, Robert, 208, 211–12
Andreev, Leonid, 45
Anglo-American readers and literature, 4, 13, 20, 35, 217–18, 221, 228
Anschuetz, Carol, 82
The Anthroposophical Society, 57
Anthroposophy, 8, 15–18, 51–61, 67, 102, 178, 191, 197
anti-Semitism, 9, 113–15, 126–27, 129, 131–35. *See also* Bely, Andrei; Jews and Judaism; *Petersburg* (Bely); race and racism
Anuchin, Dmitrii, 128–29
apocalypticism: Bely and, 45, 71, 143–45, 151–52, 178; Christianity and, 4, 138–40; Nikolai Apollonovich Ableukhov (character) and, 142–43, 147, 150–51; *Petersburg* (Bely) and, 17, 138–52, 190, 210, 241–42; Russian modernism and, 45, 139–42; Senator Apollon Apollonovich Ableukhov and, 142–46, 151. *See also* eschatology
the Argonauts, 177–78
Aristotle, 41, 189, 211
Art Nouveau, 15
"Art poétique" (Verlaine), 105, 162
Aryanism: Jews and Judaism, 124–25, 131, 133–34; Mongols and, 124–25, 134; Nikolai Apollonovich and, 117, 120; as superior, 9, 128–29, 135; Theosophy and, 66–67. *See also* anti-Semitism; race and racism

"An Astral Novel" (Berdiaev), 194
astral plane, 51, 55, 59–67, 113, 186, 194–98, 206–12. *See also* Theosophy; thought-forms
Austen, Jane, 218
Azef, Evno, 45, 47, 49–50, 127

Bakhtin, Mikhail, 91, 150
Barbershop Window (Dobuzhinsky), 192
Barca, Hamilcar, 118–19
Baroque period, 179, 190, 192–93, 198–99
Baudelaire, Charles, 162
Beardsley, Aubrey, 194
Beethoven, Ludwig van, 158
Beilis Affair, 126, 133
Bely, Andrei: aesthetics and, 211–13; Anglo-American readers and literature, 4, 13, 20, 35, 217, 221; Anthroposophy and, 16, 18, 57, 178, 197; antinomies and, 63–64, 66; anti-Semitism and, 124–28, 131–33, 136n4; apocalypticism and, 45, 71, 143–45, 151–52, 178; Bergson, Henri and, 9, 100, 103–4; Christianity and, 82, 139, 145, 177; Cubism and, 12, 188, 190–97, 199, 212; East-West opposition and, 115–16, 118–19, 146; financial troubles and, 13–15, 18; French Impressionism and, 186, 188; Freud, Sigmund and, 9, 111–22; geometry and, 105–6, 140–41, 212–14; influence of Greek mythology and culture, 74, 82, 177; Japanese art and, 193–94; Jews and Judaism, 114–15, 126, 134; Kandinsky and, 187, 196–99, 212; leitmotifs and, 6, 29, 160–67, 184, 203, 206, 213; life-creation and, 11, 171–83; modernism and, 3–4, 11–12, 52, 235; Mongols and, 66, 116–17, 134; music and, 10, 105–7, 129–31, 158, 163, 165–69; Neo-Kantianism and, 86, 89, 91–97, 103–4; Nietzsche and, 8, 70–75, 81–82, 107, 165; the occult and, 15, 178, 197–98; Oedipus myth and, 121–22; painting and, 11, 187–88; poetry and, 18, 107, 149; race and racism and, 125–28, 134; right-wing politics of, 9, 47; romantic life and, 14–15, 176–77; Schopenhauer and, 159–64; Solovyov and, 74, 111, 139–41, 174; spatiality and, 101, 105–8, 123, 187–91, 197–99, 203–7, 229–30; spirals and, 140–42, 144, 187; spirituality and, 45, 74, 111, 124, 178, 203, 212–13; Steiner and, 8, 66, 102; Surrealism and, 191–92, 199, 203; terrorism and, 40, 42–52, 143; theater and, 11, 171–84; Theosophy and, 55–56, 58, 64–66, 68n8; time and, 17, 108, 141, 164; Wagner, Richard and, 9, 15, 160–69, 186. *See also* Cubism; spirals
Bennett, Virginia, 75–77
Benois, Aleksandr, 11, 175, 187, 192
Berdiaev, Nikolai, 55, 91, 188, 194, 212
Bergson, Henri, 9, 100–101, 105–6, 108, 219, 231
Berlin Alexanderplatz (Döblin), 204–5, 211
Besant, Annie, 56–63, 191
Bethea, David M., 151n1
The Birth of Tragedy from the Spirit of Music (Nietzsche), 71–72, 74, 161, 172
Blavatskaia, Elena, 55–58, 61
Blok, Aleksandr, 5–11, 14–16, 71, 105, 107, 139–40, 173–80, 206
Blok, Liubov', 7, 11, 174
Boehme, Jacob, 55
Bogrov, Dmitrii, 126
Bolshevik coup, 139, 179
bombs, 39, 143, 151, 195–96, 198, 223, 247–49, 251–52
Book of Revelation, 80, 138–39, 143, 148, 150
Bosch, Hieronymus, 11, 191–92
Briusov, Valery, 176
Bronze Horseman, 63–64, 67, 81, 104, 133, 140–50, 192, 199, 249, 251. *See also Petersburg* (Bely)
The Bronze Horseman (Pushkin), 7, 11, 40, 65, 67, 140, 187, 192
The Brothers Karamazov (Dostoevsky), 44

Index

Buddhism, 55–56, 58, 114–16, 118, 120
Bugaev, Boris Nikolaevich (Andrei Bely), 4, 139. *See also* Bely, Andrei
Bulgakov, Sergei, 91
Burtsev, Vladimir, 44, 49

Cassedy, Steven, 100
Cassirer, Ernst, 89
Catechism of a Revolutionary (Nechaev), 41
Catherine II, 40
censorship, 19, 43, 51, 112, 115–16, 121, 172
cerebral play, 61, 167, 191, 206–7, 212, 240
Chamberlain, Houston Stewart, 125
"Characteristics of Black, Yellow, and White Races in Connection with the Question of the Russo-Japanese War" (Sikorskii), 134–35
Chekhov, Anton, 173
Chesterton, G. K., 48
China, 115, 118, 125
Chopin, Frédéric, 168
Christianity: anti-Semitism and, 9, 131–33; apocalypticism and, 4, 138–40; eschatology and, 10, 75, 138–39, 145, 152, 177, 183; race and racism, 126, 134; sexuality and, 131–33; spirituality and, 131–32, 150. *See also* eschatology
Chronos-Saturn, 115, 119, 121–22
"Circular Movements" (Bely), 103, 141, 144
cities (as text), 202–5, 207–14
"The City" (Bely), 189
Clark, Katerina, 179
Clowes, Edith, 92
Cohen, Hermann, 85–86, 89, 91–93
Colbath, Christopher, 194
colors (significant): black, 5, 62, 64–65, 132, 147, 190, 195, 197, 226; gray, 33, 62, 64, 66, 195, 197; red, 5, 46, 49–50, 62, 147–48, 182, 192–93, 198, 237–53; white, 10, 41, 67, 74, 82, 114, 147–50, 188–93, 244–45; yellow, 6, 9, 62, 77, 81, 112–17, 124–30, 134–35, 197. *See also* race and racism
commedia dell'arte, 174, 180, 183, 187
Compositions (Kandinsky), 197, 199

Comte, Auguste, 78, 86, 88, 95, 242
Concerning the Spiritual in Art (Kandinsky), 60
Conrad, Joseph, 47–48
consciousness: astral planes and, 51, 59–67, 194; Freud, Sigmund and, 112–16, 121; heroes and, 218–27; modernism and, 11–12, 102, 108, 162–64, 177, 217–20, 230–31; Nikolai Apollonovich Ableukhov and, 94–98, 223–29; *Petersburg* (Bely) and, 12, 64, 96–97, 211–12, 217–31; representations of, 222–30; Russian culture and, 47, 66, 70; Senator Apollon Apollonovich Ableukhov (character), 95–98
Cornwell, Neil, 221, 228
the cosmos, 57–59, 65, 75, 194–98, 209. *See also* St. Petersburg (city); Theosophy
Cranach, Lucas, 11
Crime and Punishment (Dostoevsky), 7, 44, 48, 203
"Criticism and Symbolism" (Bely), 92, 103
The Critique of Pure Reason (Kant), 103
The Crooked Mirror (Evreinov), 175
Cubism, 12, 188, 190, 194–97, 199, 212. *See also* Anthroposophy; Bely, Andrei; painting; Theosophy

Darwinism, 58, 124, 131
David, Jacques-Louis, 193
Dead Souls (Gogol), 14
Degaev, Sergei, 42
Demons (Dostoevsky), 44
Descartes, René, 86
"The Dissolution of the Oedipus Complex" (Freud), 123n9
the Divine, 104. *See also* Absolute Spirit
Döblin, Alfred, 204–5, 211
Dobuzhinsky, Mstislav, 187
Dolgopolov, Leonid, 19–20, 82, 97, 181, 207
Dos Passos, John, 204–5
Dostoevsky, Fëdor, 7–8, 14, 44, 71, 74, 82, 104, 207
The Dramatic Symphony (Bely), 165–66

"The Dream of the Uncle" (Freud), 112, 115-16, 119
The Dreyfus Affair, 126
Dublin, 204, 210-11. *See also* cities (as text)
Dudkin, Aleksandr Ivanovich (character): apocalypticism and, 142-50; astral plane and, 61-67, 178; cerebral play and, 183, 191-92, 197, 207-8, 210, 227; character synopsis and, 237-53; Nietzsche and, 74-83; race and racism, 8, 129-35; revolutionary terrorism and, 35, 39-40, 44-50, 102, 196
Dujardin, Édouard, 162
durée (individual experience of time), 219

East and West (tension between), 41, 47, 115-22, 127, 135, 146-49, 194, 209
East or West (Bely), 13, 18, 203, 211-12
Egypt, 108, 188, 253
Einstein, Albert, 102, 110, 184, 219. *See also* theory of relativity
Elsworth, John, 45, 93, 169, 209, 236
"The Emblematics of Meaning" (Bely), 92-93, 97
Emma (Austen), 218
epistemology, 86-87, 89, 96
eschatology, 10, 75, 138-39, 145, 152, 177, 183. *See also* apocalypticism; Christianity
the Establishment, 77, 207, 237-41, 248-50. *See also* Ableukhov, Apollon Apollonovich (character); *Petersburg* (Bely)
eugenics, 114, 135. *See also* Jews and Judaism; race and racism
European civilization, 133
Evil Shadows (Bely), 13
Evreinov, Nikolai, 173, 175
Expressionism, 187, 193, 199

Fanger, Donald, 208
Fëdorov, Nikolai, 178
Feuerbach, Ludwig, 88
Fichte, Johann Gottlieb, 88
The Fiery Angel (Briusov), 176
Fifth Symphony (Beethoven), 158
Filonov, Pavel, 212

Fleisch, Zoia (character), 9, 131-33, 237-53
The Flowers of Evil (Baudelaire), 204
Flying Dutchman, 32, 148, 166, 246
Foreign Agency of the Russian secret police, 43
"Forms of Art" (Bely), 187
Foundations of the Nineteenth Century (Chamberlain), 125
the fourth dimension, 60, 65-66, 141, 144, 150-52, 194-98, 206-9, 213
fragmentation, 12, 48, 76, 187-90, 194-95, 205, 212, 223, 231
Frank, Semën, 91
French Impressionism, 186-88, 193
Freud, Sigmund: dreams and, 112-16, 118, 121; Oedipus myth and, 121-22, 123n9; psychology and, 9, 102, 111; the Superman and, 80-81, 103, 139. *See also* the Superman
Freud's Wednesday Group, 111
Futurism, 176, 188, 194, 199, 212

Galton, Francis, 114-15
Geifman, Anna, 46
geometry, 76, 103-5, 141, 152, 194-96, 212-14. *See also* spatiality; spirals
German Idealism, 88
Gesammtkunstwerk (Wagner), 10, 21n25, 160, 162, 199, 213
Gippius, Zinaida, 45, 70
Glossolalia (Bely), 165, 214
Gnosticism, 55, 58. *See also* Anthroposophy; Theosophy
Gogol, Nikolai, 7-8, 14, 194, 208
Gogol's Artistry (Bely), 194, 197
Gorky, Maxim, 173
Great Reforms, 41
Great Russians: An Essay on the Physical Type (Vorob'ëv), 127
the Great Terror, 42
Greek mythology and culture, 72-78, 82, 131, 162, 172, 177, 191
Grünewald, Matthias, 11

Hannibal, 118, 199
Hart, Pierre, 220

Index

Hartmann, Franz, 62
Haydn, Joseph, 158
Haystacks (Monet), 186, 196, 198
Hegel, Georg, 71, 88, 100, 140, 159
Heidegger, Martin, 231
Helmholtz, Hermann von, 86
Henry, Barbara, 173
Hermeticism, 13, 55
heroes: Bely and, 5–7, 214; consciousness and, 218–27; as manifest in Nikolai Apollonovich Ableukhov, 114–17, 149, 174–77, 193; Nietzsche and, 71–73, 103; represented in *Petersburg* (Bely), 144–45; Russian modernism and, 44–45; terrorism and, 44–45, 48, 52
He Who Has Come (Bely), 172
Hinduism, 56
Hoffmann, E. T. A, 158–59
Hokusai, Katsushika, 193–94
"Holiday" (Bely), 181
Homo Sapiens (Przybyszewski), 12
Hume, David, 86–87
Husserl, Edmund, 100

The Idiot (Dostoevsky), 7, 14, 203
In Search of Lost Time (Proust), 167, 211, 214
The Interpretation of Dreams (Freud), 111–12, 118, 120–22, 123n9
Introduction to Metaphysics (Bergson), 100
intuition, 59, 101–8, 213, 231
Ivanov, Viacheslav, 71, 74, 139, 172–73
Ivanov-Razumnik, R. V., 16–17, 55

Japan, 65, 125, 139, 193–94
Jesus Christ, 67, 71–80, 131–34, 138–40, 150–51, 168, 245
Jews and Judaism, 9–10, 47–51, 78, 113, 115, 124–35. *See also* anti-Semitism; eugenics; race and racism
Josipovici, Gabriel, 3
Joyce, James, 4, 13, 20, 204–5, 209, 211, 214, 218–19, 231
"Judaism in Music" (Wagner), 130
Jung, Carl, 95, 102, 122n1

Kabbalism, 55

Kafka, Franz, 20
Kandinsky, Wassily, 56, 60, 187, 196–99, 212
Kant, Immanuel, 9, 67, 78, 85–87, 90, 92, 103, 107
Kant and the Epigones (Liebmann), 86
Kant's Theory of Experience (Cohen), 85, 89
Karakozov, Dmitrii, 41
Karma, 67
Keys, Roger, 165
Kharms, Daniil, 102
Khlebnikov, Velimir, 213
Khodasevich, Vladislav, 176
Klimt, Gustav, 122
Kobylinskii, Lev, 45
Krishnamurti, Jiddu, 57

Lakhtin, Mikhail, 111
Lange, Friedrich Albert, 86
La Revue wagnérienne (journal), 162
Lask, Emil, 93
Laughter (Bergson), 102
Lawrence, D. H., 228, 231
Leadbeater, Charles, 58, 60, 62, 191
Lectures on Aesthetics (Hegel), 159
Leibniz, G. W., 86
leitmotifs, 6, 29, 76, 160–67, 184, 203–6, 213. *See also Petersburg* (Bely)
Lenin, Vladimir, 179
Lermontov, Mikhail, 179
Letters to a Painter (Ostwald), 187
Liebmann, Otto, 86
life-creation, 11, 171–83
Likhutin, Sergei Sergeich (character), 78, 166, 174, 177, 183, 210, 237–53
Likhutina, Sofia (character), 5, 11, 50–51, 63, 75–77, 143, 237–53
"The Line, the Circle, the Spiral" (Bely), 141
Lippanchenko, Nikolai Stepanych (character): astral plane and, 63–64; character synopsis and, 237–53; influence of Greek mythology and, 78–83; race and racism, 127–34; revolutionary terrorism and, 43, 49–51, 183, 210
Livak, Leonid, 135n1, 220

Ljunggren, Magnus, 78, 111
Logos (journal), 91
Lohengrin (Wagner), 160
Lopukhin, Aleksei, 49
Losskii, Nikolai, 102
Lotman, Yuri, 178–79
Love of Three Oranges (Meyerhold), 180

"The Magic of Words" (Bely), 106–8, 145
Maguire, Robert, 20n7, 236
Mallarmé, Stéphane, 162
Malmstad, John, 20n7, 236
Man and His Bodies (Besant), 63, 102
Mandel'shtam, Osip, 45
Manet, Edouard, 194
Manhattan Transfer (Dos Passos), 204–5
Mann, Robert, 79, 82
Mansfield, Katherine, 228, 231
The Man Who Was Thursday (Chesterton), 48
Marxism, 10, 19, 47, 88, 91
masks: as metaphor, 174–75, 207; in *Petersburg* (Bely), 179–84, 239–44, 255n27; unmasking and, 45–52, 132
"The Masque of the Red Death" (Poe), 182
Masquerade (Lermontov), 179
"Masquerade" (Bely), 181
masquerades, 11, 148, 172–75, 179–87, 240, 253n11. *See also Petersburg* (Bely)
"Mass-Produced Culture" (Bely), 129
"Master and Man" (Tolstoy), 222
materialism, 49, 54–55, 66, 88–89
Matich, Olga, 48
Matisse, Henri, 11
McDuff, David, 27, 123n8
"The Meaning of Art" (Bely), 188–89
Merezhkovskii, Dmitrii, 45, 70, 139
Metamorphosis (Kafka), 20
metaphysics, 86–87. *See also* Neo-Kantianism
Metner, Emilii, 111
Meyerhold, Vsevolod, 173–74, 179
Michaelis, Karen, 111
millenarianism, 4, 138–39, 143–44, 149–50. *See also* Christianity; Second Coming (of Christ)

mimeticism, 172, 211, 219, 223–27
"Modern Fiction" (Woolf), 218
modernism: consciousness and, 11–12, 102, 108, 162, 164, 177, 217–20, 230–31; epistemology and, 218–19; literature and, 3, 12, 202–6, 211–14, 218–20; music and, 158–63; naturalism and, 12, 171; Nietzsche and, 71, 74, 80; the occult in, 54–58, 178; Steiner, Rudolf and, 15, 51–52, 58, 191; terrorism and, 44–45; theory of relativity and, 110, 184, 219–20; time, 197–99; urbanism and, 204–6. *See also* Solovyov, Vladimir
Modern Occult Revival, 54
Mommsen, Theodor, 74
Monet, Claude, 186, 196, 198
Mongolians, 66–67, 76, 78, 116–21, 127–28
Moscow Art Theater (MkhAT 2), 19
Moscow Psychological Society, 111
Moscow under Siege (Bely), 188
Mozart, Wolfgang, 158
Müller, Georg, 18
Munch, Edvard, 193
music: Bely, Andrei and, 10, 105–7, 129–31, 157–69; modernism and, 158–63; *Petersburg* (Bely), 10, 108, 129–31, 158, 165–69
mysticism, 55–56, 60, 97

Nabokov, Vladimir, 20, 221
Natorp, Paul, 89, 91, 93
naturalism, 202–3, 218–19
Nechaev, Sergei, 41, 182
Nekrasov, Nikolay, 14–15
neobaroque, 192
Neo-Kantianism, 8–9, 85–98, 120
Nevsky Prospect, 190–92, 195–96, 199, 208, 248
New Jerusalem, 150
The New Review (journal), 221
Nicholas II (Tsar), 51
Nietzsche, Friedrich, 70–75, 83, 92, 103–4, 139–41, 161–65
Nilus, Sergei, 126
Novgorodtsev, Pavel, 91

Index

occultism: Bely, Andrei and, 15, 178, 197–98; modernism and, 54–55, 58, 178; *Petersburg* (Bely), 8, 54–68
October Idyll (Dobuzhinsky), 187
Oedipus complex, 121–22
Oedipus Rex (Sophocles), 121–22
Olcott, Henry, 55, 57
Old Masters, 11, 15. *See also specific artists*
Old Pinakothek Museum, 188
"On Certain Anomalies of the Human Skull and Especially on Their Distribution According to Races" (Anuchin), 128
"On Scientific Dogmatism" (Bely), 92
"On the Spiritual in Art" (Kandinsky), 196–97
opera, 10, 15, 130, 157–61, 167
Ostwald, Wilhelm, 187

painting, 131, 139, 168, 187–99, 203, 213. *See also* Cubism; modernism
Painting with Red Spot (Kandinsky), 198
"Pan-Mongolism" (Solovyov), 134, 139
Paperno, Irina, 178
Party of Socialist Revolutionaries (PSR), 44
Pasternak, Boris, 91
Pell, Alexander, 43
The People's Vengeance, 41
People's Will, 41–42, 44
Peppovich, Pepp (character), 45, 107, 113–15, 224–25, 247
Peter I (Tsar), 40, 62, 66–67
Petersburg (Bely): abstraction and, 173, 211–14; aesthetic theory and practice, 196–99; for Anglophone readers, 4, 13, 20, 221; anti-Semitism and, 9, 49, 124–28, 244; apocalypticism and, 17, 138–52, 190, 210, 241–42; assassination and, 41–49, 229, 238, 244–46; astral plane and, 55, 59–67, 113, 186, 194–98, 206–12; Bely's love life and, 174, 177–78; Bergson, Henri and, 100, 102–6; the bomb and, 39, 46, 143, 151, 195–98, 210, 223, 247–52; Book of Revelation and, 139–40; Bronze Horseman and, 81, 104, 133, 140–50, 199, 249–51; cerebral play and, 61, 207–9, 212, 214, 240; Christianity and, 74–75, 78–80, 147–48, 245; chronology and, 235, 253n7, 253n9, 254n14, 255n34, 255n37; colors and, 197; consciousness and, 12, 64, 96–97, 211–12, 217–31; Cubism and, 12, 188, 190, 194–97; editions of, 5, 9, 13, 16–20, 235–36, 253nn3–4, 254n22, 255n28, 255nn32–33; ekphrasis and, 192–94; equine symbol and, 147–49; Flying Dutchman and, 32, 148, 166, 246; the fourth dimension and, 60, 65–66, 141, 144, 150–52, 194–98, 206–9, 213; fragmentation and, 12, 48, 76, 187–90, 194–95, 205, 212, 223, 231; Freud, Sigmund and, 111–16; geometry and, 105–6, 141, 143–44, 152, 195, 206, 214; Greek mythology and culture, 72–80, 82, 131, 172, 177, 191; history of, 13–20; inter-art text, 186–93, 197; Japanese art and, 193–94; Jews and Judaism, 9–10, 113–15, 124–35; leitmotifs of, 6, 29, 67, 76, 160–67, 184, 203, 206, 213; life-creation and, 11, 171–83; linear structure and, 235–36, 239, 254n14; logical inconsistencies and, 13, 17, 235, 253n11, 254n12, 255n26, 255n37; magic of words and, 107–8; masquerade and masks, 148, 172–75, 179–87, 239–44, 253n11, 255n27; metaphor and metamorphosis, 188–92; modernism and, 158–62, 187, 193, 199, 204–6, 212, 219–21; Mongolians and, 76, 116–35; music and, 10, 108, 129–31, 158, 165–69; narrative problems and, 211–14; narrative structure and, 5, 13–14, 17, 110, 142–45, 150, 167, 235, 252; Neo-Kantianism and, 86, 88, 93–95, 97–98; Nietzsche, Friedrich and, 70, 75, 79, 80–82, 82–83; the occult and, 8, 54–68; Oedipus complex and, 121–22; painting and, 187–88, 190–99; patricide and, 44, 78–79, 104, 120–22,

Petersburg (continued)
142, 183, 193, 228; psychology and, 110–22; race and racism, 9, 114, 124–35; Red Domino and, 20n7, 49, 157, 179–81, 240, 243–45, 247, 250, 254n14; Russo-Japanese War and, 134–35; scissors and, 63–64, 133, 146–47, 249, 251, 255n37; sculpture and, 73, 105, 159, 168, 176, 192–93; shadows and, 12–13, 47–50, 63–65, 77–81, 144, 189–92, 206–7; socio-political commentary and, 50–51, 125, 135, 142, 228, 241–42, 247, 254n17, 254n22; spatiality and, 101, 105–8, 123, 187–91, 197–99, 203–7, 228–30; spirals and, 105–7, 140–44, 150–52, 197, 226; Steiner, Rudolf and, 8, 57–58, 60–67, 102, 111, 141, 191; St. Petersburg (city) and, 178–80, 211–14; synopsis of, 235–53; terrorism and, 39–44, 47–52, 102–3, 142, 146–47, 183, 251; theater and, 11, 19, 160, 171–75, 179–84; Theosophy and, 8, 54–60, 66–68; thought-forms and, 212–13; time and, 75, 106, 108, 150, 228–29; translations of, 13, 18, 68n8, 123n8, 209–10, 236; in the transnational modernist canon, 220–21; Tsukatovs' Ball, 180–84, 243, 245; *Ulysses* (Joyce), comparisons to, 20, 204–6, 210–14, 220, 228; the unicorn and, 147–51; urbanism and, 202–9, 211–14; Wagner, Richard and, 130, 160–69, 186; White Domino, 10, 67, 82, 150, 245; World War I and, 16–17. *See also* colors (significant)
Peter the Great, 6, 96, 103–4, 133, 140, 142, 145, 246. *See also* apocalypticism; Bronze Horseman
Petrovna, Anna (character), 8, 75, 77, 166–68, 237–53
Philosophy of Symbolic Forms (Cassirer), 89
Picasso, Pablo, 102, 188, 194
Plehve, Viacheslav von, 43, 45, 47, 51
Plekhanov, Georgii, 91
Poe, Edgar Allan, 182
Populists, 41–44

A Portrait of the Artist as a Young Man (Joyce), 218, 225
positivism, 12, 54–55, 62, 71, 88, 183, 203, 211
"The Principle of Form in Aesthetics" (Bely), 164
"The Problem of Culture" (Bely), 92
projectivism, 178
The Protocols of the Elders of Zion, 126–27
Proust, Marcel, 12, 167, 211, 214
Przybyszewski, Stanisław, 12
psychology, 72–74, 89, 92, 110–22. *See also* modernism; *Petersburg* (Bely)
Punic Wars, 118
The Puppet Show (Blok), 173–74, 177, 180
Pushkin, Aleksandr, 7–8, 11, 40, 67, 140
Pygmalion, 176

"The Queen of Spades" (Pushkin), 7, 11
The Queen of Spades (Tchaikovsky), 157

race and racism, 124–26, 128–35. *See also* anti-Semitism; colors (significant); eugenics; Jews and Judaism
realism, 12, 145, 173, 190, 199–203, 217, 227–28
Reavey, George, 221
Red Domino. *See Petersburg* (Bely)
The Red Jester (Wermuth-Atkinson), 122n1
Remizov, Aleksei, 45
Repin, Ilya, 44
revolution, 31, 39–40, 46–47, 51–52, 103, 142. *See also* terrorism
The Rhetoric (Aristotle), 189
"Richard Wagner, Reverie of a French Poet" (Mallarmé), 162
Rickert, Heinrich, 89, 92–93, 97
The Ring of the Nibelung (Wagner), 160–61, 165, 167
rituals (religious), 72–74
Rosicrucianism, 55
Rozanov, Vasilii, 132
Rozenthal, Tatiana, 111
Russell, Anna, 161, 167
Russia: East and West (tension between), 41, 47, 115–22, 127, 135, 146–49, 194,

Index

209; imperialism and, 43, 117–18, 180–82, 204–6
"The Russian Joyce" (Cornwell), 221
Russian modernism: apocalypticism and, 45, 139–42; Bergson and, 100–102; commedia dell'arte and, 174, 180, 183, 187; Cubism and, 194–96; Einstein, Albert and, 183–84; the Futurists and, 175–76; life-creation and, 173, 175–80; literature and, 6–12, 107, 173, 186, 194, 207–12, 220; spirituality and, 4–6, 19, 101, 133–35; theater and, 171–72, 174, 176
Russian Orthodox Church, 126
Russo-Japanese War, 65, 125, 127, 134–35, 180, 183, 254n17

Saturn, 59, 65, 121
Savinkov, Boris, 47
Schelling, Friedrich, 88
Schoenberg, Arnold, 213
Schopenhauer, Arthur, 100, 159–62, 164
scissors (symbolism of), 63–64, 133, 146–47, 249, 251, 255n37
Scotland Yard, 43
Scream (Munch), 193
sculpture, 73, 105, 159, 168, 176, 192–93
The Seagull (Chekhov), 174
Second Coming (of Christ), 10, 134, 138, 140, 150, 177. *See also* millenarianism
The Secret Agent (Conrad), 47–48
The Secret Doctrine (Blavatsky), 56
Sections for the Protection of Public Security and Order (Okhrana), 42
Sex and Character (Weininger), 111, 125, 133
shadows, 12–13, 47–50, 63–65, 77–81, 144, 189–92, 206–7
The Shape of Apocalypse in Modern Russian Fiction (Bethea), 151n1
Shchukin, Sergei, 11, 188, 194
Shishnarfiev (character), 63–65, 80–81, 129–32, 197–98, 248–49
Shishnarfne (character). *See* Shishnarfiev
Shklovskii, Viktor, 195
"The Short Tale of the Antichrist" (Solovyov), 139

Signposts (essay collection), 47
Sikorskii, Ivan, 134–35
The Silver Dove (Bely), 13–14, 47, 117, 203
Simmel, Georg, 202
Simmons, Cynthia, 220
Sirin (publishing house), 9, 15–16
Sixth Post-Atlantean Age, 66
Skovoroda, Grigorii, 67, 104, 107
Skriabin, Aleksandr, 60
Slavs, 66, 104, 107, 128
Socialist Revolutionaries, 46, 50
Sologub, Fëdor, 175
Solovyov, Vladimir, 55–56, 71, 91–92, 111, 139–41, 174, 177. *See also* modernism
Sophia (God's wisdom in Christian theology), 66
Sophocles, 72, 121
Soviet Russia, 10, 18–19
spatiality, 101, 105–8, 123, 187–91, 197–99, 203–7, 229–30. *See also* geometry; spirals
Special Theory of Relativity (Einstein), 110
the Sphynx, 122
spirals, 105–7, 140–44, 150–52, 197, 226. *See also* Bely, Andrei; geometry; *Petersburg* (Bely); spatiality
SR Central Committee, 44–45, 49–50
SR Combat Organization, 49
Stalinism, 19
Stanislavsky, Konstantin, 173
Steinberg, Ada, 163–64, 167
Steiner, Rudolf: Anthroposophy and, 8, 16, 51, 74, 102, 178, 191; astral world and, 63–64, 67; Bely, Andrei and, 15, 56, 74; influences on *Petersburg* (Bely), 64–67, 111, 141; modernism and, 15, 51, 58, 191; Theosophy and, 56–58, 60
Stepniak-Kravchinskii, Sergei, 44
Stolypin, Pëtr, 46–47
St. Petersburg (city): astral world and, 65–67, 210–11; history of, 6, 66; as text, 6–7, 48–49, 62, 142, 150, 202–11, 236; the theatricality of, 178–80
Struve, Gleb, 221
Struve, Pëtr, 14, 91
Sudeikin, Georgii, 42–43

suicide, 7, 176, 239–40, 246, 255
the Superman, 80–81, 103, 139. *See also* Nietzsche, Friedrich
Surrealism, 191–92, 199, 203
Sventitskii, Valentin, 45
Swedenborg, Emmanuel, 55
Symbolism (Bely), 97
"Symbolism as a World View" (Bely), 163–64

Tchaikovsky, Pyotr, 157–58
terrorism, 31, 35, 39–45, 47–52, 67, 102–3, 146–47, 183, 196, 210, 251. *See also* agent provocateur; revolution
theater, 11, 19, 160, 171–75, 179–84
"Theater and Contemporary Drama" (Bely), 173
theories of reconciliation, 92
theory of relativity, 110, 184, 219–20. *See also* Einstein, Albert
Theosophical Society of New York City, 55, 57, 66
Theosophy, 8, 55–62, 66–67, 191. *See also* thought-forms
Thom's Official Dictionary, 204
thought-forms, 61–62, 67, 205–6, 213–14. *See also* Theosophy
Thought-Forms (Besant and Leadbeater), 60, 62, 191
Three Conversations about War, Progress, and the End of World History (Solovyov), 134, 139–40
Tolstoy, Leo, 8, 71, 221
Toporov, Vladimir, 207
Tristan and Isolde (Wagner), 160–61
"The Truth about the Russian Intelligentsia" (Bely), 47
Tsvetaeva, Marina, 45
Turanians, 65–67, 97, 113–20, 126–27, 130
Turgeneva, Asya (Anna), 14–16, 18
Turkic peoples, 126, 128

Ukrainians (people), 128
Ulysses (Joyce), 4, 20, 204, 206, 209–11, 214, 220–21, 228
unicorns, 147–51. *See also Petersburg* (Bely)

van Eyck, Jan, 11
Verigina, Valentina, 180
Verlaine, Paul, 105, 162
violence, 40–47, 52, 71–72, 126–27, 180, 203
Vladimir Mayakovsky: A Tragedy (Mayakovsky), 173
Voloshin, Maksimilian, 45
Voltaire, 52
Vorob'ëv, Viktor, 127–28
Vvedenskii, Aleksandr, 95

Wagner, Richard, 9, 15, 125, 130, 160–62, 166–67
Weininger, Otto, 111, 125, 133–34
Wermuth-Atkinson, Judith, 95
Western Thought and Civilization, 10–14, 55–58, 66, 91, 98, 103, 118–21, 134, 146–49
White Domino. *See Petersburg* (Bely)
Windelband, Wilhelm, 86, 89
Witte, Sergei, 50
Woolf, Virginia, 12, 211, 217–19, 228, 231n2
The World as Will and Representation (Schopenhauer), 159–60
World of Art, 175–76, 179
The World of Art (journal), 187
World War I, 4, 16–17
Woronzoff, Alexander, 221

Yeats, W. B., 140
Yellow Peril, 127, 134–35

Zarathustra, 73–75, 80–82
Zasulich, Vera, 41
Zeus, 77, 191